PENGUIN BOOKS

THE ARABIAN NIGHTS: A COMPANION

'The *Companion* is delightful; an astonishing combination of erudition, humour and quirky facts ... Robert Irwin winds his way through the labyrinth of stories and their origins, development, textual criticism, translations, commentaries and imitations with thoroughness and wit. His style is a racy and unapologetic mixture of the scholarly and the colloquial' – Emma Guinness in the *Literary Review*

'Enticing ... Every dimension of his scholarship is impressive, but most admirable of all is the easy and eloquent manner of its presentation. So I suggest that you think of this book as a true and unstealthy companion such as Dunyazade, Sheherazade's sister, was; and keep it conveniently by ... your bed, where you can follow the pleasure of the *Nights* themselves, with another from Robert Irwin's chapter on low life, or the one on marvels – whatever properly complements the story you've just concluded' – William Gass in the *London Review of Books*

'Scholarly but approachable ... does what no other study on the *Nights* has yet done: puts the tales in their cultural and historical context, as well as telling you masses of things about their world that you had never before dreamt even existed' – Robert Carver in the *Scotsman*

'A fine, elegant, learned book' – Anthony Curtis in the *Financial Times*

Robert Irwin was born in 1946. He read modern history at Oxford and taught medieval history at the University of St Andrews. He has taught Arabic and Middle Eastern history at the universities of Oxford, Cambridge and London. He is a director of a small publishing company.

Robert Irwin is the author of *The Middle East in the Middle Ages* and numerous other specialized studies of Middle Eastern politics, art and mysticism. His novels include *The Limits of Vision* (Penguin, 1986), *The Arabian Nightmare* (Penguin, 1988), *The Mysteries of Algiers* (Penguin, 1989) and *The Exquisite Corpse* (Dedalus, 1995).

ROBERT IRWIN

═══

The Arabian Nights:
A Companion

PENGUIN BOOKS

PENGUIN BOOKS

Published by the Penguin Group
Penguin Books Ltd, 27 Wrights Lane, London W8 5TZ, England
Penguin Books USA Inc., 375 Hudson Street, New York, New York 10014, USA
Penguin Books Australia Ltd, Ringwood, Victoria, Australia
Penguin Books Canada Ltd, 10 Alcorn Avenue, Toronto, Ontario, Canada M4V 3B2
Penguin Books (NZ) Ltd, 182–190 Wairau Road, Auckland 10, New Zealand

Penguin Books Ltd, Registered Offices: Harmondsworth, Middlesex, England

First published by Allen Lane The Penguin Press 1994
Published in Penguin Books 1995
1 3 5 7 9 10 8 6 4 2

Printed in England by Clays Ltd, St Ives plc

Contents

===

Introduction

═══

Beneath English trees I meditated on that lost maze: I imagined it inviolate and perfect at the secret crest of a mountain; I imagined it erased by rice fields or beneath water; I imagined it infinite, no longer composed of octagonal kiosks and returning paths, but of rivers and provinces and kingdoms . . . I thought of a labyrinth of labyrinths, of one sinuous spreading labyrinth that would encompass the past and the future and in some way involve the stars.

> Jorge Luis Borges, 'The Garden of the Forking Paths'

One feels like getting lost in *The Thousand and One Nights*, one knows that entering that book one can forget one's own poor human fate; one can enter a world, a world made up of archetypal figures but also of individuals.

> Borges, '*The Thousand and One Nights*'[1]

According to a superstition current in the Middle East in the late nineteenth century when Sir Richard Burton was writing, no one can read the whole text of the *Arabian Nights* without dying. There have indeed been times (particularly when toiling through Burton's own distinctly unattractive translation of the *Nights*) when I thought that I might slit my throat rather than continue with this enterprise. However, I am still alive. It may be that I have acquired some sort of literary stamina from a youthful reading of Gibbon's *Decline and Fall of the Roman Empire* and Proust's *A la recherche du temps perdu*. The *Arabian Nights*, applying that title in its widest and loosest sense, is a very long book. Burton's own omnium-gatherum translation, based on an uncritical collation of a variety of Arabic printed texts and manuscripts, stretched to sixteen volumes and included 468 stories (give or take a few, depending on how one counts). Moreover, a critical study of the *Nights* cannot be based on a reading of Burton's translation alone. It was of course necessary to compare his version with those of rival translators and all of them with the original Arabic. Then there were the variant versions of the canonical tales to be read, the wider context of medieval Arab literature to be investigated, the secondary critical literature to be assessed and the multifarious offspring and influences of the *Nights* to be tracked down . . .

It will probably come as a shock to most people in the West today to learn that the *Nights* is longer than Proust. In the nineteenth century, Burton's, or it might be Payne's or Lane's, translation of the *Nights* was a standard work in gentlemen's libraries. In the twentieth century, however, its popularity has declined, and only garbled versions of a handful of stories ('Aladdin', 'Sinbad', 'Ali Baba' and the story of Sheherazade herself) survive in popular consciousness and in bowdlerized children's editions. Even professional Arabists, most of them, are shockingly ignorant of the contents of the *Nights*. It is commonly regarded as a collection of Arab fairy tales, the oriental equivalent of the *Märchen* (fairy tales or household tales) of the Brothers Grimm. But, while it is true that there are items in the *Nights* which might pass as fairy tales, the collection's compass is much wider than this. It also includes long heroic epics, wisdom literature, fables, cosmological fantasy, pornography, scatological jokes, mystical devotional tales, chronicles of low life, rhetorical debates and masses of poetry. A few tales are hundreds of pages long; others amount to no more than a short paragraph.

The title of the story collection in Arabic is *Alf Layla wa-Layla*, literally 'One Thousand Nights and a Night', but the eighteenth-century English translation of Galland's French version was called *The Arabian Nights Entertainments*. In this book I shall use the term 'the *Nights*' to refer to the story collection in any of its various early and late recensions. The one thing that all the collections have in common is that the stories in them are supposed to have been told by Sheherazade to King Shahriyar. We learn from the *Nights* that Shahriyar, a mythical king in ancient times, on discovering his wife's infidelity with a kitchen servant, had the wife put to death and, from that time on, fearing further sexual betrayals, he took virgins to his bed for one night only, invariably having them beheaded on the following morning. After this deflowering and slaughtering had gone on for some time, the vizier's daughter, who was called Sheherazade, volunteered herself, much against her father's will, as the next candidate for the king's bed. Brought before the king, she asked that her sister, Dunyazade, might attend her. She had already put Dunyazade up to asking for a story. Dunyazade, inconspicuously installed in Shahriyar's bedchamber, waited until he had deflowered her sister. Then, when she judged the moment was right, she asked her sister for a story. Sheherazade obliged her with 'The Story of the Merchant and the Demon'; but, since she did not relate all of it that night, Shahriyar was impelled to postpone her execution, so that he might hear the end of it on the following night. The following night, the story continued, but it did not conclude. Instead, Sheherazade began another story, inset within the first one, and broke off with this story also unfinished as dawn was breaking. And so things continued for several years (for two years and 271 days, if we are to take the 1,001 of the title literally), with Sheherazade, night by night, talking for her life. In the end, by the time her vast repertoire of stories was concluded, she had become mother to several of Shahriyar's children, and he had repented from his original determination to execute her.

The stories in the original manuscripts are interrupted every five pages or so by narrative breaks along the lines of 'But morning overtook Sheherazade, and she lapsed into silence. Then her sister said, "Sister, what an entertaining story!" Sheherazade replied, "What is this compared with what I shall tell you tomorrow night!"' But after a while, many compilers and transcribers of the *Nights* lose patience with this device, and thereafter one story follows another with no reference back to the frame of Sheherazade telling stories to Shahriyar and Dunyazade. Not only does Sheherazade tell stories, but some of the characters in her stories tell stories, and some of the characters in their stories also tell stories. The most notable example of this boxing, or framing, technique is the Hunchback cycle of stories; here, among other things, the tailor tells a tale told to him by a lame young man, and this lame young man's tale includes within it the tales of the barber and the barber's stories of his six unfortunate brothers.

In conversations in pubs (where much of my thinking on this subject has been done), after I have finished explaining all this, I have sometimes been asked, 'Well, when was it written?' This is a 'how-long-is-a-piece-of-string?' sort of question to which the only answer must be 'It all depends what you mean by the *Nights*.' A full answer to this question will be attempted in the pages which follow, but for the moment the short (and misleading) answer must be that there was certainly a version of the story collection circulating in the tenth century (though it was entitled *The Thousand Nights*, not *The Thousand and One Nights*), but we know very little about what may or may not have been in the story collection before the fifteenth century. Moreover, the tenth-century story collection drew on older collections of stories, and further stories went on being added to the original corpus until as late as the early nineteenth century. An even shorter answer to the inquisitive person in the pub might be that nobody knows when the *Nights* began – or when they will end.

Hitherto the *Nights* has received short and rather patronizing shrift in general histories of Arabic literature (for example, those of Nicholson and Gibb).[2] In the modern Middle East, with certain exceptions, the *Nights* is not regarded by Arab intellectuals as literature at all. It is true that the literary merit of the stories is variable – and to some extent a matter of taste anyway. Some of the tales in the *Nights* are naïve and vulgar, or even, at their worst, starkly incomprehensible in the form in which they have survived. However, the best stories are artfully constructed, highly sophisticated fictions; they are works of literature in the fullest sense. Though the authors are anonymous, they were not all unsophisticated. The comparative and structural approaches of folklorists may help to bring out the full significance of some of the stories in the *Nights*, but most of them deserve to be read as the products of a highly literary culture. Some knowledge of the complex background of this culture is therefore desirable. It is one of the aims of this *Companion* to sketch in that background, to make apparent to western readers the sheer strangeness of Arab literary culture, and to indicate the existence of whole genres of writing unknown in the western literary tradition. The *Companion* also investigates the aims of the authors of the stories, how these stories were listened to by audiences at the time, and how these same stories have been translated, interpreted, imitated and parodied in Europe and America.

However, the importance of the *Nights* is not just literary, and this *Companion* is not primarily a work of literary criticism. (Mia Gerhardt's *The Art of Story-Telling* may be recommended to those who are looking for a more narrowly literary approach.)[3] The *Nights* is also a valuable source on the social history of the Middle East in medieval and early modern times. Although I have tended to concentrate, in some of the chapters devoted to the stories' contents, on seedy and bizarre aspects of life in the medieval Near East, it must be borne in mind that the vast majority of the subjects of the Abbasid caliphs and Mamluke sultans were not sorcerers, snake-charmers, drug-takers or adulterers. The *Nights* itself contains a large number of pious and edifying stories about wonder-working holy men and virtuous sages, as well as improving fables which enjoin steadfastness, caution, generosity, and so on. However, there are many books about the heroes, scholars and saints of medieval Islam. Arab chronicles and biographical dictionaries have celebrated the achievements of the great and the good at considerable length. It is much more difficult to find out anything about the criminals, the incompetent, the clowns, the beggars and the rest of the humble folk in Baghdad and Cairo, those who were not so pompous or so pious. The *Nights* is an important source on such matters as the Islamic underworld and medieval private life (though certainly a source which has to be handled with caution).

In addition to treating the *Nights* as a source on the history of society and of *mentalités*, I have also sought to give an account of the various ways in which the *Nights* has been studied and, in so doing, to give some idea, however sketchy, of what it is that translators, textual editors, structuralist critics, social historians and folklorists are engaged in. The ramifications of this enterprise are endless, and, in giving the answer to one question, I have usually found that I have uncovered other questions which are even more perplexing. This *Companion* may serve as a guide into the labyrinth, but it offers no route out. But then, having entered the maze, why should one ever want to leave?

The potential scope of a companion to the *Nights* is vast. It is a matter of opening windows on to strange vistas and then rather swiftly closing them again. Subjects only alluded to, or not mentioned at all, in the body of this *Companion* include the poetry in the *Nights*, illustrators of the *Nights*, fables and wisdom literature in the *Nights*, political theory in the *Nights*, mysticism and religion in the *Nights*, plays, films and music inspired by the *Nights*, and the influence of the *Nights* on modern Arabic and Persian literature. This is not because I regard these topics as unimportant or uninteresting. On the contrary, I hope to tackle them in some future study, or studies. However, I did not want to produce a book as bulky as the *Nights* itself, a companion which was so long that no one could read it without dying.

I am treating every story published in the four nineteenth-century editions printed in Arabic (Calcutta I, Bulaq, Breslau and Calcutta II) as part of the *Nights*. Although I believe that these stories do constitute an intelligible unit of study, my procedure is admittedly a somewhat arbitrary one, and some scholars would argue that the real canon of stories which belong to the *Nights* should be narrowly defined as those which were included in the earliest manuscript version. They will object that I am confounding the genuine *Nights* stories with a later and much larger body of, as it were, *Nights* Apocrypha. This is an issue which will be dealt with in Chapter 2.

In 1984 Muhsin Mahdi published a critical edition of an Arabic manuscript of the *Nights* from the Bibliothèque nationale in Paris.[4] With the exception of a fragmentary page from a ninth-century version, the manuscript edited by Mahdi is the oldest surviving version of the opening stories of the *Nights*, and it was the one used by Antoine Galland for his translation. The appearance of Mahdi's edition puts scholarship on a new footing. In 1990 Husain Haddawy produced a very readable translation of the text as edited by Mahdi, and this translation is strongly recommended to anyone who wishes to taste the authentic flavour of those tales.[5] However, the Bibliothèque's manuscript edited by Mahdi contains only thirty-five and a half stories. For the first thirty-five stories in the *Nights*, then, I have quoted from Haddawy's translation. But there is no entirely satisfactory translation of the rest of the stories, hundreds of them, which at one time or another have been included in editions and translations of the *Nights*. After much hesitation and doubt, I have decided to use and quote from Burton's translation of these stories. (His *Arabian Nights Entertainments* with its supplemental volumes was first published in 1885–8.)[6] There are many problems with this translation, and the reasons for both my decision to use Burton and my reluctance to do so will be spelt out more fully in Chapter 1. Here it suffices to say that Burton's edition is a comprehensive one and, though there are quite a few errors in his translation, it is more accurate and scholarly than the later Mardrus/Powys Mathers version. Burton's transliteration of Arabic now seems archaic, and his use of the English language always was eccentric. I cite the titles of stories as they are given according to Burton, but elsewhere my transliteration more closely conforms to accepted academic usage. With the exception of certain Arabic names and words which have become familiar in an English form (among them Sheherazade, Aladdin, Mamluke and caliph), I have followed a simplified form of the transliteration used in the *Encyclopedia of Islam*; I have dispensed with diacriticals, as well as with most *ayns* and *hamzas*, and I have substituted *j* for *dj* and *q* for *k*. The English versions of the Koranic citations are from A.J. Arberry, *The Koran Interpreted* (London, 1955).

I should like to thank Helen Irwin, Dr Hugh Kennedy, Miles Litvinoff, Juri Gabriel, Professor Muhsin Mahdi, Dr Peter Caracciolo and Dr Abdullah al-Udhari for suggestions and advice, as well as Peter Carson for his patience and his faith that this book would eventually get written. Donald MacFarlan's enthusiasm got the book started in the first place. I am especially grateful to Dr Patricia Crone, who read and commented on the typescript and made many valuable criticisms. However, I must emphasize that any errors in the work are my own. I also benefited greatly from conversations with the late Martin Hinds. He is greatly missed.

I

Beautiful Infidels

As Jorge Luis Borges once observed, 'Nothing is as consubstantial with literature and its modest mystery as the questions raised by a translation.' Neglected until modern times in the Near East, the *Arabian Nights* has been so widely and frequently translated into western languages that, despite the Arab antecedents of the tales, it is a little tempting to consider the *Nights* as primarily a work of European literature. Yet there is no remotely satisfactory translation of the great bulk of the *Nights* into either English or French. As we shall see, Husain Haddawy's recent translation is both accurate and fluent, but it is a translation of the first 271 nights only. Earlier English translations have failings which were, to some extent, the product of the times in which they were made and, to some extent, the product of the quirks of the individual translators who made them. But all translation from Arabic poses a range of problems not encountered in translations from European languages, and translating the *Nights* poses quite specific difficulties.

Arabic is a difficult language.[1] The alien curlicued and dotted alphabet, which so bemuses the non-Arabist, is the least of the problems which translators of the language have to master. Only a few of the more serious problems will be listed here. First, one finds almost no punctuation at all in pre-modern Arabic manuscripts and texts. A sentence will run on until the end of the paragraph, if not until the end of the book, and there are no inverted commas to signal the opening and closing of direct speech. Secondly, the absence of capital letters can lead to proper names being mistranslated as things. Yet another feature of written

Arabic which makes it easy for readers to lose their way is the relatively heavy use of pronouns. One of the commonest problems that a translator from Arabic faces is working out whether a particular pronoun belongs to the subject, the object or some other given instrument in the passage – whether, for example, the *hu* ('he' or 'it') refers to the sultan, the unlucky porter or the whip with which the porter is being flogged. Translations from Arabic are peculiarly dependent upon judgements about context and plausibility. At its most obscure, the language has some of the features of a shorthand system. Moreover, some letters in the written language are distinguished from others by little dots, or diacriticals, placed above or beneath the main form of the letter. Thus the letter *za* is distinguished from the otherwise identical letter *ra* by having a little dot on top. But the writers and transcribers of manuscripts quite often carelessly omitted some of the dots, leaving the reader or translator to guess which word or words are intended.

There are also lexical problems. We still lack a really satisfactory dictionary of pre-modern Arabic. The scholar of the language has no access to anything remotely comparable to *The Oxford English Dictionary*, where the origins and changes in use of a word over the centuries are registered. One of the best dictionaries to have been produced so far is Edward Lane's massive but unfinished *Arabic–English Lexicon* (1863–93), a work which was based essentially on medieval Arab dictionaries of classical Arabic. Hans Wehr's *Arabisches Wörterbuch* (1952, English version by J.M. Cowan in 1960) is the standard reference work for modern vocabulary. However, the *Nights*, in the form in which it has come down to us, was written neither in classical Arabic nor in modern Arabic, but in what is known, rather vaguely, as Middle Arabic. Middle Arabic, the language of common usage from about AD 1200 to 1600, had its own distinctive grammatical peculiarities and, to some extent, its own vocabulary. Its peculiarities reflected the impact of spoken colloquial and regional dialects on the older 'high' or 'classical' language. The Arabic of the *Nights* also owed a little to Turkish and Persian vocabulary and syntax. Perhaps the most important and, for the translator, most taxing feature of Middle Arabic is its tendency to dispense with mood and case endings after verbs and nouns. Inspired guesswork can be as important as a good knowledge of grammar when decoding medieval texts. Since there are no comprehensive dictionaries or grammars devoted specifically to Middle Arabic, the scholar who undertakes to translate from the *Nights* lacks some of the most elementary aids to his work, and, of course, the early translators, such as Galland and Lane, had to work with even fewer guides.

A further range of problems stem from Arabic's rigid syntax and spelling, which make it difficult, though not absolutely impossible, to register colloquial and regional spoken usage. If one tampers with the spelling of a word, then one may be altering the word beyond recognition, changing its root form and therefore its meaning. Consequently, the *Nights* features no dialogue by the Middle Eastern equivalents of Sam Weller, Joe Gargery or Mrs Gamp. It has always been difficult for Arab writers to signal class or regional origin by distinctive forms of speech, though an Arab reader, familiar with the geographic or social environment, on being told that a character in a tale is an Egyptian peasant, or a black slave, or a Maghribi (North African) king, may well supply those forms for himself.

Arabic has a rich vocabulary, notoriously so perhaps. John Julius Norwich, in his entertaining *Christmas Crackers*, had gentle fun with the Arabic word *khal*, to which are assigned the following meanings in J.G. Hava's *Arabic–English Dictionary*: 'Huge mountain. Big camel. Banner of a prince. Shroud. Fancy. Black stallion. Owner of a th[ing]. Self-magnified. Caliphate. Lonely place. Opinion. Suspicion. Bachelor. Good manager. Horse's bit. Liberal man. Weak-bodied, weak-hearted man. Free from suspicion. Imaginative man.' Professor A.F.L. Beeston's *The Arabic Language Today* despondently notes that 'in Arabic of all periods, the semantic spectrum of many lexical items is apt to Europeans to seem unduly diffuse'.

In other ways, however, the Arabic vocabulary and syntax may appear to a European eye to be arid and restricted. For instance, it is conventional to translate *wa* as 'and' and *fa* as 'then', but these two conjunctions are regularly made to do far more work than their supposed English equivalents. In certain contexts the correct translation of *wa* will be not 'and', but 'therefore', or 'while', or 'yet', or 'now', or 'many a' or even an emphatic 'by' – as in 'by the beard of the Prophet!'. Additionally, in the absence of European-style punctuation, *wa* and *fa* can do the work of full stops and commas in breaking slabs of prose. Moreover, though medieval Arab writers were at least as fond of elegant variation as their European contemporaries, a somewhat similar problem arises with *qala*, which can be translated as 'he said'. The verb *qala*, in its various forms and tenses, is used far more frequently in Arabic than the English verb 'to say'. Where an English novelist will tend, in any extended piece of dialogue, to deploy such verbs as 'he asked', 'he interrupted', 'he replied', 'he sneered', 'he mumbled', and so on, the Arabic author will tend to stick monotonously with *qala*. One important implication of this lexical austerity is that a strict word-for-word translation of any work of Arabic literature will be both unattractive and, in a sense, seriously misleading. Therefore, only a half-wit or a liar would claim that it was possible to produce a complete and faithful word-for-word translation of the *Nights*, simply changing the Arabic letters into European ones; but, as we shall see below, Mardrus made this claim for his translation.

The restricted syntactical forms and the regular patterning of word forms make rhyme and metre relatively easy to achieve in Arabic, and both rhyme and metre are heavily used for moments of high emotion and for rhetoric in the *Nights*. Arabic rhymed prose (*saj'*) was used to evoke pompous ceremonies, fierce battles, extraordinary beauty, and so on. Any attempt to register this in

English is likely to appear bizarre. Richard Burton, however, did attempt it and consequently produced many unattractive passages like the following: 'But in the stress and stowre I got sundry grievous wounds and sore; and, since that time, I have passed on his back three days without tasting food or sleeping aught, so that my strength is down brought and the world is become to me as naught.' As for poetry, the closeness and profusion of rhyming and metrical patterns cannot be mimicked in English without serious strain. Of course, translating poetry from one language to another is always difficult, but translating Arabic poetry raises so many problems that is impossible even to list them here. Just one particularly obvious and pervasive problem should be noted and that is the Arab poet's penchant for punning and word-play. Again and again, a translator will find he can translate one sense of a couplet, but only at the cost of sacrificing a second sense which the author also intended and which gave force and wit to his verse. Although there is a lot of poetry in the *Nights* and its protagonists have little difficulty in spouting it, even when faced with shipwreck, rape or death, little of the poetry which features in the stories appears to have any direct bearing on the action. Understandably, then, some translators, notably Littmann, who produced the best German translation, and Dawood, who translated a selection of the stories for Penguin Books, took the decision to omit the poetry in the *Nights* altogether.

Although all translations from pre-modern Arabic have to face problems, translations of the *Nights* have to face special problems. For one thing, the sheer length of the collection has deterred most competent Arabists from even contemplating beginning a translation. Moreover, many of the tales, perhaps because they were written to be read aloud, are weighed down with repetition and recapitulation. Most important of all, the lack of a single established source text has created problems for all translators so far. When the texts printed in Calcutta, Bulaq and Breslau all give vaguely similar but significantly different versions of what is presumably the same tale, which text should the translator work from? None of the four versions of the *Nights* printed in Arabic in the nineteenth century was an edition in the scholarly sense of the word, and here and there in all the printed versions there are passages which, as they stand, are gibberish. Moreover, some of the stories are not all that well written; they are unpolished, and their grammar is imperfect. It follows that any translation into a fluent and grammatical English will be an improvement on the original – a misleading improvement. A 'good' translation of the *Nights* will not necessarily be a 'transparent' translation.

Antoine Galland (1646–1715), the first European translator of the *Nights*, played so large a part in discovering the tales, in popularizing them in Europe and in shaping what would come to be regarded as the canonical collection that, at some risk of hyperbole and paradox, he has been called the real author of the *Nights*.[2] Galland was born in Picardy and studied classical Greek and Latin at the Collège royal and the Sorbonne in Paris. It was Galland's excellent knowledge of Greek which induced the French ambassador, the Marquis de Nointel, to take him with him in 1670 as part of a French mission to the Ottoman Turkish Sultan. From 1670 until 1675 Galland was in the Levant, working as an interpreter and studying first Turkish and modern Greek, then Arabic and Persian. Galland also hunted out rare manuscripts, coins, statuettes and precious stones for the ambassador. Back in France, Galland was appointed a curator of the royal collection of coins and medals. He visited the Levant on two further occasions, for the purpose of copying inscriptions and collecting curios, as 'antiquary to the king'. He also produced a large number of translations and treatises on oriental matters, including *Paroles remarquables, bons mots et maximes des orientaux*, *De l'origine et progrès du café* and *Contes et fables indiennes de Bidpai et de Lokman*.

In 1692 Galland became assistant to Barthélemy d'Herbelot on his great work, the *Bibliothèque orientale ou Dictionnaire universal contenant généralement tout ce qui regarde la connaissance des peuples de l'Orient*.[3] This work, with over 8,000 entries, has been described as the first attempt at an encyclopaedia of Islam. It was a somewhat quirky compilation, designed to be consulted both for reference and for pleasure. The entries on Middle Eastern people, places and things drew heavily on illustrative anecdotes, culled from Arab, Turkish and Persian chronicles and encyclopaedias. The book was a treasure-house of oriental wisdom and wit. On d'Herbelot's death in 1695, Galland took over its compilation, and he published the completed work in 1697.

The *Bibliothèque orientale* is a work which stands at the beginning of orientalism, properly speaking. It was produced in an age when the Middle East was not perceived as being part of some underdeveloped Third World (for, after all, the Ottoman Turks had advanced to Vienna and put it under siege as recently as 1683). In the preface to the *Bibliothèque orientale*, Galland asks himself why Europeans are so interested in the Islamic world, while there is so little reciprocal interest on the part of Muslims in Christian Europe's civilization and society. Galland argued that Islamic literature was so rich and of such a high quality that it was self-sufficient. The *Bibliothèque* drew on some of the best of this literature; and on its publication, the collector of fairy tales Charles Perrault praised the book for introducing its readers to a new heaven and a new earth. The *Bibliothèque* was to introduce several generations of writers and scholars to the world of Islam. The notes to William Beckford's orientalist novel *Vathek* draw heavily on the *Bibliothèque orientale* for their recondite references to eastern manners and customs, and indeed the initial inspiration for Beckford's novel seems to have come from d'Herbelot's entry on the Abbasid Caliph Wathiq in the *Bibliothèque*. The notes to Robert Southey's epic poem *Thalaba* similarly draw on the *Bibliothèque*.[4]

However, the work which gave Galland his greatest fame was, of course, his translation of the *Nights*.[5] Some time in the 1690s Galland had acquired a manuscript of 'The Voyages of Sinbad' (there is no evidence that this story cycle ever formed part of the original Arab version of the *Nights*). Galland published the Sinbad stories in 1701, and later the same year, inspired by the success of this translation, he began work on a translation of the *Nights*, having had the manuscript sent to him from Syria. Volumes one and two of *Les Mille et une nuits* were published in 1704, the twelfth and final volume appearing in 1717. Galland used a three- or four-volume manuscript, dating from the fourteenth or fifteenth century, as the basis for his translation. One volume may or may not have been lost since, but the remaining three are to be found in the Paris Bibliothèque nationale (MSS arabes 3609–11). By chance, the manuscript Galland worked from is the oldest known surviving manuscript of the *Nights* (if we exclude a single fragmentary page dating from the tenth century).

The three-volume manuscript is unlikely to have been Galland's only source; for, even in the opening frame story, there are significant discrepancies between Galland's translation and the manuscript. For example, Galland begins the story of Shahriyar and his royal brother Shahzaman by referring to their fathers, but these fathers are not mentioned in the surviving manuscript. There is no obvious reason why Galland should have made up this detail. In some cases it is likely that Galland was inserting the extra details in order to clarify the narrative for his French audience. However, other details that Galland provided are sometimes confirmed in other surviving manuscripts of the *Nights*, so not all of the additional detail can be ascribed to Galland's own whims. He must have worked also from a second parallel manuscript which is now lost.

Moreover, Galland's translation, when it was completed, included many more stories than the Bibliothèque nationale manuscript contains or could have contained even if the hypothetical missing fourth volume were to turn up. In fact, we know that Galland did not rely entirely on manuscripts for his compilation. In 1709 Galland was introduced to Hanna Diab, a Maronite

Christian Arab from Aleppo who had been brought to Paris by Galland's friend the traveller Paul Lucas. Diab acted as Galland's informant and dictated from memory fourteen stories, seven of which later appeared in Galland's edition of the *Nights*. Comparing the notes which Galland took from dictation with the final printed versions of the stories, it is clear that Galland took extraordinary liberties with the stories he received from Diab. For example, when Galland came to transmit the story of 'Prince Ahmed and the Peri Banou', he added a great deal of additional picturesque material from a non-fictional account of a visit to India by a fifteenth-century Arab called Abd al-Razzaq. In the same story, he also slipped in a speech against the eighteenth-century French custom of arranged marriages.

Les Mille et une nuits introduced the stories of 'Aladdin', 'Ali Baba' and 'Prince Ahmed and his Two Sisters' to European audiences. The puzzling thing is that none of these stories has been found in any surviving Arabic manuscript written before Galland's translation of the *Nights* was published. The story of 'The Ebony Horse' does appear in manuscripts of the *Nights*, but only in ones written after Galland had produced his translation, which leaves open the possibility that the Arab version was actually based on Galland's French story. Indeed, some eighteenth-century readers and critics went so far as to accuse Galland of having made up all the *Nights* stories himself. In 'On Fables and Romance' (1783), James Beattie wrote:

whether the tales be really Arabick, or invented by Mons. Galland, I have never been able to learn with certainty. If they be Oriental, they are translated with unwarrantable latitude; for the whole tenor of the style is in the French mode: and the Caliph of Bagdat, and the Emperor of China, are addressed in the same terms of ceremony which are usual at the court of France.

In the case of some stories there are indeed grounds for suspicion; for, although Arabic manuscript versions of 'Aladdin' and 'Ali

Baba' have turned up, they post-date Galland's *Mille et une nuits* and may have been translations into Arabic of Galland's original French prose. To complicate the story of the making of *Les Milles et une nuits* still further, not all the stories in the collection were translated or chosen by Galland. The seventh volume included the stories of 'Zayn al-Asnam' and 'Khudad and his Brothers', as translated from a Turkish manuscript by another orientalist, Pétis de la Croix. This was done without Galland's knowledge or approval by the publisher, who was in a hurry to cash in on the extraordinary success of the stories.

Perrault's *Contes de la mère l'Oye*, or 'Mother Goose's Tales', had already introduced French readers to such stories as 'Little Red Riding Hood', 'Cinderella', 'Puss in Boots' and 'Bluebeard' and had helped to create a taste for fairy stories in sophisticated circles. As it happened, Charles Perrault (1628–1703) had been one of the most enthusiastic admirers of the *Bibliothèque orientale*, and he and Galland shared the same publisher. As the *Nights* stories started to appear, they were read and discussed in the salons, and, as with Perrault's stories, society ladies were Galland's most influential partisans. The publication of the *Nights* inaugurated a mania for oriental stories, whether translated or made up (and these rivals and imitations will be discussed in a subsequent chapter).

In the eighteenth and nineteenth centuries Homer's epics provided one of the two chief battle-grounds for debate about the theory and aims of translation. (The other was the Bible.) It was not thought ridiculous in the eighteenth century for a translator to claim that he had improved on the text he had translated from. Many conceived of the translator's job as being just that, and there were Englishmen who thought that Pope's or Chapman's translation of Homer was better than the interesting but barbarous original. (Intellectual fashion has changed, but even today there are people who judge Baudelaire's translations of Edgar Allan Poe, or Nabokov's translation of *Alice in Wonderland*, to be improvements on their originals.) During the French Renaissance, humanist

translators of the literature of classical antiquity – the so-called
'beautiful infidels' – had argued that good taste took precedence
over strict accuracy in translation. Galland's decorous aim in
translating the *Nights* was not so much to transcribe accurately the
real texture of medieval Arab prose, as to rescue from it items
which he judged would please the salons of eighteenth-century
France. Therefore, the barbarous and the overly exotic were toned
down or edited out. The gallant and the pleasing were stressed or
inserted. Much later, André Gide, determined to clear a space for
his friend Mardrus's translation, was to stigmatize Galland's translation as graceful and charming, 'like the luke-warm steam room
which precedes the hot room in the hammam'. Galland's way of
working was indeed in stark contrast with that of Mardrus (or
Burton), for where Burton and then Mardrus exaggerated the
obscenity of the original, Galland censored it, though his pruning
was less extreme than that carried out later by Lane. Besides
excising most of the pornography, Galland also decided not to
translate most of the poetry. Presumably he thought that it would
not meet with the rather strict canons of eighteenth-century
French literary taste. Galland, who made only occasional use of
notes printed in the margins of his pages, did not hesitate to insert
glosses explaining unfamiliar objects or institutions into the text
itself. It is a device which many translators will judge to be
acceptable. It is clear that Galland thought of *Les Mille et une nuits*
as being, in a sense, an educational text, which continued the good
work of the *Bibliothèque orientale*, in teaching his countrymen
about the manners and customs of the Arabs – a graceful mingling
of delight and edification.

The translations which followed immediately upon Galland's
were translations of Galland rather than of any Arabic version of
the *Nights*. Even before the last of Galland's volumes had been
published in France, some of his stories had been translated into
English and were circulating as cheap chap-books on the popular
market.[6] Although many versions of the *Nights* claimed to be

independent translations made directly from the Arabic, few in fact were. Rather, they were reworkings of Galland with occasional additional material drawn from other sources.

Joseph von Hammer-Purgstall (1774–1856) was an Austrian orientalist who eventually mastered ten languages and who served as a dragoman, an interpreter and guide, in the Levant.[7] One of his early commissions in Constantinople was to seek out a manuscript copy of the *Nights* in 1799. In this he failed. He later went on a mission to Egypt and there met the British naval commander William Sidney Smith, whose service he entered. Subsequently, back in Europe, von Hammer-Purgstall was employed by Metternich and the Austrian Chancery until 1835, when he retired from the diplomatic service to devote himself to writing. It was possibly under Metternich's influence that he developed an obsession with Freemasons and with conspiratorial secret societies in general. His *The Mysteries of Baphomet Revealed* (1818) sought to demonstrate that the Templars secretly worshipped gnostic idols, including a certain Baphomet. In the same year, he published *Geschichte der Assassinen* (1818) in which he compared the medieval Shi'ite sect of the Assassins to the Templars, the Jesuits and the regicides of the French Revolution. He also published a translation of an early Arab treatise on secret and occult alphabets. However, von Hammer-Purgstall is chiefly remembered today (if he can be said to be remembered at all) for his multi-volume history of the Ottoman Empire, which, though it was published in 1827–35, is still not entirely superseded. He also made a translation of the *Divan* of the fourteenth-century Persian poet Hafiz of Shiraz, a translation which was to have a massive influence on Goethe's *West-östliche Diwan* (1819).

Although von Hammer-Purgstall's quest for a manuscript of the *Nights* in Constantinople had been unsuccessful, it seems that he did find one in Cairo. This manuscript has since been lost, but it appears to have been the first to have been discovered containing a version of the ending of the *Nights*, in which Shahriyar at last repents of his decision to have Sheherazade executed. Back in Constantinople, von Hammer-Purgstall set to work translating his text into French between the years 1804 and 1806. Both his manuscript and his translation have since been lost. However, a German translation of his French version was published in 1825 and still survives. He abridged the stories he translated, finding some of them wordy and boring. Suspiciously, his translation includes some of the stories which Galland included in his *Mille et une nuits*, but which are not known in any surviving manuscript of the *Nights* – so-called 'orphan stories'.

The publication of the earliest printed texts of the *Nights* – the Shirwanee text of 1814–18 (commonly known as Calcutta I), the Breslau text of 1824–43, the Bulaq text (printed in the Bulaq suburb of Cairo in 1835) and the Macnaghten text of 1839–42 (commonly known as Calcutta II) – gave a new impetus to the production of translations which were, or at least claimed to be, independent of Galland's. However, there are considerable problems regarding the sources and status of all these texts, and in particular with the Breslau text, the first eight volumes of which were printed under the direction of Maximilian Habicht.

Habicht, born in Breslau in 1775, had studied under the great French Arabist and philologist Sylvestre de Sacy in Paris. Habicht went on to teach Arabic in Breslau.[8] According to Habicht, he received a complete manuscript of the *Nights* sent from Tunisia by a certain Mordecai ibn al-Najjar. He began translating it into German in 1824 and published the results in 1825. Later that same year, he began publication of the Arabic manuscript he claimed to have been translating. Although he had published eight volumes by the time of his death in 1839, the edition was incomplete, and a student called Fleischer supervised the publication of the remaining four volumes (1842–3), 'improving' the Arabic as he went along. It is in fact very doubtful whether Habicht's Tunisian manuscript ever existed. What he seems to have done is patch together a collection of stories from various manuscripts of the *Nights* and from other Arabic story collections in European libraries, and when the Bulaq printed text appeared in 1835 he made use of its stories too. Habicht, like a number of his successors, was driven by a desire to produce a translation and edition substantial enough to embody the 1,001 nights promised by the title of the Arab story collection, and perhaps he dreamed of becoming rich in the process. Habicht's Tunisian manuscript is only one of a number of 'ghost manuscripts', whose alleged existence has bedevilled the study of what is in any case the complex story of the transmission of the *Nights*. As we shall see, similar frauds were perpetrated by Sabbagh, Chavis and Mardrus.

Gustav Weil (1808–89) had, like Habicht, studied under de Sacy in Paris, but he later improved his Arabic in Cairo. Early in his career as an orientalist, he made his mark by attacking the soundness of von Hammer-Purgstall's translation of the *Nights*. Weil himself produced a partial translation into German in 1837–41, which was based on the Bulaq and Breslau texts, plus manuscripts available in the Gotha library (the library of the Dukes of Saxe-Coburg-Gotha). It was not a full translation, for he omitted the rhymed prose and poetry in the stories. Weil was later to gain a great reputation for his monumental history of the Arab caliphate, but despite his status as a scholarly historian, his translation of the *Nights* has won little acclaim, even in Germany.

Jonathan Scott (1754–1829), like many other eighteenth-century Englishmen, picked up Arabic and Persian in India. (He worked for a while as Warren Hastings's Persian secretary.) Scott actually worked from Galland, making only occasional corrections and adding a few extra stories from other sources. Scott's translation, the *Arabian Nights Entertainments*, which appeared in 1811, was the first literary translation into English of Galland's work (as opposed to opportunistic translations by Grub Street hacks), and it was subsequently widely used as a basis for bowdlerized and popularized editions in English for children. The next Englishman to try his hand was Henry Torrens, who began work in Simla, translating the first fifty nights from Calcutta II, which he published in 1838. But Torrens found it hard going, for, despite his literary ambitions, his Arabic was not very good; and when he heard that E.W. Lane was beginning a rival translation, he readily ceded the field to Lane.

Edward William Lane, the son of a clergyman, was born in 1801.[9] In 1825 he went out to Egypt, intending to earn a living as a lithographer and looking for picturesque material to reproduce. On his return to England in 1828, he set to work to make a visual and written record of what he had observed during his time in Egypt. This was published in 1836 under the title *Manners and Customs of the Modern Egyptians* (revised edition 1842). This enormously influential book detailed the religious practices, domestic customs, superstitions, entertainments and material life of the citizens of Cairo. It deserves to be considered as an early work of anthropology. Although Lane had noted in *Manners and Customs* that manuscripts of the *Nights* were expensive and hard to come by, he also formed the view that its stories admirably reflected and illustrated a way of life that still continued in the city. Back in Cairo, he began work on a translation from the Arabic of the Bulaq printed text. Lane's translation appeared in monthly parts over the years 1838–41, before appearing in a three-volume bound version. Although his translation had been a considerable undertaking, he straight away began work on an even grander enterprise and from 1842 until 1849 he worked in Cairo on the *Arabic–English Lexicon*. This work entailed collecting a variety of manuscripts of the massive multi-volume dictionaries of Arabic compiled by the Arabs in the Middle Ages, collating them, arranging the Arabic root entries according to a logical system of his own devising and, of course, providing English equivalents for the words. In 1849 Lane returned to England and continued with the project there. He worked with intensity and became so steeped in this great work that he used to complain that reading English writing hurt his eyes. When he died in 1876, there were still eight letters of the Arabic alphabet on which he had done little or no work.

In the same way that Galland had intended his translation to be a continuation of the *Bibliothèque orientale*, so Lane's translation of the *Nights* was an extension of his earlier work of depicting and explaining the manners and customs of the modern Egyptians, which Lane considered to be more or less unchanged since the Middle Ages. Because he aimed to produce an instructional work, his translation carries an enormous baggage of footnotes – on cloves, graveyards, gypsum, chess, hippopotami, laws of inheritance, perspiration, polygamy, rubbish tips and much, much more. Indeed, it subsequently proved possible to publish the notes as a separate work under the title *Arabian Society in the Middle Ages: Studies from the Thousand and One Nights*.

Like most of those who followed him, Lane felt obliged to clear a space for his own translation by denigrating work that had been done before. He declared: 'I assert that Galland has excessively *perverted* the work. His acquaintance with Arab manners and customs was insufficient to preserve him always from errors of the grossest description.' Later, Lane's nephew and posthumous editor Stanley Lane-Poole was to pursue the charge, referring to the 'lameness, puerility and indecency' of Galland's translation. Lane took particular exception to Galland's style, which he felt was false to the spirit of the original. However, Lane was not a literary man, and, apart from Arabic literature, he had read little except the Bible. His own style tends towards the grandiose and mock-biblical. His text is full of people who 'sayeth' 'lo' and 'ye' and 'thou' and who 'conjure' and 'abjure' one another. Word order is frequently and pointlessly inverted. Where the style is not pompously high-flown, it is often painfully and uninspiringly literal (for example, Lane prefers to echo closely the Arabic usage by translating *ma zala* as 'ceased not', rather than as 'continued'). It is also peppered with Latinisms. True, Lane's translation is easier to read than Burton's, but that, as we shall see, is not saying very much.

Lane worked from the text printed at Bulaq in Cairo, cross-checking the text occasionally against those of Calcutta I and Breslau (though he took the unresearched view that the Bulaq text was clearly superior to its rivals and that discrepancies between the various versions were of little significance). One argument against plumping for Lane's as the best translation is that it is not a translation of the complete *Nights*. Lane designed his work for family reading. Therefore he expurgated or rewrote sections which he thought unsuitable for childish and virginal ears. In cases where he found whole tales to be obscene, he omitted them altogether. Not only did he prudishly censor his text, but in cases where he considered stories to be boring, repetitive or incomprehensible he omitted them too. A reader who has tried to wade through the whole lot, either in Arabic or in Burton's comprehensive transla-tion, may have some sympathy with Lane's procedure, but the truth is that Lane's literary judgement was erratic and his editing arbitrary. Some very good stories have been cut from Lane's version. Nor did he always indicate where his cuts fell. He also discarded most of the poetry as irrelevant. Therefore Lane's transla-tion should be regarded as a large selection from the original stories, rather than a comprehensive version of them.

Lane believed that the final version of the *Nights* as found in the Bulaq text was the work of a single author who lived in the seventeenth century. This betrays such insensitivity to matters of style and content in that certainly composite text as to raise questions about Lane's judgement in other questions. Nevertheless, Lane's translation was enthusiastically received. Leigh Hunt wrote in the periodical *London and Westminster* that 'Mr Lane's version is beyond all doubt a most valuable, praiseworthy, painstaking, learned and delightful work; worthy to be received with honour and thanks by all lovers of the "Arabian Nights" and to form an epoch in the history of popular Eastern literature.' Lane's fellow Scotsmen, headed by Andrew Lang, were particularly appreciative and they were to lead the opposition to Payne's subsequent rival translation of the *Nights*.

John Payne (1842–1906) showed an early aptitude for poetry and for foreign languages.[10] By the time he was nineteen, he had made translations of poetry from German, French, Italian, Spanish, Portuguese, Greek, Latin, Turkish, Persian and Arabic. Incredibly, it seems that Payne taught himself most of these languages – and he mastered Arabic, Persian and Turkish without ever having visited the Orient. (Although the East India Company sponsored the teaching of Arabic, and its employees who had passed an official examination in the language could qualify for higher pay, no comprehensive and accurate Arabic grammar was available in England until Thomas Wright published one in 1859–62.) Payne undertook various apprenticeships and had a short career as a solicitor. Eventually, however, he was able to earn a living as a translator and poet. He liked to work on his translations while riding around London on the top of a horse-drawn omnibus. As a young man of letters he enjoyed many literary friendships with Mallarmé, Swinburne and others. Two of his closest friendships were with Britain's leading collectors of and experts on pornography, Foster Fitzgerald Arbuthnot and H.S. Ashbee.[11] Arbuthnot was a Bombay civil servant with a strong interest in Indian pornography and oriental literature more generally. Ashbee compiled bibliographies of erotica under the pseudonym 'Pisanus Fraxi'. Some scholars believe that the latter may also have written the anonymous pornographic memoir, *My Secret Life*.

In 1877 Payne and a circle of friends set up a Villon Society, to publish in the first instance Payne's translations of Villon's medieval French verse. (The Victorian age was an age of massive scholarly publishing projects, stretching over many volumes and decades – among them Alexander Murray's *Oxford English Dictionary*, Sir Leslie Stephen's *Dictionary of National Biography* and the publications of the Hakluyt Society and the Early English Text Society. Subscription societies, like the Early English Text Society, which underwrote otherwise uneconomic publications, were a feature of the age.) It was the Villon Society which was to publish Payne's translation of the *Nights*. Not only did the society help fund the publication, it also afforded some measure of protection for Payne against charges of obscenity, as it could be pleaded that the society's publications were for subscribing members only. In the case of Payne's translation of the *Nights*, only 500 copies were printed, and all 500 were speedily taken up.

Payne began work on a translation of the Calcutta II edition in 1876 or 1877. Although Payne's translation was much fuller than Lane's, it was still not a full translation of the Arabic text, for he only included pornographic passages if they were also to be found in the Bulaq and Breslau versions. His friendship with Arbuthnot and Ashbee notwithstanding, Payne did not actually hunt out and exaggerate the obscenities he found in the original Arabic. Indeed, Payne tried to render the obscene passages in allusive paraphrases so as not to offend his readership. Payne made no attempt to render the 'doggerel' *saj'* into English rhyming prose. However, he took the poetry more seriously than his predecessors had done and he translated it all. Payne thought of his translation as a work of literature, and not as some kind of encyclopaedia of oriental manners and customs. Therefore he did not trouble to provide any annotations. It took Payne six years to complete his translation of the Calcutta II text. This was published in nine volumes over the years 1882–4. After he had completed it, he went on to translate additional stories found in the Breslau edition and Calcutta I. These he published in 1884 as *Tales from the Arabic*. When a copy of Zotenberg's manuscript of 'Zayn al-Asnam' and 'Aladdin' became available he translated these as well, publishing them in 1889.

Payne had consulted with and received help from many of the leading orientalists of the age – among them E.J.W. Gibb, author of *A History of Ottoman Court Poetry*, Dr F. Steingass, the compiler of what is still the best Persian–English dictionary, Yacoub Artin Pasha, an aristocratic orientalist of considerable eminence, and H. Zotenberg, the scholarly librarian who had made a special study of the manuscripts of the *Nights*. Nevertheless, partisans of Lane's translation, among them John Ruskin, Andrew Lang, William Robertson Smith and Stanley Lane-Poole, were fierce in their criticism of Payne's versions. On the matter of style, their criticism had some force. Payne had a passion for obscure and archaic words. The publications of the Early English Text Society and Alexander Murray's work on the *Oxford English Dictionary* had made more and more such words readily available, and Payne used them unstintingly in his translation. Though he worked hard on his translations of the Arabic poetry, little of it strikes the modern eye as satisfactory. His enthusiastic friend and biographer Thomas Wright was to claim that Payne 'as an original poet and translator was the greatest English man of letters of the late nineteenth and early twentieth centuries ... He has given to Kilburn ... a literary prominence that belongs to a Shiraz, an Avignon, a Weimar.'[12] This is not a judgement which has stood the test of time – even in Kilburn. Payne was opinionated and combative and replied to the criticisms levelled at his work by partisans of the Lane translation. He received powerful support in his combats from Sir Richard Burton.

Sir Richard Francis Burton (1821–90) was already famous as an author, adventurer and explorer.[13] He looked the part, and the young poet Swinburne, practically a disciple of his, said, 'Burton has the jaw of a devil and the brow of a god.' Burton acted the part too. According to his friend Lord Redesdale, he 'was the only man I knew who could fire the old fashioned elephant-gun from the shoulder without a rest; his powers of endurance were simply marvellous, and he could drink brandy with a heroism that would have satisfied Dr Johnson'. Burton had been British consul successively in Santos (Brazil), Damascus and Trieste. He had written extensively on such subjects as swordsmanship, falconry, Indian brothels, mining techniques, Mormons and African geography. In 1864 he had engaged in fierce controversy with his erstwhile companion in exploration, John Hanning Speke, over the location of the source of the Nile. However, Burton was above all famous for his journey in disguise to the forbidden places of the Hejaz, an account of which he had published in 1855, under the title *Pilgrimage to Mecca and Medina.*

Burton first became aware that Payne was proposing to bring out a translation of the *Nights* through a letter by Payne in the *Athenaeum* of 5 November 1881, touting for subscriptions. At the time Burton read the letter, he had been engaged for almost ten years in the dull and insignificant task of representing British interests in Trieste. He straight away wrote to Payne, offering to correct his translation and to assist in any way that Payne might find useful. He claimed that he himself had been doing preparatory work on an independent translation of the *Nights* ever since 1852, when he and the explorer Steinhauser had discussed the project in Somaliland. In fact, there is little evidence that Burton had done any serious amount of translation from any of the versions of the *Nights* prior to the 1880s, though Lord Redesdale, who had visited Burton in 1871, when the latter was consul in Damascus, claimed that Burton had shown him the first two or three of his chapters of his translation then. Nevertheless, Payne welcomed Burton's assistance, both in advising on difficult passages of Arabic and later in giving support in the controversy that raged in the literary press about the respective merits of the translations by Payne and Lane.

Besides feeling bored and cheated of recognition in Trieste, Burton was short of money. Having made contact with Payne, he learned that Payne's translation had been four times oversubscribed, but that Payne had resolved nevertheless to publish no further editions of his work. (As it was, Payne made about £4,000 from his translation.) With Payne's approval, Burton decided to produce 'his own' translation, which he could market through a subscription list of 2,000. Burton's ten-volume edition of the main corpus of the *Nights* was published in 1885. Like Payne, Burton employed the device of a subscription society, both to raise money and to diminish the risk of being prosecuted for obscenity. Burton's edition appeared under the imprint of the Kama Shastra Society, Benares. The Kama Shastra Society had been set up by Burton and Arbuthnot, initially to publish classics of Indian erotica. It had already published the *Ananga Ranga* and the *Kama Sutra*. Later Burton's retranslation of the classic work of Arab erotica, the *Perfumed Garden*, would also be published by the same press. (Benares was, of course, a fiction. The books were printed in Stoke Newington.) After Burton had finished his rendering of the Calcutta II text, he, like Payne, went on to translate and publish stories found in other printed texts and manuscripts. These appeared in six supplementary volumes in 1886–8.

In fact, a very large part of Burton's 'translation' depends closely on Payne's earlier version, though Burton went to tiresome lengths to conceal this. Thus, for example, in the opening of 'The Tale of the Second Calender', where Payne has 'seven schools', Burton has 'seven readings', and where Payne has 'science of the stars', 'handwriting', 'Ind' and 'set out'. Burton has substituted 'star-lore', 'calligraphy'. 'Hind' and 'set forth'. Burton's quest for alternatives to Payne's vocabulary was systematic and at times desperate. However, this is not say that Burton was incapable of making an independent translation of the Arabic, for his translations of the poetry in the stories do not seem to depend on Payne to any significant extent. Moreover, Burton, unlike Payne, did attempt to echo the rhymed prose of *saj'*. Burton also translated some of the supplementary stories before Payne, among them 'Zayn al-Asnam' and 'Aladdin', and there Payne's translations which follow are very similar to Burton's. Burton also translated a number of stories which Payne did not attempt at all, though it is noticeable that Burton often experienced difficulties in translating some of these. Burton adopted such a catholic attitude that he strayed quite a distance into the *Nights* Apocrypha. Finding no Arabic originals for some of Galland's 'orphan tales', he adopted the bizarre procedure of retranslating them from Hindustani translations of Galland. In this way he hoped to recapture some of the original flavour of those tales.

Similarities in style between the Payne and Burton versions are to some extent accounted for by the fact that the two men shared similar literary tastes and friends. Swinburne, Ashbee and Arbuthnot were Burton's friends too, and they all traded books and dirty jokes. Burton shared Payne's enthusiasm for archaic and forgotten words. The style Burton achieved can be described as a sort of composite mock-Gothic, combining elements from Middle English, the Authorized Version of the Bible and Jacobean drama. Most modern readers will also find Burton's Victorian vulgarisms jarring, for example 'regular Joe Millers', 'Charleys' and 'red cent'. Burton's translation of the *Nights* can certainly be recommended to anyone wishing to increase their word-power: 'chevisance', 'fortalice', 'kemperly', 'cark', 'foison', 'soothfast', 'perlection', 'wittol', 'parergon', 'brewis', 'bles', 'fadaise', 'coelebs', 'vivisepulture', and so on. 'Whilome' and 'anent' are standard in Burton's vocabulary. The range of vocabulary is wider and stranger than Payne's, lurching between the erudite and the plain earthy, so that Harun al-Rashid and Sinbad walk and talk in a linguistic Never Never Land.

Burton shared Payne's enthusiasm for Rabelais's *Gargantua and Pantagruel*. More specifically, Burton had a passion for the first three books of that work, as translated in 1653 by the eccentric Scottish Cavalier and linguistic theorist Sir Thomas Urquhart.[14] Urquhart was an advocate of logopandocie – that is, readiness to admit words of all kinds into the language – and his translation of Rabelais took on the character of a verbal riot, something resembling a surrealist reworking of *Roget's Thesaurus*. Phrases and words that had been used by Urquhart in his Rabelais translation – such as 'close-buttock game', 'the two-backed beast', 'springal', 'shite-a-bed', 'tosspot' and 'looby' – resurfaced in Burton's *Arabian Nights*. Urquhart's 'English' rendering of Rabelais was generally wordier, more colourful and more obscene than the original French. Burton followed a similar procedure in trying to improve on his Arabic original. For instance, in the opening frame story, where, in the Arabic, Shahriyar's wife gives herself to 'a black slave', in Burton this man becomes 'a big slobbering blackamoor with rolling eyes which showed the whites, a truly hideous sight'. At its best, Burton's Urquhartian rendering produces flamboyant prose; but at its worst, it is turgid and obscure. Francesco Gabrieli, who later translated the *Nights* into Italian, wryly commented that it was often necessary to consult the original Arabic in order to understand Burton's English. However, Jorge Luis Borges, in his spirited essay 'The Translators of *The 1001 Nights*', did champion Burton's translation.[15] Borges provocatively argued that a translation which is limpid or neutral makes no contribution to literature. Burton's prose, on the other hand, should be valued for its cultural weight. 'In some way, the almost inexhaustible process is shadowed forth in Burton – the hard obscenity of John Donne, the gigantic vocabulary of Shakespeare and Cyril Tourneur, Swinburne's tendency to archaism, the gross erudition of the treatise-writers of the seventeenth century, the energy and vagueness, the love of tempests and magic.' Thus, Borges concluded that Burton's is the best of the English translations of the *Nights*. Not everyone would agree with Borges here, just as not everyone would accept Borges's contention that Robert Louis Stevenson and G.K. Chesterton are two of the greatest writers in English literature. But Burton's *Arabian Nights* is certainly one of the curiosities of English literature. In Husain Haddawy's phrase, it is 'a literary Brighton Pavilion'.[16]

One of the most curious features of this curiosity of English literature is the obstrusive and often supernumerary footnotes. Burton wished to achieve recognition in the world of learning as an anthropologist or scientist of sorts, but Lane's edition with its heavy annotation had more or less done all that was necessary in setting out what the lay reader needed to know about Muslim manners and material life. Indeed, Lane had perhaps explained rather more than any common reader would wish to know. However, out of rivalry with Lane, Burton seems to have been driven to annotate more and more recondite matters in his equally copious notes.

Burton was a man of many prejudices, and they were vigorous ones. He was racist (in an age when racism was acquiring pseudo-scientific pretensions). 'Niggers', Jews and Persians got rough treatment in the notes. He was also a misogynist with a particularly strong dislike for smart society women. He was anti-Christian and he considered Islam, for all the faults he believed it had, to be a better religion, because it was more rational and more useful as an instrument of social control. The indices to Burton's notes are extraordinary specimens of rostered bigotry: 'Blackamoors preferred by debauched women . . . Blind notorious for insolence, etc. . . . Blinding a common practice in the East, how done.' In 'The Tale of the Ensorcelled Prince', Burton has the king imitate 'blackamoor' speech – 'he keeps calling on 'eaven for aid until sleep is strange to me even from evenin' till mawnin', and he prays and damns, cussing us two', and so on. As has been indicated earlier in this chapter, it is hardly possible for Arabic to accommodate 'dis kine o' lordy lordy' speech, and in fact in the Calcutta II text the king speaks an uncoloured and correct Arabic.

Above all, Burton believed himself to be an expert on sex. Cumulatively his notes add up to an encyclopaedia of curious sexual lore. It easy to find Burton's notes on sex simply salacious or quaint, less easy to remember that he was a pioneer who wrote before Havelock Ellis and Sigmund Freud. In this area, Burton was able to draw on the intellectual and bibliographical resources of Fred Hankey and Monckton Milnes, Lord Houghton. Hankey, who lived in Paris, was a wealthy sadist and collector of the works of de Sade. Monckton Milnes had played a significant part in English politics and had been made a peer by Lord Palmerston, but he abandoned political ambitions to become one of England's leading society hosts and cultural patrons. He had long been Burton's friend, and it was through Monckton Milnes that Burton first met Swinburne. (The poet and the explorer rapidly discovered that they had common interests in flagellation and alcohol.) Sexual obsession and racism often came together in Burton's would-be scientific footnotes. It is clear that Burton believed in, and feared, the exceptional virility of the black man. He also claimed to believe that the Persians were born pederasts. More generally, one of his most cherished theories was that there was a 'sotadic zone', including the Mediterranean region and most of the Islamic lands, where homosexuality was the norm. Farting rivals sex as a favourite topic for digression in the notes – and not only in the notes. As far as I can tell, there is no Arab original for the story of 'How Abu Hasan Brake Wind' (which appears in volume five). It is a European story, which Burton naughtily smuggled into his translation of the *Nights*. Something very like it appears in John Aubrey's seventeenth-century *Lives*, though doubtless the story is much older.

Sex and farting apart, Burton's footnotes are a parade of barmy erudition, interspersed with snatches of autobiography. *Bab* is the Arabic word for 'door' or 'chapter'. It is naturally one of the commoner words in that language. Two-thirds of the way through his ninth volume, Burton is able to give this word his scholarly attention and point out that it has a rare, variant (and, in the context of the passage being annotated, utterly irrelevant) meaning of 'Coptic sepulchral chamber'. A note on *shaykh* in the first volume tells us that, in Islamic lore, Abraham was the first man to part his hair and to use a toothpick. In a note in the fifth supplementary volume, he cites Swedenborg on how there will be no looking at the back of people's heads in the afterlife. In other footnotes, he remembers how he was once attacked by a dog in Alexandria and reminisces about seances he has attended. Doubtless such excursuses enlivened the dull slog of transcribing his translation and collating it with Payne's work. Burton's notes are obtrusive, kinky and highly personal. It is tempting to speculate that they might have furnished one of the models for Kinbote's egocentrically deranged annotative scholarship in Nabokov's marvellous novel, *Pale Fire*. (There is, however, no evidence that Nabokov ever read Burton.)

It has become fashionable in recent years to discuss Burton, the author, as if he were the spokesman for Victorian Britain and its empire, one of those orientalists who provided a blueprint for colonialism. From this sort of perspective, studies by Burton and other nineteenth-century orientalists can be seen as amounting to acts of cultural violation. According to Rana Kabbani, for example, Burton bears a heavy responsibility for fostering the myth of the erotic and exploitable East.[17] It is indeed true that Burton attempted to justify his labours and peddle his edition by pointing out that the British Empire, with its millions of Indian and African Muslim subjects, was the largest Muslim empire the world had ever known, and went on to claim that the stories of the *Nights* gave an unrivalled insight into their customs and institutions. It is also true that Burton seized on the racist and sexist elements in the *Nights* and embroidered them. However, he did not invent them. Moreover, it is obvious that Burton's *Nights* was the work of an eccentric and embittered outsider, at odds with the Foreign and Colonial offices, as well as with the Church and with most of the literary and academic world. He had little reward from the Empire and not much regard for it.

Predictably, Burton's work was attacked, as Payne's had been, by partisans of Lane's translation. Burton had done quite a lot to invite controversy. His notes and appendices were peppered with corrections of and sneers at the work of Scott, Torrens and Lane. The orientalists who had advised and supported Payne supported Burton too in a new round of polemic on the subject. Swinburne wrote (bad) verse celebrating the appearance of Burton's translation. Payne himself, while supporting Burton in public, had private reservations about the new version. He thought that Burton had a cloth ear for poetry. More important, Payne thought Burton's concentration on the obscene passages excessive. It amounted to a 'general rubbing of noses in the sewage of depravity'.

Henry Reeve, writing in the *Edinburgh Review*, characterized the then available translations as follows: 'Galland is for the nursery, Lane is for the library, Payne for the study and Burton for the sewers.'[18] Many agreed with him in preferring Lane's staider prose; for, as T.E. Lawrence put it much later, 'It doesn't matter missing if you don't aim; thereby Lane's *Arabian Nights* is better than Burton's.' Others criticized the Burton translation for being excessively literal, the word-for-word translation (noun for noun, and verb for verb) often giving rise to quaint and ugly effects. However, Burton's version survived these onslaughts fairly well, and his criticisms of Lane's selective procedures were on the whole justified. Burton had provided a full edition of the tales, even to the point of including in the supplementary volumes variants of tales he had already translated. His judgement of the respective merits and failings of individual tales was on the whole good, and he had a much saner view of the likely history of the formation of the corpus of the *Nights* than Lane had.

Unsurprisingly Galland's translation of the *Nights* retained a strong hold on the affections of his countrymen, and it was not until the eve of the twentieth century that a retranslation into French was attempted. However, the man who set out to do this was not French himself. Mardrus's grandfather was a Mingrelian, a native of the Caucasus, who had fought with the Muslims under Shamyl to resist the Russian annexation of the Caucasus. After the final defeat of Shamyl, the Mardrus family fled to Egypt, and the head of the Mardrus clan became head of the Mingrelian community there. Joseph Charles Mardrus was born in Cairo in 1868 and grew up in an Arabic-speaking environment, but, as will become obvious, Arabic can never have been his first language.[19] Subsequently, the young Mardrus moved to France and pursued a career in medicine. As a sanitary officer for the Ministry of the Interior, he did much of his work in the French colonies, especially in North Africa. His translation of the *Nights* came out in 1899–1904. (A very readable English translation of Mardrus's French by

Powys Mathers appeared in 1923.) Mardrus also produced a number of exotic and mystical effusions, quite forgotten today, among them *La Reine de Saba* and *L'Oiseau des hauteurs*. Mardrus's wife, Lucie Delarue-Mardrus, was a poet of some note and presided over a coterie of literary lesbians. Unsurprisingly, Proust in his last years was a frequent visitor to her circle, and there are several references to her husband's translation of the *Nights* in Proust's *A la recherche du temps perdu*. Although Lucie published her *Mémoires* in 1938, her husband and his work scarcely feature in those scrappy and egocentric jottings. Joseph Charles Mardrus died in 1949.

Mardrus's sixteen-volume translation, *Le Livre des mille nuits et une nuit*, has a brief preface which boasts of its stark, literal, word-for-word accuracy: 'Pour la première fois en Europe, une traduction complète et fidèle des *Mille nuits et une nuit* est offert au public. Le lecteur y trouvera le mot à mot pur, inflexible. Le texte arabe a simplement changé des caractères: ici il est en caractères français, voilà tout.' (There is something rather attractive about such presumption.) At the time of its appearance, it was hailed as a triumph. However, those who acclaimed its appearance were literary men, not scholars. Mardrus's translation (which was really more of a loose adaptation) caught the literary mood of the time. André Gide was a personal friend of Mardrus, and in an article devoted to '*Les Mille nuits et une nuit* du Dr Mardrus' he argued that Galland's shaping sensibility, his ever present *bon goût*, had so infused his translation that it really told us more about the world of Louis XV than about that of Harun al-Rashid. However, Gide had no access to the original Arabic, nor was he able to step outside the *bon goût* of his own time. He was unaware therefore how much Mardrus's translation spoke to and of its own time. Mardrus took elements which were there in the original Arabic and worked them up, exaggerating and inventing, reshaping the *Nights* in such a manner that the stories appear at times to have been written by Oscar Wilde or Stéphane Mallarmé. Mardrus's version of the Arabian tales was a belated product of *fin-de-siècle* taste, a portrait of a fantasy Orient, compounded of opium reveries, jewelled dissipation, lost paradises, melancholy opulence and odalisques pining in gilded cages.

When Mardrus began his translation, he claimed that he was translating from the 'best' version of the *Nights*, the Bulaq text. However, after some criticism from Arabists who noticed discrepancies between Mardrus's translation and the Bulaq version, Mardrus changed his story. Thereafter he claimed to be translating from a seventeenth-century North African manuscript of the *Nights*, which he alleged had served as the basis of the Bulaq printed text; but it is clear that Mardrus was lying and that this manuscript never existed. The new elements in Mardrus's translation derive from the translator's own fancies. Mardrus embroidered the original Arabic and inserted whole new stories. Many of Mardrus's interpolations were erotic ones, for he shared Burton's unspoken conviction that the *Nights* was not dirty enough and he seems to have thought that the stories would be improved if the erotic element in them could be heightened. At other points Mardrus added revolting little anti-Semitic embellishments of his own. More generally, he made all sorts of 'improvements' to the stories, his inventions often tending towards the fey or ironical. For example, Gide found a snatch of dialogue between Shahriyar and Sheherazade particularly charming. This was where Shahriyar asks Sheherazade what language the animals speak. 'In purest Arabic verse and prose,' replies Sheherazade, but this is really Mardrus having fun, for the exchange does not appear in any of the original Arabic manuscripts or texts. Additions apart, Mardrus also omitted some stories and rearranged others to suit his own taste.

Mardrus's translation of the actual Arabic, when he really was translating the Arabic, has also attracted criticism. At times it was painfully literal; at other times it was simply wrong. Mardrus's dogged literalism led him to turn perfectly ordinary Arabic into the most grotesque sort of French. For example, the Arabic word *ayn*, which means 'eye', can also mean 'well', 'spring' or 'essence'. But in contexts where *ayn* clearly means a well or other source of water, Mardrus translates it as 'the eye of water'. Then again *din* means both 'faith' and 'debt', but Mardrus regularly renders it as 'faith' regardless of whether it is correct in the context or not. It is just possible that for some readers such literalisms may help to give an air of exoticism to the text, but much of this exoticism is simply spurious, owing little to the original Arabic text, but much to the eccentricity of the translator. Moreover, quite apart from Mardrus's monocular practice of matching Arabic words with French words regardless of sense, there are also many simple errors of translation in his version. His translation was heavily criticized by academic Arabists. In response, Mardrus promised to produce a fat tome of learned commentary and justificatory pieces which would conclusively demonstrate his accuracy and scholarship. It is not surprising that this volume failed to materialize. D.B. MacDonald, possibly bending over backwards to be fair to Mardrus, was kind enough to point out that not all Mardrus's mistakes were his own; some of them were directly copied from Galland. However, MacDonald was forced to conclude that 'The Arabic scholarship of Dr Mardrus is beneath criticism.' Suhayr al-Qalamawi, author of one of the best studies in Arabic of the *Nights*, remarked of Mardrus's translation that 'With great regret, we cannot regard this translation as scholarly because of its vulgarity and distortions.'

In 1923 the publisher Jonathan Cape proposed to T.E. Lawrence that he translate Mardrus into English. Lawrence replied enthusiastically, describing the Mardrus version as 'Much the best version of the "Nights" in any language (not excepting the original which is in coffee-house talk!) and it's ambitious to make a still-better English version: and yet I think it's possible. Better, I mean, as prose. The correctness of Mardrus can't be bettered. The rivalry in English isn't high. Payne crabbed: Burton unreadable:

Lane pompous.'[20] T.E. Lawrence's breezy praise of Mardrus's translation calls his judgement into question (not for the first time, of course) and it makes one wonder how good Lawrence's knowledge of Arabic really was. For all his love of the Arabs of the desert, Lawrence showed little knowledge of or interest in Arabic literature. In the end, nothing came of the Lawrence/ Mardrus edition, and Mardrus's French was translated by E. Powys Mathers. Powys Mathers did a good job on Mardrus's French, but whether the job was worth doing in the first place is another matter.

Although the key translations of the *Nights* were into English and French, the stories have of course been translated into most of the world's written languages (though not often directly from the Arabic). In the twentieth century, German readers have been well served by Littmann's complete and very capable six-volume translation (1921–8). Enno Littmann (1875–1958) was an academic philologist with a good grasp of Arabic – and of Hebrew, Amharic, Syriac, Persian, Italian, Latin and Greek. He translated the whole of the *Nights*, except for the poetry, though he translated the most obscene bits not into German but into Latin. His translation was based on Calcutta II, and he seems to have made use of Burton as a crib for his rendering. Despite this partial dependence on Burton, Borges, while conceding that Littmann's translation was accurate and perfectly scholarly, still condemned it for its colourlessness: 'In Littmann, like Washington incapable of lying, there is no other thing than German probity. It is little, it is so little. The intercourse between the *Nights* and Germany should have produced something more.'[21] (German readers I have talked to tend to confirm Borges's judgement.)

In Italy, the distinguished Arabist Francesco Gabrieli presided over a team of anonymous translators who translated Bulaq collated with Calcutta II. Gabrieli took a bracingly critical view of the material which was being translated, criticizing the stories for their intellectual poverty, their puerility, their psychological shallowness, their lack of internal logic and their too easy resort to magic and marvels.[22] Gabrieli's view of the stories is excessively downbeat. However, both Gabrieli's introduction and his translation can be recommended to Italian readers. Russian readers too are apparently well served – in their case by a translation by M.A. Salier, which appeared in the years 1929–33. This translation was published by the Akademia publishing house in Moscow under the patronage of Maxim Gorky. The Akademia project was set up by Gorky in order to save writers and academics from starvation.

As has been noted in the Introduction, most recently we have a translation into English by Husain Haddawy of the Mahdi edition of the Galland manuscript. Published in 1990, Haddawy's translation covers only 271 nights, ending with 'The Story of Jullanar of the Sea', and of course it does not include any of the 'orphan stories' or any of the *Nights* Apocrypha. Some readers may therefore prefer the wider range of tales translated for Penguin from the second Calcutta edition by N.J. Dawood.[23] However, Haddawy's translation is both accurate and a pleasure to read. Moreover, the Mahdi text, from which Haddawy translates, contains many artful details which have been lost in the versions printed in Calcutta and Bulaq. For those wishing to sample the *Nights* and get a true impression of the style and art of the stories, Haddawy's translation cannot be too highly recommended.

2

The Book without Authors

===

Can textual criticism add anything to our pleasure in reading 'The Story of the Three Apples' or 'The Barber's Tale'? It seems doubtful. However, arguments about the oral or literary nature of the *Nights*, its folk sources and oriental prototypes, its narrative techniques, its social and political content and much else are arguments conducted in a vacuum unless one has some notion of what early versions of the *Nights* may have looked like and some notion too of how this corpus of tales came together in an Arab compilation. Besides, it will become apparent (I hope) that the arcanum of textual criticism and editorial technique has its own dry charm. Textual criticism is detective work, a mixture of routine foot-slogging and the occasional inspired deduction, at the end of which the suspects are narrowed down, identities are unmasked, and there are even 'criminals' to be apprehended; for, as we shall see further, the history of the textual transmission of the *Nights* has been muddied by forgers and compilers of pastiche manuscripts of the stories.

The very existence of the *Nights* was unknown in western Europe until Galland began to publish his translation in 1704 (even though, as we shall see, individual stories from the *Nights* had been included in medieval and Renaissance story collections). At first the stories were read for entertainment and studied only as a source for parodies and pastiches of eastern fairy tales. The investigation of such matters as the source or sources of the stories, the date of their compilation and the identity of their possible author only began in the early decades of the nineteenth century. That is to say, the serious study of the *Nights* coincided with the development of orientalism as an academic discipline. Bonaparte's brief occupation of Egypt in 1798-9, the East India Company's need for good linguists, the growing interest of theologians in Semitic languages related to Hebrew, and the foundation of the Société Asiatique in 1821 and the Royal Asiatic Society in 1823 all helped to stimulate a growing interest in the language and literature of the Arabs.[1]

It was European interest in the work that led to the production of the first printed Arabic text of the Nights. This was printed in two volumes in India in 1814-18 under the patronage of the East India Company's College of Fort William.[2] The text, which covered the first 200 nights, is known today as Calcutta I. Sheikh Shirwanee, a teacher at the college and the compiler of Calcutta I, did not indicate what his manuscript source was. Shirwanee was not attempting to produce a scholarly text, but rather an entertaining text to be used by Englishmen and others learning Arabic. Indeed, he believed the tales had originally been produced by a Syrian Arab for the use of people learning Arabic. As we have seen, the next printed version was produced in Breslau by Habicht and Fleischer (1824-43).[3] The availability of these and yet later printed versions of the Arabic stories helped fuel scholarly debate about their origins.

Louis Mathieu Langlès was the founder, in 1795, of the Ecole des langues orientales vivantes in Paris. In 1814, in a preface to a text and translation of Les Voyages de Sinbad le marin et la ruse des femmes, Langlès had suggested that the stories of the Nights had ultimately an Indian origin, and he cited evidence from al-Mas'udi to this effect. His suggestion was developed further by Baron von Hammer-Purgstall (whose career and translation of the Nights have been discussed in Chapter 1). In articles in the Journal asiatique in 1826 and 1839, von Hammer-Purgstall stressed the role of Persia and the Persian language as the conduit by which the Indian stories had reached the Arab lands (no later than the tenth century). Von Hammer-Purgstall's arguments did not impress Silvestre de Sacy. Baron Antoine Silvestre de Sacy (1758-1838), Jansenist, royalist, positivist, great linguist, expert editor of texts, author of the *Grammaire arabe* (1810) and successor to Langlés as director of the École des langues orientales vivantes, was the teacher of a whole generation of Arabists. (His protégés and pupils included Maximilian Habicht, Heinrich Fleischer, Jean Warsy and Michael Sabbagh.) In 1817 Silvestre de Sacy published a review of the Calcutta I edition. In the review, he rather offhandedly discounted the evidence from al-Mas'udi that the stories had a Persian and, ultimately, an Indian source. The stories seemed to him to be too Arab and too Islamic ever to have come from India. In a subsequent article published in the *Mémoires* of the Académie des inscriptions et belles-lettres, he argued that the work had been composed in Syria in the thirteenth century, but that its author had left the work unfinished.[4]

In 1835 a new recension of the *Nights* was printed in two volumes by the Bulaq press in Egypt.[5] Although an Arabic printing press had been set up briefly in Cairo by Bonaparte when the French invaded Egypt in 1798, the printing press set up under the direction of Muhammad Ali's regime in 1821 in the Bulaq suburb of Cairo was the first indigenous printing press in Egypt and one of the first in the Arab world. A certain Sheikh Abd al-Rahman al-Safti al-Sharqawi saw the *Nights* through the press. His edition of the stories gave no indication of its manuscript source, but the Bulaq text was to be the source of most subsequent printed versions of the *Nights* and was the basis of Lane's translation. Unlike the other printed versions of the *Nights*, the Bulaq text does not look like a composite one. Rather, it is thought to have been based on a single Egyptian manuscript of the eighteenth century, now lost. The Arabic of Bulaq's source was generally more correct than the garbled and semi-colloquial renderings given by the manuscripts used in the compilations of Calcutta I and Breslau. The Bulaq text was also used as a source for the fourth and last of the historically important printed versions. This was produced in Calcutta in four volumes (1839–42) and is usually referred to as Calcutta II.[6] Macnaghten, who compiled it, made use not only of the Bulaq edition, but also of the two other printed versions, as well as of an eighteenth-century Egyptian manuscript. Since it used more source manuscripts, Calcutta II appeared to be the 'fullest' version of the *Nights* and hence it was chosen by Torrens, Payne, Burton and Littmann as the basis for their translations. Although scholars of sorts were involved in the production of these printed texts, none of the editions were scholarly editions in any meaningful sense. Their 'editors' simply put the script into type, correcting what they judged to be errors of grammar and spelling, while adding new errors of their own.

The appearance in 1838–41 of Lane's abridged and expurgated translation of the Bulaq text provoked a new flurry of speculation about the provenance and nature of the tales. Lane's own opinion was that, while the collection may have had a Persian prototype, the work, as we now have it, was that of one or two authors writing in Egypt around the end of the Circassian Mamluke period – that is, around 1500. When Burton produced his translation, he denounced Lane's theory with characteristic vigour.[7] Burton argued that the original core of the stories had come into the Arab lands from Persia. The stories had no single author, but were the work of many hands over a long period of time, the last additions probably being made in the sixteenth century. Burton, who can now be seen to have had the better of the argument, in coming to the conclusions that he did, was greatly assisted by his friendship with Hermann Zotenberg. Zotenberg, who looked after oriental manuscripts in the Bibliothèque nationale in Paris, was the first scholar to attempt a comprehensive survey and comparison of the surviving manuscripts of the *Nights*.

At least twenty-two Arabic manuscripts of *Alf Layla wa-Layla* are known to have survived to the present day, and most of these were examined by Zotenberg.[8] The majority of the surviving manuscripts were identified by Zotenberg as having been written in Egypt, but a few were produced in Syria, and one manuscript seemed to be a copy of a Baghdadi prototype (and hence of particular importance, for most scholars were agreed that the first Arabic version of the *Nights* must have been put together in medieval Iraq). A large proportion of the manuscripts were of a late date and had ended up in European libraries. It is possible that many of those written in the eighteenth and early nineteenth centuries were produced to meet the demands of European manuscript-hunters in the Near East. (That relatively few manuscripts survived in the Near East might be taken as an indication that the work was not particularly popular there. On the other hand, one can argue that it was precisely the popularity of the work which led to the disintegration of its manuscripts in the hands of avid readers and hard-working professional storytellers.)

Zotenberg has many discoveries to his credit. Perhaps his most important achievement was to identify the main manuscript source used by Galland in his translation. This was a three-volume manuscript (though, as has been noted, there was perhaps once a fourth volume, now lost). These were the volumes which had been sent to Galland from Syria in 1701. Not only was this manuscript the main source for most of Galland's stories, but Zotenberg (correctly) judged it to be the oldest surviving manuscript of the *Nights*. The script, paper and language of the manuscript all pointed to it having been produced in Syria in the Mamluke period (mid-thirteenth to early sixteenth centuries). Furthermore, an inscription in the margin listed several of the work's owners. The earliest was a Sheikh Taj who had lived in Hama in (probably) the late fifteenth century. His grandson certainly possessed the manuscript in the Muslim year 943, corresponding to the Christian year AD 1536 or 1537. On the basis of the script, however, Zotenberg deduced that the manuscript was actually written in the late fourteenth century, and he later pushed this back to the early fourteenth century.

However, the three-volume manuscript in the Bibliothèque

nationale did not include all the stories that had appeared in Galland's translation, nor did it include more than a minority of the stories known to readers of Lane's or Burton's translations of the *Nights*. The Galland manuscript contained 281 nights or about forty stories (give or take a few, depending on what one judges to be a story unit), and the third volume of the manuscript broke off halfway through the story of 'Qamar al-Zaman'. The stories about Aladdin, Ali Baba, Sinbad, Crafty Dalilah and Prince Ahmed, and scores of others, are not included in it. It seems fairly clear that Galland also had access to another early manuscript which has since been lost. Galland's translation gives a fuller version of the opening frame story than the Bibliothèque nationale manuscript does, and the additional details furnished by Galland (such as the name of Shahriyar's father) are unlikely to have been invented by him (and in fact they also appear in later Egyptian manuscripts). John Richardson's *A Grammar of the Arabick Language . . . Principally Adapted for the Service of the Honourable East India Company* (1776) casually refers to Galland's work as 'an imperfect translation of not quite one half', before giving an Arabic text for 'The Tale of the Barber's Fifth Brother'. The manuscript which Richardson quoted from in his grammar, which once belonged to the notable orientalist Sir William Jones but is now lost, seems to have resembled the surviving Syrian group of manuscripts while being twice their length.

Other Syrian manuscripts, in the Vatican and the British government's India Office, break off where the Bibliothèque nationale manuscript does, and their texts are so similar to it that all three manuscripts must ultimately derive from a common manuscript source. Zotenberg also examined the more numerous Egyptian manuscripts. He found that they had many more stories, but that they tended to give more condensed versions of the story-line than did the Syrian manuscripts (though this is not always the case). Moreover, some of the stories were so garbled that they hardly made any sense at all. The Egyptian manuscripts (which are known collectively as Zotenberg's Egyptian Recension, or ZER) were mostly produced around 1800, almost a hundred years after Galland's translation. Zotenberg also discovered an Arabic version of 'Aladdin' in a manuscript copy of a Baghdadi version of the *Nights*. However, as we shall see, this discovery was not what it seemed.

In the 1880s and 1890s a lot of work was done on the *Nights* by Zotenberg and others, in the course of which a consensus view of the history of the text emerged. Most scholars agreed that the *Nights* was a composite work and that the earliest tales in it came from India and Persia. At some time, probably in the early eighth century, these tales were translated into Arabic under the title *Alf Layla*, or 'The Thousand Nights'. This collection then formed the basis of *The Thousand and One Nights*. The original core of stories was quite small. Then, in Iraq in the ninth or tenth century, this original core had Arab stories added to it – among them some of the tales about the Caliph Harun al-Rashid. Also, from perhaps the tenth century onwards, previously independent sagas and story cycles were added to the compilation, such as the epic of *Omar bin al-Nu'uman* and the *Sindibadnama* (or, as the latter cycle features in the Burton translation, 'The Craft and Malice of Women'). Then, from the thirteenth century onwards, a further layer of stories was added in Syria or Egypt, many of these showing a preoccupation with sex, magic or low life. In the early modern period yet more stories were added to the Egyptian collections so as to swell the bulk of the text sufficiently to bring up its length to the full 1,001 nights of storytelling promised by the book's title. At the same time older stories were modernized in small ways, so that one finds references to guns, coffee-houses and tobacco in some stories which certainly pre-date the invention or discovery of those things.

The debate about the origins and early form of the *Nights* was not dependent only on evidence found within the manuscripts themselves. Other medieval works referred to the existence of the

Nights or something very like the *Nights* in the Middle Ages. Al-Mas'udi (896–956) wrote a delightfully rambling history entitled *Muruj al-Dhahab*, or 'Meadows of Gold'. In a digression on stories, he had occasion to remark that there

are collections of stories which have been passed on to us translated from the Persian, Hindu and Greek languages. We have discussed how these were composed, for example the *Hazar Afsaneh*. The Arabic translation is *Alf Khurafa* ('A Thousand Entertaining Tales') ... This book is generally referred to as *Alf Layla* ('A Thousand Nights'). It is the story of a king, a vizier, the daughter of the vizier and the slave of the latter. These last two are called Shirazad and Dinazad. There are also similar works such as *The Book of Ferzeh and Simas* which contains anecdotes about the kings of India and their viziers. There is also *The Book of Sindibad* and other collections of the same type.[9]

Al-Mas'udi's observations are supported in general terms by Ibn al-Nadim (who died around the year 990). Ibn al-Nadim was a bookseller and the compiler of a catalogue of all the books that were known to have been written up to his own time, called the *Kitab al-Fihrist*. According to Ibn al-Nadim, the writing and collecting of entertaining stories (which it is clear he does not rate very highly) first became fashionable in pre-Islamic Sassanian Persia:

The first book to be written with this content was the book *Hazar Afsan* which means 'A Thousand Stories'. The basis for this [name] was that one of their kings used to marry a woman, spend a night with her and kill her the next day. Then he married a concubine of royal blood who had intelligence and wit. She was called Shahrazad and when she came to him she would begin a story, but leave off at the end of the night, which induced the king to ask for it the night following. This happened to her for a thousand nights, during which time he [the king] had intercourse with her until because of him she was granted a son, whom she showed to him, informing him of the trick played upon him. Then, appreciating her intelligence, he was well disposed towards her and kept her alive. The king had a head of the household named Dinar Zad who was in league with her in this matter.

Ibn al-Nadim says that, although *Hazar Afsan* means 'A Thousand Nights', there were only about 200 stories in the collection, and he adds that 'it is truly a coarse book, without warmth in the telling'.[10] Elsewhere in the *Fihrist*, when he lists the 'Names of the Books of the Byzantines about Evening Stories, Histories, Fables, and Proverbs', he includes 'Shahriyar the King and the Reason for his Marrying Shahrazad the Storyteller'.[11]

Then there is evidence from the Geniza (a medieval Egyptian Jewish archive to be discussed later). The Geniza contains a fragmentary record of loans made by a twelfth-century Jewish bookseller and notary in Cairo. One of the books lent out was *The Thousand and One Nights*.[12] (Here for the first time we get the title in its final form.) That these stories were circulating in Egypt at about this time is confirmed by al-Maqrizi, an Egyptian historian of the early fifteenth century, who quotes a thirteenth-century Spanish author, Ibn Said, who in turn quotes a certain al-Qurtubi ('the Cordovan'), to the effect that tales from *The Thousand and One Nights* were circulating in Fatimid times, that is, in the late eleventh century.[13]

Finally, in the preface to a late-eighteenth-century Turkish story collection, *Phantasms of the Divine Presence*, Ali Aziz Efendi the Cretan claims to be translating from, among other sources, *Elf Leyle* (i.e. 'The Thousand Nights') by al-Asma'i. Ali's story collection does indeed contain versions of stories that are common to the Arabic *Nights*, but he provides no supporting evidence that al-Asma'i, the distinguished ninth-century Basran philologist and companion of the Caliph Harun al-Rashid, did indeed compile such a collection; and in general, scholars have been chary of attributing the *Nights* to a single author.[14]

Although such external sources suggested that something like the *Nights* was circulating in the ninth or tenth century, it took scholars a long time to identify any text or fragment of the text which could have been written earlier than the thirteenth century. However, an important discovery was made after the Second World War. This was a couple of fragmentary sheets of paper, which had been preserved in Egypt's dry air, dating from the ninth century. The fragment was acquired by the University of Chicago and published by the distinguished papyrologist Nabia Abbott. It is one of the oldest surviving literary manuscripts from the Arab world, and by great good fortune the fragment which was preserved bears the title *Kitab Hadith Alf Layla*, or 'The Book of the Tale of the Thousand Nights', plus some fifteen lines of the opening of the book, in which Dinazad asks Shirazad, if she is not asleep, to tell her a story and give 'examples of the excellencies and shortcomings, the cunning and stupidity, the generosity and avarice, and the courage and cowardice that are in man, instinctive or acquired, or pertain to his distinctive characteristics or to courtly manners, Syrian or Bedouin'.[15] Obviously, the title is different, and there is no reference to the misfortunes of Shahriyar and Shahzaman in this opening fragment of the frame story; yet, equally obviously, here we have a prototype version of *The Thousand and One Nights*.

It seems probable from all the above that the Persian *Hazar Afsaneh* was translated into Arabic in the eighth or early ninth century and was given the title *Alf Khurafa* before being subsequently retitled *Alf Layla*. However, it remains far from clear what the connection is between this fragment of the early text and the *Nights* stories as they have survived in later and fuller manuscripts, nor how the Syrian manuscripts related to later Egyptian versions. In the absence of a critical text of the *Nights*, all opinions were at best speculative. Duncan Black Macdonald first formulated the project of producing a critical edition of the *Nights* in the earliest form which could be deduced from the surviving manuscripts.[16] Macdonald was born in Glasgow in 1863. He studied Semitic languages at Glasgow and Berlin and subsequently taught in the United States at the Hartford Theological College. His main academic interest was in Muslim theology and spirituality. His interest in the *Nights* really developed as a subsidiary to his main interest, for he believed that the stories could be used to illustrate the concerns and imagery of Muslim popular piety. Macdonald himself was particularly interested in the invisible world and in parapsychology.

Macdonald followed Zotenberg's trail, examining the manuscripts of the *Nights*, and he began to publish studies on the subject in 1908. Among his achievements in the field of *Nights* scholarship was the discovery in the Bodleian Library, Oxford, of a unique Arabic manuscript of the story of Ali Baba. ('Ali Baba' does not feature in the Bibliothèque nationale manuscript, and some had therefore speculated that Galland himself had made up the story.) Macdonald also demonstrated in devastating detail that Habicht's 'Tunisian manuscript', the basis for the Breslau edition, had never existed, the printed text being based on a variety of manuscript sources. Macdonald also planned to publish an edition of the Galland manuscript, collating it with another early manuscript of Syrian provenance which was preserved in the Vatican. However, this project does not seem to have got very far by the time he died in 1943.

The techniques involved in editing medieval texts, whether western or eastern, are based on those pioneered for the production of editions of the literature of classical antiquity.[17] These techniques depend heavily on what may be called the psychopathology of scribal error. The textual critic, working from a number of late and variant copies of a no longer extant original manuscript source, seeks to reconstruct as accurately as possible the appearance of the original manuscript. He does this by establishing a stemma, or hypothetical pedigree, in which some manuscripts are shown to descend from one or several earlier manuscripts. Common errors are crucial in helping to establish the mutual dependence of manuscripts upon a common source; for, while scribal mistakes which are shared between an early and a late manuscript of the same work may be the result of coincidence, this is not likely. It is much more likely that the later manuscript was directly copied from the earlier one (or from a copy of the earlier one), or that the two manuscripts had a common parentage and that they derive their shared errors from a manuscript from which both were copied. Common errors in scribal psychopathology include haplography (writing once what should have been written twice), dittography (writing twice what should have been written once) and *saut du même au même* (moving to the same word or phrase further down the page). Through the detection of shared errors, a family tree of manuscripts is established (curiously similar to the system devised by the eighteenth-century naturalist Linnaeus for classifying biological organisms).

The textual critic seeks, among other things, to establish which is the earliest manuscript. However, it is important to remember that the earliest manuscript is not necessarily the best, for a late manuscript might easily turn out to be a good copy of a now lost manuscript of an even earlier date. More importantly, the textual critic seeks to establish and date the archetype of the stemma, that is, the hypothetical manuscript from which all the surviving manuscripts with their different chains of transmission of error descend. According to the textual scholar Paul Maas, the archetype is defined as 'the exemplar from which the first split originated'. The archetype, however, is not necessarily and not often the same as the very first version of the manuscript, and the textual critic may attempt to go beyond the archetype, to divine what the source looked like when it was first written down, with all errors and deliberate interpolations removed (that is, to present a hypothetical *constitutio textus*).

A stemma gets a bit complicated if it can be demonstrated that cross-contamination has taken place – that is, if more than one manuscript has been consulted when making a copy of the work in question; with the result that one finds a confluence of readings (and scribal errors) deriving from two or more branches of the stemma. Textual criticism is, by its nature, a conjectural science, and the results it produces are often controversial. Several textual critics have noted the suspiciously frequent production by textual scholars of bipartite stemmata. E.J. Kenny has argued that what often happens in such cases is that one group of manuscripts has been treated as the chief chain of descent, while all the rest have been (unjustifiably) lumped together in a single divergent group, even though members of the divergent set are a miscellaneous residue rather than a genuine group with significant common characteristics.

It is worth noting finally that the great pioneers of textual criticism, among them Bentley, Pasquali and Lachman, worked on texts which had, or were presumed to have had, a single author and of which there was once in truth a single original manuscript (perhaps even an autograph written in the writer's own hand), from which all surviving manuscripts ultimately derived. Moreover, those scholars worked on authors like Homer, Callimachus and Lucretius, whose works were treated with reverence by later generations, with the consequence that copyists were often at considerable pains to transcribe them accurately. When faced with a problematic reading, reverentially careful scribes might even go so far as to compare the manuscript they were copying with another manuscript of the 'same work (and hence there was a possibility of cross-contamination).

Muhsin Mahdi, a professor of Arabic at Chicago and later at Harvard and at one time a colleague of Nabia Abbott, inherited the project – first conceived of by Macdonald – of editing the Galland manuscript and reconstructing the archetypal manuscript of the *Nights*, from which the Galland manuscript and all other surviving Syrian and Egyptian manuscripts derived. It involved him in years of back-breaking work, making a word-for-word, diacritical-point-by-diacritical-point comparison of widely dispersed and sometimes hard-to-read Arabic manuscripts. Mahdi began work in 1959, and the impressive outcome of his labours was published in 1984.[18]

Mahdi took as his base text the three-volume Syrian manuscript which had been used by Galland. He compared it with the other surviving Syrian manuscripts, paying attention to variants and errors. He compared the Syrian family of manuscripts with a parallel, though on the whole later, family of Egyptian manuscripts. Some of the Syrian manuscripts showed signs of contamination from the Egyptian branch; but, by relying mainly on the early versions, Mahdi was able to reconstruct the common ancestor of all the Syrian manuscripts (their archetype or, in Arabic, *al-dustur*), purged of all later additions and corruptions. He then carried out a similar though more cursory operation examining the mainly later Egyptian manuscripts and posited the existence of a common ancestor for this group too. Finally, he compared the two reconstructed manuscripts – the Syrian and the Egyptian – which were the sources of all surviving manuscripts of the *Nights* and deduced the form of their common ancestor, the ultimate archetype. It was not possible to go beyond the text of the archetype, but Mahdi was able to offer some plausible speculations about the circumstances of composition of the original or 'mother' source (in Arabic, *al-nuskha al-umm*) from which the archetype derived. According to Mahdi, the 'mother' source was produced in Syria, some time in the thirteenth or early fourteenth century, probably not many years before the archetype was in turn copied from it (and the Galland version followed on close behind the archetype). The 'mother' source manuscript was in turn based on an earlier version of the *Nights*, composed in Iraq, but Mahdi did not think it profitable to speculate on what form this Iraqi version would have taken.

For the first time, an authentic medieval text of the *Nights* has been made readily accessible to Arabists; and, for the first time, it is possible to make detailed criticism of the language, style and narrative technique of the *Nights*. The style of the *dustur* archetype (and of the Galland manuscript) displays a remarkable variety, ranging from dialect and common colloquial to a high-flown and very correct classical Arabic. Mahdi argues that this range is the product of design and that the 'author' adjusted his language according to the social context of the stories and the rank of his speakers. It is also possible that this variation in language merely reflects a haphazard and unintelligent compilation from diverse sources. Mahdi, however, does not believe that the compiler of the Syrian *Nights* was unintelligent or acted haphazardly. The stories in the Syrian recension were not thrown together, but have been linked to one another to fit an underlying design. In particular, Mahdi has argued that the exemplary tales that come framed within the main narrative are carefully placed to give a covert message about the fatuity of exemplary tales. In other words, the 'author' has used this genre of stories to undermine itself.[19]

It might also be added in support of Mahdi's thesis that, if one takes the first 270 to 280 nights as a unit (that is to say, the stories found in the Galland manuscript), it is possible to detect the recurrence of certain common devices and images in them. The crucial device is, of course, the framing one of a person talking to save a life. Sheherazade does it. So do the sheikhs who tell stories to a jinn (or genie) in order to save the merchant's life, and so do the guests in the house of the three ladies of Baghdad, and so do those who are arrested after the death of the hunchback. Then there is a preoccupation with mutilation (the three one-eyed dervishes; the young men who lost their hands in 'The Christian Broker's Tale' and 'The Jewish Physician's Tale'; and the various deformed brothers of the barber). The breaking of an interdiction often sets the story in motion or keeps it moving along. Underground spaces are associated with sex and danger. The 'author' has a playful, Shandyesque tendency to promise stories which are in fact never told (for example, the allusions to the *Sindibad* cycle and to 'the story of the crocodile' in 'King Yunan and Sage Duban'). Then there are the careful enumerations of things to be shopped for, something which features at the beginning of the story of 'The Porter and the Three Ladies of Baghdad' and at the beginning of the Hunchback cycle.

However, while it is possible that even more common themes and images can be found in this small core of stories, the existence of a common author or compiler is impossible to prove. Be that as it may, Mahdi contrasts the coherence of this early group of Syrian stories with the ragbag of tales which make up ZER and of which he has written that 'copyists who missed what [the Syrian compiler] was after and thought the book was like a hole in the ground in which one could dump one story after another regardless of their styles, structures or contradictory aims, disfigured the book'.[20] In Mahdi's opinion, the old idea that the *Nights* had no original designer and that its structure had always been fluid is based on nothing more than insufficient research.

Mahdi believes that the Galland manuscript incorporates all or very nearly all of what was available in the early Mamluke period, some forty stories related over 282 nights and written down in Syria. Subsequently in Egypt more and more stories were added to meet consumer demand and perhaps to match the number of nights to the title. While Mahdi's main achievement lies in his critical edition of the Galland manuscript, he has also made some interesting discoveries along the way. Mahdi shows that the Baghdad manuscript, which would have been the sole survivor of an Iraqi tradition of transmission and was allegedly copied by the Lebanese copyist Michael Sabbagh in the early nineteenth century, was a fake. What Sabbagh actually did was put his manuscript together by copying from various Egyptian and Syrian manuscripts of the *Nights* that he found lying around in Paris. Since he was a good writer, Sabbagh added little touches of his own, and, not having an Arabic original for 'Aladdin', he translated a French version of the tale back into Arabic. His 'discovery' of this alleged Baghdad manuscript earned him money as well as some academic fame. Similarly, Mahdi has shown that another manuscript, which purported to be the old continuation and completion of the Galland manuscript, was actually a fake perpetrated by a Syrian priest called Chavis, who in fact copied an eighteenth-century Egyptian manuscript. Chavis, like Sabbagh, also seems to have translated Galland's French version of 'Aladdin' into Arabic. A similar case arises with the manuscript of 'Ali Baba', which Macdonald had discovered in the Bodleian and which was in the hand of Jean Warsy, a French pupil of de Sacy's who had settled in Egypt as a merchant in the late eighteenth century. This too has been shown to be a retranslation back into Arabic of Galland's French version of the story.

Mahdi's meticulous editing and research have led him to some interesting conclusions. However, those conclusions, particularly with regard to the stemma and archetype, raise problems and doubts. He has employed a method pioneered by classicists for the study of highly regarded works of literature written by, for the most part, known authors (such as Manilius or Lucretius). Even in the Middle Ages, European scribal copyists took trouble to produce what they hoped would be accurate texts of Latin authors by comparing one manuscript with another and by correcting what seemed to them obvious errors in the manuscripts they were copying from. The case is perhaps a little different when we turn to a medieval Arab work of popular fiction. The *Nights* cannot have been seen as a canonical text which deserved special care or demanded accurate transmission; nor was it written to be read by scholars. It is unlikely that medieval copyists of manuscripts of the *Nights* had any great reverence for the text they were transcribing. Mahdi himself has noted the evidence, provided in the marginalia of a manuscript of the *Nights* now in the British Library, of a book dealer, Ahmad al-Rabbat, who traded in Aleppo in the late eighteenth century, who used to hire out copies of collections of stories and poetry – and when these collections began to suffer from wear, al-Rabbat would insert new pages, sometimes with new stories.

There was no reason for a scribal copyist of the *Nights* to take special pains to get the Arabic right, for it was never written in immaculate classical Arabic in the first place. Nor was there any reason to hesitate in adding or deleting stories, incidents or glosses. If there was no compelling reason for scribes to treat this anonymous work of popular fiction with reverence, then there was no reason for them to consult other manuscripts in order to ensure the accuracy of their copying. Yet Mahdi has argued that the later Syrian manuscripts show signs of cross-contamination, that readings from the Egyptian tradition appear in them. But why should Syrian scribes go to this sort of trouble?

In fact, it is likely that many copies of the *Nights* were written to be read aloud, whether by professional or amateur storytellers, and it may be that the storyteller had no need of the full text (never mind an accurate one!); he needed only an outline of a story on which he could embroider. Moreover, if storytellers themselves made copies of the text, they would very likely have added favourite elaborations of their own devising to stories in their repertoire. And, of course, while the Galland manuscript is the oldest surviving one, it is not possible to prove beyond any shadow of doubt that relatively late Egyptian versions of the *Nights* were not copied from an even older version of the tales. Classical text criticism tends to produce a stemma which leads back to a single source with a single author – and this is the result that Mahdi has achieved. However, the *Nights* are really more like the New Testament, where one cannot assume a single manuscript source, nor can one posit an original fixed canon. Stories may have been added and dropped in each generation. Mahdi's stemma suggests that there were very few thirteenth-century manuscripts of the *Nights*; for, in the end, the stemma narrows down to one single manuscript source. The references in the Geniza and in al-Maqrizi's topography of Cairo suggest, however, that the work was quite well known in the eleventh and twelfth centuries. Is it conceivable, then, that only one thirteenth-century manuscript served as the basis for all subsequent copies? It certainly seems unlikely.

Mahdi argues for a Syrian origin of the 'mother' manuscript, but the Galland manuscript, though it was written in Syria, seems to show a more detailed familiarity with Cairo than with anywhere in Syria. Moreover, Mahdi's stemma depends heavily on manuscripts in European libraries – for the most part the ones collected in Egypt and Syria by European travellers. Must the (longer) Egyptian manuscripts be judged inferior just because they are later? (While on the subject of Egyptian versions, why assume that Bulaq, alone of all the printed texts, was based on a single Egyptian manuscript source?) All the manuscripts, both Syrian and Egyptian, have three old men who offer to tell amazing stories to the jinn in order to save a merchant's life. However, none of the Syrian manuscripts give the third old man's story, while manuscripts in the Egyptian tradition do. Surely this suggests that the Egyptian tradition here was based on a fuller source? If the Egyptian manuscripts were right in including a third old man's tale, perhaps they were also right in including other material. It is also noteworthy that the Syrian group of manuscripts begin the story of 'Qamar al-Zaman' but break off at the 283rd night with the story barely begun. In completing the text of 'Qamar al-Zaman' for his edition of *Alf Layla wa-Layla*, Mahdi was obliged to make use of an Egyptian manuscript in the Bodleian. (This is the Wortley Montagu manuscript, brought to England in the late eighteenth century by the so-called 'Man in the Iron Wig', Edward Wortley Montagu, a notorious charlatan, necromancer and Arabist.)[21]

Although Mahdi's stemma suggests that everything comes from a single thirteenth- or early-fourteenth-century Syrian manuscript, it would appear that there was at least one other early Syrian version of the manuscript which was longer than the Galland manuscript and was available for Richardson to use when he prepared his Arabic grammar. Then again, can Mahdi be right in supposing that the Galland manuscript dates from the fourteenth century, and can the (now lost) source copy of the Galland manuscript be dated back to as early as the thirteenth century?[22] Most of the internal evidence suggests otherwise. It is true that a thirteenth-century dating might be suggested by an incident in 'The Barber's Tale', in which the barber uses his astrolabe to set up a horoscope in the Muslim year 653, that is, AD 1255.[23] However, notwithstanding this (and discounting Zotenberg's and Mahdi's impression of the date of the manuscript hand), other references in the Galland manuscript suggest that it cannot have been written any earlier than the fifteenth century. The Christian broker meets someone in Cairo at the Caravanserai of al-Jawli, which was founded only in the early fourteenth century.[24] In 'The Jewish Physician's Tale' there is reference to a large house in Damascus, known as the house of Sudun Abd al-Rahman. If this is a misrendering of Sudun min Abd al-Rahman, then the reference is to Sayf al-Din Sudun min Abd al-Rahman, who became Governor of Damascus in 1424 and died in 1438.[25] Finally, and most conclusively, in 'The Jewish Physician's Tale', a payment is made in the Ashrafi dinar, a coin which was first put in circulation in 1425 during the reign of the Sultan al-Ashraf Barsbay.[26]

From all the above, it must be apparent that complex problems remain to be resolved. There is still a great deal of work to be done. In particular, a number of manuscripts in Middle Eastern libraries need to be looked at. It would be useful if an edited version of the ZER recension could be produced (though that would certainly be a difficult and time-consuming task). It is also desirable that more research should be done on individual stories or story cycles, tracing their history prior to their incorporation in the corpus of the *Nights* and comparing their renderings in parallel and rival story collections. It is possible also that research into the history of Ottoman Turkish and Balkan popular fiction may produce interesting results. We have already had occasion to refer to Ali al-Effendi's story collection and his belief that the *Nights* were written by al-Asma'i. There seems also to be evidence that, by the seventeenth century at least, there was a version of the *Nights* in Romanian. The Romanian version had been translated from Greek and the Greek from Syriac, and the Syriac version was allegedly based on an Arabic translation made from Persian by Musa ibn Isa al-Kasrawi, a ninth-century scribe.[27]

Evidently, the issues raised in dating an anonymous, slowly evolving, composite work like the *Nights* are complex. The answer to the question how old is *The Thousand and One Nights* will depend, among many other things, on what one counts as the first version of the *Nights*. Should it be the Persian prototype, the *Hazar Afsaneh*? Or the ninth-century *Thousand Nights*, of which a few scrappy lines survive? Or *The Thousand and One Nights*, referred to in the twelfth century, but of which not even a few scrappy lines survive? Or the purely hypothetical thirteenth-century Syrian source manuscript? Or the Galland manuscript, which was written in either the fourteenth or the fifteenth century? Or the fuller versions of the *Nights*, translated by Lane and Burton, which were filled out with all sorts of ancient and recent stories (including 'Sinbad', 'The Ebony Horse', 'Ali Baba' and the rest) some time between the fifteenth and the early nineteenth centuries?

3

Oceans of Stories

===

Very deep is the well of the past. Should we not call it bottomless?

Thomas Mann, *Tales of Jacob*

Two rogues, pretending to be traders, attached themselves to a journeying merchant, having agreed to rob him of everything he had. However, each of the thieves had privately decided that he wanted all the spoils for himself, so each poisoned the other's food. Thus they perished, and the merchant proceeded on his way unharmed. This is how the tale features as 'The Merchant and the Two Sharpers' in the *Nights*. A more elaborate and more satisfyingly structured version of essentially the same story appears in *The Canterbury Tales* as 'The Pardoner's Tale', in which three rioters set out to find Death, who has killed the fourth man in their company. A mysterious old man tells them that they will find Death under a certain tree. But, instead of Death, they find treasure under the tree. Each man then plots to kill his fellows. The story ends with their success and the death of all three of them. An earlier and simpler version of this story-type is found in the ancient Indian story collection known as the *Jataka*. A more recent reworking can be found in John Huston's film *The Treasure of the Sierra Madre* (1947).[1]

A man approached an aged bawd and asked her to arrange an assignation with a woman in the town. The bawd had a certain woman in mind, but the trouble was that this woman was a virtuous wife. So the bawd devised a stratagem. She made cakes full of pepper and fed them to a bitch puppy, so that the dog's eyes were scalded with tears. Then the bawd took the bitch along with her when she went to visit the virtuous woman. When the woman asked why the dog was weeping, the bawd told her that this was a woman who had been transformed by sorcery into a dog for refusing the advances of a young man and so the dog wept as she remembered her previous state and the pleasures that she had so foolishly refused. In this way the hitherto virtuous wife was persuaded to let the bawd make an assignation for her with the man. When the hour of the assignation came, the wife's horror was great to discover that the man she had been brought face to face with was her own husband. But she kept her presence of mind and swiftly started abusing him, claiming that she had set this trap to test him and teach him a lesson. The husband promised to mend his ways and keep faithful to his wife thereafter. This story, which really consists of two linked story elements, the weeping puppy trick and the wife's quick-thinking stratagem, is found in the *Nights* as 'The Tale of the Woman who Wanted to Deceive her Husband', one of the *Sindibad* cycle of tales. But both halves of essentially the same tale are found elsewhere: in the eleventh-century Sanskrit *Katha Sarit Sagara*, in the twelfth-century Latin *Disciplina clericalis*, in the Middle English fabliau, or short tale in verse, of 'Dame Sirith', in the fourteenth-century Persian *Tutinameh* by al-Nakhshabi, in the fourteenth-century *Decameron* by Boccaccio, and in Thomas Mann's twentieth-century novel *Doctor Faustus*.[2]

Similar exercises can be performed on many other tales in the *Nights*. For example, the Ebony Horse in the *Nights* is unmistakably the same horse as the one featured in Chaucer's 'The Squire's Tale'. The same horse takes to the air again in the North African *One Hundred and One Nights*, in the thirteenth-century French romance of *Cleomades* and in the *Katha Sarit Sagara*.[3] Indeed, there is scarcely a tale in the whole of the *Nights* which does not have its precursors, derivatives or analogous versions. Tales evolve into other tales and they replicate, elaborate, invert, abridge, link and comment on their own structure in an endless play of transformation – but was there ever the first version of any story? It is almost always impossible to tell when a story was first told and when it was first written down, or how it was transmitted, and impossible too to say what the last telling and final version of a story will be. Good stories pay little attention to cultural or linguistic frontiers. The student of story collections finds himself adrift on an ocean of stories, an ocean which is boundless, deep and ceaselessly in motion.

What follows is a brief, all too brief, survey of those story collections which are *not* the *Nights* – as it were, the presentation of a jigsaw puzzle with its central piece missing. However, every one of the story collections to be discussed stands in some relation or another to the *Nights*, and the Arab collection can be better understood when it is placed in a global setting and compared with its Sanskrit, Greek, Latin and other rivals.

To begin where some scholars believe all great stories began, in India,[4] the *Jataka* is a Pali collection of 547 fables, stories, romances, maxims and legends that purportedly relate to previous incarnations of the Buddha. It is not known when this anthology was compiled. While it survives in a fifth-century version in Pali, it is probably much older. The tales are for the most part moral tales with an ethical purpose. 'The Tale of the Bull and the Ass' and the linked 'Tale of the Merchant and his Wife', in which a man knows the language of the beasts and takes warning from their conversation not to reveal the secret of his knowledge, are found in the *Jataka* and in the frame story of the *Nights*. (The vizier tells these stories to his daughter, Sheherazade, in the misguided belief that it will deter her from offering to become Shahriyar's next bride.) The same story, or one or other of its halves, is also found in the Sanskrit *Vetalapanchavinsati* and in the medieval Latin *Gesta Romanorum*, as well as in Estonian and Javanese folklore. Similarly, others of the *Jataka*'s tales can be found both in later Sanskrit story collections, like the *Panchatantra*, and in western collections like Aesop's *Fables*.

The *Panchatantra*, or 'Five Books', composed in Sanskrit no later than the sixth century, is a collection of stories in which the framing device is that of a wise brahmin who instructs three young princes in the wisdom that they must learn if they are ever to rule well.[5] It belongs, then, to the genre of 'mirrors for princes'. However, it is clear that the stories were aimed at a wider audience than one just composed of princes; and though, as in the case of the *Jataka*, it is claimed that the stories have been strung together for a moral purpose, it is clear that these were at least as often read for entertainment as for edification. The stories are concerned with losing and gaining friends, with war and peace, with the loss or gain of property and, finally, with ill-considered action. Animals form the cast of these stories – the lion who is the ruler, the two jackals who are his good and bad advisers, the stupid monkey, and so forth. The *Panchatantra* was a popular story cycle and it travelled far. In the sixth century it was translated into Pahlavi (Old Persian) as *The Fables of Bidpai*. In the eighth century Ibn al-Muqaffa translated it into Arabic as *Kalila wa-Dimna* (the title referring to the names of the two jackal viziers). From Arabic it was translated into Syriac, Hebrew and, ultimately, most of the European languages.

The stories of the *Panchatantra* were eventually incorporated in the *Katha Sarit Sagara*. This much grander compilation was translated from the Sanskrit into English by C.H. Tawney (published in 1880–84), and more accessibly republished by Norman Penzer under the title of *The Ocean of Story* (1928), and in this English version it runs to ten fat volumes.[6] It is perhaps because this extraordinary work was translated later than the *Nights* that it has found less fame in the West than the Arab stories. The Sanskrit collection of moral, humorous and horrific tales was originally compiled by Somadeva, a Kashmiri court poet, in the eleventh century. Bulky though the collection is, it seems that it is only the abridgement of a yet bulkier work, the *Brihat-Katha*, or 'Great Tale', by Gunadhya, which was put to-

gether some time before the seventh century but has since been
lost. Taken as a whole, one of the most obvious features of the
Katha Sarit Sagara is its misogyny. 'Woman has fickleness
implanted in her by Nature like the flashings of lightning': murderous women, faithless women and shrewish women proliferate in
its pages. (However, this is a general, almost invariable, feature of
pre-modern story collections and their frame stories in particular.
Why this should be so deserves further investigation.)

As the medieval Dutch proverb has it, 'Big fish eat little fish.'
Individual stories are swallowed up in story collections, and these
story collections in turn are swallowed up in yet larger collections
of story collections. Besides the moral fables of the *Panchatantra*,
the *Katha Sarit Sagara* also contains within it the *Vetalapanchavinsati*,
or 'Twenty-Five Tales of a Vampire'.[7] A *vetala* is an evil spirit that
haunts cemeteries. In this story collection within a story collection,
the somewhat curious framing device is the story of a king who
owes a beggar a favour. He agrees to fetch a corpse for the beggar.
The corpse is hanging from a tree in a cemetery. As the king
approaches the corpse, it emits a sinister laugh, for it is inhabited
by a *vetala*, or vampire. The vampire-ridden corpse settles on the
king's shoulder, and the vampire, knowing that the beggar plans
to kill the king when he arrives, keeps telling the king stories with
the aim of delaying his progress. Finally the vampire advises the
king on how to outwit the sinister beggar. A version of some of
these stories was translated from Hindu by Burton under the title
Vikram and the Vampire: or Tales of Hindu Devilry (1870). Again –
and this may have appealed to Burton – the misogynistic tenor of
the tales is striking. This story collection contains the tale about
the merchant who knew the language of animals, which eventually
ended up in the frame story of the *Nights*. What is essentially an
early form of the *Nights* tale of 'The King who Kenned the
Quintessence of Things' is also found in this vampire's repertoire.

The *Sukasaptati*, or 'The Seventy Tales of the Parrot', was put
together in India no later than the twelfth century. A parrot, by

telling a string of stories, prevents a woman from committing adultery. Although the parrot is telling stories to preserve the wife's virtue, a large number of the tales it tells are of cunning, faithless women. This parrot collection reached the Middle East via a fourteenth-century translation from Sanskrit into Persian by al-Nakhshabi (d. 1350) entitled the *Tutinameh*.

The idea that the ultimate ancestor of the *Nights* was an Indian story collection has a long history. As we have seen, von Hammer-Purgstall argued that the *Hazar Afsaneh*, the presumed Persian original of the core of the earliest version of the *Nights*, was itself a translation or an adaptation of an Indian original. In the course of the nineteenth century the quest for the eastern, and usually Indian, origins of western culture continued to be an obsession in certain scholarly circles. Diffusionism – the notion that aspects of culture start from a single source and spread from there to other civilizations – was the fashion, and the theory tended to discount the possibility that things could be independently invented in several civilizations. The study of the history of language and of Sanskrit philology, of which Max Müller (1823– 1900) was perhaps the most distinguished practitioner, provided a paradigm in which India was the fountain of culture. Theodor Benfey (1809–81), similarly a German Sanskrit scholar philologist, argued in the introduction to his translation of the *Panchatantra* (1859) that 'a great number of *Märchen* and other folk-tales have spread out from India over almost the entire world'. He went on to suggest that, prior to the tenth century, such stories were usually transmitted orally (although he believed the tales of the *Panchatantra* to be a rare exception). Thereafter, however, stories were commonly transmitted from India to Europe, via Persian and Arabic, in written texts. Benfey also believed that some Indian story collections reached the Mongols via Tibet and that the Mongols brought some of those stories to Europe in the thirteenth and fourteenth centuries. It seemed that stories, like the sun, always travelled in a westward direction. Since the stories of the

Panchatantra had been transmitted from Sanskrit to Persian, then to Syriac and Arabic and then to various European languages, Benfey believed that the same applied to the other stories that students of literature and folklore had found to be common to Europe and India. Benfey and his disciples also argued that the idea of framing stories within stories to provide a pretext for their telling was peculiarly Indian.

As far as the history of the study of the *Nights* is concerned, Emmanuel Cosquin (1841–1921) was the most important of Benfey's disciples, though he was not uncritical and he rejected the idea of the Mongols as the medieval bearers of Indian folk-tales to Europe. Also Cosquin did not believe in the Indian origin of almost everything. He preferred to think of the subcontinent, not as a fountain, but rather as a reservoir, a place which both supplied and received stories. However, Cosquin did believe in the Indian origin of the *Nights*. In 'Le Prologue-cadre des *Mille et une nuits*, les légendes perses et le Livre d'Esther' (*Revue biblique*, 1909), Cosquin first argued against the theory of a Persian origin for the frame story of the *Nights*, and against the idea that a lost ancient Persian tale had also been reworked in the biblical Book of Esther (in which Esther becomes the bride of King Ahasuerus and saves the Jews). Secondly and more importantly, Cosquin attempted to show that the frame story of the *Nights* derived from the reworking and stringing together of older Indian stories.[8] At least three elements from Indian sources were used in this manner: first the king who despairs of the possibility of woman's fidelity; secondly the woman who is guarded by a supernatural being in order to keep her faithful but who nevertheless eludes his guard to sleep with men; and thirdly the tireless telling of stories in order to delay an evil. The first two of these motifs were found in a Chinese Buddhist text of about AD 250, the *Kieou Tsa P'iyu King* of Seng-Houei, which Cosquin believed to have been translated from the Sanskrit. That text has the story of a prince who is unhappy because of the evil conduct of his mother; he is cheered up when he finds a brahmin magician who keeps his wife sealed in a pot which he can swallow or spit out at will; but the magician does not know that, when he sleeps, his wife, who has similar magical powers, can spit out a pot in which she keeps her secret lover. The affinity between this tale and the adventures of King Shahriyar is evident. As for the storytelling of Sheherazade, this had its precedent in the Jain legend of Kanakamanjari, who keeps the love of her king for six months by telling stories every night which have to be concluded on a following night.

Cosquin presumed that the Chinese story of Seng-Houei was based on a lost Sanskrit original, but there is no evidence for this. As Professor B.E. Perry has pointed out, the Chinese might just as well have taken it from an ancient Persian story, one which was later recycled in the *Hazar Afsaneh*.[9] The transformation of men and women in the *Nights* into animals has been held to be an indication of an Indian origin, a reminiscence of Buddhist and Hindu ideas on reincarnation. However, this motif is pervasive in the world's folklore, and such a basic fantasy as the transformation of a man into an animal does not need to have a single point of invention. After all, it even features in the myths of the North American Indians. When in the *Nights*, in 'The Second Dervish's Tale', the prince is transformed into a monkey, but a monkey who can write, the point of derivation may well be a reminiscence not of anything Hindu or Buddhist, but rather of the ape's form of the ancient Egyptian god of the scribes, Thoth. The theme of a man magically transformed into an animal is also at the heart of Apuleius' Latin novel *The Golden Ass*. One might refer also to Ovid's *Metamorphoses*, which, as its title suggests, is concerned with little else but the possibilities of shape-shifting. Moreover, going further back, when, in the Greek *Odyssey*, Circe transforms Odysseus' companions into beasts, must we look for some ancient Sanskrit model of inspiration?

India was in any case not the only possible source from which the Arabs could have derived the device of the framing story, for the frame story was also a familiar device in the western world. The insertion of smaller stories within the framework of a larger story is a basic technique. In the *Odyssey*, Homer has Odysseus telling tales at the court of King Alcinous, and Ovid's *Metamorphoses* also makes much play with stories within stories. Nor can Indian storytellers claim a monopoly on misogyny. Early Christian storytellers were also fond of tales with this theme. Since even Benfey thought that animal fables, of the Aesopic kind, originated in the West, in Greece, a western origin for other sorts of stories is also possible.

Here and there throughout the *Nights*, one comes across what seem to be survivals of stories and images from the literature of ancient Greece and Rome. Galland was the first to consider this question and he noticed that Sinbad's encounter, on his third voyage, with a giant, whom he blinds before making his escape, was an echo of the incident in the *Iliad* in which Odysseus encountered Polyphemus. Similarly, Galland found a reworking of Circe's enchantment of Odysseus' companions in the *Nights* story of 'Julnar the Sea-Born and her Son King Badr Basim', in which the sorceress Queen Lab uses a drug to transform her former lovers into birds. (The ninth-century translator, Hunayn ibn Ishaq, was able to recite sections of Homer by heart, presumably in Greek, yet he never translated him into Arabic. Although there are indications in the *Nights* and in the writings of al-Biruni, al-Shahrastani and others that the contents of Homer's epics were known to some, Homer was only a name to the cataloguer Ibn al-Nadim, and neither the *Iliad* nor the *Odyssey* was translated into Arabic until the present century.)[10]

Julnar the Sea-Born herself may owe something to Thetis, the sea deity and mother of Achilles. 'The Cranes of Ibycus' (the story of how a Greek poet of the sixth century BC was murdered and avenged) is recycled as 'The Sixteenth Constable's Story' in the cycle of tales told by Sultan Baybars's policemen. A prototype of the *rukh* (a huge mythical bird reputed to be able to carry a man through the skies) in 'The Voyages of Sinbad' may be found in Lucian's *True History* (second century AD). Images and incidents from *The Romance of Alexander* by Pseudo-Callisthenes crop up in a wide range of romances and adventures that were incorporated in the *Nights*.

In the third or second century BC, the Roman playwright Plautus wrote *Miles gloriosus*, or 'The Braggart Soldier', a play about two lovers in adjoining houses who make use of a hole in a common wall to meet. The resemblances of this story to the *Nights* story of 'Qamar al-Zaman and the Jeweller's Wife' are much too close for coincidence, and Gustave von Grunebaum argues that both the Roman play and the Arab story go back to an older Greek source. However, it may well be that an Arab author worked on a version of Plautus' play, transmitted via Greek and Syriac, and turned it into a story; and it is possible that more links between the dramatic tradition of classical antiquity and collections of stories in Arabic remain to be discovered. As we shall see in a later chapter, there is a certain family resemblance between the themes of plays acted out by classical mimes and the subject-matter of some of the stories of the *Nights*.

One could go on and on listing particular instances of potential Greek and Roman prototypes for the plot structures, themes and motifs of the later Arab stories.[11] Instead, one intriguing possibility should be considered. In the tenth-century *Fihrist*, or 'Catalogue', of the Iraqi bookseller Ibn al-Nadim, under the general heading 'The Names of the Books of the Byzantines about Evening Stories, Histories, Fables and Proverbs' is included a book called *Shatariyus the King and the Reason for his Marrying Shazad the Storyteller*.[12] What follows from this unique reference is that the frame story of King Shahriyar and Sheherazade the storyteller may be of Greek origin. While this is possible, it does not seem particularly likely. Even so, the alleged existence of a tenth-century, or earlier, Byzantine Greek version of the story is intriguing and it makes one wonder if a version of the *Nights* was not transmitted, via the Greek, to the various Balkan languages. Some at least of the *Nights* stories seem to have been known in Romania prior to Galland's translation of them.[13] Although it is improbable that the frame story of Sheherazade had a Byzantine origin, nevertheless, many of the romantic tales in the *Nights*, such as 'Uns al-Wujud and the Vizier's Daughter Rose-in-Hood', show signs of having borrowed from the conventions of Byzantine romance.

Of course, large areas of classical Greek and Latin literature were not imitated or reworked in the literature of the Arabs, and the works of Euripides, Aeschylus, Petronius and Marcus Aurelius have left, I think, no traces in the later literature of the Middle East. The question of why once popular stories or even whole genres of literature may fail and die out is an interesting one. For example, wisdom literature and fables were taken by the Arabs from their Hebrew, Greek, Roman and, above all, Persian precursors, and in turn medieval Christendom took much of that material from the Arabs. However, there is no market for such stuff now. La Fontaine and his seventeenth-century fables came very near the end of a line. While *The Seven Voyages of Sinbad* has survived to the present day and (even if in a highly mutated form) has made the leap on to celluloid, the once popular and highly improving discourse of the slave girl Tawaddud has been forgotten by all, save specialist scholars. We shall return to the survival of stories and the reason for their survival in the next chapter.

The Arabs became heirs by conquest not only to the storytelling lore of Greece and Rome, but also to that of the Copts, Hebrews, Berbers and Persians. Primitive prefigurations of some of the stories of the *Nights* have been found in the literature of Pharaonic Egypt, and it seems likely that some of those stories or parts of stories reached the Arabs via the folklore of the Coptic Christian inhabitants of Egypt. For example, the germ of 'The Tale of the Envious and the Envied' (narrated in the *Nights* by the second dervish to the wrathful jinn) is found in the ancient Egyptian story of 'The Blinding of Truth by Falsehood', which in its written form appears in the thirteenth century BC. Then again, the Twelfth Dynasty papyrus of 'The Tale of the Shipwrecked Man' anticipates some of the themes of *The Seven Voyages of Sinbad*. When Crafty Dalilah, in the *Nights*, gets a gang of her rivals drunk so that she may commit a theft, and then marks the success of her enterprise by shaving the right cheeks of the sleeping drunks, she repeats actions which Herodotus in his *Histories* ascribes to a thief in the reign of the Pharaoh Rhampsinitis (Rameses III). Finally, while on the topic of ancient Egyptian fiction, those who believe that only the Indians could have invented the frame story should consult *The Magical Stories Told to King Cheops* (the Westcar Papyrus, written between the eighteenth and sixteenth centuries BC) in which the king asks his sons for stories about the wonders worked by magicians.[14]

Other ancient civilizations of the Near East also made their contributions to the *Nights*. Most strikingly, there are many obvious echoes in 'The Adventures of Bulukiyya' (which is the tale of the quest of a pre-Islamic king for immortality) from the Babylonian *Epic of Gilgamesh* as it is known to us in a version of the first millennium BC.[15] Similarly, the Sumerian tale of 'The Poor Man of Nippur', in which a man who has been insulted avenges himself with three ingenious pranks, was passed on for over two millennia in a multitude of tongues and scripts to resurface in Arabic in the *Nights* as 'The Tale of the First Larrikin'.[16] It is also worth noting that 'The Say of Haykar the Sage', which Burton included in his *Nights* – though it really belongs to the *Nights* Apocrypha, since it comes from the manuscript put together by Chavis – is a medieval Arab version of the ancient Assyrian *Book of Ahiqar*.[17]

The contribution of the pre-Islamic literature of Persia to the story lore of the medieval Arabs is both more obvious and more pervasive than the legacies of the ancient Semitic civilizations and of classical antiquity. Stories, fables and wisdom literature were much appreciated under the Parthians and the Sassanians, and it is unfortunate that (possibly because of the switch to Arabic script after the seventh-century Islamic conquest) relatively little has survived of early Persian fiction in its original form. The *Hazar Afsaneh*, or 'Thousand Stories', the presumed Persian prototype of the *Nights*, has already been discussed in the previous chapter. Ibn al-Nadim reported that that book was alleged to have been composed for Humai, daughter of King Bahram (a legendary ancient king of Persia). According to al-Mas'udi, Sheherazade was the mother of Bahram. The bookseller and cataloguer Ibn al-Nadim and the historian al-Mas'udi were always inclined to ascribe a Persian or an Indian origin to works of fiction. Often they were right to do so. However, in the case of the important *Sindibadnama* cycle of stories, al-Mas'udi's belief that they had an Indian origin led nineteenth-century scholars headed by Benfey to look in the wrong direction.

The *Sindibadnama*, or 'The Craft and Malice of Women', no longer survives in the pre-Islamic Persian version, and the oldest surviving manuscript is in Syriac.[18] From Syriac it passed into Hebrew and a wide variety of European languages. It was also translated into Arabic and incorporated into the *Nights*. In this compendium of moralizing tales (which have nothing to do with the cycle of stories concerning Sinbad the Sailor) the framing device is that of seven viziers who tell stories to a king in order to dissuade him from killing his son, Sindibad, on the insistence of his wicked wife. Meanwhile the son has to keep silent in the face of all accusations for seven days. The wicked stepmother who denounces the prince has a precedent in the ancient Buddhist *Jataka*. However, Professor Perry, an expert on ancient story collections, has discounted al-Mas'udi's vague claim that the collection had an Indian origin and has argued instead for a western origin in the Latin legend of Secundus the Silent.

Secundus the Silent is said to have been a philosopher living in the reign of the Emperor Hadrian. Having heard someone remark that there is no such thing as a faithful woman, he decided to test the truth of this statement by attempting to sleep with his mother. She, failing to recognize him after his many years' absence, proved ready enough to go to bed with him, but then he backed off. Since she pressed him hard for an explanation, he told her, whereupon she hanged herself. Horrified by the mischief his words had wrought, Secundus thereupon took an oath of silence. When asked by the Emperor Hadrian to answer some philosophic questions, Secundus refused, even though he was unaware that the emperor had secretly resolved to excute him if he broke his vow of silence. Secundus' silence saved him, and he was eventually able to answer the emperor's knotty questions in writing. This legend, with its message about the evils of fleshly pleasure and its stress on the virtue of silence, seems indeed to come from an authentic Pythagorean tradition. As a frame story, in various later and distorted forms, it was much imitated in Persian literature and then in Arab literature, so that the misogyny of the Pythagoreans came to mingle with that of the ancient Buddhists and Hindus in the Arabian tales of the *Nights*.

Another Persian story collection incorporated in the *Nights* is 'King Jali'ad of Hind and his Wazir Shimas', a cycle of stories with a frame story which loosely imitates that of the *Sindibadnama*. In the Jali'ad cycle, the king's viziers tell stories against a hostile woman, in order to preserve the life of the son of the sage Shimas.[19] As with the *Sindibadnama*, the original Persian version no longer survives. Again somewhat similar is the seventh-century Persian *Bakhtiyarnama*, which, since an Arabic version is included in the Breslau text, appears in the first of the supplementary volumes of Burton's translation of the *Nights* as 'The Ten Wazirs: or the History of King Azadbakht and his Son'. In this collection it is the viziers who are the villains, and Prince Bakhtiyar has to tell stories to save his life against the ten viziers, until a robber chief arrives with proof that Bakhtiyar is truly the king's son.

Mention has been made here of only a handful of Persian collections of stories which happened to be translated into Arabic and ended up in the *Nights*. The range of Persian storytelling was much wider than this, and it is tempting to explore and explain the plots of the *Marzubannama,* the *Haft Paykar* and the old Pahlavi romance of Vis and Rahmin (which may have furnished the original template for the European romance of Tristan and Isolde). But to do so would be to turn what should be a short and selective chapter into an ocean of summaries and theories. One can wander for ever, if one wishes, adrift on this sea of ancient stories, looking for Berber, Georgian, Syriac, Armenian, Turkish and Malay prototypes, analogues and derivations for one or other of the Arabian tales of the *Nights*. But it may be that a great weariness will come upon one, and then there is the temptation to ask, did the Arabs never invent a story? It is true that the Arabs were heavily indebted to their precursors and neighbours for their stories, but that is a universal cultural characteristic; and, as we shall see shortly, European literature, with its individual geniuses (among them Dante, Boccaccio and Chaucer), was in turn heavily indebted to the anonymous storytellers of the Arab world. The Arabs originated and exported at least as much story lore as they imported, and the Christians took their stories while often removing from them all their specifically Islamic features.

Evidently it is difficult, and usually it is impossible, to trace individual stories or collections of anonymous stories decisively to some single originating place or time. Attempts by folklorists to establish the rules by which stories migrate have not been successful. Much of their difficulty stems from the fact that, while they are dedicated to studying stories which were, more often than not, carried across the world by gypsies, sailors and merchants in oral versions, they nevertheless are reduced to studying the track of the migrating stories on the basis of the potentially very misleading evidence of surviving written versions. It has therefore been the argument of this chapter so far that there are no conclusive grounds for thinking that either the frame story of Sheherazade and Shahriyar or the original core of stories contained within that frame originated in India, and were then transmitted to the West via Persia; for India received stories as well as transmitted them.

It is also true, of course, that similar circumstances will give rise to similar stories. Certain basic plots will frequently occur to fiction-makers. Thus, essentially the same story may be created quite independently in different parts of the world (polygenesis). If sometimes the oldest surviving written version of a story is found in India or China, this does not necessarily mean that the story began life in the East. It is well to remember that the manufacture of paper was introduced to the Middle East from China in the ninth century, and its use seems to have become widespread only in the tenth century. As paper became more widely available, there was (or, at least, appears to have been, on the basis of what has survived) a corresponding explosion in the production of written collections of stories and other works of fiction in Arabic.

Writing some time in the 1950s, John Walsh, a lecturer in Turkish at the University of Edinburgh, observed that a 'society which does not paint pictures or carve images does not invent stories, and so the folk-tales and romances of Islam are all either pre-Islamic or borrowed from other peoples, and, like the looted portraits and statues, defaced of their specifically human features'.[20] Such crass orientalist theorizing betrays an ignorance of the achievements of Islamic art, which is only balanced by a corresponding unfamiliarity with the characteristics of Islamic literature. Admittedly, medieval Arab story collections plundered freely from Sanskrit and Persian precursors (and that is indeed one of the main themes of this chapter). But the transmission of folk-tales and similar materials across cultures is a global feature; and, as we shall see, European literature plundered Arab literature at least as ruthlessly as Arab writers had ransacked the writings of their neighbours.

Although the translation of works from other languages began under the Umayyad caliphs, Ibn al-Muqaffa, killed during the reign of the Abbasid Caliph al-Mansur (754–75), may have been the first to translate a work of fiction (the Persian version of *Kalila wa-Dimna*) into Arabic. Subsequently, the translation movement gathered momentum under the Caliph al-Mamun (reigned 813–17).[21] Al-Mamun, the son of Harun al-Rashid, founded the Bayt al-Hikma, or House of Wisdom. One of the main activities of that research-institute-cum-library was to translate books from Greek, Indian, Persian and other languages. However, the works given priority by al-Mamun's team of translators dealt with mathematics, medicine, chemistry, philosophy and other subjects which were perceived as being useful. Al-Mamun and his successors do not seem to have been interested in sponsoring translations of the world's great works of fiction, and the development of an Arab literature of entertainment seems to have owed little or nothing to caliphal patronage.

As has already been suggested, Ibn al-Nadim and al-Mas'udi were keen to ascribe Indian or Persian origins to the great story collections. However, Perry has concluded that the

proliferation of story-books in the Near East in the time of the Abbasid Caliphate (750–1258 AD) was not due to the importation of materials or models from India, as is too often supposed, but to the recognition of prose fiction on its own account as a legitimate form of literature, which came about with the new Persian–Arabian culture.[22]

Arab versions of Persian books were rarely slavish translations. When Ibn al-Muqaffa translated *Kalila wa-Dimna*, he made substantial additions and amendments of his own.[23] His translation, in turn, inspired many later Arab authors to try their hands at producing collections of animal fables with moral or political messages. The prestige of *Kalila wa-Dimna* was immense, and every courtier and court functionary was expected to be familar with its stories and adages. Throughout the Middle Ages it was widely recognized as one of the two great works of fiction in Arabic.

The second great work was undoubtedly the *Maqamat*, or

'Sessions', by al-Hariri (1054–1122). Al-Hariri's work was inspired by and loosely modelled on a similar work with the same title by al-Hamadhani, 'the Wonder of the Age' (968–1008).[24] Al-Hamadhani's *Maqamat* was probably the first entirely original work of prose fiction in Arabic (as opposed to an adaptation from another language), but, despite its great success with al-Hamadhani's contemporaries, its fame was to be eclipsed by al-Hariri's more elaborate and finished specimen of the genre. The *Maqamat* genre embraces episodic anecdotal works of fiction, written in rhymed prose, in which the sessions, or episodes, furnish pretexts for the display of wit and eloquence. In the case of al-Hariri's *Maqamat*, the protagonist is Abu Zayd, a wily, scrounging, hard-drinking rogue who makes his living by the swiftness of his wits and the fluency of his tongue. The fifty sessions in which Abu Zayd features are set-pieces of rhetorical eloquence and special pleading. As R.A. Nicholson put it in *A Literary History of the Arabs*, Abu Zayd offers his audience 'excellent discourses, edifying sermons, and plaintive lamentations mingled with rollicking ditties and ribald jests'.[25] As we shall see, the trickster enjoyed a high status in the culture of the medieval Arabs. Abu Zayd has much in common with the wily beggars, thieves, prostitutes and religious charlatans which fill the pages of other works of Arabic fiction, but his chief claim to distinction is that he is, before anything else, a grammatical trickster and master of linguistic artifice, making use of metaphors, puns, parallelisms, alliterations and *hapax legomena* to talk himself out of scrapes. Al-Hariri's work was the model for those who thought that high literature should be allusively obscure and complex.

Kalila wa-Dimna and the *Maqamat* were the two prose classics that every civilized Arab might be expected to have read. If a civilized Arab happened to have read the *Nights*, he probably kept quiet about it, since the vulgarity of that work's subject-matter, and even more the vulgarity of its style, rendered it unworthy of serious consideration.

Yet if the *Nights* was not regarded as a work of literature, neither in a sense were its more sophisticated rivals, for there was no word for 'literature' in medieval Arabic. The modern word for it, *adab*, is also used to refer in the more restricted sense to *belles-lettres*. But in the Middle Ages, *adab* referred neither to literature in general nor to *belles-lettres* in particular. It originally meant mental discipline, etiquette, polite accomplishments. In time and by extension, *adab* came to be applied to the literary and conversational culture of a gentleman and especially to the intellectual repertoire of the *nudama*, or cup-companions of the princes. Court scribes were also expected to have mastered an *adab* which encompassed, among other things, a knowledge of protocol, history, geography, poetry, proverbs, good jokes and entertaining stories.[26] However, although a knowledge of stories might form part of a courtier's *adab*, fiction had in general a very low status in the medieval Arab world. Stories, such as those found in the *Nights*, were classified as *khurafa*, lies or fantasies, tales fit for women and children, and only suitable for telling in the evenings when serious work had been done. Ibn al-Nadim gives a list of such stories of which nothing more was known than their names, including such intriguing titles as 'The Foot Bone of a Giant Lizard', 'Lover of the Cow' and 'Bird Droppings'. Ibn al-Nadim was generally contemptuous of prose fiction, regarding it as 'cold'.[27] He shared the common Arab prejudice in favour of poetry. Poetry was the most noble and challenging of literary forms and the one that attracted the most ambitious, sophisticated and enterprising practitioners.

The *Nights*, being full of *khurafa* and for the most part written in a fairly simple prose which was littered with colloquialisms, had a low status in medieval Arabic literature. It is almost certain that only the accident of its early translation into French and its finding favour with eighteenth-century European taste rescued this particular story collection from obscurity and possible oblivion. (Even today, with the exception of certain writers and academics, the *Nights* is regarded with disdain in the Arab world. Its stories are still regularly denounced as vulgar, improbable, childish and, above all, badly written.) However, despite the low status of the *Nights*, the story collection had several rivals in the Abbasid period.

As has been noted in Chapter 2, Ibn al-Nadim relates that a certain Muhammad ibn Abdus al-Jahshiyari (d. 942), a distinguished writer on politics and a vizier's aide, otherwise best known for his biographical dictionary of viziers,

> began the compiling of a book in which he was to select a thousand tales from the stories of the Arabs, Persians, Greeks and others. Each section (story) was separate, not connected with any other. He summoned to his presence the storytellers (*musamirun*, literally the evening folk, or people who tell stories in the evening), from whom he obtained the best things about which they knew and what they did well. He also selected what pleased him from the books composed of stories and fables. As he was of a superior type, there were collected for him four hundred and eighty nights, each night being a complete story, comprising more or less than fifty pages. Death overtook him before he fulfilled his plan for completing a thousand stories. I saw a number of sections of this book.[28]

Alas, nothing seems to survive of al-Jahshiyari's mighty compilation, though some would identify it with the *Hikayat al-Ajiba wa'l-Akhbar al-Ghariba*, or 'Tales of the Marvellous and News of the Strange'.[29] This anonymous work survives in Istanbul in a single manuscript copy probably made in the fourteenth century. Although the surviving manuscript seems to be of a relatively late date, the content of the tales suggests that the collection was originally put together in Egypt some time in the tenth century. The title page lists forty-two stories, although only eighteen are still extant. Of these, several stories are common to the *Nights* collection, most notably the stories of the barber's six brothers and of 'Julnar the Sea-Born' (which appear in the Galland manuscript), as well as 'Abu Muhammad Called Lazy-Bones'. Among the tales which the *Hikayat* contains and which are not found in the *Nights*, perhaps the most striking is that of 'The Story of the Forty Girls' to be discussed later.

The *Hikayat al-Ajiba* also contains 'Su'l and Shumul', a strange story about the love of two Yemenis for one another and about how Shumul is spirited away and how Su'l travels through the Levant, seeking for her in one convent after another. Interestingly enough, this story also survives in an independent manuscript version dating from the sixteenth century. In that manuscript, the story is at first broken up into nights, with mornings overtaking Sheherazade, and her sister urging her to continue on the following evening. Evidently, the scribe intended to insert 'Su'l and Shumul' into the *Nights*, but, after the thirty-fifth page, he lost interest in this enterprise and continued the tale without breaks.[30]

Al-Tanukhi (939–94), a retired judge resident in Baghdad, was, like al-Jahshiyari, a collector of stories.[31] His most important work, *Al-Faraj ba'd al-Shidda*, or 'Relief after Distress', is a collection of stories on the theme promised by the title, and it draws on both literary and oral sources. From the ninth century onwards, books on the theme of 'joy after sorrow' came to constitute a sub-genre of Arabic literature, though al-Tanukhi's compilation is the best-known specimen of that sub-genre. These fictions of consolation deal with recovery after sickness, wealth after poverty, victory after defeat. Many of the tales in the *Nights* are on the theme of joy after sorrow (or 'all's well that ends well'), for example 'The Ruined Man who Became Rich Again through a Dream' and 'The Tale of the Envier and the Envied'. There are important comparisons to be made between *Al-Faraj ba'd al-Shidda* and the *Nights*, and it is unfortunate that the former work has not been translated. Part of one work by al-Tanukhi, the *Kitab Nishwar al-Muhadara wa-Akhbar al-Mudhakara*, has been translated into English (alas in an expurgated form) as *The Table Talk of a Mesopotamian Judge* (1922). Here again al-Tanukhi drew on oral sources, as emerges from his preface: 'It is my purpose to collect in this work such stories as are current on men's lips, and which have not hitherto been transferred from the custody of their memories to perpetuation in notebooks.' One important type of tale found in al-Tanukhi's *Table Talk*, in the *Nights* and in other story collections is the story of princely or vizieral generosity (for examples in the *Nights*, see 'Hatim of the Tribe of Tayy', 'Ma'an Son of Zaidah and the Three Girls' and 'Generous Dealing of Yahya Son of Khalid with a Man who Forged a Letter in his Name'). Many of these stories focused on the semi-legendary generosity of the Barmecide dynasty of viziers, in the service of the Abbasid caliphs. It seems that this sort of story was used by beggars to attract an audience and wheedle hand-outs from them. This sub-genre of stories therefore tended towards brevity. When Egyptian copyists and compilers set to swelling out the bulk of the *Nights*, they seem to have made liberal use of stories from al-Tanukhi's anthologies.

For reasons which are far from clear, the first wave of story collections were put together in Iraq in the ninth and tenth centuries, but then there was a renewed fashion for such anthologies in Syria and Egypt in the late Mamluke period. It is possible that in the latter period such collections of stories catered to the literary tastes of the Mamluke élite. Al-Ghuzuli (d. 1412) was a Berber who moved from North Africa to Mamluke Damascus and who wrote in Arabic.[32] His *Matali al-Budur fi Manazil al-Surur*, or 'Rising Places of Full Moons in the Places of Delights', is an *adab* treatise whose chapters are devoted to things that delight the senses, among them flowers, breezes, food, drink, parties, music, women and slave girls. One of his lengthy chapters is devoted to the *musamara*, or tales told by the night. Of the seven stories or 'nights' related in this chapter, at least four have parallel versions in the *Nights*; and elsewhere, embedded in other chapters of al-Ghuzuli's sprawling compendium, there are more tales to be found which are common to the *Nights*. Not only are the stories essentially the same, but sometimes there is a word-for-word correspondence, and it seems probable that compilers of later recensions of the *Nights* plundered al-Ghuzuli just as they had plundered al-Tanukhi.

Badr al-Din al-Ayni (1365–1451), a Turk born in Ayntab (a town in the Turkish-speaking part of Mamluke Syria), was a religious scholar and historian who found success in Cairo.[33] He became Cairo's market inspector and the court historian to a succession of sultans. Writing in both Turkish and Arabic, he was chiefly famous for his great Arabic chronicle, the *Iqd al-Juman*, but he also wrote an anthology of entertaining tales about different classes of people, the *Majmu Mushtamil ala Hikayat wa Ghayriha*.

After the sack of Damascus by the Turkish empire-builder Tamerlane in 1401, the young Ibn Arabshah (1392–1450) was taken as a captive to Tamerlane's Central Asian capital, Samarkand. Subsequently, he spent time at the court of the Ottoman Sultan Mehmed I, before returning to the Mamluke lands in the 1420s.[34] Ibn Arabshah is chiefly remembered today for his venomous life of Tamerlane (in which is embedded a tale also to be found in the *Nights*). He also translated a thirteenth-century collection of Persian beast fables, the *Marzuban-nama*. He later produced a greatly expanded and heavily reworked version of the Persian work, which he entitled *Fakihat al-Khulafa wa-Mufakahat al-Zurafa*, or 'The Caliph's Delicacies and Jests of the Refined', which, although it purports to be a 'mirror for princes', is full of entertaining tales which have no obvious educational value. The outer frame of the collection owes something to *Kalila wa-Dimna*, but, although the frame stories concern animals and birds, the stories the creatures tell are mostly about humans. Again, the *Fakihat* has stories in common with the *Nights*, among them the story of the slave who tells lies once a year and a variant of 'The Merchant and the Two Sharpers'.

Some of the stories found in the *Fakihat* are also to be found in yet another anthology of short fictions put together in Egypt during the Mamluke period, the *Mustatraf fi Kull Fann Mustazraf*. Its author, al-Ibshihi, who died some time after 1446, produced a vast rambling collection of improving stories, traditions, proverbs, fables and moralistic reflections.[35] Some of his tales are common to the *Nights*, and it is probable that he and the late Egyptian compilers of manuscripts of the *Nights* drew on a common source. Magic, marvels and adulterous liaisons featured prominently in the *Nights* and in rival story collections, but one should not lose sight of the fact that all these works contained a lot of edifying tales about virtuous deeds and holy men. Some anthologies were devoted exclusively to edifying themes. One such was *Rawd al-Rayahin fi Hikayat al-Salihin*, or 'Garden of Sweet Basil regarding Tales of Holy Men', by al-Yafi'i, a fourteenth-century Yemeni Sufi mystic.[36] His collection of improving and wondrous tales of the Sufis was plundered both by al-Ibshihi and by those who sought to swell up the bulk of the *Nights*.

After the end of the Mamluke period, there were few Arab writers of note in any genre until the late eighteenth century. Then al-Jabarti (d. 1825), one of the greatest Arab historians, began his masterful history of Egypt from the Ottoman conquest of 1517 until his own times. He also chronicled the French invasion of Egypt under Bonaparte in 1798. Al-Jabarti met with French scholars at their institute in Cairo. It may be that the French communicated some of their enthusiasm for the *Nights* to al-Jabarti. In any event, he later attempted to produce an expurgated version of the *Nights*. Alas, it has not survived.[37]

A curiosity, which has in the past been numbered among Arab story collections, perhaps deserves mention. This is the *Contes du Cheykh el-Mohdy* (1835), which purports to be a translation of an Arab collection of stories with the title 'The Present to the Awakened Bachelor for the Delight of the Somnolent Sleeper', by a certain Sheikh Muhammad al-Mahdi, a contemporary of al-Jabarti. This work was 'translated' by Jean-Joseph Marcel, an Arabist who accompanied Bonaparte to Egypt in 1798. The opening frame story is about a young man who keeps sending his audience to sleep with his stories. He irritates people so much that he ends up in the Cairo *maristan* or lunatic asylum, which becomes the bizarre setting for yet more storytelling. However, although there really was a Sheikh Muhammad al-Mahdi, there can be little doubt that the stories are fakes, European pastiches of the *Nights* tales; and it is all but certain that the motif of the storyteller who regularly sends his audience to sleep was plagiarized by Marcel from Cazotte's *Mille et une fadaises*.[38]

The above has been a somewhat haphazard sampling of once famous but now mostly forgotten writers of the 'Abbasid, Mamluke and Ottoman periods. However, what this fragmentary evidence suggests is that the stories contained in the *Nights* were not the exclusive property of anonymous storytellers. In many cases they were known and transmitted by scholars and belletrists of considerable distinction in anthologies which purported to do more than entertain idlers in coffee-houses. Despite the opinion generally held among educated Arabs that prose was inferior to poetry, and despite their frequently proclaimed contempt for prose fiction, it is evident that some members of the élite interested themselves in storytelling. It is possible that sometimes they took stories from the *Nights* and made use of them to convey political or religious messages. What is also apparent is that the scholars were well placed to introduce new and foreign items into the repertoire of Arab storytelling. Al-Ghuzuli was a Berber by origin, al-Ayni was a Turk, and Ibn Arabshah was a polyglot who had spent much of his life in Turkish- and Persian-speaking centres of culture. However, these writers 'wrote' their stories only in the sense of transcribing them (or at best adapting them). They did not invent stories – or, if they did, they kept quiet about it. In medieval Arab society, one did not boast of inventing stories: one claimed only to be transmitting them. (Sheherazade herself does not invent tales; she relates what she has heard. We should take it that she has been blessed with an excellent memory, rather than with a creative imagination.)

The stories edited by, say, al-Tanukhi or Ibn Arabshah would usually have been accessible only to a literate and sophisticated élite, though of course it is easy to imagine that there may sometimes have been public readings from their works. However, the taste for their works, and indeed even for the stories of the *Nights*, was eclipsed by the popularity of the great prose epics. It is clear that the latter appealed to quite unsophisticated audiences. The twelfth-century North African Jewish polygraph, Samwal ibn Yahya al-Maghribi, recorded his delight as a schoolboy in the popular epics:

At the age of between ten and thirteen, I was very much attracted by historical information and stories. I was very eager to read what happened in ancient times and to know what had taken place in past centuries. I read the different collections of stories and anecdotes. From that I transferred my predilection to the long fanciful tales, and then to the big novels, such as the stories of Antar, Dhu'l-Himmah, and al-Battal, the story of Alexander Dhu'l-Qarnayn ('the two-horned'), of al-Anqa' (the Phoenix), and Taraf ibn Ludhan, and others.[39]

Eventually, Samwal ibn Yahya moved on from these romantic pseudo-histories to the serious study of Islamic history, and, impressed by that history, he ended up by converting to Islam.

Although many of the popular folk-epics had a basis in history, that basis was invariably pretty shaky.[40] Centuries and wars were confounded in tales which tended to stray into fairyland at their topographical edges. The long rambling plots of these epics, in which crisis follows crisis, are characteristic of stories composed for serial delivery over a period of weeks and days (and have much in common with nineteenth-century European *feuilleton* literature). The straggling medieval sagas drew much of their inspiration, first, from the frontier wars with Byzantium from the mid-eighth century onwards and, secondly, from the struggle against the Crusaders from the 1090s onwards. 'The Tale of Omar bin al-Nu'uman', which started out as an independent work but eventually found its way into the *Nights*, is fairly typical of the genre. This sprawling epic (it occupies almost 250 pages in the Burton translation, not counting the stories framed within it) offers a pseudo-historical account of the seventh-century wars of the King of the Muslims and the Christian King of Constantinople against the Christian King of Caesarea. The career of the fictional hero may be very loosely based on the deeds of a historical Umar who was Emir of Malatya (a town in what is now eastern Turkey) in the ninth century, in a period of fierce frontier warfare between the Arabs and the Byzantines. Vague memories of his struggles and other Arab wars against the Byzantines were later conflated with the twelfth-to-thirteenth-century jihad against the Crusaders. The Franks feature prominently, and the villainous Jawfran is surely a distorted rendering of Godfrey – that is, Godfrey of Bouillon, one of the leaders of the First Crusade and the first of the Franks to rule over Jerusalem.

In this and similar epics, garbled and transposed reminiscences of events between the tenth and the thirteenth centuries are embedded in fantastic stories of high chivalry and sorcery. The taste for epic tales about superhuman heroes who undertake peril-ous journeys, fight battles against hopeless odds and survive the plots of evil wizards was not restricted to the Arabs. Indeed, it seems that various details in the Byzantine poem *Digenis Akrites* (which is difficult to date but was probably given clear literary form in the twelfth century) were taken from 'The Tale of Omar bin al-Nu'uman'. This poem about a heroic frontier warrior fighting for Byzantium strikingly resembles the Arab epic in many of its motifs and devices. (It also seems likely that Arab storytelling influenced similar works in other areas, such as the anonymous eleventh-century Armenian epic tales of *David of Sasun* and the Georgian Shota Rustaveli's twelfth-century *Knight of the Panther Skin*, but more research is needed in these areas.)

Returning to the *Nights*, the 'History of Gharib and his Brother Ajib' is, like 'The Tale of Omar bin al-Nu'uman', a preposterous and perfunctorily plotted farrago of magic, warfare and romantic intrigue. Like 'Omar Bin al-Nu'uman' too, it was originally an independent epic which was eventually incorporated as a bulky makeweight into the later Egyptian recensions of the *Nights*. However, many similar popular epics, which circulated in the medieval Arab world, were not included in the *Nights*, among them those of 'Dhat al-Himma' (or 'Delhemma') and 'Sayyid Battal'. These sagas, like those discussed above, are ostensibly set in the time of the early Arab–Byzantine wars; yet once again distorted but unmistakable reflections of the wars against the Crusaders appear.

In the chapter on storytelling in *Manners and Customs of the Modern Egyptians*, Lane observed that oral recitations from the *Nights* in early-nineteenth-century Cairo were rather rare; much more popular with the storytellers and their audiences were the epics devoted to the exploits of Abu Zayd, al-Zahir Baybars and Antar.[41] Abu Zayd, according to the storytellers, was the dark-skinned son of an Arab chief of the Hilali tribe. The romance of Abu Zayd (or rather romances, for there are several variant versions) is (are) devoted to the exploits of the Hilali Arabs and their victories over the Berbers in North Africa in the eleventh century. Although this cycle of stories probably first took shape in the eleventh century, it both drew on older plot motifs and devices and, as the centuries passed, added incidents and names which derived from the later Muslim jihad against the Crusaders. The exploits of Abu Zayd and the Hilali tribesmen were usually recited to a musical accompaniment.

The *Sira of al-Zahir Baybars* was the next most popular story cycle in nineteenth-century Cairo. This saga, which perhaps began to take shape in the fifteenth century, is ever so tenuously based on the exploits of the real-life Sultan al-Zahir Baybars I of Egypt (reigned 1260–77). Vague memories of that sultan's wars against the Crusaders and the Mongols are jumbled up with low-life adventures, mystical fantasies and marvels generally. (We shall have more to say about this *Sirat* when we come to examine how crime was treated in the *Nights* and in other works of medieval fiction.)

By contrast with these two epics, which were popular in every sense, the *Sirat Antar*, a picturesque romance about a pre-Islamic poet and warrior, half Arab and half Abyssinian, was not much in demand. Lane says that the coffee-house audience found the poetry a bit difficult. The *Sirat Antar* is mostly in rhymed prose, but Antar's poems, amounting to about 10,000 verses, are embedded within the rhymed prose. Another off-putting feature of this *Sirat* may have been its length. The modern printed edition is in thirty-two volumes. The Antariyya (who made a living from telling the story of Antar) read the story from a book, and if there was not much demand for the tale then they might read from another book, for example the *Nights*.

Although *The Thousand and One Nights* could not compete with the heroic epics in popularity, it retained a precarious hold on the favour of nineteenth-century Egyptian café society. Further to the west in the North African territories, however, a rival but similar collection seems to have been more popular. This was *The Hundred and One Nights* (in Arabic *Mi'at Layla wa-Layla*).[42] Although the oldest surviving manuscript was transcribed in 1776, this collection seems to have been put together in North Africa some time during the Middle Ages. It contains stories which are similar or occasionally identical to those found in the larger and more famous story collection. In its frame story, 'Flower of the Gardens', the eponymous young man is blessed with a luminously beautiful face, but it loses its beauty when he discovers the adultery of his wife. Flower of the Gardens' face only regains its former sheen when Flower of the Gardens learns through later experience (spying on a queen and her attendants) that all women are unfaithful. Flower of the Gardens warns the king, his host, that he is being cuckolded by the queen. The king promptly has his wife slaughtered and thereafter takes a virgin to bed every night, having them beheaded in the morning, until Sheherazade is brought to his bed and succeeds in breaking the cycle. *The Hundred and One Nights* also includes 'The City of Brass', 'The

Ebony Horse' and the *Sindibad* cycle, but some of its tales were unknown to the compilers of *The Thousand and One Nights*. This North African story collection is much shorter than its eastern prototype, for Sheherazade only has to tell stories for eight months, until it is obvious that she is pregnant (the Gaudefroy-Demombynes translation into French runs to less than 260 pages).

The great Arab epics borrowed from each other, threading their way through a great swamp of plot motifs, converging on and diverging one from another. They offered a vision of the Arab past which featured individual deeds of heroism undertaken by poetry-spouting warriors, as well as captive princesses, battles and single combats, enterprising gangsters, disguises and mistaken identities, marvellous poisons, Amazons, talismans and automata. The epics and shorter fictions found in the great story collections provided medieval Islam with a mythical past. However, as we have seen, plot motifs and incidents crossed cultural frontiers with considerable ease, and the Arabs borrowed from the Indians, among others, while lending to the Byzantines, among others. It is time now to consider medieval Europe's debt to Arab fiction and, more specifically, to investigate the possibility that all or part of the *Nights* may have been circulating in translation in one or other of the European languages centuries before the birth of Antoine Galland.

Although a certain amount of material was translated in Byzantium, Spain and Sicily were the main corridors for the translation and transmission of Arab learning – and the Arab literature of entertainment – into medieval Europe.[43] Arabic versions of Greek works of science and mathematics were being translated into Latin in Spain as early as the tenth century, but the translation movement really got under way in the twelfth century, with Toledo as one of its main centres. The translators continued to be interested mainly in Greek works of philosophy and mathematics which had been preserved in Arabic. Although the Koran was also translated into Latin in 1143, the translation was of course intended for use in anti-Muslim polemics. Probably the first Latin work to draw heavily on Arabic fiction was the *Disciplina clericalis*. This anthology was put together by Petrus Alfonsi in twelfth-century Toledo. Petrus Alfonsi was a Jew with a good knowledge of Arabic who had converted to Christianity in 1106. In the *Disciplina* he assembled thirty-four exemplary tales in a frame structure. In the prologue, Petrus Alfonsi announced that he had produced this work in order to give men a better knowledge of their Creator and to guide them to a virtuous life. However, he had broken up the book into small sections to prevent boredom setting in, and he claimed:

I have been mindful of the fact that in order to facilitate remembrance of what has been learnt, the pill must be softened and sweetened by various means ... For that reason then have I put together this book, partly from the sayings of wise men and their advice, partly from Arab proverbs, counsels, fables and poems, and partly from bird and animal similes.[44]

Not only did Petrus Alfonsi rely heavily on Arab fables and stories; his apologetic prologue also follows the pattern of his oriental sources. His compilation drew on a variety of works in Arabic, including *Kalila wa-Dimna* and the *Sindibad* cycle. Mention has already been made of the appearance of the 'weeping bitch' story in the *Disciplina clericalis*. The *Disciplina* was immensely popular. It was widely translated and became the vehicle for the transmission of many of the Arab tales found in later European story collections. For example, much of the *Disciplina*'s material was incorporated in the *Gesta Romanorum*, which was probably produced in thirteenth-century England and relates the mostly legendary lives of saints in Roman times.[45]

In the course of the thirteenth century and particularly at the court of Alfonso the Wise (reigned 1252–84) there was a partial shift to translating Arabic into vernacular Spanish.[46] Alfonso commissioned a translation of *Kalila wa-Dimna* into Spanish. (However, a rival Latin version made by John of Capua circulated more widely throughout Europe, being eventually translated into numerous other vernaculars.) The *Sindibad* cycle of stories was also translated into Spanish as *Sendebar* or *Libro de los enganos e los asayamientos de las mugeres* (1253) under the patronage of Alfonso's brother Prince Fadrique.

Alfonso the Wise's nephew, the Infante Don Juan Manuel (1282–1348), collected fifty-one exemplary tales under the title *Conde Lucanor*.[47] The rather naïve frame story is that of a tutor instructing the young pupil Lucanor. Juan Manuel knew Arabic and drew on Arab literature for many of his moral tales. One story in particular, about the sorcerer Don Illan and the Dean of Santiago (a story centred on the years-of-experience-in-an-instant-of-time motif), was subsequently rediscovered by the Argentinian short-story writer Jorge Luis Borges and retold by him under the title 'The Sorcerer Postponed'. It may be that, in the Borges tale, Don Illan stands in for the storyteller, who, just like the sorcerer, can unroll the whole of a man's life in less than an hour. (Nai-tung Ting, who has made a special study of this tale-type, points to a relatively recent example of it in C.S. Lewis's novel *The Lion, the Witch and the Wardrobe*.)[48] The *Nights* rendering of this motif is found in 'The Tale of the Warlock and the Young Cook of Baghdad'. Juan Manuel's story about the king who desired to test his three sons is also based on a famous oriental tale and is found both in the ninth-century chronicler al-Tabari's universal history and in the *Nights*, where it is called 'The Story of the Sultan of al-Yaman and his Three Sons'. The *Conde Lucanor* also contains a variant of the barber's story of his fifth brother.

The Catalan Ramón Lull (1233–1316) wrote poetry in the style of the troubadors and led a fairly dissolute life as a youth, but he later converted and became a Franciscan friar.[49] Thereafter, everything he wrote was intended to advance the faith. He produced a prodigious amount – according to one estimate, 243 books. He studied Arabic (with a view to converting the infidel) and came to know the language well enough to write books in it. *The Book of the Beasts* is a collection of animal fables, many of which seem to have an oriental origin. Lull certainly made use of *Kalila wa-Dimna* in either its Arabic version or its Spanish translation. More intriguingly Lull's book has a version of 'The Tale of the Merchant and his Wife' much like the one in the frame story of the *Nights*, where Sheherazade tells it to her father, the vizier. Then again, it is possible that the baroquely romantic *La vida es sueño*, or 'Life Is a Dream', by the great Spanish dramatist Calderón de la Barca (1600–81) may derive ultimately from 'The Sleeper and the Waker' (or 'The Sleeper Awakened' as it is often known). But where the *Nights* story is merely an entertaining farce, the play by Calderón examines the nature of human identity, as its protagonist Prince Segismondo learns to distinguish between dream and waking, between truth and reality. In prison, Segismondo meditates:

> I dream that I am here,
> Chained in these fetters. Yet I dreamed just now
> I was in a more flattering, lofty station.
> What is this life? A frenzy, an illusion,
> A shadow, a delirium, a fiction.
> The greatest good's but little, and this life
> Is but a dream, and dreams are only dreams.

(A much more lightweight reworking of the plot of 'The Sleeper Awakened' can be found in the first act of Shakespeare's *The Taming of the Shrew*. Shakespeare almost certainly took the gist of the plot from a sixteenth-century English collection of tales. Whether that collection took the story from an oral or a written source is not known.)[50]

The influence of Arabic literature on medieval European literature was not confined to Spain. Motifs and plots which look as though they must have been taken from stories in Arabic have been identified in twelfth- and thirteenth-century fabliaux (short verse treatments of what are usually comic subjects), in the *Lais* of Marie de France (1154–89), in *Tristram and Iseult*, in *Floire et Blanchefor*, in *Aucassin and Nicolette*, in Adenet Le Roi's *Cleomades* and in *Pierre de Provence et la belle Maguelonne*. (The resemblance between the last and 'The Tale of Kamar al-Zaman' is particularly striking; among other features, both the Arab and the French stories make play with the motif of a female bird abandoned by a male, a motif that was later to be picked up by Chaucer.) In eleventh-century Germany the epic poem *Herzog Ernst* has details which are curiously similar to those in the adventures of Sinbad the Sailor. In the thirteenth century, the anonymous *Nibelungenlied* and Wolfram von Eschenbach's *Parsifal* similarly drew on oriental motifs.[51]

In England 'The Squire's Tale' in *The Canterbury Tales* by Geoffrey Chaucer (*c.* 1345–1400) features a mechanical flying horse of brass on which an Arabian knight travels to the court of King Cambuscan. Chaucer may have been introduced to the motif of the Ebony Horse by Adenet Le Roi's *Cleomades*. However, this is not the only element of Arab origin in 'The Squire's Tale'; for the episode in which Princess Canacee (who has acquired a magic ring that allows her to understand the language of birds) eavesdrops on a female falcon which tells of its desertion by a tercel, or male hawk, must derive ultimately from 'The Tale of Taj al-Muluk and the Princess Dunya' in the *Nights* (possibly via *Pierre de Provence et la belle Maguelonne*). Then again 'The Merchant's Tale', the bawdy story about the cuckold, the lovers and the pear-tree, has a Persian precursor in the *Mathnawi Discourses*, mystical sermons delivered by Jalal al-Din al-Rumi, the thirteenth-century Sufi master in Konya, as well as an Arab precursor in 'The Tale of the Simpleton Husband' in the *Nights*.[52]

The story of the pear-tree and the lovers also features in that other great collection of framed tales produced in fourteenth-century Europe, Boccaccio's *Decameron* (1353).[53] This work hardly pretends to originality in content. Of the stories – told by courtiers who have fled from Florence to escape the Black Death – nine-tenths have identifiable precursors. The *Decameron* has many stories in common with the *Nights* and other Arab story collections. For example, Boccaccio's tale of how Calendrino was fooled into thinking that he was pregnant probably derives ultimately from the *Nights* story 'The Qadi who Had a Baby', just as the story about Federigo and the falcon has its precursor in the older Arab tale about legendary generosity, 'Hatim Tayyi'. Likewise, in the fifteenth century, Masuccio Salernitano's *Novellino*, a collection of fifty tales from southern Italy put together in loose imitation of the *Decameron*, contains 'The Tale of the Ill-Fated Corpse', which is in essence the same as the story of the hunchback which frames the Hunchback cycle in the *Nights*. (One should be a little cautious about assuming a genealogical relation between Salernitano's story and the *Nights* story. The story of the unlucky corpse also circulated among the North American Indians.)

So much material which is common to the *Nights* has been found in collections of stories put together in Europe in the centuries prior to Galland's translation that it has led some scholars to speculate that the *Nights* did circulate in Europe in an earlier translation – perhaps a translation into Latin made in Spain in, say, the twelfth century. However, no such translation has been found, and there is no reference to such a translation ever having been commissioned. Although there is plenty of evidence for items like parts of the *Sindibad* cycle and the odd individual story like 'The Ebony Horse' being recycled in Latin or one or other of Europe's vernacular languages, most of those stories were added to the *Nights* only in the later stages of its growth, from the fifteenth century onwards. European versions of stories which formed part of the early core of the *Nights*, such as 'The Tale of Kamar al-Zaman' or 'The Story of the Hunchback', are much rarer – though, as has been noted above, there seems to be a relation between the former and *Pierre de Provence et la belle Maguelonne* and between 'The Tale of the Hunchback' and one of Salernitano's tales. However, there was nothing to prevent either of these stories being imported to Europe, perhaps by oral transmission, as independent, free-standing tales.

It is perhaps more significant that something like the frame story of the *Nights* seems to have been known in medieval Italy. The *Novelle* by Giovanni Sercambi (1347–1424) comprises 155 tales told by characters who have left Lucca, fleeing from the plague of 1374. Evidently Sercambi took the idea of the frame story from the *Decameron*, and a few of his tales are also taken from Boccaccio and are not very interesting. However, the 'Novella d'Astolfo' should intrigue the student of Arabic literature. In this story, the king recovers from a melancholy, brought on by his being cuckolded, when he succeeds in making love to a woman kept in a casket by a Siennese merchant. After making love to her, the king gives her his ring. Here there are unmistakable echoes of the frame story of the *Nights* and the adventure of Shahriyar and Shahzaman with the lady kept in a casket by a jinn. (Since a similar version of this story exists in a Hungarian folk-tale, it is possible that it reached Italy via some Balkan version, rather than directly from an Arab text.)[54]

There seem to be further echoes of the adventures of Shahzaman and Shahriyar in Ariosto's sixteenth-century masterpiece, the epic poem *Orlando Furioso*. In Canto 28, an innkeeper tells Rodolfo the story of King Jocondo, who set out on a journey with his brother Astolfo to the latter's kingdom but, having forgotten something, returned unexpectedly to observe his beloved wife in the arms of a low-born page. With difficulty he restrained himself from killing the pair, slipped away and rejoined Astolfo on the road. Not long after arriving at Astolfo's court, Jocondo discovered that his brother's wife too was adulterous and delighted in the embraces of a humpbacked dwarf. Jocondo, cheered up by the discovery that he was not alone in his cuckolded state, revealed all to his brother. When the latter calmed down, he agreed to set out with his brother on a voyage of exploration in which it would be demonstrated that there is no such thing as a faithful woman. Thereafter the story-line diverges somewhat from that in the *Nights*, though the conclusion is still that, no matter what precautions are taken, it is impossible to guard a woman's chastity; and the moral is picked up by Rodolfo: 'I do believe that there is no limit to woman's wiles; not all the books in the world could record a fraction of them.'[55]

Other reflections of the *Nights* and of other Arab anthologies continued to appear in European story collections of the sixteenth and seventeenth centuries, such as the *Piacevoli notti* by Gianfrancesco Straparola, the *Heptameron* by Marguerite of Navarre and Giambattista Basile's *Pentamerone*. The *Pentamerone*'s fifty stories are mostly fairy stories and tales of wonder, divided into sessions of ten nights. Though Basile drew on the folklore of southern Italy, he was himself a highly literary nobleman in love with the fantastic. The twentieth-century novelist Italo Calvino wrote of the *Pentamerone* that 'it resembles the dream of an odd Mediterranean Shakespeare, obsessed with the horrible, for whom there were never enough ogres or witches, in whose far-fetched and grotesque metaphors the sublime was intermingled with the coarse and sordid.'[56] Basile was one of the pioneers of the fairy tale. In pre-modern times the genres of literary fiction and the folk-tale, or fairy tale, were not clearly separated. It is probable that many of the 'folk-tales' circulating in medieval and early modern Europe were really orally transmitted reminiscences of individual literary creations, while on the other hand compilers of works of literature (such as the *Decameron* and *The Canterbury Tales*) drew on both literary and oral folk sources. Generally, stories passed backwards and forwards between written and oral versions.

With the publication in 1697 of Charles Perrault's *Contes de la mère l'Oye* (or 'Tales of Mother Goose'), the fairy tale emerged more clearly as a distinct genre. This collection of eight stories, of the type that French peasants allegedly used to tell their children, created a vogue for such stories at court and in the salons of fashionable ladies. The vogue for tales about fairies and other marvels, created by the appearance of *Contes de la mère l'Oye*, was part of the background to the favourable reception accorded to Galland's translation of the *Mille et une nuits*. Perrault, D'Aulnoy, Galland and others aimed at cultivated adult audiences. (Of course, in the nineteenth and twentieth centuries, the tales collected by Perrault, Galland and the Brothers Grimm, which had been fashionable among intellectuals and society folk, sank in status to become the staple fare of children in the nursery. Why this happened remains mysterious, but part of the answer may be that science fiction has usurped the role of the fairy tale as the purveyor of marvels to adults.)

Although Perrault and his French imitators drew on peasant and oral source material, they did not hesitate to improve and write up that material to make it suitable for discerning literary tastes. The brothers Jacob and Wilhelm Grimm did similarly when they published their collection of folk-tales transcribed from oral informants, the *Kinder und Hausmärchen* (1812–22).[57] Most of the stories were subsequently further revised by the brothers in later editions. The Grimms' tales were a product of the age of Romanticism, in Germany the age of Wieland, Herder and the cult of medieval and folk poetry. The German cult of folk poetry had been stimulated in its turn by the success of James Macpherson's presentation of the ostensible works of a third-century Gaelic bard, Ossian, under the title *Fragments of Ancient Poetry Collected in the Highlands of Scotland and Translated from the Gaelic or Erse Language* (1760). The works of Ossian were a forgery of Macpherson's, but this was not at first detected.

In Germany the cult of the folk was more specifically the cult of the German *Volk* and its communal soul. Nineteenth-century German folklorists aimed to give Germany, divided as it was between hundreds of princely states and independent municipalities, a sense of cultural identity and a mythic past. The Brothers

Grimm claimed to have collected their stories from a wide area of Germany, to have sought out illiterate or at least ill-educated peasant informants and to have transcribed exactly what they were told without editing or improving them in any way. Although these precepts must have had a beneficial influence on later folklorists, the Brothers Grimm did not in fact practise what they preached. In recent times, careful study of their working methods suggests that they relied on rather few informants, and that these were mostly literate and middle class, residing in Kassel. The Grimms also reworked their tales to improve their readability and moral content. Two of their 'best' informants in Kassel had a French background, and their memories of childhood stories from Galland may account for the appearance of distorted but still recognizable versions of 'Aladdin' and 'Ali Baba' in the Grimms' collection of German folklore. The Grimms themselves identified the *Nights* as the ultimate source of eight of the tales they had been told. Additionally 'The Sea Rabbit' probably derives from 'The Story of Prince Calaf and the Princess of China' in the *Mille et un jours*, an oriental story collection produced by Pétis de la Croix. ('The Story of Prince Calaf' was also to inspire Gozzi's drama and Puccini's opera *Turandot*.)

Tales from the *Nights*, albeit stripped of their specifically Islamic and oriental features, circulated orally in Germany in pre-modern times, and for that matter in Italy, France and Spain too. In most cases it is impossible to determine whether those tales passed into Europe first by word of mouth or in manuscript form. The Grimm brothers were great admirers of the *Nights*, which for Jacob Grimm described 'the poetic geography of the East'. Hans Christian Andersen, who as a child was regularly read to from the *Nights*, was similarly devoted to its tales, but he made more deliberate use of its stories as a source of creative inspiration. His 'Tinder Box' certainly owes something to 'Aladdin', while his 'Little Mermaid' may be modelled on the story of 'Julnar the Sea-Born'. Similarly, his story of 'The Emperor's New Clothes' seems to be based on a story in the Turkish collection *The History of the Forty Viziers* (or a variant version in *Conde Lucanor*).

Deliberate literary plundering of the *Nights* by western novelists and short-story writers is the subject of a subsequent chapter. Returning to the main theme of this chapter, in Europe the rise of folklore studies and the new enthusiasm for collecting fairy tales (to which the works of the Brothers Grimm gave an enormous impetus) were concurrent with the rise of nationalism and the development of a science of philology. This is in marked contrast to what happened in the Middle East. As Ernest Gellner has put it: 'Arab nationalism defines itself and the limits of the nation in terms of the old literate High Culture and in opposition to its folk variants, whereas in Central and Eastern Europe it had been the other way around.'[58] That is to say, Arab intellectuals identify folk culture with regionalism and dialectal differences, whereas for the most part they conceive of the 'Arab nation' as transcending the national boundaries delimited by the European powers in the Near East in the twentieth century. The Arabs were slow to take an interest in the oral prose tale, though folklore institutes do now exist in Baghdad and Cairo. Hasan El-Shamy, director of archives at the Cairo Folklore Centre, has observed that 'Modern nationalistic ideologies have shunned local folk dialects and hold classical Arabic to be a major unifying force among the Arabic-speaking countries. It is not surprising that the novel and the short story emerged only in the late nineteenth century as a direct transplant from European literature.'[59] Yet, as this chapter may suggest and a future chapter will confirm, the paradox is that the way both the European novel and the short story developed owed an immense amount to the *Nights* and to other Arab works of fiction and folklore.

4

The Storyteller's Craft

They were words that held no meaning for me, hammered out with fire and impact: to the man who spoke them they were precious and he was proud of them. He arranged them in a rhythm that always struck me as highly personal. If he paused, what followed came out all the more forceful and exalted. I sensed the solemnity of certain words and the devious intent of others. Flattering compliments affected me as if they had been directed at myself; in perilous situations I was afraid. Everything was under control; the most powerful words flew precisely as far as the storyteller wished them to.

Elias Canetti, *The Voices of Marrakesh*[1]

As Elias Canetti, the novelist, watches the storytellers at work in the market-place of Marrakesh, he seems to be engaged in meditation on the mysterious origins of his own art. It is indeed tempting to think of the storyteller in the market-place as a precursor or primitive type of novelist. But the relationship between oral narrative and written fiction is more complex than at first appears.

It has often been assumed that the stories collected in the *Nights* derived from oral storytelling, but, as we have seen, this assumption is at best only partially true. Again, it has often been assumed that the stories in the *Nights* formed part of the stock-in-trade of the professional street-corner storyteller. As we shall see, this was only occasionally the case. Little or no systematic research has been carried out into the history of storytelling in the Middle East, and indeed that history is very obscure. From the first, storytelling has been rated as a low-grade and slightly disreputable activity. According to early Islamic tradition, one of the Prophet's contemporaries,

a man called Khurafa, from the tribe of Udhrah, was visited by
the jinn and carried off by them. When he returned, he went
around telling stories about his encounter with the jinn, but people
disbelieved him, saying that his stories were impossible. Khurafa
then allegedly gave his name to the Arabic word for a fable or
silly story (khurafa), though it is obvious that this is a case of back-
formation, the legendary fabulist having been invented to provide
an etymology for the word.[2]

Although nothing certain is known about storytelling in the
first two centuries of Islam, it is likely that the profession had a
twofold ancestry, religious and secular. On the religious side, the
popular preacher was certainly one of the precursors of the
storyteller. The khatib, the man who preached the sermon in the
main mosque on Fridays at noon, was usually a man noted for his
piety and learning. But in the early centuries, besides the khatibs,
there were also popular storytellers, qussas, who specialized in
telling religious stories in the mosques. Many of the qussas were
learned in the interpretation of the Koran and of irreproachable
orthodoxy. However, they also included some less reliable narra-
tors who specialized in telling tales from what may be reckoned to
be the Muslim Apocrypha – marvellous and doubtful tales about
the pre-Islamic prophets, about Muhammad and about the heroes
of the early Islamic conquests. In the centuries which followed the
initial preaching of Islam, Muslim scholars slowly reached some
sort of consensus about what was fantastic and legendary in tales
which purported to be religious. Eventually the qussas came to be
looked on with suspicion by the religious establishment, both
because of the doubtful orthodoxy of some of their edifying
stories and because many of these storytellers cared less about
edification than they did about increasing their personal income.

The qussas moved out from the mosques and into the market-
places. The worst of them were not really distinguishable from
buffoons or beggars. Alleged sayings of the Prophet were
manufactured for profit and entertainment. 'He who can touch

the tip of his nose with his tongue will not go to hell' was one such saying attributed to Muḥammad by a popular preacher. While the preachers worked on their audiences with sob stories, confederates went among the people collecting money. Ibn al-Jawzi described the popular preachers in thirteenth-century Baghdad and commented that 'it is an evident way of making the stories a source of livelihood and of getting gifts from tyrannical princes and obtaining the like from the gatherers of unlawful imposts . . . Some of them go to the cemeteries where they dilate upon affection and parting with friends drawing tears from the women, but not exhorting them to take warning.' The *qussas* competed for pitches. Hence the saying 'One *qass* does not love another.'[3]

Islamic storytelling's second line of descent derives from acting. Until very recently it was thought that there was no live theatre in the Islamic world until the nineteenth century – apart, that is, from the Shi'ite passion plays which commemorated the martyrdom of Hasan and Hussein. The only known play scripts in Arabic to have survived from the Middle Ages are scripts for shadow plays. Therefore the scholarly consensus has been that the classical theatrical tradition was brought to an end by the Arab conquest of much of the Eastern Roman Byzantine Empire, or perhaps had withered away a century or two before the Arab invasions. However, the classical scholar Professor B.E. Perry has observed that

Put into narrative form, instead of dialogue, many of the mimes which were acted on the stage in late Alexandrian and early Roman imperial times would read very much like the clever stories of adulterous intrigue, the outwitting of husbands, the clever devices of women, the picaresque adventures of rogues, the tricks played by sharpers on simpletons, etc., which we find in the *Arabian Nights* and in *Sindbad*.[4]

What is implied here is that it is possible that some of the old classical farces continued to be played in Islamic times, and that some of the content of the *Nights* is based on the plots of those plays. In the last few years, moreover, the researches of an Israeli scholar, Dr Shmuel Moreh, have uncovered evidence of the survival of acting and specifically of classically derived perform-ances of mime in the Arab lands.[5] Mime in its original Greek and Roman sense does not refer to a drama without words in which actors use only gestures and facial expressions to get over the drama's meaning; the classical mime was a short play, often about everyday life, or at least a farcical and bawdy version of everyday life, in which the actors did use speech. Indeed, they often entertained their audiences by mimicking the accents and speech patterns of certain stock types, such as doctors, peasants and barbarians.

Mimics and companies of actors did not actually disappear with the coming of the Arabs. The mimics merely added to their repertoire. *Hikaya* in modern Arabic means 'story', but originally the word meant mimicry, and the *hakiya* was a mimic. The *hakiya*'s art lay in his skill in imitating anything – birds, animals, natural disasters, famous people and social types. The ninth-century essayist al-Jahiz ('Goggle-Eyes') wrote a treatise on eloquence, the *Kitab al-Bayan wa'l-Tabyin*, in which he praises the expressive genius of mimics. They are

capable of producing in perfect detail the pronunciation of Yemenis; and they can equally well imitate Khurasanis, Ahwazis, Zanjis, Sindis or Ethiopians. They even seem more natural than the originals! When they imitate a man with a stammer, it is like all the peculiarities of all the world's stammerers rolled into one. They imitate blind men, making up their faces and eyes and affecting movements of their limbs such that not one blind man in a thousand exhibits all these peculiarities; the mimic seems able to catch all the characteristic movements of the blind man at the same time.[6]

Al-Mas'udi tells the tale of Ibn al-Maghazili, a ninth-century *hakiya* in Baghdad who was famous for his jokes, stories and imitations of 'Bedouin, grammarians, transvestites, judges, gypsies, Nabateans, Sindi, Zanj, eunuchs and Turks'. A eunuch in the service of the Abbasid court arranged to bring him before the Caliph al-Mu'tadid in return for a half-share in the reward that the *hakiya* would get for entertaining the caliph. When al-Maghazili came before al-Mu'tadid, it was agreed that he should receive 500 dirhams if he made the caliph laugh. However, it was stipulated that, if the caliph did not laugh, then the mimic would receive ten heavy blows on the neck. The mimic ran through his entire repertoire, but the unsmiling caliph kept his composure. The desperate mimic prepared to receive his punishment and in fact asked to have it doubled. Then, as soon as the beating had been administered, the sore and giddy mimic asked that the eunuch should receive his half-share too. Now indeed the caliph did burst into peals of laughter.[7]

Although the *hakiya* was not in the first instance a storyteller, it is easy to imagine how, as he developed the patter to go with imitations of ignorant bedouin or rich Persian merchants, this patter, designed to carry grotesque accents and mannerisms, might evolve into a full-blown story or series of stories. In the thirteenth century the distinguished Christian historian writing in Syriac, Barhebraeus, put together a collection entitled *Laughable Stories*, within which the fifteenth chapter is devoted to 'Amusing Stories of Mimics and Comedians'.[8] In fact, by the early fourteenth century at the latest, *hikaya* had come to mean 'story', and the storyteller had replaced the mimic in the market-places. Competing with the individual storyteller, small companies of actors continued to give open-air, street-corner performances of short comedies, just as they had done in Greek and Roman times. Although references to actors and live theatre are rare in the sober medieval chronicles, it seems that the shows which were put on were often bawdy farces somewhat similar to the Latin comedies of Plautus, though less sophisticated. Perhaps some performances were based on themes derived ultimately from Plautus. It is even possible that such *Nights* tales as 'The Tale of the Ugly Man and his Beautiful Wife' or 'The Tale of the Fuller, the Wife and the Trooper' (the plots of which have similarities with Plautus) may be the transcriptions of farces which had been acted out in medieval Baghdad or Cairo.

In the medieval Arab lands the professional Arab storyteller enjoyed (if that is the word) a very low status. He competed with snake-charmers, jugglers and pedlars of quack medicines for the attention and the money of the crowds. Like these other low-life entertainers, many of the storytellers in twelfth-century Cairo were to be found in the Bayn al-Qasrayn. The Bayn al-Qasrayn ('Between the Two Palaces') was originally the military parade ground between the two great Fatimid palaces in the heart of old Cairo. After the suppression of the Fatimid dynasty in the late twelfth century, the palaces fell into ruin, and by Mamluke times they had largely been built over, while the open space between them had become a market-thoroughfare and a place of popular entertainment. According to al-Qurti, the storytellers in the Bayn al-Qasrayn 'told stories of the Bedouin Girl and Ibn Mayyah and about al-Hakim bi-Amr Allah [a historical personage to whom many fantastic stories were attached]. These stories are comparable to the stories of al-Battal [a semi-legendary hero of the early Islamic conquests] and to *The Thousand and One Nights* and similar stories.'[9] The northern suburb of al-Husayniyya, an area settled by Kurds and Turks, was another favoured stamping ground of the storytellers. In medieval Fez, storytellers were normally found working close to the city's gates. Their stories were often accompanied by music, and the Moroccan storytellers sometimes supplemented their earnings by selling talismans.[10]

Because of their low status, individual storytellers were rarely noticed by the historians and compilers of biographical dictionaries. A rare passing mention of a storyteller comes in an obituary notice of a jurisprudent, Shams al-Din al-Fa'alati, in a fifteenth-century chronicle, whose author, Ibn Taghribirdi, notes that this man rose from humble and even disreputable origins, for one of his brothers was a geomancer and the other an astrologer, while his father earned his living by telling stories and by selling astrological predictions to professional wrestlers.[11]

The professional storyteller makes a rare appearance in the *Nights* itself. In 'The Tale of King Muhammad Bin Sabaik and the Merchant', the king has been criticized by his vizier for spending too much on his court poets, cup-companions and storytellers (*shu'ara wa'l-nudama wa arbab al-hikayat*); nevertheless he commissions Hasan the Merchant to seek out the most marvellous story ever. Hasan sends his mamluke slaves out on the quest. One of the mamlukes achieves success, for in Damascus he finds an old man who tells stories every day, seated on his storyteller's throne (*kursi*), and this old man knows the wondrous story of 'Sayf al-Muluk and Badia al-Jamal'. When the mamluke agrees to pay a fee of 110 dinars, the old man takes him to his home and allows him to make a copy of his book of the story. But the sale is on five conditions, which are as follows: 'that thou tell not this story in the beaten high road nor before women and slave-girls nor to black slaves nor feather-heads; nor again to boys; but read it only to Kings and Emirs and wazirs and men of learning, such as expounders of the Koran and others'.[12] The king is indeed pleased with the story, has his scribes copy it out in letters of gold and has it placed in the treasury. (The treasury, the *khizana*, was normally used as a book depository in Muslim palaces.) We need not take the old man's stipulations very seriously. An announcement that the story to come was fit only for crowned heads or for the very learned was a stock way of crying up one's wares. We may safely assume that the story of 'Sayf al-Muluk and Badia al-Jamal' was regularly listened to by the common people in the market-places, including slaves and women. A twelfth-century Andalusian Muslim market inspector's manual indeed warns of the dangers of unaccompanied women entering the booths or homes of story-tellers and fortune-tellers.[13]

The prelude to the story of 'Sayf al-Muluk' suggests that the professional storyteller commonly worked from written sources (and, as we shall see, Lane's testimony suggests the same). It also suggests that stories which were written had a higher status than those which continued to be transmitted orally. Remarkable stories deserved something better than oral transmission. That the story is so good that it must be written down is in fact a recurring topos in the *Nights*: 'Your story must be written down in books, and read after you, age after age.' Only writing guarantees survival, and writing makes the best claim on the attention of those who should marvel at or take warning from the stories.[14] A rather oddly phrased formulation of this recurs frequently: 'Verily my adventure is wondrous and were it graven with needle gravers on the eye corners it would be a warning to whoso would be warned and a matter of thought to whoso would think.'

With the Ottoman conquest of Egypt and Syria (1516–17), most crafts and trades in the cities of those provinces were organized into guilds.[15] (This was done mainly to facilitate the collection of taxes.) At about the same time, coffee drinking and coffee-houses spread through the Ottoman lands. The storyteller moved off the streets and into the coffee-house. The clientele of the Middle Eastern coffee-house was entirely male and often somewhat disreputable, numbering the unemployed, off-duty soldiers and drug addicts among its patrons. The most rigorous theologians held that coffee was an intoxicant and tried to get it banned, but learned opinion was divided, and coffee was rarely unavailable for very long in any Muslim city. From the seventeenth century onwards, coffee-houses were also where one went to smoke tobacco – another activity regarded with disapproval by religious rigorists. The seventeenth-century Turkish belletrist Katib Chelebi sourly remarked in an essay on the moral menace of coffee that 'Story-tellers and musicians diverted the people from their employments, and working for one's living fell into disfavour.'[16] A list of guilds compiled in 1801 includes two corporations of storytellers who worked in cafés. Besides tips from the customers, the storyteller sometimes also received a small weekly fee from the proprietor of the café. In the early nineteenth century one of these guilds held weekly meetings in a coffee-house. The Madkhana, the 'Place for Laughing', was a particularly famous coffee-house in Cairo where the leading storyteller acted as a sort of president and chose other people to tell stories. Although most professional storytelling was done in coffee-houses, the storytellers were also summoned to the houses of the rich to perform at weddings or other important social functions.

Alexander Russell's *The Natural History of Aleppo* (1794) described a storyteller at work in a Syrian café in the mid-eighteenth century:

He recites walking to and fro in the middle of the coffee room, stopping only now and then, when the expression requires some emphatical attitude. He is commonly heard with great attention; and not unfrequently in the midst of some interesting adventure, when the expectation of his audience is raised to the highest pitch, he breaks off abruptly and makes his escape, leaving both his hero or heroine and his audience in the utmost embarrassment. Those who happen to be near the door endeavour to detain him, insisting upon the story being finished before he departs; but he always makes his retreat good; and the auditors suspending their curiosity are induced to return at the same time the next day to hear the sequel. He has no sooner made his exit than the company in separate parties fall to disputing about the characters of the drama or the event of an unfinished adventure. The controversy by degrees becomes serious and opposite opinions are maintained with no less warmth than if the fall of the city depended on the decision.

This 'Perils of Pauline' approach to storytelling may account for the rambling and crisis-punctuated narrative structure of some of the stories in the *Nights*. However, although Russell found that storytellers flourished in eighteenth-century Aleppo, he noted that the *Nights* collection was scarcely known to them.[17]

In Tangiers in the 1880s, Burton tracked down a storyteller
weaving his enchantments in an extremely squalid suburb of the
city: 'a foul slope; now slippery with viscous mud, then powdery
with fetid dust, dotted with graves and decaying tombs, unclean
booths, gargottes and tattered tents, and frequented by women,
mere bundles of unclean rags, and by men wearing the haik or the
burnus, a Franciscan frock, tending their squatting camels and
chaffering over cattle for Gibraltar's beef eaters'. The storyteller, a
disreputable-looking figure, carried a stick and an hourglass-shaped
tom-tom. This man 'speaks slowly and with emphasis, varying the
diction with breaks of animation, abundant action and the most
comical grimace: he advances, retires and wheels about, illustrating
every point with pantomime; and his features, voice and gestures
are so expressive that even Europeans who cannot understand a
word of Arabic divine the meaning of his tale'.[18] However,
Burton never heard any stories from the *Nights* recited in
Tangiers.

It is Edward Lane who, relying on his long sojourn in Cairo,
gives the fullest and most useful information about the storyteller
and his relationship to the *Nights*. Lane devoted three chapters of
his *Manners and Customs of the Modern Egyptians* to the professional
storytellers who worked in the Cairene coffee-houses, and the
Nights features prominently in his account.[19] According to Lane,
there were then few copies of the book to be found in Cairo, and,
perhaps because of this, there were few reciters of its stories. Far
more common were the *shu'ara* (literally, 'poets') who specialized
in reciting the *Sira of Abu Zayd*, a popular romantic epic, half
prose and half poetry. There were approximately fifty of these
shu'ara who had memorized the book and who gave recitations
from it, sometimes with a musical accompaniment on the viol.
Some of them specialized in recitations of only part of the story
(for it was very long). Next most numerous were the *muhaddithun*
who specialized in telling stories from the *Sira of Baybars*. Finally,
the smallest group specialized in chanted recitations from the *Sirat*

Antar, an epic celebration of Arab heroism and warfare in pre-Islamic times, most of which was put together between the eighth and the twelfth centuries. Lane observed that *Antar*, a distinguished example of rhymed prose in classical Arabic, was not really popular in the coffee-houses; and consequently there were only about half a dozen of the Antariyya in the whole of Cairo. It was the Antariyya who occasionally varied their repertoire by reading stories from the *Nights*. All these professional storytellers worked the Cairo coffee-houses and normally told their tales from the *mastaba*, or stone platform outside. The proprietor would pay them a small sum for the added custom which their stories brought, and the reciters could also hope to collect voluntary contributions from the audience.

The professional storyteller, or *hakawati*, did not always rely on memory, but often worked from a text. At the beginning of this century, the *Nights* scholar Duncan Black Macdonald purchased several scrappy manuscripts of prompt-texts that had belonged to a professional *hakawati* in Damascus. Macdonald also watched a professional storyteller at work in a Cairo coffee-house and noted how the audience preferred action and jokes to the poetry which the storyteller wished to insert into the narrative.[20]

Evidently the medieval *Nights* was a kind of cultural amphibian. Although the story collection should not be considered only in literary terms, it would be still less correct to consider it as merely oral folklore slapped down on paper. It is true that many of its stories first circulated as orally transmitted folk-tales, before being written down, but the point is that they *were* written down, and those who wrote them down almost invariably gave them a literary shaping. It is occasionally possible to detect the rhythms of oral delivery in the prose of the stories, and David Pinault (whose work will be discussed in a subsequent chapter) has identified the survival of the characteristics of verbal delivery in some parts of the text. However, there are only occasional traces in the *Nights* of such important features of oral transmission and delivery as sterotyped adjectives, mnemonic formulas and recurrent summaries of the plot so far. Therefore methods developed for the study of such things as the transmission of African tribal genealogies or the preservation of English country lore are not very useful when one turns to study the *Nights*.

It is true that most of the stories were told by storytellers (of a rather low social status) to illiterate audiences, but, as we have seen, the storytellers usually worked from a written text. Moreover, this was not the only way the stories continued in circulation, for some people borrowed the *Nights* and similar works from small private lending libraries. Anyway, it would be a mistake simply to equate oral transmission and delivery with some sort of 'low' culture. Poetry enjoyed the highest status in medieval Arabic culture, as it does in the modern culture, and poems were more often recited than read in private. People regularly committed enormous swaths of poetry to memory. Also, the only proper way that *hadiths*, traditions concerning the Prophet Muhammad and his contemporaries, could be passed on to students was by word of mouth, and it was not thought acceptable simply to mug up all that religious material from a book.

Turning to books, the normal way of 'publishing' a book in the early centuries of Islam was to take it along to the mosque and read it out loud there. Most people were familiar with such works of high literature as Ibn al-Muqaffa's *Kalila wa-Dimna* and al-Hariri's *Maqamat* from hearing them read out aloud. One might think that the lack of a fixed canonical text of the *Nights* in the Middle Ages was in itself a sign of its low status, but a great many important works had no fixed text, including *Kalila wa-Dimna*. It is very hard indeed to draw any sort of boundary between a 'high' Arabic culture and a 'low' culture; for example, vulgarly obscene stories, *mujun*, did not circulate exclusively among some sort of Arab lumpenproletariat, since the *nudama*, the drinking companions of the caliphs and sultans, were commonly expected to have a fund of such stories committed to memory and ready for use as after-dinner entertainment. Not only did street-corner storytellers gather some of their material from scholarly books, but scholars and literary men in their turn reworked much of the material that was the stock-in-trade of the storytellers. Al-Hariri's *Maqamat* deals with the low-life themes of begging and small-time confidence tricks, but it does this in an elaborate and technically brilliant high style. Such cultural cross-overs defeat attempts to draw a boundary between the culture of the literary élite and that of the masses. Finally, it must be remembered that the Arab literary élite was not co-extensive with the politico-military élite. Many of the sultans, emirs and governors who ruled over the Arab lands in the Middle Ages were Turks, who had grown up in a culture of the steppes in which legends and histories circulated orally. Members of this Turkish élite were often illiterate.

Although information about the professional Arab storyteller in pre-modern times is fairly sparse, the activities of his Turkish and Persian counterparts are better documented. The *ashiks* (literally 'lovers') were poet-minstrels who wandered through Turkey in early Ottoman times, singing or reciting poems about love and heroism. The *meddah*, or Turkish storyteller, may be a descendant of the *ashik*. *Meddah* literally means 'praise-giver', and the earliest *meddahs* specialized in heroic epics about Turkey's past. Only subsequently did they add fantastic, comic and bawdy tales to their repertoire. The *meddah* was a normal fixture at the courts of the Turkish princes. Lalin Kaha, the *meddah* of the Ottoman Sultan Mehmed III (reigned 1595–1603), was a particularly famous court storyteller.[21]

However, most Turkish storytellers were not part of a court establishment but, as in Egypt, were organized in a guild and normally told their stories in the coffee-houses. The *meddah* usually spoke from a chair in the café, using a handkerchief and wand as props. The handkerchief was sometimes used to muffle his voice for effect. The tales he told tended to be rich in dialogue and offered many opportunities for mimicry. The *meddahs* of Istanbul were renowned for their female impersonations. Some *meddahs* gave improvised performances, others read from texts. The story was told in an oddly stylized way, for first the *meddah* would announce that the story he was going to tell had a moral; next he would list the story's characters; then he would advertise the poetry and give the setting of the story; finally he would tell the story.

In medieval Persia, the *naqqal* (literally, the 'transmitter') used to recite from the great national epic, the *Shahnama*, produced by Firdawsi in the eleventh century. Since the *Shahnama* is over 50,000 couplets long and has claims to be the longest poem ever produced in world literature, most *naqqals* specialized in recounting different sections of the poem. (In serial form the *Shahnama* could take a whole year to recite). But as in Turkey, by the nineteenth century, if not earlier, these storytellers had added to their stock by telling folk-tales, as well as more recently coined stories. By the late nineteenth century, the *naqqals* had been organized into a guild headed by an imperial official, the *naqibolmalek*, who also doubled as the head of the official dervish order.[22] It was the *naqibolmalek*'s job to tell the Shah stories every evening until he fell asleep. (In much the same way, the Russian Tsar Ivan the Terrible used to employ three blind men to tell him stories until he drifted off.) Sir John Malcolm, who visited the court of Fath Ali Shah in 1801, reports Mullah Adeenah, the court storyteller, as saying: 'Besides my own invention, I have a great book, containing anecdotes on all subjects, and an infinite quantity of amusing matter, which I select at pleasure, and adapt my story to the circumstances of the moment, and to the characters of those who form the audience.'[23]

More generally, storytelling was closely associated with Sufism and the dervish orders. Jalal al-Din al-Rumi, the thirteenth-century Persian Sufi who taught and preached in Konya (Anatolia), was steeped in Arabic and Persian poetry and prose. Rumi used familiar stories from, for example, *Kalila wa-Dimna* and recast them as mystical parables. He left the world a rich legacy of story lore in his *Mathnawi Discourses*, a great sprawling series of stories within stories, cast in poetic form, in which the inner stories comment on and indicate the mystical meanings of the outer stories.[24] C.J. Wills, a medical officer of the British Telegraph Department in nineteenth-century Persia, described the outlandish gear of the dervish storytellers – their short trousers of animal skin, their skull-caps and their huge axes or clubs: 'I frequently, on passing through the Maidan, or public square, of Shiraz, saw Aga Nusserulla surrounded by a gaping crowd of peasants, porters, and muleteers squatting in a circle, he striding up and down and waving his axe as he told his story of love or fairyland.'[25] A special sort of storyteller, the *pardadar*, made use of an additional prop, a large, gaudy painting featuring episodes from the story he was going to tell and which he pointed to as he progressed with his narrative.

In Persia the *naqqals* with their repertoire of entertainment and adventure tales sometimes had to compete with the *rowzeh khans*, who preached and told edifying stories. In particular, the *rowzeh khan* specialized in describing the martyrdom of Hasan and Hussein, the grandchildren of the Prophet Muhammad, and working on the audience's emotions to bring them to a state of repentance and religious fervour. However, sometimes the *naqqal* doubled as a *rowzeh khan*, telling secular stories most of the time, but switching to tales of martyrdom and piety on religious holidays. An American researcher, Mary Ellen Page, made a study of storytelling in Shiraz in the 1970s. She found that there were four professional *naqqals* working in the city. Each had his set rota of coffee-houses and could draw audiences of between 100 and 200 for performances which tended to go on for an average of an hour and a half, breaking off at a point of suspense. The stories they told were drawn from the *Shahnama*, large sections of which they had committed to memory. However, while the storyteller's apprenticeship consisted of rote memorization of a text, once embarked on his career he felt no obligation to stick closely to the text he had memorized. Rather, he embroidered and abbreviated at will to suit his personal style, as well as the tastes of his particular audience.[26]

Although professional storytelling still seems to flourish in modern Iran, it looks as though the profession has died out in all the Arab lands except Morocco, where tourism has helped keep it alive. In recent years Nacer Khemir, a Tunisian, has single-handedly revived the craft, telling tales from the *Nights* and from local Tunisian folklore to Arab and European audiences, building up a repertoire of about twenty-four hours of stories. But Khemir's performances are an individual creation rather than the perpetuation of a living tradition. Indeed, he has described how, some time around 1970, he hunted through the old part of Tunis for the last surviving practitioner of his chosen craft: 'It took us a long time before we eventually dug out an old, old storyteller, who, to earn his living, had had to take a job as a watchman at a charcoal depot. But we couldn't get him to talk of the past, and the mere mention of it threw him into agony.'[27]

The professional storyteller makes a unique appearance in 'The Tale of Sayf al-Muluk' and he is heavily outnumbered in the *Nights* by talented amateurs who tell tales in order to save their lives, make moral points, confuse suspicious husbands, win beautiful princesses or simply pass the time. Here fiction accurately models reality. Most storytelling has always been done by amateurs. Medieval Arab intellectuals, who espoused poetry and *belles-lettres* in opposition to prose fiction, often claimed that fanciful stories, or *khurafa*, were only suitable for women and children. In twentieth-century Egypt the researches of the folklorist Hasan El-Shamy have indeed revealed that fantastic stories are usually told by women to other women and to children.[28]

Storytelling is often regarded as a time-wasting activity and therefore as something which is rather sinful and may consequently attract the jinn. Therefore storytellers may begin their stories with some sort of evil-averting formula. (On the other hand, it is also common to finish with some ritually authenticating phrase such as 'I was there and just returned and I did not even have supper'.) Storytelling becomes less sinful when the day's work is over, and so wonder-stories were also known as *samar*, or 'things of the evening'. Also, at certain times of the year, there was less work to be done in the fields, and then again storytelling became a more respectable activity. El-Shamy notes that there is a particular demand for long stories in Egypt in July and August, when the flooding of the Nile means that the work-load is light. In Morocco, on the other hand, the winter months are the ones when one has some time to sit about and listen to stories. The novelist Richard Hughes, who resided in Tangiers in the 1920s, kept a cook who was an expert, if amateur, storyteller. Hughes transmitted some of his cook's narratives in a volume of short stories, *In the Lap of Atlas*, but he noted that each story was 'embellished with a wealth of detail that would have filled an ordinary-sized novel. The Arab story-teller excels at this long spinning-out of detail: he will begin the morning with a description of the hero's bridle as he starts out on the journey, and by the afternoon be still describing the horse's tail.'[29]

More recently the American novelist Paul Bowles has enjoyed a similar relationship with another amateur (in formal terms, that is) storyteller, Mohammed Mrabet. Mrabet's stories are tape-recorded and translated by Bowles before being published as books. Mrabet, who used to listen to the tales told by old men in cafés, comes almost at the end of a line. These days, according to Bowles,

practically every café has a television. The seats are arranged differently and no one tells any stories. They can't because the television is going. No one thinks of stories. If the eye is going to be occupied by a flickering image, the brain doesn't feel a lack. It's a great cultural loss. It's done away with the oral tradition of storytelling and whatever café music there was.[30]

5

Street Entertainments

===

There are more stories in the *Nights* about princes and sons of wealthy merchants than there are about street-corner layabouts and petty criminals. It could therefore be argued that it makes more sense to use the *Nights* as a source for the high life of the rich and powerful than for low life. However, when Arab storytellers described the world of the palace, its rituals, its intrigues and its fabulous wealth, whether in old Baghdad or Peking, they were conjuring up a fantasy vision of the lives of the great – a vision of ceremonies conducted behind high walls, of harems which could not be penetrated without the risk of being apprehended and executed and, above all, of days spent without having to do a hand's turn of work. They were describing a milieu which was no more familiar to them than it was to their audience. Such fantasies are gently mocked in the barber's story about the day-dream of his fifth brother. That brother, having invested what little capital he had in buying some glass, leaned against a balustrade and began to fantasize about selling the glass at a good profit, recycling the profits to buy more glass, using further profits to buy a great house and slaves and horses, then seeking and gaining the hand of the vizier's daughter. He saw himself making his new bride kiss his feet and subjecting her to various other humiliations; then, as she submissively presented herself to him once more in his reverie, he spurned her with his foot. Acting out what he was imagining, the barber's brother kicked out and smashed that small quantity of glass which he had acquired at such cost and which he had imagined would be the foundation of his fortune.

When storytellers talked about small shopkeepers, petty

criminals and beggars, however, they were able to draw on their own experience of life. Moreover and more important, modern students of the medieval Near East can find plenty of other sources to tell them about the lives of the princes, viziers, emirs and members of the merchant oligarchy.[1] High life is a matter of official record, of court panegyric and of pious chronicle. Such sources, of which there are thousands, offer an exhausting amount of detail on how great sultans, viziers, emirs and scholars lived. Very few sources shed any light on the lives of ordinary people (still less those of street-corner entertainers and criminals) in the pre-modern Islamic lands. The stories of the *Nights*, many of which deal with the lives of humble folk and were written down with that audience in mind, are an outstanding source, though not, as we shall see, a unique one. Of course, there are problems in mining fiction for facts; but, though the stories are fantasies, the settings – the buildings and their interiors, the costumes, the streetlife and the gestures – are, or rather were, facts faithfully transmitted. The small touches of background detail, such as the brokerage fees transmitted by the Christian broker, or the hunchback's 'tall green hat, with knots of yellow silk stuffed with ambergris', were used precisely to lend verisimilitude to the bizarre stories in which such details featured.

The stories of the *Nights* are urban stories, written for the most part by people in the cities about people in the cities for people in the cities. The urban nature of the collection as a whole is well illustrated by the themes of 'Abu Kir the Dyer and Abu Sir the Barber', a story about two wily Arab townsfolk who leave Alexandria and set sail from Egypt to seek their fortune. They end up penniless in a strange non-Islamic city, but after various twists and turns of the plot, Abu Kir, who has first made and lost a fortune by introducing different-coloured dyes to the city, finally finds favour with the king and makes his fortune by building the first *hammam* (public bath) in the place. Although the story is a fantasy (surely directed at an audience of Egyptian merchants) about the fortune that could be made using urban Muslim know-how in foreign parts, nevertheless it is a fantasy with some relationship to reality; for Muslim dyestuffs and other finished goods were successfully sold in markets throughout the known medieval world, from Britain to China; and wherever Muslims settled in any numbers, they invariably built *hammams*, as well as mosques and souks.

The peasant and the nomad feature only occasionally in the stories, and, when the nomadic Arab or Kurd does have a part in the stories, it is often an unflattering one. For example, in 'The Rogueries of Dalilah and her Daughter Zaynab', the guileless bedouin is persuaded by Dalilah to change places with her on the cross in the hope of thereby securing some honey fritters. The Kurd in 'Ali Shar and Zumurrud' is a villainous thief. In 'Ali the Persian' the Kurd is a rogue and a fool. It is true that in 'The Fellah and his Wicked Wife' we get a vivid picture of peasant life – ploughing, sowing, harvesting, milling and baking – but this story is almost unique and in any case is not one of the early core stories. The original core stories are pre-eminently set in Baghdad, Cairo and Damascus.

Baghdad, in the days of the Abbasid Caliph Harun al-Rashid (reigned 786–809), is the setting of 'The Story of the Porter and the Three Ladies' and of 'The Story of the Three Apples'. Although the Sinbad the Sailor cycle of stories was not added to the *Nights* until the early modern period, they were certainly composed in the Abbasid period, when Basra served as Baghdad's port on the Gulf. Many of the great love stories in the *Nights*, such as 'The Story of the Slave-Girl Anis al-Jalis and Nur al-Din Ali ibn Khaqan', show signs of having been composed in Abbasid Baghdad. Other shorter tales and anecdotes can also be shown to have originated in Baghdad, some time between the ninth and the eleventh centuries, for they feature in other works of that period such as al-Mas'udi's chronicle *The Meadows of Gold* or al-Isfahani's literary anthology *The Book of Songs*.

In the years 762–6 the Abbasid Caliph al-Mansur caused the perfectly round city of Baghdad to be built on the banks of the Tigris.[2] It was a planned city, and the essayist al-Jahiz remarked that 'It is as if it was poured into a mould and cast.' At the centre of the city was the caliph's residence, the Palace of the Golden Gate. The palace's dome was allegedly capped by a bronze horseman whose lance pointed in the direction from which enemy invasion might next be expected. (This bronze horseman may make one think of the brass horseman in 'The Third Dervish's Tale'.) Outside the palace compound, different concentric sectors of the city were at first reserved for the residences of specific functionaries, such as the palace guards, the water-carriers and the muezzins. It is hard to distinguish truth from legend in the earliest accounts of the city, and certainly no more remains of original Baghdad than of the mythical City of Brass. However, in the lifetime of al-Mansur, the Palace of the Golden Gate was abandoned in favour of the Palace of Eternity, which al-Mansur had founded beyond the walls of the original round city. Baghdad as a whole grew and spilt beyond those walls, and in time the formal layout at the centre of the city was eroded and built over, with the streets coming to assume the higgledy–piggledy layout that is characteristic of so many other medieval Islamic cities. In the centuries which followed, palaces proliferated, and so did suburbs, as the city drifted eastwards. In its heyday Baghdad had a population of at least half a million, making it the largest city west of China. The great slums which grew up came under the control of gangs of riff-raff (or *ayyarun*, of which more later). As for the inhabitants of the slums, lists have survived of the disapproved occupations in Abbasid Baghdad – disapproved of either because of their immorality or because of the noise and smells intrinsic to their practice: blacksmiths, butchers, conjurors, policemen, night-watchmen, tanners, makers of women's shoes, dung collectors, well diggers, bath stokers, masseurs, pigeon racers and chess players.

Few in the city had access to the palace. There, the caliphs conferred and caroused with their *nudama*, cup-companions or intimates, wits and virtuosi, experts on literature, art and human beauty. Beautiful page boys and singing girls waited on the caliph and his companions. The Abbasid palace was an enclosed world, to be fantasized about. Oleg Grabar has eloquently written of it that

> the notion of a prince living in a separate world appears at its best in literature, where it is often connected with a secondary theme, that the interior of the forbidding and forbidden palace consists of a labyrinth of separate elements secretly and mysteriously related to each other. Such a world of courts, pavilions, baths, strange doors, and fantastically elaborate decorations appears in the story of the City of Brass from *The Thousand and One Nights*. It is from this kind of slightly immoral, if exciting, realm that Harun al-Rashid escapes for his forays into the living city. For ... the world of the prince – secluded, rich, and mysteriously complicated – was seen by the Muslim as an evil, and the just man, if called to it, never penetrated it without his own shroud.[3]

In 'Harun al-Rashid and Abu Hasan the Merchant of Oman', the latter is described as going to a brothel in Saffron Street in the quarter of Karkh.[4] However, whereas the storytellers often seem to know their way around Cairo or Damascus, it is rare to find even the pretence of any detailed knowledge of the topography of Baghdad. When one finds stories set in Baghdad during the caliphate of Harun al-Rashid, the notional setting should be read as an expression of nostalgia for a lost golden age, located in the early ninth century, when the Arabs still controlled their own destiny, before the Turks took control over the army and administration, and when almost all the Islamic lands were united under one ruler, the Abbasid caliph. Even though Baghdad is the setting for 'The Porter and the Three Ladies', and the story may well have been composed in that city in Abbasid times, it would be foolish to assume that this is the case; at the very least, the story shows signs of rewriting elsewhere; for it is suspicious how much of the lady's shopping bag, carried by the porter at the beginning of the story, consists of Syrian produce (Hebron peaches, Aleppo jasmine, Ba'albakk figs, Syrian cheese, etc.), and how almost none of the comestibles seem to come from Iraq or points further east.[5]

By the late twelfth century, Baghdad was in full decay. The Spanish Muslim traveller Ibn Jubayr, who visited the place in 1184, remarked: 'In comparison with its former state, before misfortune struck it and the eyes of adversity turned towards it, it is like an effaced ruin, a remain washed out or the statue of a ghost. It has no beauty that attracts the eye, or calls to him who is restless to depart to neglect his business and to gaze.'[6] The last Abbasid caliph to rule in Baghdad fell into the hands of the Mongols when they captured the city in 1258. He was executed by being wrapped up in carpet and trampled to death under the hoofs of the Mongol cavalry.

From the late thirteenth century, Cairo, governed by the Mamluke sultans, was effectively the religious and intellectual capital of Islam.[7] It is evident that many of the contributors to the *Nights* knew and loved this city, and they show detailed familiarity with its topography. For example, in 'The Christian Broker's Tale', in the Hunchback cycle of stories, it is told of the Broker how he lodged in the al-Jawli Caravanserai and how he came to hear the story of the man with the severed hand and how the latter had lodged at the Masrur Caravanserai. (The Masrur Caravanserai was a huge hostelry, chiefly for the use of visiting merchants, located on the Bayn al-Qasrayn, or broad central highway, that runs through the heart of old Fatimid Cairo.) He then walked up the Bayn al-Qasrayn to the Jerjes Market, where he attempted to sell his fabrics. Later this young man, having arranged an assignation with a mysterious lady, walked out through the Zuweyla Gate, heading towards the Habbaniyya Quarter, in search of the house of the Naqib Barqut Abu Shamah, which was close to the al-Tawqa Lane.[8] Most, though not all, of these places can be located with the help of old handbooks or maps of the city. The storyteller has ensured that his audience will have no difficulty in visualizing the setting of his tale by placing it in the urban environment with which they were probably all familiar. Again, in 'The Jewish Physician's Tale', the young man's kinsmen argue about which is the most beautiful city in the world. Someone suggests Baghdad, but the man's father is emphatic that there is nowhere to match Cairo and he recites verses in praise of the Nile and the Ethiopian Pleasure Pond, before concluding:

And what is this compared with the observatory and its charms, of which every approaching viewer says, 'This spot is full of wonders'; and if you speak of the Night of the Nile-Flooding Feast, open the floodgates of words and release the bow; and if you see al-Rauda Park in the shade of late afternoon, you will be thrilled with wonder and delight; and if you stand at the river bank, when the sun is sinking and the Nile puts on its coat of mail and shield, you will be refreshed by the deep and ample shade and gentle breeze.[9]

By the beginning of the fourteenth century, Cairo had a population of perhaps a quarter of a million. The city was a sprawling and poorly policed agglomeration of commercial and residential quarters. It has been calculated that over half its narrow and intricately twisting streets ended in cul-de-sacs.

Looming over the southern end of the city, the Citadel enclosed within its walls not only the sultan's palace but also the barracks of the élite mamluke slave soldiers. Beneath the Citadel there was a parade ground and arms market. Proceeding north, one came eventually to the Bab al-Zuweyla. According to local folklore, the Bab al-Zuweyla, one of the gates into the core of old Cairo, was the invisible seat of the Qutb, 'the Pole', a mystical figure who presided over a secret brotherhood of Sufi saints. The open space before the gate was also the place of public execution, and severed heads were set on spikes over the gate. Strangely this was no deterrent to the disreputable, and the Bab al-Zuweyla was one of their favourite meeting places. Here one could buy musical instruments, consult astrologers, take lessons in single-stick fighting and listen to stories from the *Nights* and similar collections. From 'The First Constable's History', one learns that the Zuweyla Gate was shut at night, thus protecting the greater part of commercial Cairo from night attacks by bandits. Ma'aruf the Cobbler had his shop in the Darb al-Ahmar, or 'Red Street', just outside the Zuweyla Gate.

The Zuweyla Gate was at the southern end of the Bayn al-Qasrayn. Bayn al-Qasrayn literally means 'Between the Two Palaces', and in earlier times this broad highway did indeed run between the palaces of the Fatimid caliphs. However, by the time the Christian broker's interlocutor went walking up this highway, it was lined by mosques, teaching colleges and shops. The great religious foundations provided an imposing backdrop to Mamluke ceremonial. The Bayn al-Qasrayn was Cairo's biggest shopping street, and, according to the fifteenth-century chronicler al-Maqrizi, storytellers and entertainers were to be found along its length. So were stalls serving cooked foods. Although restaurants were more or less unknown in medieval Cairo, many citizens availed themselves of take-away dinners which they either consumed as they continued walking or took back to their houses.

Smaller streets leading off the Bayn al-Qasrayn provided access to specialized markets, among them those of the sellers of knives, of books, of candles and of woodwork. Such markets are well described by Lane:

These streets are called, in Arabic, 'Sooks'; and are generally termed by us 'Bazars' [sic]. A whole street of this description, or a portion of such a street, commonly contains only or chiefly shops appropriated to that particular trade; and is called the Sook of that trade. In general, the shop is a small recess or cell, about six or seven feet high, and between three and four feet wide, the floor of which is even with the top of a raised seat of stone or brick, called 'mastabah', between two and three feet high and about the same in breadth; upon which the shopkeeper usually sits. The front of the shop is furnished with shutters; which when closed at night, are secured by a wooden lock.[10]

Such shops furnished the settings for what is a leitmotif in the *Nights*, the story which opens with the shopkeeper, who is minding his business in his shop, when a mysterious woman pauses to examine his stock. In 'The Christian Broker's Tale', the mysterious woman raises her veil to reveal a large pair of black eyes, before asking after a piece of silk fabric. In 'The Steward's Tale', she enters the young merchant's shop, raises her veil and begins a conversation. In 'The Story of Nur al-Din Ali Ibn-Bakkar and the Slave Girl', Nur al-Din was sitting with a friend in a shop when 'there came up ten full-bosomed virgins, looking like moons, with a young lady riding upon a gray she-mule with trappings of red silk set with gems and pearls'. Such commercial encounters are invariably the prelude to bizarre and wonderful adventures.

The slave market, or *suq al-raqiq*, usually took the form of a rectangular building with an open courtyard in the centre, with the stalls of the slaves ranged around the courtyard. Voyeurs were discouraged, and thus only those judged wealthy enough to be serious potential customers were admitted to this market. In 'The Tale of the Damsel Tuhfat al-Kulub', Harun al-Rashid goes to watch the buying and selling in the slave-dealers' quarters, which was 'a building tall of wall and large of lodgement, with sleeping-cells and chambers therein, after the number of slave-girls, and folk sitting upon the wooden benches'.[11] More public slave auctions, however, feature in 'Ali Shar and Zumurrud' and in 'Ali Nur al-Din and Miriam the Girdle-Girl'.

Shops and markets tended to be clustered close to the central axis of the Bayn al-Qasrayn, while residential quarters were located further out. Customarily the houses of the wealthy were closed in upon themselves, giving little evidence of wealth or even comfort to those who passed by on the street. Inside, however, was another matter, as the porter discovered in 'The Story of the Porter and the Three Ladies':

The shopper and the porter went in, and the doorkeeper locked the door and followed them until they came to a spacious, well-appointed, and splendid hall. It had arched compartments and niches with carved woodwork; it had a booth hung with drapes; and it had closets and cupboards covered with curtains. In the middle stood a large pool full of water, with a fountain in the center, and at the far end stood a couch of black juniper wood, set with gems and pearls, with a canopylike mosquito net of red silk, fastened with pearls as big as hazelnuts or bigger. The curtain was unfastened.[12]

As one moved away from the central highway of the Bayn al-Qasrayn, the streets became narrower. The narrow zigzag streets, the alleys going up in staircases and the frequent cul-de-sacs meant that the unwary traveller was always at risk from false guides and thieves. On the other hand, this pattern of street layout made it easier to barricade off parts of the city in times of civic disturbance and protect respectable neighbourhoods from the gangs of thugs and beggars which dominated the outer slums. The worst slums were located on the northern and western fringes of the city, beyond the old Fatimid walls. There the houses, or shanties, were made from sun-dried brick and palm-leaves. The quarters of al-Husayniyya and Bab al-Luq were dominated by criminal gangs and will be discussed later in that context.

The cemeteries, which in Cairo mostly lay to the east of the city, were places for pious meditation, amorous encounters and pickpockets. Lovers trysted in the underpoliced cemeteries. People who could find no homes elsewhere slept in the shelter of the tombs in the City of the Dead and begged or conducted their nefarious trades there. They shared their territory with ghouls. Also to the east of the city were the vast hills of rubbish which provided a living of sorts for scavengers, both animal and human.

A string of ponds, or pleasure pools, were to be found to the

west of the city between the Nile and the Cairo Canal. The
Ezbekiyya Pond, dug out in 1476 by a Mamluke emir called
Ezbek, became the most popular place of entertainment in the late
Middle Ages. People used to go there after the noon prayer on
Fridays to relax. To the south of Ezbekiyya, the Elephant Pond
was first dug out in Fatimid times, but it dried up subsequently
and had to be re-excavated. Its surface is described as being
covered with pleasure craft and yellow water lilies. It had a horse-
racing track beside it, which is mentioned in story of 'Sayf al-
Muluk and Badia al-Jamal'. The houses of the élite lined the edge
of the pool. One of those buildings, the House of Kafur, was
notorious as a haunted place to which the jinn fled to escape the
conjurations of magicians. Further south was the Qarun Pond,
noteworthy for the extraordinary adventures that Judar the Fisherman had with three Maghribi sorcerers on its bank. Further to the
south yet was the Ethiopian Pond. As has been noted, the delights
of the Ethiopian Pond are extolled by the father in 'The Jewish
Physician's Tale'. He even recites a series of verses, beginning with
the couplet:

> O what a day by the Ethiopian Pond
> We spent between the shadows and the light

and concluding:

> Soft carpets made and spread for us to rest,
> As we sat passing the refreshing wine,
> Which of all drugs for sorrow works the best,
> Quaffing deep draughts from large and brimful cups
> For they alone can quench our burning thirst.

The pleasances and public spaces were thronged with entertainers, storytellers and their competitors. In his extraordinary treatise
on the philosophy of history, the *Muqaddima*, the fourteenth-
century thinker Ibn Khaldun suggested that entertainers flourished
when a civilization decayed:

They become excessive when civilization develops excessively. Thus, we learn that there are Egyptians who teach dumb creatures like birds and domestic donkeys, who produce marvellous spectacles which give the illusion that objects are transformed, and who teach the use of a camel driver's chant, how to dance and walk on ropes in the air, how to lift heavy animals and stones, and other things.[13]

To those entertainers listed by Ibn Khaldun one might also add the storytellers, the snake-charmers, the contortionists, the shadow theatre players, the jugglers, the wrestlers and the *darrats* ('Pétomanes' or professional farters').[14] The storyteller's mode of working has already been discussed in the previous chapter. It is time now to turn to his rivals.

In the *Nights* 'Story of Woman's Wiles' (which is set in Damascus), the wily woman instructs a mamluke (a slave soldier) in the following terms: 'Arise and go straight away to the Takht al-Qala'a, seek out all the Banu Sasan, ape dancers, bear leaders, drummers, pipers.' The Takht al-Qala'a was an open space beneath the Damascus Citadel where people went to be entertained. For reasons which are mysterious, Banu Sasan, or 'Children of Sasan', was the term used to designate the loose community of low-life entertainers, spongers, beggars and thieves.[15] If the reference is to the Sassanian dynasty who ruled over Iran before the coming of Islam, the reference is still mysterious. Members of the Banu Sasan do not feature prominently in the texts on religion, law and history produced by Islam's clerical élite. However, a few long poems have survived which commemorate their achievements. Moreover, treatises were written to expose rogues' tricks. The most famous of these was the *Kashf al-Asrar*, or 'Unveiling of Secrets', by al-Jawbari, who wrote the work to a princely commission in thirteenth-century Iraq.[16] Although al-Jawbari's work was ostensibly written as a caution to the virtuous and a warning to the prudent, there can be little doubt that his retelling of famous confidence tricks, set-ups and practical jokes was written to entertain. Indeed, the genre he was writing in closely resembles the sixteenth- and seventeenth-century literature in English devoted to the exploits of coney catchers, bawdy baskets, Abraham men and other assorted rogues. Al-Jawbari himself, before he took to literature, had travelled and performed throughout the Islamic lands as a conjuror. In those days the conjuror's repertoire included acts which we would now regard as being the province of the juggler on the one hand and of the fraudulent occultist on the other. In the *Kashf al-Asrar*, al-Jawbari exposed not only the tricks of the conjuror, as broadly interpreted, but also the dodges of wonder-working monks, lasciviously pederastic Sufis, itinerant preachers, alchemists, fire-walkers, prostitutes, horse doctors and treasure-hunters.

In one chapter devoted to the frauds of the Banu Sasan, al-Jawbari relates how, when he was in the city of Harran, he saw an ape whose master had trained it to make the human gesture of salutation, to perform the ritual ablutions, to pray and to weep. The ape's master then brought the ape, accompanied by a retinue of servants in Indian costume, to the mosque, where the ape performed the ablutions and the prayer. When the curious in the congregation pressed him to explain this wonder, the ape's master replied that this was in truth no ape but an ensorcelled Indian prince. The king who was his father had married off the prince to a princess. All had gone well in the marriage, until the prince's wife became jealous, suspecting that he had fallen in love with a slave girl. His protestations were useless, and in a rage she used a spell to turn him into an ape. Ever since that moment, the prince had wandered the world in this unhappy form. The ape's master then took a collection on behalf of the 'prince'. Then he and his team scarpered from the town. Although al-Jawbari claims to have been an eyewitness to all this, it bears a certain affinity with 'The Second Dervish's Tale' in the *Nights*. It is an open question whether the *Nights* story inspired the confidence trickster or vice versa. We shall return to the conjuror, and to al-Jawbari's treatise, in the context of medieval Arab crime.

Conjuring, or *sha'badhah*, spawned a specialized literature of its own.[17] In the preface to his *Flowers of the Gardens Concerning Knowledge of Juggling*, the fifteenth-century street-corner conjuror al-Zarkhruri writes of having seen many works on his craft. Al-Zarkhruri's own treatise provided directions for the performance of an impressive range of tricks, some of which are quite elaborate. For example, he describes how a little wax model of a man clutching a scroll can be thrown into a basin of water by the conjuror, who claims that he has sent him as a messenger to the King of the Jinn. Then, when the manikin fails to reappear, the conjuror feigns annoyance and dispatches another wax figure, this one armed with a sword, to punish the messenger for his tardiness. In a little while the water in the basin is coloured red, the swordsman and the severed head of the messenger reappear on the surface, and everyone is amazed. Al-Zarkhruri instructs the neophyte in the mechanics of the trick and the patter to go with it.[18]

Towards the end of his curious treatise, al-Zarkhruri briefly describes the sort of competition that the street-corner conjuror had to face in medieval Cairo from fellow members of the Banu Sasan. First he mentions the professional treasure-hunters. Then there were the alchemists, who pretended to make gold from gypsum and had many other tricks up their sleeve. Then there were the fake ascetics, venerable sheikhs who pretended to go into isolation without food or water for forty days, so as to impress the piously credulous – whereas, in fact, food was being delivered to them by accomplices, who passed it up through a hidden trapdoor in the floor. Finally, there were the Saramitis, who travelled about with a great tabernacle covered with mystical signs, specialized in staging bogus manifestations of poltergeists and performed equally bogus exorcisms for a fee.[19]

Sometimes conjuring was put to pious purposes, as Sufi preachers might perform tricks in order to attract an audience, to whom they would then preach. Al-Hallaj, the great tenth-century Iraqi mystic, having produced an apple, seemingly out of the empty air, told the people around him that he had just plucked it from a tree in paradise. When one man, sharper-eyed than the rest, commented that the paradisal apple seemed to have worm holes in it, al-Hallaj's reply was swift: 'How could it be otherwise? I plucked the apple from a tree in the Mansion of Eternity and brought it into the House of Decay, and that is why it is touched with corruption!' Al-Hallaj is said to have travelled to India to study the rope trick and other magical feats. Hostile contemporaries accused al-Hallaj of having rigged up a special room, the 'Expanding Chamber', in which concealed pipes and partitions allowed him to fake the appearance of a living lamb from out of a flaming furnace, to conjure a fish out of thin air and to make his own body seem to swell until it filled most of the chamber.[20]

The word *la'ab*, which literally means 'play', was used to refer to both conjuring and juggling. According to those mysterious tenth-century encyclopaedists the Brethren of Purity, juggling 'is not anything real but just quickness of movement and concealment of the means (whereby the tricks are executed) ... The fools laugh, but the reasoning marvel at the skill of the performer.' The *hawi*, or snake-charmer, juggled with snakes. He also doubled as a kind of environmental health officer, getting rid of snakes from people's houses. According to Lane, members of certain dervish orders specialized in this activity. Maxime du Camp, Flaubert's travelling companion in Egypt in 1849, included a vivid account of the snake-charmer's *modus operandi* in the narrative of his travels. The young man, after letting the snake curl around his body several times, spat into its mouth and pressed upon its head, so that it became stiff (as stiff as the serpents conjured into rods by Pharaoh's sorcerers in the Old Testament). Then du Camp invited the snake-charmer into his room. The young man immediately divined the presence of a viper and, after stripping naked, he walked about the room whistling monotonously and tapping the walls. Then, invoking God, he conjured the snake to appear, ending with the words, 'If you are within, show yourself! I adjure you in the name of one so great that I dare not say it! If it is your will to obey, appear! If it is your will to disobey, die! die! die!' Sure enough, a snake did appear and come slithering towards the boy, who caught it. Du Camp, however, concluded that he had been fooled by sleight of hand.[21] The Rifa'i dervishes, in particular, specialized in snake handling, going so far as to eat the snakes they handled. They also had a remunerative sideline in fire-walking (for all their 'miracles' were staged for money). In the early fourteenth century, the fundamentalist religious thinker Ibn Taymiyya mounted a campaign against them in which he revealed how they smeared frogs' fat, pieces of orange peel and talc on their feet to protect them from the burning coals.

Then there were the *bahluwans*. A *bahluwan* (literally, a champion) could be an acrobat, a tight-rope walker or a master of one or other of the martial arts. Wrestling was particularly popular in the Mamluke period. The Sultan al-Muzaffar Hajji (reigned 1346–7) loved the common people and common sports and he used to take part in wrestling matches, wearing only the leather trousers of the professional wrestler. (Hajji's other enthusiasms included single-stick fighting, pigeon racing and polo.) Fencers and the stagers of fights between animals also contended for the attention of pleasure seekers and loafers.[22]

Live theatre (*khayal*) was not entirely unknown in the Islamic lands, but shows seem to have been vulgar affairs, which were neither patronized by the élite nor treated as if they were part of Arab high culture.[23] (In the nineteenth century, Lane was particularly dismissive of the 'players of low and ridiculous farces, who are called "Mohabbazzen"'.) The little evidence that there is about live drama in the medieval Arab world suggests that many of the plays were crude farces, not very different from the stories of cuckoldry, roguery and low life that abound in the *Nights*; and, as we have seen, it is possible that some, at least, of both the plays and the stories derive from themes that were first developed in the

Hellenistic drama of late antiquity. One of the rare literary references to an actor occurs in a poem recited by Zumurrud in the story of 'Ali Shar and Zumurrud': 'You go with one beard and return with another / As if you were one of the performers of *khayal*.'²⁴ (Burton mistranslates the couplet in question, believing that *khayali* had to refer to a puppeteer.) Shadow plays (*khayal al-zill*) seem to have been staged more frequently than dramas using actors. Both types of presentation were staged by the disreputable for the vulgar and commonly comprised bawdy romps featuring buffoons, cuckolds, procuresses and hashish eaters. It was all closer in spirit to the music hall than to Molière. Shadow plays seem commonly to have been staged in *khans* or taverns.²⁵ Despite their bawdy nature, the pious head of Saladin's Chancery, al-Qadi al-Fadil, was able to perceive a mystical message in the performance of shadow plays: 'I have had a lesson of great significance. I have seen empires coming and empires going, and when the screen was folded up, I discovered that the prime mover was but one.' More generally, the illusory imagery of the shadow theatre often provided mystical poetry with a repertoire of metaphor.

The thirteenth-century texts of shadow plays written by Ibn Daniyal are an important source on entertainers and low life generally. Ibn Daniyal (1248–1311), by profession an ophthalmologist, had a reputation as a serious poet and was the friend of members of the mamluke élite in Cairo. However, there was another side to him; he wrote scripts (in colloquial Middle Arabic) for shadow plays, and three of these have survived. His play *Ajib wa Gharib* parades some of the seedier denizens of the market-place. In it, the characters appear one after another in front of the Zuweyla Gate. Gharib (literally 'Strange') is a fraudulent occultist, who keeps body and soul together by selling bogus talismans, by faking epileptic fits to solicit charity, by gumming his eyelids together to feign blindness, by training performing apes and by other similarly dubious skills. He is followed by Ajib (literally 'Amazing'), a half-educated and fanciful preacher, the chief aim of whose sermons is to raise money for himself. Then come the snake-charmer, the seller of folk medicines, the herbalist, the surgeon, the tight-rope walker, the conjuror, the geomancer, the amulet seller, the lion tamer, the elephant handler, the man with the marvellous goat, the man who trains cats and mice to be friends, the dog trainer, the bear leader, the Sudanese clown, the sword-swallower, the ape dancer, the self-mutilator, the bogus pilgrim and the lamplighter who is also a beggar. They all make speeches, in which they reveal the tricks of their trade and lament the hardness of their lot. (Ibn Daniyal's collection of Banu Sasan types is not a comprehensive one, and al-Jawbari's *Kashf al-Asrar* lists many more, including stone-swallowers, thimble riggers, wrestlers, singers and galli-galli men.) A second play, *Tayf al-Khayal* ('Shadow of the Imagination'), actually has a plot, in which a soldier, the Emir Wisal, is trapped into an unsuitable marriage; but the plot is a vehicle for satire on contemporary manners and events – such as the Mamluke Sultan Baybars's much publicized (though ultimately ineffective) attempt to ban hashish, pubs and prostitution. The third of Ibn Daniyal's surviving plays, *Al-Mutayyam* ('The Love-Stricken One'), is a curious narrative dealing with the homosexual love of al-Mutayyam and a series of animal fights that he and his beloved stage.

Together with the works of Ibn Daniyal and al-Jawbari, some *adab* treatises and less well-known rival story collections, the *Nights* is one of few sources on the small-time and the seedy, and we have concentrated in this chapter on the disreputable street-corner rivals to the storyteller. However, the *Nights* has plenty to tell us about more ordinary trades. One only needs to think of the porter, the barber, Ma'aruf the Cobbler, Judar the Fisherman, Badr al-Basim the Blacksmith, the Ferryman of the Nile and a whole tribe of cuckolded *qadis* and foolish schoolmasters who crowd the pages of its stories. Such people furnished much of the subject-matter, as well as most of the audience, for the stories of the *Nights*. The real-life counterparts of these characters led lives which were largely ignored by the medieval Arab compilers of chronicles and biographical dictionaries, which focused rather narrowly on a military, administrative and religious élite.

It is fortunate that the *Nights* is not a unique source on the lives of humbler folk, for then one would have to be uneasy about using without corroboration a work of fantasy as a source about private life, commercial practice and *mentalités*. However, besides the literary sources already mentioned, there is also a vast and curious archive known as the Geniza. This huge hoard of documents, over 10,000 pieces of paper, was discovered in the sealed lumber-room of a synagogue in old Cairo in the 1890s. Because of the medieval Jewish reverence for the name of God, they were afraid to throw away anything that might bear his name. Therefore these papers and fragments of paper, written in the Arabic language but in the Hebrew alphabet, had been preserved, rather than being tossed out on to the rubbish heap. The Geniza, or store-room of papers, includes documents of all sorts – wills, laundry lists, letters, poems, deeds of sale, marriage contracts, prayers, legal contracts, and so on. As we have mentioned in Chapter 2, the Geniza even contains the earliest reference to the full title of the *Nights* (in a Jewish bookseller's record of books lent out). The Geniza has proved to be an extraordinarily rich historical source for everyday life in Egypt from the tenth to the thirteenth centuries. The evidence it provides has been brilliantly marshalled and interpreted by S.D. Goitein in his magisterial five-volume synthesis, *A Mediterranean Society: The Jewish Communities of the Arab World as Portrayed in the Documents of the Cairo Geniza* (1967–88). Goitein's study presents the world-view of a vanished society of merchants, shopkeepers, artisans and their families. (It is incidentally noteworthy that now and again Goitein drew on the *Nights* to supplement or confirm the data provided by the Geniza.)

The *Nights*, other literary sources and the Geniza documents offer us countless insights into the material life and *mentalité* of medieval Arab townsfolk: about eating, sleeping, child rearing and cooking. For the social historian, the detailed shopping lists provided at the beginning of both 'The Porter and the Three Ladies' cycle and the Hunchback cycle are as exciting as any fantasy about jinn and flying carpets. The stories are also a rich source for the proverbs and maxims which furnished the common currency of social intercourse: 'He broke his lance on the very first raid'; 'Be kind to him who wrongs you'; 'In love all are alike'; 'The jar cannot be saved every time'; 'A lie may save a man, but the truth is better and safer.' One also finds a range of slang and metaphor in the stories which is almost totally absent in the literature of officials and belletrists. The material contained in the Nights might further provide the basis for a study of the medieval Arab language of gesture. For example, to strike the left hand against the right signified regret (the Calcutta II version of 'The Jewish Physician's Tale'), while to bite one's hand signified repentance ('Abu'l-Husn and his Slave-Girl Tawaddud'). There is no space in the present study to explore this, or a thousand other tempting avenues, but, in the chapters which follow, we shall examine the themes of crime, sex and magic, as they feature in the Nights and in related sources.

6

Low Life

In pre-Islamic Arabia camel-raiding was not regarded as theft, and successful camel-raids were frequently celebrated in poetry. In general, theft was not considered to be a highly reprehensible crime. However, with the coming of Islam and the promulgation of the shari'a, or religious law, fixed penalties were instituted for theft; and a persistent thief, if he was caught, was liable to have one or both of his hands cut off. However, the attitudes persisted, and in certain circles thieves were admired and celebrated, so long as they were cunning and successful. The chronicles, biographical dictionaries and legal treatises which were produced by the medieval Arabs tell us little about the criminal underworld.[1] For that we are forced to turn to fiction. Tales about criminals and confidence tricksters abound in the *Nights*. Although Baghdad is occasionally the nominal setting of these stories, most of them seem to have been composed, or at least rewritten, in Egypt in the Mamluke and Ottoman periods.

Even so, though most 'Baghdadi' crime stories in the *Nights* are really about Cairo, Abbasid Baghdad did produce its own semi-legendary criminals. Many tales were told of the ingenious exploits of the ninth-century master-thief, al-Uqab ('the Eagle'), among them the story of a bet he had with a certain doctor that within a set period of time al-Uqab could steal something from the doctor's house. Although the house was closely guarded, al-Uqab drugged the guards. Then, posing as an apparition of Jesus and making use of hypnotism, he succeeded in stealing off with the doctor himself.[2]

Medieval treatises on crime recognized several categories of thief. One group of housebreakers, the burrowers, simply dug their way through the mud-dried bricks in order to force an entry into the house they wanted to burgle. Other thieves employed hooked poles and grappling irons to fish things out of windows. Others used to make use of a tortoise with a lighted candle placed on its back. They sent this creature ahead of them into the house they proposed to burgle. If the house was currently occupied, then the owner would surely exclaim in surprise on seeing the tortoise (something along the lines of, 'Oh, look! There's a tortoise with a candle on its back. I wonder what it's doing in my house'), and the thieves would be warned off. If, however, the house was unoccupied, then the candle on the tortoise's back would help to guide the thieves as they went about their work. The tortoise was not the only creature to be of use to the professional criminal. In the course of his bizarre and lengthy treatise that purported to discuss the respective merits of the cock and the dog, *Kitab al-Hayawan*, the ninth-century essayist al-Jahiz remarks that the stranglers, who always work in gangs, make use of dogs. Whenever they strangle a victim, at the same time they beat their dogs, so that the barking of the dogs drowns out the screams of the victim, and the suspicions of respectable people in the neighbourhood are not aroused.[3]

It seems that it was common in medieval Baghdad for retired thieves to join the police force as *tawwabun* or 'repentants'. According to the tenth-century historian al-Mas'udi, 'The Repentants are old thieves, who, as they get on in years, give up their profession. When a crime is committed, they know who did it and can point out the culprit. It does, however, often happen they share with the thieves the fruits of their thefts.'[4] What al-Mas'udi has to say about the *ayyarun* is no less curious. In Baghdad, *ayyarun* – gangs of ruffians and vagabonds – armed with cudgels collected protection money from shops and policed their neighbourhoods, controlling the local rackets and protecting them from rival gangs based in other quarters. These gangs were sufficiently organized and armed to provide sizeable militias in times of civil strife. Al-Mas'udi describes how the *ayyarun* 'went into battle almost naked, wearing only short trousers or drawers. They had made themselves a sort of helmet out of plaited palm-leaves, which they called *khudh*. Their shields were made of these same leaves and of reed mats covered with tar and stuffed with sand and gravel.' Bizarrely, the leaders of the *ayyarun* went into battle riding on human mounts, that is to say, the chiefs rode piggy-back on the shoulders of lesser vagabonds who had decked themselves out as horses in fancy harnesses. Gang warfare and factional strife, which plagued Baghdad from the tenth century onwards, played a part in reducing the authority of the caliphate; and, for a while, the caliphs removed themselves from Baghdad and settled in Samarra, in order to bring the clashes between their soldiers and the city's mobs to an end.[5]

The fame of some of the great criminals of Abbasid Baghdad survived the fall of that city to the Mongols in 1258. In Mamluke Egypt popular stories were produced about villains of both sexes who were alleged to have flourished under the Abbasid caliphate, and some of those stories eventually found their way into the later compilations of the *Nights*. However, Cairo itself was the scene of many spectacular crimes, crimes which were a cause of marvel and the source of inspiration to storytellers. For example, some time in the year 1264, in the reign of the Mamluke Sultan Baybars, a dresser was summoned to a house at the Bab al-Sha'riyya on the Khalij al-Masri (a canal that ran through Cairo into the Nile), on the corner of the Husayniyya Quarter. There her assignment was to dress and make up a woman called Ghazia, famed in the city for her beauty and the extravagance of her apparel. The dresser went into Ghazia's house, but never came out again. However, unknown to the people in the house, the dresser had been accompanied by a female slave, who had been left to wait outside. After waiting a long time, this slave girl went off to report her mistress's disappearance to the Governor of Cairo. He promptly had the place raided. Inside, they found not only the dresser's corpse, but a whole cellar full of corpses. The *shurta*, the police force, arrested the entire gang, and in a series of painful interrogations the gang's *modus operandi* was disclosed. Ghazia had made use of an old crone as a bawd or procuress. Ghazia used her beauty and the crone used encouraging words to lure gullible men back to the house. Inside the house, two male confederates would jump on the lusty and unsuspecting victims, killing them and stripping them of everything they had. A fifth confederate, a brickmaker, had a furnace, and at regular intervals the corpses would be taken along to be fed into the furnace. At the end of the investigation, the five were sentenced to death by crucifixion, and the house was confiscated. Somewhat incongruously the house was turned into a mosque, the Masjid al-Khanaqa, or Mosque of the Strangleress.[6]

In the case of Ghazia, robbery was the motive for murder. In times of famine, however, people were murdered in Cairo for the meat that was on their bodies. Abd al-Latif al-Baghdadi, an Iraqi physician who visited Cairo in the years 1200–1201, reported that small children were being boiled or roasted alive while he was there, despite the governor of the city's decree that any cannibals who were caught would be burned alive. Abd al-Latif's narrative abounds with tales calculated to make the flesh creep. 'One night after, a little after the sunset prayer, a young slave played with a newly weaned child which belonged to a wealthy person. While the child was at her side, a beggar, seizing a moment when the slave had her eyes turned from him, slit the child's stomach and began to eat its flesh raw.'[7] Similar stories of kidnap, body-snatching and cannibalism recurred in the 1290s when Egypt was again stricken by severe famine.[8]

At its best, a good crime was *ajib*, a marvel and something as wonderful to hear about as rain of blood or the birth of a two-headed calf. This fascination with crimes and their detection spawned a considerable literature, both factual and fiction. Al-Jawbari's thirteenth-century treatise, the *Kashf al-Asrar*, or

'Revelation of Secrets', has already been referred to.[9] It is one of our most important sources on criminal deceits. Al-Jawbari's book was ostensibly written to warn honest people of the dangers they faced from crooks and charlatans. (The unconvincing piety of this boast can be compared to that of the prologue to the *Nights*, in which it is claimed that the latter contains 'splendid biographies that teach the reader to detect deception and to protect himself from it'.) However, there can be little doubt that al-Jawbari's retelling of famous confidence tricks, set-ups and practical jokes was really put together for the sake of entertaining the reader rather than warning him. A considerable portion of the *Kashf al-Asrar* is devoted to criminal activities – among them the tricks of bogus holy men, bandits, fraudulent alchemists, horse fakers, muggers, body-snatchers, highwaymen and housebreakers.

'The Romance of Baybars', an anonymous late-medieval folk-epic about the legendary exploits of the thirteenth-century Mamluke Sultan Baybars, made only light use of the facts of Baybars's reign.[10] In their place a glorious farrago was conjured up concerning Baybars's youthful association in Syria and Egypt with all sorts of genial low-life types – wrestlers, grooms, cudgel-men, repentant thieves and, above all, the Isma'ilis. In historical reality, the Isma'ilis, Shi'ite heretics who came to use assassination to promote their aims, were among that Sultan's greatest enemies. In the 'Romance', however, the Isma'ilis are Baybars's greatest allies – and very valuable ones too, for they are expert cat burglars and skilled also in the use of drugs for overpowering enemies. The 'Romance' celebrates the cunning of the Isma'ilis and other semi-criminal friends of the Sultan in a struggle against corrupt officials and soldiers who are secret enemies of Islam.

More generally, a cult of cunning and tricks (*hiyal*) is pervasive in Arab literature, and tales of the cunning thieves or rogues constituted a sub-genre in the broader genre which celebrated the cunning of soldiers, women, uninvited guests and even animals. The celebration of artfulness or tricksiness, whether in the commission of crimes, in arguing points of law or in inserting puns in poems, is one of the most striking features of medieval Arab culture. The anonymous *Raqa'iq al-hilal fi Daqa'iq al-hiyal*, or 'Cloaks of Fine Fabric in Subtle Ruses', written in the Mamluke period, is a fairly typical example of the genre.[11] It includes sections on the cunning dodges of jinn, prophets, kings, viziers, lawyers, holy men, and so on. A further specialized sub-genre of the literature of cunning celebrated the disreputable though not exactly criminal activities of the *tufayli*, the uninvited guest or gate-crasher. In medieval Baghdad, gate-crashing was an organized way of earning a living, and the professional *tufaylis* formed a kind of guild under the direction of a sheikh, who each evening would allocate selected dinner parties to his following of gate-crashers.[12] In the *Nights* story of 'Isaac of Mosul and the Merchant', Isaac sees a singer in the street, falls in love with her and follows her into a house where a dinner is being held. The host, who has spotted that Isaac is a gate-crasher, merely remarks, 'This is a parasite [*tufayli*]; but he is a pleasant fellow, so treat him courteously.'

Whereas highwaymen and other robbers outside the towns were usually presented in the *Nights* tales and in other stories as pretty stupid (Jawan the Kurd, for example, in 'Ali Shah and Zumurrud') the urban criminal was generally reputed to be a cunning man. He was admired for his guile and the success which his guile brought him. (Robin Hood and Dick Turpin have comparable reputations in British culture.) Independent stories about real or legendary criminals, among them Mercury Ali, Crafty Dalilah and Ahmad the Sickness, circulated among the people prior to being gathered up into the *Nights* collection.[13] Ali Zaybak, or Mercury Ali, seems to have been a real brigand in eleventh-century Baghdad, before he became the hero of a loosely linked series of fictional exploits, some of which eventually found their way into the *Nights*. Similarly, Dalilah was already known of in Abbasid Baghdad, for al-Mas'udi refers to this 'famous female confidence trickster' in his tenth-century chronicle *Meadows of*

Gold. Al-Mas'udi, indeed, incorporated several allegedly true tales of crime and roguery in his chronicle.

Ahmad al-Danaf, or Ahmad the Sickness, like Ali Zaybak, may have been a historical figure. Inconsistent information is given by two Mamluke chroniclers. According to Ibn Taghribirdi, Ahmad the Sickness was the hero of a popular romance current in the fifteenth century, but his story was based on a certain criminal called Hamdi who lived in Cairo in the tenth century. According to Ibn Iyas, on the other hand, the bandit known as Ahmad the Sickness was captured by the Mamluke authorities in 1486 and executed by being sawn in half. Most likely the fifteenth-century criminal had taken to calling himself Ahmad the Sickness in reference to his legendary precursor in crime.

A brotherhood of crime flourished in medieval Cairo. With its own hierarchy and a code of honour (of sorts), the Cairene underworld presented a dark mirror to the ruling establishment. It would appear that gangsters sometimes messed and slept together in *tibaq*, or barracks. A hierarchy of respect among thieves is suggested in the story of 'The Sandalwood Merchant and the Sharpers', in which a merchant who has been swindled is advised to visit a certain Sheikh of Thieves, an old man 'versed in craft, magic and trickery', pre-eminent among the city's sharpers for his cunning, who adjudicated and delivered judgement on the exploits of his juniors.

The organization of criminals and rogues was not simply a fictional convention. It reflected elements of historical reality. Guilds were unknown in Mamluke Egypt, but when after the Ottoman occupation in the early sixteenth century guilds were established to regulate crafts and trades, the guilds of the thieves and the beggars were found among their number. In the Ottoman period (sixteenth to eighteenth centuries), Egyptian crime was organized and, to some extent at least, placed under state supervision. There were guilds for every craft in Cairo. Hence, thieves, prostitutes, entertainers, beggars and cheaters at cards had their recognized guilds. In most Ottoman cities it was possible for the victim of a robbery to go to the commander of the janissary regiment garrisoned in the town and report what had been stolen. The janissary commander would in turn contact the sheikh of the thieves' guild, and the stolen property might be returned – for a price. Thieves' guilds survived into the nineteenth century in Egypt. Edward William Lane, writing in the 1830s, informed his readers that 'Even the common thieves used, not many years since, to respect a superior who was called their sheykh. He was often required to search for stolen goods, and bring offenders to justice; which he generally accomplished.'[14]

In the Middle Ages a great deal of the criminal activity in the cities was controlled by the members of *futuwwa* lodges. *Futuwwa* is sometimes translated as 'chivalry', though it is more accurately translated as 'youngmanliness'. The history of *futuwwa* is somewhat obscure.[15] In tenth- or eleventh-century Iraq, lodges were formed initially at least by unmarried young men. These young men, perhaps because they were unemployed or underemployed, or perhaps because they had not accumulated enough capital to marry and therefore felt obliged to seek male companionship, came together in such associations. One was initiated into a *futuwwa* lodge by drinking a cup of salt water and donning a special pair of trousers, the trousers of *futuwwa*. Subsequently *futuwwa* lodges spread throughout the Middle East, and many of them were devoted to respectable and even idealistic purposes. They might help ensure high standards of artisanship and commercial practice; they might devote their resources to offering hospitality to passing strangers; or they might assemble to perform mystical exercises. In medieval Cairo, however, the lodges, or most of them at any rate, came under the control of criminal elements and provided the basis for the organization of protection rackets in the city's suburbs. Such gangsters proliferated in the Husayniyya, the north-eastern area of Cairo, and they congregated in special meeting places, 'the halls of *futuwwa*'. They organized

themselves in lodges called 'villages'. The rogues who called
themselves 'the sons of Husayniyya' feature prominently in 'The
Romance of Baybars'. Moralists denounced the *futuwwa* groups
for their assemblies during which wine was drunk and where it
was suspected that sexual, especially homosexual, activities took
place. Members of *futuwwa* groups carried knives, and having
sworn always to help one another, if one of their number should
be arrested, then they would mass outside the prison to enforce
their fellow's release. According to one fourteenth-century critic
of *futuwwa*, its members took their vows of brotherhood so
seriously that a member of a lodge might force his wife into
prostitution in order to support a fellow lodge member who had
fallen upon hard times.[16]

Somewhat similar to the *futuwwa* lodges were the hunting
lodges. *Shatir* (pl. *shuttar*) has a range of meanings. Most commonly
it means a loose, immoral person, a cunning man, a sharper. The
Nights abounds with tales of the 'sharpers' or 'larrikins'. However,
in the Mamluke period *shatir* was also used to refer to archers who
were members of hunting lodges. While members of *futuwwa*
lodges tended to rely on the knife and the cudgel, the *shuttar* were
specialists with the crossbow and expert hunters of birds. These
hunting clubs, which effectively constituted a disreputable kind of
militia, were regularly denounced by the *ulema* because of the
criminal elements who tended to attach themselves to the *shuttar*.
In one version of 'The Romance of Baybars', the young Baybars
is inducted into a league of men who hunt birds with crossbows.[17]

In the *Nights*, *shatir* tends to be used in the wider sense of 'crafty
rogue'; for example, the Egyptian Ali Zaybak is described as a
shatir. Always one step ahead of the police, he is perhaps the
greatest of all the *shuttar*. For Ali Zaybak stealing is an art, and he
steals from fellow criminals simply to demonstrate to them his
skill in this art. Ahmad al-Danaf, his rival in Baghdad, maintains a
barracks in Baghdad from where he directs the activities of his
forty *shuttar*. In a story outside the Ali Zaybak cycle, 'The tale of

Nur al-Din Ali and his Son', the benevolent pastry cook in Damascus, who takes in Badr al-Din Hassan, is a former *shatir* and thief: 'but Allah had made him repent and turn from the evil of his ways and open a cook-shop'. Despite his repentance, it is evident from the story that he was still an intimidating figure and not the sort of person one would want to pick a fight with.

Fidawiyya are defined in Lane's *Arabic–English Lexicon* as 'those who undertake perilous adventures, more particularly for the destruction of enemies of their party; as though they offered themselves as ransoms or victims'. The expression was used to refer to religious devotees, in particular members of the Isma'ili Assassin sect who were prepared to use murder and to sacrifice their lives in order to further the interests of their particular Shi'ite sect.[18] Although the Isma'ili Assassins were reputed to carry out their murderous missions under the influence of hashish (and hence the derivation of the western word 'assassin' from *hashashin*), there is no good evidence that this was ever the case. It is more likely that the enemies of the heretical Isma'ilis, when they called them *hashashin*, meant that they were low-grade riff-raff. As has already been noted, in 'The Romance of Baybars' the sultan was assisted by Isma'ili heretics, called *fidawis*, who offered their criminal skills in the service of the Sultan and Islam. In medieval Arabic, however, *fidawi* could be used much more loosely to refer to any sort of desperado. In the *Nights* 'History of the First Larrikin', when the larrikin (or *shatir*) encounters forty *fidawis*, the sense is that he has encountered a gang of criminal vagabonds. In another tale, 'The History of the Lovers of Syria', a pirate crew are described as *fidawis*.

The *zu'ar* are a little difficult to distinguish from some of the more disreputable *futuwwa* lodges. In medieval Cairo, *zu'ar* referred to a loose association of criminal bands. They constituted a sort of organized criminal lumpenproletariat which 'protected' or controlled the slum areas of Cairo, such as al-Husayniyya, Bab al-Luq and Ard al-Tabala. Members of these bands used to hire themselves out to the emirs as cudgelmen and, like the *ayyarun* in earlier centuries, they could provide powerful armed militias to whoever was prepared to employ them. Sometimes *zu'ar* gangs played at a game called *shalaq*, or beggar's bag, a low-life form of rugby in which some of the players might die.[19]

Then there were the *harafish* (sing. *harfush*). Burton, in 'The Story of the Larrikin and the Cook' (a tale about one of the destitute whose wits are sharpened by hunger), translates the word *harfush* as 'larrikin' (nineteenth-century Australian slang for an urban layabout) and annotates it as 'blackguard'. This is a little inaccurate. The *harafish* were actually beggars who in Mamluke times lived on the patronage of emirs or on hand-outs from mosques. They were sturdy beggars and, like the criminal *zu'ar*, could provide powerful armed militias. In Mamluke Egypt there was a Sultan of the Harafish, a King of the Dregs, who spoke to the authorities on behalf of the mendicants and layabouts.[20] In Ottoman Egypt there was a guild for beggars, and its members paid tax on their income. Sometimes *ju'adiyya* ('curly-haired ones') replaces *harafish* as the word for beggars. In 'The Story of the Three Sharpers', the three destitute men who rummage around on rubbish heaps for salvageable scraps are called *ju'adiyya*.

The world of the beggar was a highly competitive one, and all sorts of dodges were adopted to stay alive in it. Al-Jawbari tells us that beggars used to take blood squeezed from camel ticks and mix it with gum arabic before smearing it over the eyelids in order to fake the appearance of congenital blindness. Al-Jawbari also gives a recipe for a peculiar concoction which those who wanted to fake the appearance of elephantiasis used to put in their bath. Other beggars pretended that they were mute, or insane, or had been wounded in the war against the infidel. Moralists deplored the habit of some beggars of solemnly cursing those who failed to give them alms. A literary genre developed, known as *adab al-kudyah* or the etiquette of mendicancy, in which beggars were instructed in how to go about their business and how to trick or wheedle money out of passers-by.[21] In al-Hariri's *Maqamat*, for example, the aged and wily rogue Abu Zayd preaches to his son on the merits of the beggar's way of life and exhorts his son to be alert, cunning and always on the move. Literary folk were rather inclined to romanticize the carefree raggle-taggle life of the professional mendicants. Al-Jahiz, who wrote a treatise on vagrants and their tricks, puts these words in the mouth of one old beggar:

Pray listen to me. Do you not know that vagrancy is a noble, enjoyable, pleasing calling? Vagrants enjoy boundless happiness; their task it is to rove the world by stages, and to pace out the earth; they need fear no harm. They go wherever they wish, getting the best there is to be had in every town . . . They are serene and content with their lot, and have no worries about families, possessions, houses or property.[22]

Lane gave an unsympathetic account of Cairo's beggars in *Manners and Customs of the Modern Egyptians*. According to him, there were 'many beggars, who spend the greater part of the day's gains to indulge themselves at night with the intoxicating hasheesh, which, for a few hours, renders them, in imagination, the happiest of mankind'.[23] Although opium, hashish and henbane (in Arabic *banj* can refer to either hashish or henbane) had long been used in the recipes of occultists as ingredients in medicines, poisons and aphrodisiacs, drug-taking does not seem to have become popular as a recreation among the common people until the twelfth or thirteenth century. The theologian and religious polemicist Ibn Taymiyya blamed the introduction of drugs into Syria on the entry of the Mongols into the Near East. In the centuries before the introduction of tobacco, drugs were either eaten or drunk in special cakes or decoctions, flavoured to remove the bitter taste of the drugs. In the *Nights* 'Tale of the Kazi and the Bhang-Eater', the Sultan enquires about hashish. His better-informed vizier replies: "Tis composed of hemp leaflets, whereto they add aromatic roots and somewhat of sugar: then they cook it and prepare a kind of confection which they eat.'

Drug-taking was regarded with abhorrence by the orthodoxly pious and the wealthy.[24] The consumption of hashish or opium was forbidden by most Muslim jurisprudents, since the effect of the drugs was held to be analogous with that of wine. However, the Hanafi law school tolerated their consumption. Moreover, hashish was very cheap and it was one of the few pleasures of the poor. According to the thirteenth-century historian Ibn Abd al-Zahir, hashish was so cheap that one silver dirham's worth of hashish had as much effect as one gold dinar's worth of wine. In fourteenth-century Damascus, it was low-grade occupations such as falconers and dog handlers who ran and profited from the hashish parlours. The stereotypical consumer of hashish is portrayed in 'The Rogueries of Dalilah and her Daughter Zaynab'; he is 'an ass-driver, a scavenger who had been out of work for a week and who was an Hashish-eater to boot'. In Mamluke Cairo, the area round the Bab al-Luq, an impoverished and disreputable quarter, was the best place to buy hashish. Opium, on the other hand, most of which was grown in Upper Egypt, was rather more expensive, and some respectable people indulged in it. Although drugs were always denounced by the pious and occasionally banned by the sultans, most of the time they were sold and consumed openly. In the *Nights* story of 'Ala al-Din Abu al-Shamat', when the Cairene merchant Shams al-Din seeks a drug to increase his fertility, he goes to the bazaar, where there was 'a man who was Deputy Syndic of the brokers and was given to the use of opium and electuary (*barsh*) and green hashish'. The deputy syndic then goes to a drug seller in order to buy opium and some other, more reputable substances in order to mix the wonder-working medicine.

'The wine of the *fuqara*' (that is, of the poor before God, i.e. the Sufis) was one of the nicknames of hashish. In some of the less respectable Sufi groups, poetry was written in praise of hashish or opium. The sixteenth-century Turkish poet al-Fuzuli wrote a treatise in praise of hashish. It was argued that drug-taking could provide an artificially induced taste of divine ecstasy, or that a temporary derangement of the mind might bring the drug-taker closer to a God, who transcends all rationality.[25] According to al-Jawbari, members of the Haydariyya dervish order took hashish before staging their performances of self-mutilation, in order to numb the pain.

Drugs feature in the *Nights* and other specimens of popular fiction in two contexts. First, *banj* (either henbane or hashish) and opium are rather naïvely called upon by the storyteller as a kind of Mickey Finn, or early form of chloroform, available for the use of villains. For example, in 'Ali Shar and Zumurrud', the sinister Nazarene uses *banj* (hashish) mixed with opium on Zumurrud in order to overpower her and steal her away. Then again, in 'The Rogueries of Dalilah and her Daughter Zaynab' the two women use *banj* to knock out Ahmad al-Danaf and his following and steal their clothes in a game of competitive cunning. In 'The Tale of the Enchanted King', the prince is knocked out night after night by *banj* which is secretly administered to him by his monstrous wife. Robbers who were supposed to use *banj* or other drugs to overpower their victims were known as *mubannij*, and al-Jawbari provides considerable detail about their activities. For example, in his supposedly factual compendium of rogues' tricks, he claims that hashish was used by the kidnappers of children to keep their little victims quiet. It is really very doubtful that henbane, hashish or opium can be used in this way, but plainly it was useful as a fictional convention.

Secondly, there was a sub-genre of *Nights* stories of the late Egyptian period devoted to the buffooneries of simple folk who have temporarily lost their wits on drugs. For example, in 'The Tale of the Kazi and the Bhang-Eater', the hashish-addicted poor fisherman mistakes the reflection of the moon on the ground for a river and a dog for a fish, whereupon he sets about trying to hook the dog, and then further absurdities ensue. In 'The Tale of the Hashish Eater', a beggar who has eaten a lump of hashish fancies that he has found his way into a palace where servants have washed and massaged him before he goes to bed with a beautiful girl ... but then suddenly he awakes to find himself surrounded by a small crowd, lying naked with an erection beside one of the public water troughs. Stories about hashish eaters in the *Nights* tend to be simple, crudely constructed tales, aimed at an audience which had a taste for bawdy or even lavatorial humour.

As has already been noted above, it was much cheaper to get intoxicated on hashish than on wine, and in the *Nights* it tends to be the princes and merchants who indulge in wine.[26] Alcohol is, of course, formally banned by Islam, but the ban was widely disregarded by the more easy-going believers. Some argued that only wine made from grapes was banned by the Koran, so it was all right to get drunk on alcohol made from, say, figs. Doctors, many of whom were Christians and Jews, regularly recommended wine to their patients for all sorts of ailments. In Egypt, the Turkish Mamluke élite used to get drunk on *qumiz*, a potent brew of fermented mare's milk. Drinking at court had a long ancestry. Although Harun al-Rashid features in the *Nights* as a genial and convivial lover of evening drinking sessions, in fact the historical Harun al-Rashid seems to have been a pious and austere figure, and there is no good evidence that wine ever touched his lips. However, other Abbasid caliphs were notorious for their evening drinking bouts. (Contrary to modern western practice, wine and conversation followed the meal, rather than accompanying it.) A class of courtly participants in these activities was the *nudama*, or cup-companions, who were expected to sing for their supper by entertaining their patron with poems, songs and witty anecdotes. Abu Nuwas, the ninth-century poet who was patronized by the Barmecid clan and later became the *nadim* of the Caliph al-Amin, was the greatest of the poets who celebrated both the joys of wine and the beauty of the boys who served that wine. Abu Nuwas also features in several of the *Nights* stories as the hero of a number of unedifying adventures, and several of his poems are inserted in the stories. Poems in praise of wine constituted a literary genre in their own right, *khamriyyat*. Examples of such poems abound in the *Nights*. In 'The Story of the Porter and the Three Ladies', the porter recites the following:

> Drink not the cup, save with a friend you trust,
> One whose blood to noble forefathers owes.
> Wine like the wind is sweet if o'er the sweet,
> And foul if o'er the foul it haply blows.

The porter follows this up with more verses in praise of wine. Then again, in the Hunchback cycle of stories, the Jewish physician's father recites verses in praise of idle pleasure and drinking wine beside the Ethiopian Pond in Cairo.

Poems were written in praise of intoxication, good fellowship and beautiful cup-bearers. Wine drinking and pederasty tended to go hand in hand – in literature at least. Sufi poets wrote poems in praise of wine and beautiful boys. Perhaps images of the cup of wine and of the beautiful boy were intended as metaphors for the intoxication of divine ecstasy and divine beauty, but many Muslims were doubtful, and controversy raged over whether the verses of Sufi poets like Umar ibn al-Farid (1181–1235), in particular his *Khamriyya*, or 'Hymn of Wine', were to be read literally or not. Often taverns (*khans*) were attached to Christian monasteries. Boys served the wine, and entertainments such as shadow plays might also be provided. In the *Maqamat*, al-Hariri describes the interior of a wine-hall in Damascus, where there was an 'old man in a gaily coloured dress among casks and wine-vats. There were around him cup-bearers of surpassing beauty, and lights that glittered, and the sweet scents of myrtle and jasmin, and pipe and lute.'[27] Despite the convivial scene evoked by al-Hariri, it was also possible to drink alone. In 'The Adventures of Mercury Ali of Cairo', Ali in a depressed state of mind goes to the wine shop and is given a room where he can get drunk alone.

Medieval Muslims gambled on many things, including horse-races, pigeon-races, backgammon, wrestling matches and egg-knocking.[28] Betting on how long a man could stand on one leg (*al-wuquf ala rijl wahidah*) attracted the disapproving attention of some Islamic jurists. In medieval Cairo there were sporting astrologers who specialized in predicting such things as the outcome of wrestling matches. The religious authorities prohibited gambling, because *maysir*, a pre-Islamic game of chance based on the flight of arrows and associated with pagan worship, was banned in the Koran. While some Muslims justified the game of chess on the grounds that it was good training in strategy (and hence something that could be put to the service of the jihad), other sterner Muslims disapproved, because it was customary to bet on the outcome of the game. In 'The Tale of King Ins bin Kays and his Daughter', for example, the prince, al-Abbas, and the merchant stake vast sums on the outcome of a series of games of chess.

It is possible that the cult of the criminal in popular literature was given additional impetus by the unpopularity of the judiciary and the police force.[29] In such *Nights* tales as 'The Lady and her Five Suitors', 'The Story of the Qadi and the Bhang Eater' and 'The Story of the Qadi who Had a Baby', the *qadis*, or judges, are relentlessly lampooned as corrupt, foolish, incompetent and lascivious. The police receive no better treatment in the *Nights*. Indeed, the police force was commonly known as *al-zalama*, or 'the tyrannous', and this is what the young man in 'The Christian Broker's Tale' calls them. (In that story the young man, who has been driven to theft in order to support his mistress, is apprehended and has his right hand cut off.) Arbitrary arrests, strippings, beatings and tortures inflicted by the police feature frequently in the *Nights*. So does police corruption. As has been mentioned already, many of the police in medieval Egypt and even as late as the early nineteenth century were pardoned thieves. The police force, or *shurta*, as it was officially called, was officered by a *wali*, who wrote regular reports for the sultan. In 'Al-Malik al-Zahir

Rukn al-Din Baybars and the Sixteen Captains of Police', and in 'Al-Malik al-Nasir and the Three Chiefs of Police', the police are regularly portrayed as corrupt and incompetent.

The *muhtasib*, or market inspector, supervised weights and measures as well as the quality of goods in the market, and he chased up debt defaulters. But he also had policing duties and was responsible for public morality. He tried to ensure that all Muslim men attended the noon Friday prayer at the main mosque and that the month-long Ramadan fast was observed. He also had to patrol secluded spots, lest they be used for adulterous assignations or frequented by drunks, beggars or prostitutes. Last but not least, the *muhtasib* levied commercial taxes on the markets. The opportunities for corrupt profit were immense, and in fact the office was often sold by the sultan. In 'Ali Nur al-Din and Miriam the Girdle-Girl', Miriam, who is being sold in the slave market, recklessly improvises verses which mock the *muhtasib*, who is a man of power in the town.

The *masha'ili*, or cresset-bearer, brings up the end of the procession in Ibn Daniyal's shadow play *Ajib wa Gharib* and boasts of his membership of the Banu Sasan. Historically, the *masha'ili*, who was under the supervision of the *muhtasib*, acted as night-watchman, lamplighter and town crier. He also collected night-soil, cleared the corpses of animals from the streets and escorted condemned criminals to execution. In the Hunchback cycle, it is the *masha'ili* who puts the rope round the neck of the Nazarene broker after the latter has been judged guilty of murdering the hunchback. In 'The Story of the Three Sharpers', the *masha'ili* again features as the executioner. In 'Ala al-Din Abu al-Shamat', the *masha'ili* is sent round the town to proclaim the elevation of the eponymous hero to the rank of Provost of the Merchants.

In the early Mamluke period, the Khizanat al-Bunud (literally Storehouse of Banners) was the main prison for common (i.e. non-political) prisoners. The Khizanat al-Bunud was also, incongruously, the officially sanctioned centre for licensed prostitution and the sale of wine and pork. It was then the custom (and it still is in some Middle Eastern countries) to make the prisoner chargeable for his upkeep. Those prisoners who could not find support from their own families were liable to be sent out in chain-gangs to beg for their sustenance in the streets. Alternatively they might be used on construction work or be entrusted with organizing the sale of wine at the Khizanat.

However, prison populations in pre-modern Muslim societies were usually small, and fines, floggings and amputations were also part of the armoury of social control. The young man in 'The Christian Broker's Tale' has his hand cut off at the Zuweyla Gate, the normal place for executions and amputations in Cairo, and is given a cup of wine after the operation has been carried out. One encounters many such unlucky one-handed men shuffling through the pages of the *Nights*. In Abbasid times, it had been common practice to pillory lesser offenders not deserving of death, and to tie them to a frame attached to the humps of a Bactrian camel which was then paraded around the city. The frame was known as a *lu'ba*, or manikin. The Mamlukes, more ruthless, used to crucify criminals and political failures on the backs of camels. Those criminals who had been condemned to be sawn in half were similarly displayed.[30] Executions were a form of street theatre and highly popular as such. When the Emir Qusun was condemned to be crucified, street vendors cashed in by selling lollipops in the shape of the crucified victim. After Tumanbay, the last Mamluke Sultan of Egypt, was hanged before the Zuweyla Gate in 1517, his execution was re-created by the masters of the shadow theatres, much to the delight of Egypt's new master, the Ottoman Sultan Selim the Grim.

7

Sexual Fictions

The stories from the *Nights* which have survived in popular memory, in the West at least, are stories like 'Aladdin' or 'Ali Baba', which have little or no sexual content. But sexual themes – incest, adultery, sadism, and so on – are pervasive in the *Nights*. Indeed, a series of sexual incidents furnishes the pretext for their narration. The two kings of the frame story, Shahriyar and Shahzaman, discover that their wives are adulterous and prefer black slaves and grooms to their husbands. Subsequently, the two kings set out on a quest for someone who has suffered the same kind of betrayal that they have. At length they approach and spy on a terrifying jinn who keeps his woman captive in a chest bound with seven padlocks. Yet even the jinn's precautions are of no avail; for, while he sleeps, the woman escapes from the casket and blackmails Shahriyar and Shahzaman into having sex with her. She takes their seal-rings as tokens and shows them the 570 seal-rings that she has already collected from men who have slept with her. Returning to his kingdom, Shahriyar decides that from now on, he will sleep only with virgins and that each virgin will be killed after he has spent a night with her. Sheherazade's never-ending tales are of course designed to delay her execution and abate the king's wrath. But the tales are designed also to teach, and it is striking how many of the tales feature adulterous women, virtuous women, dominant women and wily women. From some of the tales Shahriyar may learn that there can be such a thing as fidelity in love and marriage. From other tales he may conclude that women are infinitely lustful and will deceive their husbands if they can, and he may derive a melancholy sort of consolation from this. Then again, after listening to yet other stories, he may simply laugh and conclude that sex is not such a serious matter anyway. The sheer diversity of the stories can be seen as providing a therapy of a kind.[1]

In a study of the way western writers and artists have portrayed and usually travestied the Middle East, Rana Kabbani claimed that the *Nights* 'were originally recounted to an all male audience desiring bawdy entertainment'. As we have already seen, this account of the origins and audience of the tales is an oversimplification. However, Kabbani went on to claim that the women in the tales fall into two categories: on the one hand, the adulteresses, witches and prostitutes, a lascivious and devious lot; and, on the other, pious and prudent women 'who are not disturbingly sexual' and whose virtues 'are usually a decorative foil to the story-line but of no great dramatic value'.[2] Thus we are to understand that the stories were popular with the low fellows in the Cairo coffee-houses, because of the misogynistic stereotypes they promoted and because of the implication of feminine inferiority underlying the tales as a whole.

It is, however, possible to take a very different view. Mme Lally-Hollbecque's *Le Féminisme de Scheherezade* (1927) provides an extreme example of a different approach. Lally-Hollbecque argued that the collection of stories had a single author-compiler and, moreover, that the author was an ardent feminist. Lally-Hollbecque's Sheherazade teaches by stories, and what she teaches above all justifies and exalts women and their virtues. She initiates Shahriyar into love and civilizes him. Lally-Hollbecque's position seems as extreme and partial as that of Kabbani. (It is also somewhat undermined by her dependence on the thoroughly unreliable Mardrus translation of the *Nights*.)

In fact, it is difficult to argue that the story collection as a whole, with its diverse constituents, presents a case for either misogyny or feminism. It is even difficult to make deductions from the erotic content of the tales about actual sexual behaviour in the medieval Islamic lands, and anyone who wishes to make use of incidents in the stories as 'data' about Arab sexual practices faces serious problems. In the first place, obviously, many of the tales are not of Islamic origin. They have been translated into Arabic and lightly Arabized and Islamicized; characters have been given Arab names; the locale has been shifted to Baghdad or Cairo; but the structure of many of the stories and their inspiration come from elsewhere. For example, the nymphomaniac captive in the jinn's casket in the frame story of the *Nights* may derive from an earlier Indian prototype. Certainly, there are Indian precursors of 'The Woman who Wanted to Deceive her Husband' and of 'The Lady of Cairo and her Four Lovers'. Then again, the behaviour of the soldier in 'The Tale of the Fuller, the Wife and the Trooper' almost certainly owes more to a reworking, several times removed, of Plautus' Latin play *Miles gloriosus* than it does to scandalous goings-on in medieval Baghdad. At a more elevated level, romances concerning the separation of lovers, fidelity and heroic tests of lovers' prowess can often be traced back to Byzantine fictions. However, it remains true, of course, that the fact that such tales were translated and narrated in the Arab lands means that the attitudes and practices conveyed in those tales were not wholly alien to Arab knowledge and taste.[3]

In any case, the romantic and erotic fiction of any culture is always constructed from conventional plot motifs, literary stereotypes and stock themes. (Lovers often swooned in medieval fiction, but did they do so in medieval reality?) The way erotic fiction is put together makes it difficult to assign any hard documentary value to it; and, for example, a story that is overtly about a woman's scheme to get her husband out of the house, so that her lover may join her in bed, may be really a story about ingenuity, rather than female sexual needs. Adultery is often used as a plot mover in the stories of the *Nights* (rather like Uncle Tom's silver cow-creamer in the P.G. Wodehouse stories), and thus the incidence of adultery in the stories tells us little or nothing about the incidence of adultery in medieval society. The picture of Cairo's thriving bawdy low life, teeming with randy women, cuckolded husbands and lucky virile porters, may be as much a fantasy as the stories about the kingdoms of the jinn and the marvellous goings-on in caliphal palaces.

Even so, it is still likely that some of the tales, particularly those about low life in Cairo, composed in the Mamluke period, do reflect social and sexual practices of the time. A few of the stories may even be based on real incidents. Historical chronicles, legal judgements, records of table talk and satirical poems composed at the time all indicate that sexual scandals occurred frequently and that actual practice was often at odds with the religious ideal. The public face of Islam was austere and restrictive. Religious leaders and the sultans who sometimes listened to them sought to enforce a strict religious code. From time to time, particularly in years of famine or plague, when a need for public repentance was generally felt, women were banned from going out of doors unaccompanied, brothels were closed down, licentious festivals were suspended, and so on. In most years, though, an easy-going pragmatism prevailed. There were limits to what the regime could enforce or what the public would accept. Sultans tended to prefer to tax brothels and hashish concessions rather than to abolish them.

Puritanical Muslims urged that a woman should obey her husband and that she should be confined as much as possible to the harem, or women's part of the house. If a woman had to go out, she should be accompanied and wear a veil. But of course not all women did obey their husbands; some dominated them. The veil was not really practicable for women who worked in the fields and it seems rarely to have been worn in the countryside. Even in the cities the veil was not always worn (and Christian, Jewish and slave women were exempt from that prescription anyway). The seclusion of women in harem quarters was a pious or precautionary measure that only wealthy men could indulge in. As S.D. Goitein has observed: 'At the other end of the social spectrum [the lower end], the people who were not *mastur* – literally "not covered", not protected by their means, family or social standing, in short not respectable – had little power to seclude their wives, and no cause to restrain their tongues. Their voice is heard in the chronologically later parts of *The Arabian Nights*.'⁴ Moreover, much of Islam's teaching concerning sex and women is based not on the Koran but on *hadith*, the orally transmitted sayings and practices of the Prophet and his Companions. The vast number of *hadith* allowed both restrictive and permissive interpretations of Islam's social code to flourish. For example, *hadith* can be quoted both for and against the practice of coitus interruptus, so that the Prophet was quoted as approving of it, as in his reply to an enquiring companion, 'Practice coitus interruptus with her if you so wish, for she will receive what has been predestined for her', and yet disapproving of it, as in the statement, 'It is hidden infanticide.'⁵ Then again, while a misogynist might quote the Prophet's saying, 'Hell is mostly populated by women', a feminist might retort with his saying, 'Paradise is under the heels of the mothers.'

The *Nights* was not the only story collection with a strong sexual content. For example, the *Hikayat al-Ajiba wa'l-Akhbar al-Ghariba* ('Tales of the Marvellous and Information about the Strange'), which was probably put together in the tenth century, is a collection which includes several highly erotic tales.

The most notable of these is 'The Story of the Forty Girls', in which a prince, wandering across a desert, stumbles across a palace, which he enters. The place is deserted, though there are forty thrones and in the centre of the great chamber a golden table with food and water set out for forty people. The prince takes a little from the food and water of each setting. Then he is disturbed by the sound of horses' hoofs and, looking out of the window, he sees forty cavalry in full armour approaching. The prince conceals himself and spies on the warriors. It is only when they take off their armour that he discovers that these warriors are in fact women. They are all beautiful and *hur al-ayn*. (A woman who is *hur al-ayn* has eyes in which there is a strong contrast between the black and the surrounding white. To be *hur al-ayn* is one of the attributes of houris in paradise.) When the forty women sit to dinner they discover that their bread has been broken and they are disturbed by this; but, after one of their number promises to investigate the matter, they spend the night drinking, reciting and telling stories until the break of day. Then thirty-nine of the girls don their armour to set out hunting, while one of their number remains behind to solve the mystery. When the young man comes out to steal more food from the table, she pounces on him. She is at first uncertain whether he is human or a jinn, but eventually they eat and drink together and have sex. The following day the prince has essentially the same adventure, but with a different girl, and so it goes on until he has separately and secretly slept with all the women in the castle and made them all pregnant. 'The Story of the Forty Girls' is a joyous and graphic celebration of sex. It may be that stories about 'the castle of women' (and one finds this motif also in the *Nights*) were based ultimately on Muslim fantasies about what went on in convents. The *Hikayat al-Ajiba* certainly deserves to be translated into English.[6]

The *Nights* and the *Hikayat al-Ajiba* are mixed story collections, and many of their stories are perfectly proper; some are even edifying. However, the *Nights* had also to compete with the *kutub al-bah*, or books dedicted to pornography, in the form either of sex manuals or of collections of exclusively erotic tales.[7] The author of one such work was Ahmad ibn Yusuf al-Tayfashi, who was born in Tunisia but settled in Cairo and died there in 1253.[8] His *Nuzhat al-Albab* ('Delight of the Hearts') is an obscene collection of observations, stories and poems about debauchery. Al-Tayfashi was particularly interested in stories about homosexuals and pederasts, and some of his scabrous anecdotes concern named contemporaries. Al-Tayfashi's book, despite its obscenity, was intended as a work of *adab* – that is, a work of *belles-lettres* furnishing suitable material for table talk – and it was written at a time when homosexuality and homosexual mannerisms seem to have been fashionable in intellectual circles.

Unlike al-Tayfashi, Ali al-Baghdadi concerned himself exclusively with women.[9] Almost nothing is known of his life, but he seems to have been a hanger-on at the Mamluke court in the early fourteenth century. His *Kitab al-Zahr al-Aniq fi'l-Bus wa'l-Ta'niq* ('The Book of the Delicate Flowers Regarding the Kiss and the Embrace') is a twenty-five-chapter compendium on the wiles of women (*kayd al-nisa*) and deals with the tricks they use to deceive their husbands and lovers. The narrative is written in a vulgar Middle Arabic, and the sexual encounters are detailed with relish. Like al-Tayfashi, Ali included adventures which are ascribed to named contemporaries or to recently deceased personalities, usually men who were accustomed to receiving respect, like emirs and qadis. Though he provides a great deal of circumstantial detail about persons and places which serve to locate these stories firmly in Mamluke Egypt and Syria, nevertheless one should not take it for granted that all his stories can be used to provide documentary evidence about the sexual practices of Ali's time. Some at least of the stories are plainly fictions. (It is noteworthy that Ali's story of how the deputy governor of Bahnasa came to lose his clothes to a wily prostitute is found in the *Nights* in an abridged and less artful form as 'The Third Constable's History'.)

Al-Tayfashi and Ali al-Baghdadi were inventing or compiling fictions for entertainment. But the most famous of all pornographic manuals written in Arabic, the *Rawd al-Atir*, or 'Perfumed Garden', was primarily an instruction manual, with chapters on the various positions which can be used in copulation and advice on such matters as the treatment of sterility and impotence, increasing the size of the penis and getting rid of underarm odour. Its author, Sheikh al-Nafzawi (*c.* 1410), wrote in Arabic and prefaced the work with a pious Muslim's apologia which celebrated sex and women as wondrous works of God.[10] However, *The Perfumed*

Garden was clearly influenced by the notable Indian genre of sex manuals, of which the most famous example is the *Kama Sutra*; and, like its Indian precursors, *The Perfumed Garden* gives highly technical and sometimes intimidatingly athletic accounts of possible sexual positions. Nevertheless, even *The Perfumed Garden* carries a considerable freight of anecdotal and fictitious material (particularly in the inevitable chapter 'On the Deceits and Treacheries of Women'). Middle Eastern pornography is a field which has received little serious academic attention. Many works of Arab erotica have been falsely and mischievously ascribed to distinguished religious thinkers and philosophers. Some books which have the same title turn out to have different contents, or vice versa.

It is clear that the strong sensual, even pornographic, content of the *Nights* can be paralleled elsewhere in Arabic literature. Thus, drawing on rival works of erotic fiction and on sex manuals as well as on the *Nights*, one can get some sort of impression of the prevailing sexual practices and prejudices of the medieval Islamic world. In his excellent book *Arab Painting*, Richard Ettinghausen suggested that the medieval Arabs' image of the ideal woman can be reconstructed from early Arab poetry:

In these love lyrics one reads that the ideal Arab woman must be so stout that she nearly falls asleep; that she must be clumsy when rising and lose her breath when moving quickly; that her breasts should be full and rounded, her waist slender and graceful, her belly lean, her hips sloping and her buttocks so fleshy as to impede her passage through a door. Her legs are said to be like columns of marble, her neck like that of a gazelle, while her arms are described as well rounded, with soft delicate elbows, full wrists, and long fingers. Her face with its white cheeks must not be haggard, her eyes are those of a gazelle with the white of eye clearly marked.[11]

Essentially the same pneumatic image can be reconstructed from the *Nights*. When, in 'The Tale of Omar bin al-Nu'uman', the Muslim warrior Sharrkan wrestled with the Christian princess Abrizah, he found that his fingertips 'sank into the soft folds of her middle, breeding languishment'. Sharrkan was so overmastered by desire that he lost this wrestling bout, for Abrizah took advantage of his fainting passion, threw him and 'sat upon his breast with hips and hinder cheeks like mounds of sand'. Great attention was paid to women's bottoms. When Hasan of Basra spied upon the princesses in the pool, he saw that the most beautiful of them 'had thighs great and plump, like marble columns twain or bolsters stuffed with down from ostrich ta'en'. The male bottom too: Prince Kamar al-Zaman's waist 'was more slender than the gossamer and his back parts than two sand-heaps bulkier, making a babel of the heart with their softness'. The piously superstitious warned men against sitting on a place recently warmed by a female bottom, fearing that some sort of illicit sexual pleasure might be derived therefrom. The sixteenth-century Egyptian religious scholar Jalal al-Din al-Suyuti argued that in paradise people would have no behinds.[12] In some areas of the Middle East until quite recent times, women might choose to overeat systematically (the practice of *tasmina*) in order to acquire the sexually attractive fat.[13] A woman could draw attention to her bottom by adopting a distinctive waggling gait known as the *ghunj* – a term also used for the waggling of the hips during sexual intercourse. Sleepiness was also considered to be sexually attractive, and drowsy charms and languorous airs are frequently commended in the poems embedded in the *Nights*.

However, sexual tastes in the medieval Islamic world were not absolutely uniform, and rival ideals coexisted. The plump, panting languid woman faced plenty of competition from her more active sisters – in both fiction and fact. Indeed, one of the striking features of the *Nights* (especially if one compares it with western literature in the same period) is how active and vigorous the heroines of the stories are and, contrariwise, how passive and idle many of the nominal heroes are. How could Kabbani have missed

Tawaddud, who defeats the court sages in an intellectual form of strip-poker; Dunya, who kicks the vizier in the groin; Budur, who, having become a king (*sic*), revenges herself on her enemies and threatens her lover with sodomization; Marjana, who rescues Ali Baba and engineers the death of the forty thieves; or Miriam the Girdle-Girl, who rescued her lover from captivity in Christendom – not to mention such warrior-princesses as Princess al-Datma and Abriza, and the legions of Amazon warrior-women who troop through the pages of the *Nights*, as well as the specialized variant the *kahramat* (armed female harem guards)? The taste for boylike women (*ghulumiyyat*) in fiction may have reflected the actual sexual tastes of Cairo men. According to the fifteenth-century historian and moralist al-Maqrizi, the women of his day, finding that they were having to compete with attractive young men, had themselves taken to dressing like boys in order to retain the affection of their husbands.[14]

Al-Maqrizi had been a student of the philosopher-historian Ibn Khaldun, who held that the spread of homosexuality was a sign of the decay of civilization.[15] Despite al-Maqrizi's almost apocalyptic dread of the spread of homosexuality in medieval Cairo, it is in fact difficult to gauge the degree of acceptance accorded to homosexuals.[16] Indeed, it may be a mistake to think of there being one reified condition, 'homosexuality', which has remained more or less constant in its characteristics from century to century and from culture to culture. There is some evidence to suggest that in medieval Arab society active homosexuality was regarded as an acceptable way of finding relief from sexual tension, but that passive homosexuals and those who cultivated effeminate traits were scorned.[17] However, the evidence does not all run in one direction, and there are indications in medieval texts that some Arabs thought of homosexuality as a single condition and even as a form of illness.

In chapter 6 of his *Nuzhat al-Albab*, al-Tayfashi deals with the characteristic features of homosexuals (*la'ita*) and of those who hire themselves out.[18] The homosexual should have a pleasant lodging, well furnished with books and wine, and made pleasanter yet by the presence of doves and singing birds. A homosexual can be recognized by the way he stares directly at one, this direct gaze often being followed by a wink. The typical homosexual has thin legs with hairy ankles and tends to wear robes which reach right down to the ground. When he walks, his hands and his legs sway. ('A man's second face is his leg' was a saying of the time.) A subsequent chapter is devoted to entertaining and funny stories about homosexuals. Al-Tayfashi is almost exclusively concerned with mature men who pursue beardless boys. However, he does note the existence of a minority group of men who went looking for sex with mature bearded men. He comments that these latter were known as 'men with short lives', because of the risks they ran of being mugged and murdered. As has already been noted, homosexuality seems to have been fashionable in literary circles in thirteenth-century Egypt and Syria. But homosexual practices (*liwat*, or the crime of Lot's people) were proscribed by the religious law, and those found guilty of a homosexual act might face the death penalty. In practice, while there were occasional instances of successful prosecutions, resulting in execution or castration, there is also evidence, at certain times and in certain places, of homosexuality being more casually accepted. Several of the Mamluke sultans were known to be homosexual, and the tastes of homosexual sultans and emirs were a factor behind the high prices paid for beautiful boys in the slave market.

Because the *Nights* is an omnium gatherum, one can use its texts, through selective quotation from the stories, to support the argument that homosexuality was widely approved of, or to argue that it was indifferently accepted, or to demonstrate that it was absolutely abominated. It was certainly openly discussed, and 'The Man's Dispute with the Learned Woman Concerning the Relative Excellence of Male and Female' in the *Nights* presents fiercely contrasted arguments. The (pederastic) man argues that it is better to love men than women, since men are superior to women, and the Koran itself declares that 'Men are the managers of the affairs of women for that God has preferred in bounty one of them over the other' (IV, 38). Man is active, woman passive. Somewhat eccentrically, the man cites a saying of the Prophet that warns against looking too long on young boys, because of their resemblance to the houris of paradise. He also cites the poet Abu Nuwas, to the effect that boys are better because they do not have periods and they do not get pregnant. He points out how common it is in poetry to praise women by comparing them to beautiful boys.

However, the woman replies by describing the beauties of the ideal girl, calling to her support the numbers of kings and rich men who have squandered fortunes to acquire beautiful women. She points out that, in the saying of the Prophet already quoted by the man, boys are praised only by being compared to houris, who are female. In any case, the Koran unequivocally condemns homosexuality: 'What do you come to male beings, leaving your wives that your Lord created for you? Nay, but you are a people of transgressors' (XXXVI, 165). Also, a woman has more to offer in the way of pleasure, since she can be taken both ways; and the first wispy beards of young men are unattractive. The woman quotes another saying of the Prophet: 'Three things I have valued in this world, perfume, prayer and women.' Finally, she winds up by reciting some rather explicit verses about the messiness of anal intercourse.

Grosso modo, the debate reverberates throughout the *Nights*. Some stories cheerfully celebrate homosexual seductions, particularly those in which Abu Nuwas features as the raffish hero. Abu Nuwas was a historical figure, a familiar of the court of Harun al-Rashid and a poet famous above all for his verses in praise of wine (*khamriyyat*) and beautiful boys (*mudhakkarat*). He is the hero of a number of (fictional) adventures in which his sexual tastes may be sometimes a subject for teasing, but never for vilification. On the other hand, some tales present the paedophile as a villain, and Ali Zaybaq, Nur al-Din Ali and Ala al-Din Abu Shamat, among others, are menaced by sinister male seducers. In 'The Rogueries of Dalilah', Hajj Muhammad, who as the slang had it loved 'to eat both figs and pomegranates' (i.e. he was a bisexual), is described as 'a man of ill-repute'. A leitmotif in the *Nights* is the seclusion of a beautiful boy by his parents in order to protect him from lascivious men. Although Princess Budur, disguised as a man, makes a stirring speech in favour of homosexuality to Kamar al-Zaman, whom she threatens to bugger, the interest of the story at this point lies in Kamar al-Zaman's fear and shame at the prospect of being homosexually raped. The pursuit of beardless boys by likeable or villainous rogues features fairly frequently in the *Nights* (just as it does in al-Tayfashi's work of literary erotica). However, love or buggery between two mature men is not, I think, dealt with anywhere in the *Nights*.

Lesbians do not seem to have been persecuted in medieval Islamic societies. However, lesbianism, or 'rubbing' (*musahaqa*), was associated with witchcraft in the popular mind. Leo Africanus reported that there was a notorious circle of lesbian witches operating in Fez at the end of the fifteenth century.[19] The anonymous storytellers of the *Nights* went along with popular prejudice, and the presentation of lesbianism in the stories is consistently hostile, with the lesbians usually doubling as witches. The dowager witch, poisoner and wrestler Zat al-Dawahi in 'The Tale of Omar bin al-Nu'uman and his Sons' is identified as a lesbian who used saffron to add spice to her masturbatory sessions. The description of her is not a flattering one: 'wanton and wily, deboshed and deceptious; with foul breath, red eyelids, yellow cheeks, dull brown face'. Unfortunately for Zat al-Dawahi, her smelly armpits made her unpopular among the young women of the harem. Shawahi, the 'lady of calamities' in the story of 'Hasan of Bassorah', is again a witch as well as a lesbian.

Although cross-dressing features in a number of stories, this is as a literary device and not as a statement of sexual preference. (Shakespeare, of course, used transvestism in the same way.) Budur disguised herself as a man, and Zumurrud did similarly, but they did so in order to travel in security and to advance their fortunes. Niama bin Rabia put on women's clothes, but he did so only in order to gain access to his beloved, who was immured in a harem. Bestiality features in a handful of the foulest and most vulgar tales. Necrophilia is something that ghouls indulge in, but the wide range of fetishes and perversions which feature commonly in western pornography seem to have been unknown to the Arab storyteller.

In 'The Story of the Porter and the Three Ladies', the women interrogate the porter about the correct name for their private parts; each time he gets the answer wrong, the porter is slapped and pinched. In the Barber cycle, in 'The Tale of the Second Brother, Babaqa the Paraplegic', Babaqa is led on and slapped about by the mysterious lady and her maidservants, before being thoroughly humiliated and cast out into the street. Al-Tayfashi devoted a chapter in his treatise to the subject of slapping, arguing, among other things, that it was good for the health of the recipient.

While there are a handful of stories in the *Nights* which focus on the joys of wedlock and domesticity, illicit sexual adventures, involving adulteresses, prostitutes, concubines and singing girls, furnish more of the staple fare of the *Nights*. In those stories it is often the singing girl (*qaina*, pl. *qiyan*) who is provided with the wittiest lines and most appropriate verses. The stories of 'Harun al-Rashid and the Two Slave-Girls' and 'Harun al-Rashid and the Three Slave-Girls' commemorate the bawdy wit of these accomplished entertainers. In historical fact, singing girls were much in demand at the court of the Abbasid caliphs and in the houses of other rich men, particularly as after-dinner entertainers and as a female counterpart to the learnedly witty *nudama*, or cup-companions. The most famous essayist of the Abbasid period, al-Jahiz, wrote a treatise sarcastically entitled *In Praise of Singing Girls* in which he warned against those wily, greedy, faithless seductresses, who stole first a man's senses and then his money: 'As soon as the observer notices her, she exchanges provocative glances with him, gives him playful smiles, dallies with him in verses set to music, falls in with his suggestions, is eager to drink when he drinks, expresses her fervent desire for him to stay a long while, her yearning for his prompt return, and her sorrow at his departure.'[20]

These accomplished courtesans, who may remind one of the ancient Greek *hetairai*, or of the Japanese geisha girls, might be free women or slaves. They usually accompanied their singing on the lute. The slave girl Tawaddud, at the end of a gruelling interrogation which ranged widely through the Muslim sciences, was presented with a lute by Harun al-Rashid: 'She laid her lute in her lap and, with bosom inclining over it, bent to it with the bending of a mother who suckleth her child; then she preluded in twelve different modes, till the whole assembly was agitated with delight, like a waving sea.' The annals of the Abbasid court abound with anecdotes illustrating the wit and learning of the singing girls, and though Tawaddud was a heroine of fiction her accomplishments can easily be paralleled by those of historical courtesans. For example, Mahbuba, before she was acquired by the Caliph al-Mutawakkil, had been trained by her first master. According to the chronicler al-Mas'udi, he 'had taken great care with her education, cultivated her mind and had enriched her with knowledge on the most varied subjects. She composed poetry which she sang to her own accompaniment on the lute and, in a word, she excelled in all those things which distinguish people of talent.'[21] Singing girls also flourished in the Mamluke period. Many of the songstresses were black, like Ittifaq, who started out as a concubine in the harem of the Egyptian Sultan al-Nasir Muhammad in the early fourteenth century. Ittifaq, who was famed not just for her beauty, but also for her intelligence and her singing voice, went on to marry successively four sultans and a vizier.[22] However, not many female singers enjoyed such distinguished careers, and in the Mamluke period there was an overlap between the profession of singer and that of prostitute. Both were taxed at the Daminat al-Maghani, or Tax Farm of the Singers.

In the early sixteenth century, any woman who wanted to become a prostitute registered her name at the above-mentioned office, and as long as she paid her taxes she could ply her trade undisturbed. Medieval Egypt knew three types of prostitute (or *baghiya*): the 'wild cow' who had her own room, the 'free cow' who went to the client's room and the 'milk cow' who had sex out of doors. Many of the Cairene prostitutes worked the *funduqs*, or travellers' hostels. However, a large group had their beat in and around the wax candle market, in the shadow of the Mosque of Aqmar. In 'The Story of the Chief of Police of Cairo', the policeman, seeking information about two criminals who frequent prostitutes, makes his enquiries among 'the taverners, and confectioners, and candle-makers and keepers of brothels and bawdy houses'. Prostitutes could be identified by their custom of wearing red leather trousers and carrying little daggers. They used to cough to attract the attention of clients. In the port of Alexandria many of the prostitutes were reported to be of European origin.[23] In 'The Tale of Harun al-Rashid and Abu Hasan, the Merchant of Oman', the latter visits a brothel in Baghdad, 'a tall and goodly mansion, with a balcony overlooking the river-bank and pierced with a lattice-window', and a standard tariff of between ten and forty dinars a night is quoted.[24]

Syphilis seems to have first appeared in Egypt in the first decade of the sixteenth century. The chronicler Ibn Iyas called it the *al-habb al-Franji*, or the European pimple. However, although coffee, tobacco and artillery feature in some of the later additions to the *Nights*, venereal disease does not, and its absence contributes to the sense of freedom and amorality in so many of the stories. Medieval

Muslims were none the less far from free of fear and superstition regarding sexual matters. It was believed that worms in the vagina caused nymphomania, that intercourse with a menstruating woman gave a man leprosy and that sex with old people was also dangerous. The beautiful young slave girl Tawaddud warned her audience on the danger of sex with 'old women, for they are deadly', and she was able to quote several authorities in support of this. Men travelling in the desert also feared the *udar*, a monstrous creature which raped men and left them to die of worm-infested anuses.[25] Only marginally more rational were the widespread fantasies on the part of medieval Arabs about the sexual powers of black men and their lusting after Arab women. Blacks were believed to be exceptionally virile, and fears of black virility are evident in the frame story of the *Nights* about the cuckolding of Shahriyar and Shahzaman. In *Race and Slavery in the Middle East*, Bernard Lewis comments that 'King Shahzaman and King Shahriyar were clearly white supremacists, with sexual fantasies, or rather nightmares, of a sadly familiar quality.'[26] Sexual and racist paranoia is fairly widespread throughout the *Nights* (see, for example, 'The Tale of the Enchanted King' and 'The Story of the Three Apples' among many others).

Turning away now from the perverse and fantastic, to consider more ordinary sexual practices, the well-off seem to have slept in separate beds. Wives in medieval Egypt were accustomed to demand money for coming to their husbands' beds and granting them sex – the *haqq al-firash*, or bed fee. Coitus interruptus was sanctioned by most Islamic jurists, but some also argued that the woman was entitled to financial compensation if early withdrawal was practised. People slept either naked or in their daytime clothes. Anal intercourse with women was vigorously disapproved of by the religious and therefore presumably sometimes practised by the less religious. More detailed information about normal copulation is hard to glean from the *Nights*, because of the linguistically ingenious and metaphorical modes of describing the sex act favoured by the storytellers, as they move smoothly from the description of foreplay to word–play. What we are offered are displays of rhetorical skill, not documentary accounts of fucking.

In the typical ideally romantic tale, the hero falls in love with a princess, merely by seeing her portrait, or just by hearing her name. They are predestined to love one another. Fate brings them together, and fate separates them. The hero, who swooned when he first saw the princess, swoons again when he discovers she has vanished. He will, or should, recite verses of lamentation. Then there are adventures, perhaps featuring storms, pirates, infidel armies and sorceresses. The princess may fall sick and begin to starve herself to death. The hero may think of suicide, but in the end fate reunites the lovers, and they live happily together until they are 'overtaken by the breaker of ties and the destroyer of delights'. It is all rather silly; but such stories, despite their patent lack of realism, may have served an educational purpose, and those who listened to these tales were instructed in the symbolic language of love – a surreptitious code devised to get round the proscriptions of society: In 'The Tale of Aziz and Azizah', for example, the woman's putting her finger into her mouth signifies that the man she gazes on is like her own body's soul to her; and when she strikes upon her breast with her palm and outstretched five fingers, it means that the man should come back in five days.

More generally, stories like 'The Tale of Taj al-Muluk and the Princess Dunya', 'The Tale of Ali bin Bakkar and Shams al-Nahar' and 'Masrur and Zayn al-Mawasif' set forth an *adab* of love, in which amorous young men and women were instructed in how to feel and behave.[27] Such stories not only provided a vocabulary of gestures, flowery compliments and verse couplets through which sexual attraction could be expressed, but they also gave guidance on how to dress and what gifts to offer the loved one. In 'Uns al-Wujud and the Vizier's Daughter Rose-in-Hood', Rose-in-Hood's nurse tells her that love is a sickness which can only be cured by passionate enjoyment:

'And how may one come by enjoyment?'

'By letters and messages, my lady; by whispered words of compliment and by greetings before the world; all this bringeth lovers together and makes hard matters easy.'

However, it was not always so easy to cure the sickness of love. In 'The Lovers of Banu Tayy', the pining and ill-starred bedouin drops dead even while he is running towards his beloved (who, like Juliet, belongs to the wrong tribe). Members of the pre-Islamic bedouin of the tribe of Banu Udhra, martyrs to chastity, espoused the cult of a platonic sort of thwarted love from a distance, even unto death, and a handful of stories in the *Nights* explore similarly gloomily romantic themes.[28] However, most of the romantic tales in the *Nights*, while they borrow plot motifs, gestures and postures from the old Udhrite literary tradition, tend to end happily, with the lovers brought together in the same bed after all their turbulent and improbable adventures.

8

The Universe of Marvels

=====

> The pen is the most powerful sorcerer.
>
> Balinus[1]

In an essay on 'Narrative Art and Magic', Jorge Luis Borges contrasted the slow-moving and realistic psychological novel with the adventure novel and the short story. The two latter, he argued, are ruled by a quite different sort of order, 'one based not on reason but on association and suggestion – the ancient light of magic'.[2] Certainly, the medieval storyteller and the sorcerer worked in parallel trades, manipulating words and phrases to achieve their effects, and the medieval Islamic sorcerer was pre-eminently a man with a book. In 'Judar and his Brethren', the Maghribi sorcerers dispute the possession of a volume entitled *Fables of the Ancients*, 'whose like is not in the world, nor can its price be paid of any, nor is its value to be evened with gold and jewels; for in it are particulars of all the hidden hoards of the earth and the solution of every secret'. In 'The Tale of the Wazir and the Sage Duban', the sage, who has been condemned to death by beheading on the orders of the foolish king, bequeaths to the king a book which, he claims, has the power to make his severed head speak. However, in reality, his legacy to the king is a poisoned book, and the king dies when he licks his ink-stained fingers. (Centuries later, the device of the poisoned book was to resurface in Umberto Eco's novel, *The Name of the Rose*.)

The storyteller and the sorcerer are professionals who know the power of the phrase, the word and the letter.[3] Knowledge of the name, the *mot juste*, can mean the difference between life and death. Ali Baba escapes from the perilous cave because he remembers the magical password 'Open sesame'; his brother does not and consequently perishes. The study and manipulation of words may confer knowledge of the future, as in 'The History of Mohammed, Sultan of Cairo', where the Maghribi sorcerer in the market-place has before him some leaves with writing on them which he uses to make predictions about the bystanders. Letter magic, *ilm al-huruf*, was one of the most important sub-sciences in Islamic occultism. In 'The Story of the Sage and the Scholar', for example, the sage controls the jinn and performs supernatural feats by virtue of his knowledge of the magical powers of letters. Finally, of course, the storyteller and the sorcerer, rivals in the market-place, are both traders in illusion. The sorcerer who has mastered the art of illusion, *ilm al-simiyya*, is able to offer his customers and victims visions of what is not — that is, he has become a creator of fictions.

Serious treatment of magic in the mainstream of modern European fiction is rare, and when magic does feature it often does so as a transparent metaphor. For example, Balzac's *The Ass's Skin* and Robert Louis Stevenson's *The Bottle Imp*, both tales which are ostensibly about the wish-conferring powers of a magical object, are really parables about the price paid for success and the diminishing options in life as one grows older. On the whole, stories about magic now seem to be considered to be most suitable for children. Edith Nesbit's cycle of stories about the Bastable children, C.S. Lewis's Narnia cycle and Ursula Le Guin's *Earthsea Trilogy* were all written for children (though adults may read them with guilty pleasure). Tanya Luhrmann in her penetrating and wide-ranging anthropological account of modern British witchcraft, *Persuasions of the Witch's Craft*, observes that 'Magical books encourage an embracing, dream-like absorption, a dissociated daydream of dragons, powers and higher realms. This sense of imaginative absorption, quite apart from any themes which it encompasses, is one of the most striking elements in magical fiction.'[4] Cardinal

Newman remarked in his autobiographical *Apologia pro Vita Sua* (1864): 'I used to wish the Arabian Tales were true: my imagination ran on unknown influences, magic powers and talismans.' It is a childhood dream of omnipotence. However, what also emerges from Luhrmann's survey of the modern witch is that novels about magic (by Dennis Wheatley, Dion Fortune and others) are widely read by practising occultists and enjoyed by them as fictions, yes, but as fictions about something that is real. For them, a story about magic is not *per se* purely fantasy.

Similarly, in the pre-modern Middle East, a story about magic and the supernatural may have had a double aspect; it may have been a wonderful piece of nonsense designed to enthral an audience of children, yet, at the same time, the adults listening to the same story could recognize social facts and aspects of everyday reality. There were, after all, practising sorcerers, alchemists and treasure-hunters in medieval Baghdad and Cairo. Geomancers were consulted regarding business trips and the outcome of sporting events. The powers of magic and the jinn were not to be doubted. They were attested to by the Koran:

> they follow what the Satans recited
> over Solomon's kingdom. Solomon disbelieved not,
> but the Satans disbelieved, teaching
> the people sorcery.

> (II, 96)

And again:

> Say: 'I take refuge with the Lord of the Daybreak
> from the evil of what he has created,
> from the evil of darkness when it gathers,
> from the evil of the women who blow on knots,
> from the evil of an envier when he envies.'

> (CXIII)

In this sort of social and intellectual context, the frontiers between occult fiction and non-fiction were so weak as to be more or less indistinguishable, and we find tales which would not be out of place in the *Nights* embedded in such 'non-fictional' works as sorcerers' manuals. For example, in an eleventh-century *grimoire*, or sorcerer's manual, the *Ghayat al-Hakim* ('The Goal of the Sage', later translated into Latin as *Picatrix*), the story is told of how in old Harran, when the demon worshippers who dwelt there were desirous of knowing what was to happen in the future, they would hunt out a dark-complexioned man with eyebrows that joined together and blue eyes. This man would be overpowered and stripped. The unhappy victim was then plunged into a barrel containing sesame oil with only his head remaining above the surface of the oil. The head inhaled stupefying drugs which were burnt before it while certain rituals were performed. The blue-eyed man was then macerated in the oil for forty days until all the flesh had fallen from his bones. After forty days it was possible to detach the head from the rest of the body at the first vertebra. The head (whose blue eyes no longer blinked) was set in a niche where it gave out prophecies. The philosopher-historian Ibn Khaldun, who gave a condensed account of the procedure, commented: 'This is detestable sorcery. However, it shows what remarkable things exist in the world of man.'[5]

Even more striking, some tales of marvel included in the *Nights* for the purpose of entertainment appear in other books as reports of sober fact. 'The Caliph al-Maamun and the Pyramids of Egypt', an account of the inaccessible treasures contained in the pyramids and the magical guardians appointed by the ancients to protect those treasures, is only a retelling of one of the standard wonder-stories about the pyramids found elsewhere in medieval Arab histories and topographies.[6] Again, in 'The Tale of the Warlock and the Young Cook of Baghdad', a vizier enters a cauldron of water at the urging of the warlock, and during the brief instant he is in the water he experiences years of an alternative life. The vizier's fictional ordeal is paralleled by the allegedly true experience of the fifteenth-century Egyptian Sultan al-Ashraf Qaytbay. The sultan was visited by the famous Sufi Sheikh al-Dashtuti and fell into an argument with that great saint about whether it was possible for Muhammad to have visited all the heavens on a winged steed in a single night. Al-Dashtuti made the sultan plunge his head into a bowl of water for what seemed to onlookers to be only an instant. But when the sultan raised his head he declared that he had experienced several lifetimes of experience. It is most probable that this story, in its various forms, derives ultimately from an Indian fable, very likely Buddhist, about the illusory nature of time.[7]

The taste for the fantastic was so pronounced in the medieval Arab lands that it spawned a distinctive genre of literature, that of *aja'ib* (marvels), and books were written on the marvels of Egypt, of India and of the cosmos as a whole.[8] Such books were hugger-mugger compilations of improbable information about the stupendous monuments of antiquity, strange coincidences, the miraculous powers of certain plants, stones and animals, and feats of magic. Many of the marvels first found in 'non-fiction' works on cosmography eventually made their way into the *Nights*. The Sinbad cycle, which is a fictional reworking of mariners' yarns about the wonders to be found in the Indian and China seas (among them the wak-wak tree with its human-headed fruit, the Old Man of the Sea and the fish as large as an island), is the most obvious example of this process.[9]

Of course, readers and writers in medieval Christendom also had a taste for marvels and loved to read of monsters, of strange cities and of supernatural events. However, medieval Christendom and Islam did not share the same supernatural world. This is most strikingly apparent in the cases of the ghost and the witch. Ghosts and ghost stories feature prominently in medieval European culture.[10] This was not the case in the Islamic lands. In Christendom, ghosts were commonly conceived of as unshriven souls who sought revenge, absolution or Christian burial from the living. The Christian doctrine of purgatory implied that the prayers and acts of the living could aid the dead, and the restless souls who spoke to the living provided valuable testimony about the accuracy of the Catholic Church's vision of life after death. Purgatory does not feature in the orthodox Muslim's concept of the afterlife. However, though ghosts had no proper role in the Islamic vision of the world, native Christians in the Middle East believed in them, and it is possible that their fears sometimes infected their Muslim neighbours. In medieval Cairo it was customary to abandon a house where a murder or a suicide had occurred, and let the house fall to ruin, rather than run the risk of sharing the dwelling with a tormented spirit. Felix Fabri, a Christian pilgrim who visited Egypt in the fifteenth century, described a house on the banks of the Nile whose owner had been driven out by 'nymphs', nocturnal spirits, which threw out first the owner's furniture and then the owner and his companions. Despite subsequent attempts to let it, the haunted house had remained untenanted. However, these punctilious 'nymphs' did leave a monthly rent for the owner.[11] One is tempted to characterize such lodgers as ghosts, but this may be a mistake; for, as Burton observes: 'Haunted houses [in the Middle East] are there tenanted by Ghuls, Jinns and a host of supernatural creatures; but not by ghosts proper; and a man may live for years in Arabia before he ever hears of the "Tayf".'[12] *Tayf* may be translated as 'ghost'. So may *khayal*. But *tayf* also carries the sense of 'fantasy', and *khayal* that of 'shadow', both words implying that what is seen is not really there.

In the tales of the *Nights*, the title 'Ali the Cairene and the Haunted House of Baghdad' seems to promise a ghost story, but the story itself is no such thing. In the story, a young Egyptian, down on his luck in Baghdad, is offered temporary lodgings by a merchant. The merchant owns two houses, but Ali is warned that one of them 'is haunted, and none nigheth there but in the morning he is a dead man'. No one even dares enter the house to retrieve the corpses; instead they get the bodies out by hauling them on to another roof with ropes. As an opening for a traditional ghost story this seems promising, but, as the narrative makes clear, the locals believe the place to be haunted by jinn rather than by ghosts. As the story develops, the jinn who haunts the house is never seen. Only the voice of the jinn is heard, and, far from doing Ali harm, the jinn showers him with gold as the chosen one whose coming was expected.[13]

Medieval Christendom was haunted by fear of the witch. Witches were both numerous and dangerous. They flew by night, they destroyed cattle and livestock, they met in covens and they rendered obscene homage to the Devil. The Christian Inquisition devoted vast resources to hunting down, interrogating and burning witches. In the Middle East, however, there was no institution comparable to the Inquisition (although an *ad hoc* tribunal, a *mihna*,[14] might occasionally be established to try a heretic). Nor was there an obsessional fear of witches. Nevertheless, there were thought to be witches in the medieval Near East. (Instead of broomsticks, they flew about on jars.) Two types of witch feature in the tales of the *Nights*, and each type presents a sexual threat to men. First, there is the nymphomaniac man-killer (see, for examples, the sorceress-wife in 'The Ensorcelled Prince' or Jan Shah, the 500-year-old queen who forces men to sleep with her and then kills them in 'The History of Ghaib and his Brother Ajib'). The second type of witch was a lesbian, and as we have already seen, lesbians are several times maligned as witches in the pages of the *Nights*. Despite all the above, witches played a far smaller part in the demonology of the Arab lands than they did in the Christian West.

On the other hand, some occult pursuits were much more popular in the Middle East than in Europe. In Europe, magic was occasionally used to divine the whereabouts of buried treasure. The Elizabethan magus John Dee and his shady colleague Edward Kelley wasted a great deal of time in quest of the alleged ten great treasures buried in Britain by lords of King Arthur. In the Arab lands, however, treasure-hunting was both a sophisticated occult science and a popular obsession. The number of tales on the subject in the *Nights* bear witness to this. Of course, a treasure-hunt – the quest and the ordeals endured during the search for the goal – has been a popular theme in western storytelling. One only has to think of such books as *The High Quest of the Holy Grail*, Edgar Allan Poe's *The Gold Bug*, Robert Louis Stevenson's *Treasure Island* and J.R.R. Tolkien's *The Hobbit* and such films as *The Treasure of the Sierra Madre* and *Raiders of the Lost Ark*. What is striking about Arab fiction on the subject, however, is the central role of occult knowledge in the search for the treasure.

'Alaeddin, or the Wonderful Lamp', is surely the best known of all the *Nights* tales featuring a treasure-hunt. In the story, the Maghribi (i.e. North African) dervish, who is also a sorcerer, determines by astrology that the boy, Aladdin, is the only person who can bring a certain hoard of treasure out from its hiding place. The sorcerer brings the boy to the astrologically determined place and performs a ritual fumigation with incense in order to create a hole in the ground. Then the sorcerer consults his geomantic tablet. (Islamic geomancy will be discussed later in this chapter.) A copper ring attached to a marble slab is revealed by the cleaving open of the earth. The sorcerer bids Aladdin raise the slab (for it is the boy alone who can do this) and descend into the vaults below. The vaults are filled with treasures, but Aladdin is warned not to touch any of them or he will be turned into black stone – and in fact the sorcerer's quest is not for mere silver and gold, but for a magical lamp which confers power over a genie. There is no need here to follow the development of this famous story any further.[15]

The story of 'Judar and his Brethren', however, deserves to better known than it is. It is a more interesting story than 'Alaeddin' and succeeds better in creating an atmosphere of the uncanny. Judar is a young man who fishes to support his family.

One day he goes out to fish on Lake Karun, on the edge of Cairo, but before he can cast his net upon the waters he is approached by a Maghribi who salutes Judar by name and asks him to do him a service. He asks Judar to recite the first chapter of the Koran and to tie him up by his elbows and throw him into the lake. If and only if Judar subsequently sees the two hands of the Maghribi raised above the surface of the water is Judar to use his net to rescue him. If only the Maghribi's feet appear, then Judar will know that the Maghribi is dead. In that case Judar is to take the Maghribi's mule and precious saddle-bags to a certain Jew dwelling in Cairo and report to him, whereupon the Jew will give him 100 dinars. In the event, the Maghribi's bizarre escapological feat fails, and Judar sees the ill-fated man's feet rising above the surface of the water. So begins a long and complex story of Judar's involvement with four brother sorcerers from the Maghreb who are using a book known as *The Fables of the Ancients* to guide them in their quest for the magical treasures of al-Shamardal. Eventually it emerges that, like Aladdin, Judar is the appointed one, and only he can descend underground to retrieve the treasures of al-Shamardal.

Judar's ordeal is a curious one. In the wilderness, the Maghribi sorcerer (brother of the two magicians who have drowned in Lake Karun) conjures up two jinn who are enjoined to obey Judar and open up to him the treasures of al-Shamardal. Then he instructs Judar on what he must face when the door to the subterranean hoard is revealed. First, the man who opens the door will demand that Judar offers his neck for execution. Judar must agree to this, for only if he does so will the apparition vanish without doing any harm. Secondly, Judar must face a horseman with a lance and Judar must offer his chest to be run through, whereupon the horseman will disappear. At the third door, an archer will threaten Judar. At the fourth door, Judar must offer his hand to be bitten by a lion, and at the fifth he will be challenged by a black slave. At the sixth door, two dragons must be suffered to bite at Judar's hands. Finally, when he comes to the seventh door, he will see his mother welcoming him, but here he must draw his sword and force her to strip, for only by these means can this apparition be disarmed, and then Judar will able to proceed into the hall of treasures. Having received his instructions, Judar descends and outfaces all his ordeals until he comes to the seventh door, where he confronts the thing which appears to be his mother. Sword in hand, he forces her to strip down to her pants. At this point she (or should it be it?) cries out, 'O my son, is thy heart stone? Wilt thou dishonour me by discovering my shame?' Judar hesitates, and in his hesitation he is lost; the supernatural guardians of the treasures set upon him, flog him and expel him from the vaults. A year has to pass before the astrological conjunctions are once again favourable and Judar is able to make the attempt on the treasure again. This time he forces the vision of his mother to strip completely, and, as he does so, the thing turns into a body without a soul. The treasures are now his for the taking.[16]

Judar's subterranean ordeals seem vaguely reminiscent of an initiation rite into some sort of secret society, for which courage, readiness to die and a willingness to renounce both one's family and traditional social constraints are demanded. Alternatively, it is possible to read the story of Judar's ordeal as a thinly veiled psychodrama about descent into the unconsciousness to face the monsters waiting there before attaining the treasures of maturity. However, it is hard to say whether such subtexts could have been picked up by the story's medieval audience. There are many tales featuring treasure-hunts in the *Nights*, among them 'King Ibrahim and his Son', 'The City of Brass', 'The City of Labtayt', 'The Queen of the Serpents', 'Maamun and the Pyramids of Egypt', 'Zayn al-Asnam' and 'Hasan of Basra'. Most of these stories are of Egyptian origin; for Egypt, where tomb robbers had searched for thousands of years for the lost treasures of the Pharaohs, was pre-eminently the home of *mutalibun*, or professional treasure-hunters.

Treasure-hunts in medieval Egypt were not just the stuff of fantasy and fiction. In fact, treasure-hunting was both an occult science and a professional occupation. As a science, it demanded from its students a knowledge of ancient lore and sorcery. As a profession, it demanded courage. It was universally recognized that the *mutalib* (treasure-hunter) was engaged in a high-risk occupation. Al-Jawbari warned in his thirteenth-century treatise *Kashf al-Asrar* of the real perils that the treasure-hunter might face: 'Imagine you are in a long narrow passage descending into the deeps of the earth and the passage is lined by sword-bearing statues. Beware! Beat out the ground in front of you with a stick, so that the swords fall on emptiness.' Al-Jawbari went on to explain how the sword-wielding arms of the statues are activated by tubes of mercury attached to trip-wires. Readers of *Kashf al-Asrar* are instructed on how to avoid fire-traps by making magical fumigations, and to beat out the ground in front of one with a stick so as to avoid being pitched into a silo of sand by a revolving flagstone. A treasure-hunter needed patience, courage, occult knowledge and artisanal skill. Al-Jawbari spoke from personal experience. He and some friends excavating in a cemetery near Cairo found the gateway to a subterranean passage. They avoided the collapsing staircase by sounding it out with sticks, and they avoided the revolving flagstone by throwing a lump of lead on to it. Al-Jawbari does not say whether they found any treasure.[17]

While al-Jawbari was himself a *mutalib*, and respected the skills of the genuine treasure-hunter, he also warned of the dangers posed by confidence tricksters who posed as treasure-hunters, who used spurious maps and talismans, and salted away caches of 'treasure' and drugs for separating their clients from their money. In the *Nights*, 'The Tale of the Sharpers with the Shroff and the Ass' concerns a team of rogues who trick a shroff (money-changer) into believing that a donkey belonging to a confederate of theirs is the only creature which can guide them to a certain hoard of treasure. The shroff is persuaded to act on their behalf and offer their confederate a vast sum of money for the donkey, whereupon the sharpsters all disappear with the money.

While there were many frauds associated with treasure-hunting, nobody doubted that there were real fortunes to be won – and real perils to be encountered. Besides the threats posed by booby-traps and by jinn, the *mutalib* often had to encounter homicidal automata. A great deal of the ancient Greek expertise concerning ingenious mechanical devices (powered by wind, water, weights or springs) had been handed on to the medieval Arabs, and Arab engineers continued to develop and refine devices for telling the time, dispensing drinks and playing music.[18] However, in popular belief such automata – primitive robots – were powered by magic, and it was widely believed that ancient kings and wizards had set magically driven automata to guard over their hidden treasure hoards.

The automaton, a creature who is neither living nor dead, features frequently in the *Nights* as an uncanny accessory in its tales of wonder. The brass oarsman who bears a tablet of lead inscribed with talismanic characters on his breast and who rows the Third Dervish over to the Islands of Safety; the little manikin which a dervish fashions out of beeswax and which plunges into the river to retrieve the sultan's lost signet ring; the air-driven statues which seem to speak to Omar bin al-Nu'uman and his son in the palace of the Christian princess; and the Ebony Horse, which is powered by wind and, when the right lever is pulled, carries a man through the air: they all simulate life, but there is no life in them. Devised for the most part by masters long dead, they are remnants of a poorly understood and therefore dangerous past. In the idolatrous stone city in 'Abdullah bin Fazil and his Brothers', the idols are man-made, but, as the prophet sent by God points out, 'the Satans clad themselves therewith as with clothing, and they it is who spake to you from within the bellies of the images'.[19]

In order to find treasure, recourse might be had to oracles and divination. Treasure could be dowsed for, just as one dowsed for water, and the treasure-hunter might have recourse to the linked sciences of astrology and geomancy. In the course of her

examination by the sages of the caliph's court, the learned slave girl
Tawaddud, the heroine of the *Nights* story which bears her name,
gives an impromptu lecture on the mansions of the moon, the
benevolent and sinister aspects of the planets and the auspicious
and inauspicious days of the week. However, she is careful to
point out the limits of divination. Foreknowledge of certain things
is reserved for God alone. Tawaddud's reservations about the
powers of astrology were shared by many medieval thinkers. In
fiction, however, what is prophesied by the astrologers always
comes to pass. In 'The Third Dervish's Tale', the prince, hidden
on the island, tells Ajib ibn Khasib 'how the astrologers and wise
men, noting my birth date, read my horoscope' and then told his
father that 'Your son will live fifteen years, after which there will
be a conjunction of the stars, and if he can escape it, he will live.'[20]
But there is no escaping the doom of the astrologers; and, though
Ajib ibn Khasib has no wish to kill the prince, he still does kill
him, just as the astrologers have foretold.

In both Christian and Muslim lands, astrology was closely
linked with geomancy. In the Mamluke lands, diviners usually
made use of a combination of geomancy and astrology to
formulate their prophecies. 'I am the ready Reckoner; I am the
Scrivener; I am he who weeteth the Sought and the Seeker; I am
the finished man of Science; I am the Astrologer accomplished in
experience! Where then is he that seeketh?'[21] This is the cry of the
eponymous hero of 'The Tale of Kamar al-Zaman' when, to gain
access to the king's daughter, he dons the guise of a geomancer
and wanders through the streets, carrying the precious tools of his
trade: 'a geomantic tablet of gold, with a set of astrological
instruments and with an astrolabe of silver, plated with gold'. At
its least sophisticated level, geomancy involved the diviner in
nothing more than guessing the future from random marks in the
sand. In 'Ali Shar and Zumurrud', Zumurrud, who pretends to be
a geomancer, needs nothing more than a tray of sand and a brass
pen to allow her to divine the figure of a baboon from the

random markings made by her pen in the sand. However, as both Kamar al-Zaman's boasting and his impedimenta suggest, geomancy at a more sophisticated level involved complex astrological calculations. A geomantic figure was formed by making four random lines of dots. Then the number of dots in each row was counted to determine whether the row was even or odd. The combination of even and/or odd lines generated one of sixteen possible geomantic figures. The horoscope of the enquirer, the dominant planets at the time of enquiry and other astrological considerations all also played a part in determining the geomancer's final prognosis.[22] (Medieval Muslim and Christian geomancy is not to be confused with Chinese geomancy, which is concerned with 'the subtle currents in the earth' and the flow of the occult forces of *yin* and *yang* through landscapes and buildings.) In the *Nights*, geomancy is the most widely employed means of discovering the unknown. Crafty Dalilah casts a geomantic figure in order to discover Mercury Ali's true identity. Geomancers predict the future of Zayn al-Asnam. Geomancy reveals to the sorcerer that Aladdin is still alive.

Firasa, physiognomic divination, or divination from appearances, was a science or skill on the edge of the occult. Its practitioners might draw on occult lore to perform inexplicable feats of deduction, but they also used common sense and humdrum detective work. The word *firasa* comes from the same root as *faras*, meaning horse, and it may be that the skill of *firasa* was first developed by the bedouin to evaluate horses and see through the deceits of swindling horse-dealers. In later centuries, one of the chief practical uses of *firasa* was in the examination and assessment of slaves offered for sale in the market.[23] In a brilliant and wide-ranging essay, 'Clues, Roots of an Evidential Paradigm', the cultural historian Carlo Ginzburg has discussed the related techniques of art connoisseurship, psychoanalysis, detection and *firasa*. As Ginzburg observes: 'Ancient Arabic physiognomics was rooted on *firasa*, a complex notion which generally meant the capacity to leap from the known to the unknown by inference on the basis of clues.'[24]

'The King who Kenned the Quintessence of Things' and the 'Story of the Sultan of Al-Yaman and his Three Sons' are both tales about *firasa*. In the former tale, the king, who has lost his kingdom and has had himself sold as a slave, is able to amaze his successor on the throne by his ability to determine, just by looking, that a certain pearl is rotten inside, that, superficial appearances to the contrary, the older of a pair of horses offered for sale is a better buy, and that, finally, the king, his master, is the son of a baker. In 'The Story of the Sultan of Al-Yaman and his Three Sons', three gifted princes, wandering in the wilderness, are able to deduce that a one-eyed, tailless camel laden with halva and pickles has passed that way before them. This early detective story is of considerable antiquity. A variant version appeared in al-Tabari's tenth-century chronicle of Islamic history. Versions of essentially the same tale feature in Sercambi's fifteenth-century *Novelle*, in Voltaire's *Zadig* and, most recently, in Umberto Eco's *The Name of the Rose*. References to *firasa* abound elsewhere in the *Nights*. In 'The Night-Adventure of the Sultan Mohammed of Cairo', the sultan's disguise is penetrated by the youngest of the girls he visits, for she looks at him 'with the eye of the physiognomist'. To the ignorant such deductions must have seemed positively miraculous, but often it was only a matter of close observation coupled with logical reasoning. There was nothing necessarily occult about the process. However, certain Sufi sheikhs taught how interior truths might be deduced by occult intuition, a mystic might transform himself into a 'spy of the heart', and *firasa* might easily shade into thought-reading (*ilm al-mukashafa*). Outward appearances betrayed inner truths, and it is one of the commonplaces of the *Nights* that 'a man's destiny is written upon his forehead'.

The broad science of divination embraced some quite strange sub-specialisms, such as urinomancy (featured in 'The Tale of the

Weaver who Became a Leach', where the weaver pretends to skill as a urinomancer, but is actually using the broader skills of the physiognomist), divination from palpitations, divination from wounds, divination from beauty spots and *qiyafah* or divination of ancestry. Even predicting rainfall from examining the sky's appearance was classified as divination (perhaps rightly so, for modern attempts to turn meteorology into a fully fledged science are not entirely convincing).

However, astrology and geomancy apart, dream interpretation was probably the most commonly employed technique of unveiling the secrets of the future.[25] Despite the weirdly dreamlike quality of so many of the stories within the *Nights*, the dreams actually featured in the stories are rather simple ones and they are easily interpreted. It is a feature of popular stories that the dreams that the characters have always carry messages that are true. When, in 'The History of Gharib and his Brother Ajib', Gharib dreams that he and his companion are swept up from a valley by two ravening birds of prey, the dream's content is not that of a mystifying riddle with latent sexual content to be teased out and decoded. Rather, the following day Gharib and his companion are in a valley when two great birdlike creatures swoop down and carry them away. Medieval Arab storytellers did not make use of sophisticated dream symbolism. If a sultan in a story is warned of something, then the warning will come true. The dream in medieval Arab fiction was a storyteller's device, used to foreshadow what is going to happen – and, as such, a special form of literary adumbration or prolepsis. But dreams were not only used to prefigure what would happen later on in the story; as often as not, they also made the story happen. For example, in 'The Ruined Man who Became Rich Again through a Dream', the man in question is told to leave his native city of Baghdad and go to Cairo, where he will discover the whereabouts of some hidden treasure. In Cairo he experiences a series of misfortunes and ends up in gaol. There he tells his dream to the police chief. The police chief mocks the idea of veridical dreams and tells the man how he himself has dreamed of a certain house, a courtyard and a fountain in Baghdad and of treasure buried under that fountain. The imprisoned man recognizes that house as his own and, on his release from gaol, he goes back to Baghdad and digs up the treasure. (A variant of the same story in English folklore is known as the story of the Pedlar of Swaffham.)[26] In the above story and in numerous others, the dream not only predicts the future, it makes it happen. Most of the dreams in the *Nights* turn out to be self-fulfilling prophecies.

In medieval Islamic reality, as opposed to fiction, the science of dream interpretation was highly sophisticated, and not all dreams were regarded as being veridical. There were dreams which came from God and which were a portion of prophecy, and it was widely held by Muslims that no dream in which the Prophet appeared could be false or misleading. Then there were enigmatic dreams, which did not come directly from God but might never-theless, if sensitively interpreted, give useful guidance about the present and future state of the one who had had the dream. Finally, there were very confused dreams, which were the product of nothing more than indigestion or a poor sleeping posture. Much depended on one's choice of dream interpreter, for the dream was not regarded as having any meaning until it had been assigned one by its interpreter. 'The dream follows his mouth.' Once the dream had been interpreted, however, its meaning was fixed. Thomas Mann made play with this ancient Semitic concept in his remarkable novel *Joseph the Provider*: 'For it may well be that dreaming is a single whole, wherein dream and interpretation belong together and dreamer and interpreter only seem to be two separate persons but are actually interchangeable and one and the same, since together they make up the whole.'[27] Dreams were also ranked according to the status of the dreamer. Thus, a king's dream was more to be believed than a commoner's, and a man's dream was more creditworthy than a woman's.

According to an ancient Arab tale (not included in the *Nights*), a man was walking down the street one morning when he saw Death looking at him strangely. In a panic, the man fled his native city, seeking to place as much distance between himself and Death as possible. In the evening he arrived in Samarra, but he found Death waiting for him there. The reason Death had looked so strangely on the man in the morning was that he was surprised to see him in that place, for Death knew that they had an appointment in Samarra that night. Here complementary actions combine to bring about the predestined fate. The structure of the story of 'The Appointment at Samarra' is essentially the same as that of 'The Ruined Man who Became Rich Again through a Dream', discussed above. Such tales offer perfect examples of the mysteriously satisfying symmetries of fate and fiction.

Qada and *qadar* play a determining role in the Muslim universe. *Qada* means decree, or fate in general (which is God's decree), while *qadar* is a particular application of *qada*. Although it has been contested by many Muslim thinkers and some sects, the notion of predestination, of the control of the lives of men and women by God's decree, has been fairly widely accepted by Sunni Muslims. If God's will is omnipotent, then human will counts for nothing – or rather, a man's will is determined by God's will, so that, somewhat subtly, a person of his or her free will chooses the fate that God has already predetermined for that person. The damned are damned because God has predetermined their damnation. 'God has set a seal on their hearts and on their hearing, and on their eyes is a covering, and there awaits them a mighty chastisement' (Koran, II, 7); and 'God leads astray whomsoever He will' (Koran, XIII, 27). According to Islamic folklore, when God made Adam, he took out all Adam's future descendants (they looked like little ants) and divided them into those with good futures and those with evil futures. The good were replaced on the right side of Adam's body and the evil on the left side.

The above is rather by way of an excursus, for the way that fate performed in medieval Arab fiction owed little to speculative theology. Al-Tanukhi's *Faraj ba'd al-Shidda*, or 'Relief after Distress', a tenth-century collection of stories to illustrate the workings of divine providence, was compiled with the aim of inspiring its audience to bear their tribulations with fortitude and pious resignation.[28] The *Nights* contains many stories and fables which share this 'you-can't-beat-fate' attitude and advocate a sort of religious quietism. In the fable of 'The Fishes and the Crab', the fishes, threatened by the drying up of their pool, go to the crab for advice. The crab urges resignation, for 'Know ye not that Allah (extolled and exalted be He!) provideth all His creatures without account and that He foreordained their daily meat ere He created aught of creation and appointed to each of His creatures a fixed term of life and an allotted provision, of His divine All-might?' And, as the trapped sparrow in one of the fables observes, 'It availed me not to beware of the stroke of fate and fortune, since even he who taketh precaution may never flee from destiny.' However, seeking to avoid fate makes for a better story than listening to the wise old crab and waiting for the rain to fall again. In most *Nights* stories, the protagonists refuse to heed the warnings of the wise old sages and astrologers, and they make their bids to beat fate.

To resign oneself to God's will is evidently laudable. Sometimes, however, one feels that the doctrine of predestination is being used to serve less laudable aims, and resignation to divine decree can serve as an apologia for idleness. Certainly, some of the stories in the *Nights* can be read in this way. 'The History of Khawajah Hasan al-Habbal', for example, is about the debate between two neighbours about whether hard work or luck makes man rich. Inevitably, it concludes that 'wealth cometh not by wealth; but only by the Grace of Almighty Allah does a poor man become a rich man'.[29] More generally, it is striking how many of the stories in the *Nights* (stories designed to entertain the idlers of Cairo's cafés) feature heroes who are idle and feckless, but who attain great fortunes through amazing good luck. Aladdin is perhaps the best-known example of these unimpressive heroes. Destiny is capricious and favours the humble, the talentless and the lazy. Consider also Ali Baba, Ma'aruf the Cobbler and a string of poor fishermen who haul up bottled jinn, talking fish and magic rings. What could be more chancy than casting one's net upon the waters? Fate, or destiny, under God, is the poor man's omnipotent ombudsman. 'Think not, O King, that thou art safe from the shifts of Time and the Strokes of Change which come like a traveller in the Night,' warns the wazir in 'The Tale of Kamar al-Zaman'. Destiny, like death, is a great leveller, and 'Death, the Destroyer of all Delights' is everybody's destiny. We are all eventually pulled through that dark and infinitely small hole.

'Character,' as the German poet Novalis cryptically observed, 'is destiny.' Novalis probably meant that each individual, through exercise of his particular qualities and in pursuit of his own particular ambitions, is the architect of his fortunes and misfortunes. In the *Nights*, however, the sense of this equivalence of character and destiny is reversed; for, as Todorov has observed in an essay on 'Les Hommes-Récits', 'characters' like Sinbad and Ali Baba seem to have no character, no inner depth and no psychological consistency. They are what they do, or, rather, they are what fate (working hard on behalf of the storyteller) makes them do.[30]

From the stories of the *Nights* we learn that fate is 'that which is written on the forehead'. Indeed, fate is written all over the place. *Maktub*, it is written. Fate is a thoroughly literary affair. Each man has his story, and it is written on him. The poet Zuhayr ibn Abi Sulma once compared fate to 'a night-blind camel'. It may be true that in real life fate is blind. But when we turn to fiction, we find that the blindness of fate is a thoroughly misleading metaphor. As we shall see, fate is far from blind. It watches over everything and meticulously arranges it all. There is no random fumbling on the part of fate. Though fate is always omnipresent and active, it is discoverable only by certain clues, such as marks on the forehead or in the sand, or by the operation of amazing coincidence (*ittifaq*). Though largely invisible, Fate is a leading character in the *Nights*. As we have already seen, in 'The Second Dervish's Tale', Fate, helped along by the astrologers, is the architect of the misfortunes of Khasib and the prince he slays. Similarly, in 'The Story of King Ibrahim and his Son', the king is warned by his astrologers that his new-born son, when he reaches the age of seven, will be attacked by a lion, and moreover that, if the boy survives the lion's onslaught, he will grow up to slay his own father, the king. The king has his son secluded and carefully guarded against such an eventuality. But seven years later, 'the time of the Fate foreordered and the Fortune graven on the forehead' arrives. The son's nursemaid is slain by a lion, and the son vanishes. He reappears later inadvertently to slay his father. With his (rather prolix) dying breaths, the king forgives his son, for as he tells his courtiers, 'Know that what Allah hath writ upon the forehead, be it fair fortune or misfortune, none may efface, and all that is decreed to a man must perforce befall him.'

Again, in 'The Merchant's Daughter and the Prince of al-Irak', the merchant is warned by an invisible voice, first that 'Predestination overcometh Prudence and resignation to the trials sent by Allah is foremost and fairest', and secondly that his daughter will bear an illegitimate child to an Iraqi prince. In an (inevitable) attempt to avoid the decree of fate, the merchant takes steps to hide his daughter on a remote mountain. But the very steps that the merchant takes to secure his daughter's virtue ensure her fall; for the Iraqi prince goes out hunting one day and comes across a stallion which 'under decree of Destiny was influenced by the Lord and directed towards the Prince for the sake of that which was hidden from him in the World of Secrets', and this stallion eventually takes the prince to the maiden secluded on the mountain. And so the fate-laden story continues. In 'The Tale of Attaf' (also known as 'The Power of Destiny'), Harun visits a

library, consults a volume at random, falls to laughing and weeping
and dismisses the faithful vizier Ja'afar from his sight. Ja'afar,
disturbed and upset, flees Baghdad and plunges into a series of
adventures in Damascus, involving Attaf and the woman whom
Attaf eventually marries. Returning to Baghdad, he reports back
to Harun, who takes him into the library. Now Ja'afar is allowed
to consult the book which caused his master such grief and mirth,
and in it Ja'afar finds the story of his own adventures with Attaf,
those same adventures which were provoked by Harun's reading
of the story in the book. Even so was the doom of destiny
fulfilled. A form of reverse causation operates in these stories, in
which the prophecy gives birth to what is prophesied. C.S. Lewis
has written of this type of tale (the legend of Oedipus comes in the
same category):

Such stories produce (at least in me) a feeling of awe coupled with a
certain sort of bewilderment such as one often feels in looking at a
complex pattern of lines that pass over and under one another. One sees,
yet does not quite see, the regularity ... We have just had set before our
imagination something that has always baffled the intellect: we have
seen how destiny and free will can be combined, even how free will is
the *modus operandi* of destiny.[31]

Fate is fond of symmetry and economy in stories, Fate standing
here for the storyteller, of course. One way for the storyteller to
achieve economy is through the canny deployment of coincidence,
but what is coincidence? In Julian Barnes's novel *Flaubert's Parrot*,
the narrator roundly denounces coincidences: 'There's something
spooky about them: you sense momentarily what it must be like
to live in an ordered, God-run universe, with Himself looking
over your shoulder and helpfully dropping coarse hints about a
cosmic plan.' And Barnes's curmudgeon continues: 'And as for
coincidences in books – there's something cheap and sentimental
about the device; it can't help seeming cheap and gimcrack. That
troubador who passes by just in time to rescue the girl from a

hedgerow scuffle; the sudden but convenient Dickensian bene-
factors; the neat shipwreck on a foreign shore which reunites
siblings and lovers.' However, Barnes's narrator allows that
coincidence may have a proper place in picaresque narratives, and,
of course, the medieval Arab was quite sure that he was living in
'an ordered, God-run universe' and he had no objection to the
storyteller assuming similar powers over his fictional universe.[32]

In 'Julnar the Sea-Born and her Son', Princess Jauharah flees
from a palace coup to a certain island and hides up a certain tree.
Surely no one will discover her there? But, in fact, 'destiny from
eternity fore-ordained' drives Badr al-Basim, who is fleeing for his
life, to the very island where the princess has taken refuge, and
Badr lies down to rest under the very same tree. The coincidence
is ludicrous, and Barnes's spokesman would hate it, but without
the coincidence there would be no story. Without pattern, there is
no meaning. Coincidences, however, hint at a hidden meaning in
the world's ordering. Destiny promises – no, demands – adventures
and, having called up adventures, eventually resolves them. The
Italian film director Pier Paolo Pasolini, one of the most intelligent
of modern interpreters of the *Nights*, observed that

every tale in *The Thousand and One Nights* begins with an 'appearance of
destiny' which manifests itself through an anomaly, and one anomaly
always generates another. So a chain of anomalies is set up. And the
more logical, tightly knit, essential this chain is, the more beautiful the
tale. By 'beautiful' I mean vital, absorbing and exhilarating. The chain
of anomalies always tends to lead back to normality. The end of every
tale in the *The Thousand and One Nights* consists of a 'disappearance' of
destiny, which sinks back to the somnolence of daily life ... The
protagonist of the stories is in fact destiny itself.[33]

Consciously or unconsciously, Pasolini's reflections on destiny
echo and elaborate on those of the social and cultural theorist
Walter Benjamin, who observed in an essay on 'Fate and
Character' that misfortune is a category of fate, but that 'happiness

is, rather, what releases a man from the embroilment of the Fates and from the net of his own fate'.[34] Pasolini's reflections may also remind one of Vladimir Propp's ideas about the functions of violation and resolution in Russian fairy tales (which will be discussed in the next chapter).

In *Chance and Necessity*, Jacques Monod, when considering which ideas are most likely to lodge themselves in people's heads and therefore survive, argues that 'What is very plain, however, is that the ideas having the highest invading potential are those that explain man by assigning him his place in an immanent destiny, a safe harbour where his anxiety dissolves.' As with ideas, so, surely, with stories. A story which has begun by conjuring up a problem (or an anomaly, or a violation), and which has ended by conjuring the problem away, will have commended itself to those in its audience who are worried about their own destiny and place in the universe. Fiction here has some of the same soothing powers as religion.[35]

Each man has his own fate, and one man's fate may conquer another. In 'The Adventures of Mercury Ali of Cairo', the sinister Jewish sorcerer, Azariah, discovers through geomancy that Ali's fortune conquers his, so he refrains from killing him and turns him into an ass instead. In the medieval Near East, Jews were often credited with magical powers, and, in fact, one can find features in surviving Arab magical texts from the Middle Ages which have obvious Jewish origins – the stress on letter-magic and the cabalistic manipulation of letters, the imagery of Solomon's seal, staff and ring, and Hebrew or at least Hebrew-sounding names of the spirits who could be conjured to do the sorcerer's bidding.

However, although Jews frequently featured as sorcerers in popular literature, the Maghribis – Arab or Berber Muslims from North Africa and Spain – were more commonly assigned roles as sorcerers in the *Nights* and in popular folklore. The best known of these Maghribi sorcerers must be the one who sought to make use and then dispose of Aladdin, but there are many others, among them the three brothers who make Judar tie them up and cast them into the Karun Pool and the Maghribi encountered by Sheikh Muhammad in 'The History of Mohammed, Sultan of Cairo', who had before him 'some written leaves and was casting omens for sundry bystanders' and who helps Muhammad against a deceitful jinn. It was not only the authors of fiction who assigned Maghribis a role as sorcerers. Ibn Iyas's history of Mamluke Egypt tells how a Maghribi sorcerer conjured up a garden which he sold to a citizen of Cairo, before vanishing, together with the garden. Of the two most important medieval Arab magical treatises, one, the *Ghayat al-Hakim*, or 'Goal of the Sage', was attributed to the tenth-century Spanish Muslim mathematician al-Majriti; while the other, *Shams al-Ma'arif*, or 'Sun of Gnosis', was attributed to al-Buni, a thirteenth-century North African Sufi who had settled in Alexandria. Al-Zannati, a key figure in the history of geomancy, was a Berber, and the Arabs thought, probably rightly, that geomancy came to them from the Berbers. Persians also occasion-ally feature as magicians. For example, there is the geomancer in 'Hasan of Bassorah', of whom Hasan's mother warns him: 'O my son, beware of hearkening to the talk of the folk, and especially of the Persians, and obey them not in aught; for they are sharpers and tricksters, who profess the art of alchemy.'[36] Bahram the Guebre (that is, the Zoroastrian) does indeed use the promise of teaching the alchemic arts to lure Hasan into his power (he really intends to sacrifice the youth to the fire which, as a Zoroastrian, he worships).

As has been noted above, there were no witch-hunts of any consequence in medieval Islamic history. The sorcerer, no matter how wicked he might be, was thought of not as the servant of the Devil, but rather as the master of the jinn. The sorcerer worked through books, swords, talismans and lamps to force the unseen legions to his will. In 'The Tale of the Warlock and the Young Cook of Baghdad', the warlock makes use of a metal flask, seven needles, a piece of aloes wood, some clay, a sheep's shoulder-blade, some felt and some silk. Having used these objects to make a curious bundle pierced through with needles, he recites over it: 'I have knocked, I have knocked at the hall doors of the earth to summon the Jann [a variant plural of Jinn], and the Jann have knocked for the Jann against the Shaytan.'

The jinn (sing. jinn or genie) were thought of as supernatural creatures with bodies of flame. They were normally invisible (and so it was that the merchant in the *Nights* inadvertently killed the son of a jinn by throwing away a date stone). However, they frequently make themselves visible in the *Nights*. Though they normally appear as human beings, this was not always the case. In 'The Tale of Zayn al-Asnam', Zayn al-Asnam is ferried across the lake by a jinn with the head of an elephant and the body of a lion. The hosts of jinn assembled on the other side of the lake are hideous to look upon; only the King of the Jinn has assumed the form of a handsome young man. Such accounts of meetings with the kings of the jinn and their legions can easily be paralleled in medieval Arab sorcerer's manuals which purported to be non-fiction. In the treatises of the thirteenth-century sorcerer Abu'l-Qasim al-Iraqi, for example, there are a variety of spells for summoning jinn, for learning their secrets and for using them as treasure-hunters. (Abu'l-Qasim also knew spells for flying, walking on water, mastering telepathy, giving people dogs' heads and giving women beards.) Another magician, writing under the name Ibn al-Hajj, produced a treatise called *Suns of the Lights*, which contains among other things a spell for having sex with the daughter of the White King of the Jinn. After twelve days' fasting and uttering of conjurations in the desert, first a dragon appears (which must be ignored) and then a very pale woman who approaches with an undulating walk and who is laden with gold and jewels. The trouble is, if you agree to marry her, this will make you impotent with ordinary women.[37]

The jinn were shape-shifters,[38] as emerges from the shape-shifting battle in 'The Second Dervish's Tale'. Very commonly jinn

travelled about as whirlwinds. The society of the jinn was rather
like human society. It had its own kings, courts and armies. In
'The Adventures of Bulukiya', Bulukiya comes before Sakhr,
King of the Jinn, who is attended upon by lesser kings and princes
of the jinn, as well as by counsellors, emirs and officers of state.
There are good Muslim jinn, like Sakhr and his following, and
there are evil, infidel jinn. (The evil jinn are sometimes characterized as *shaytans*, or devils.) Since jinn often move about in the
world of men and transact business with humans, a significant
body of law was elaborated by religious jurisconsults, dealing with
such matters as the property rights of jinn and cases of mixed
marriages between jinn and women. Ritual hygiene was another
potential issue. Although women have to perform the major ritual
ablution (the *ghusl*) after having had sex with men before they can
perform the prayers, according to the legal compilation *Al-Fatawa
al-Hindiyya* there is no need for the ablutions after having had sex
with jinn.[39]

Some considered Iblis, the Devil, to be a jinn; some thought of
him as an angel.[40] (Angels are made of light, while jinn are made
of fire.) The majority opinion appears to have been that he was a
fallen angel and that he had been punished for his pride. Specifically, he had refused God's command to bow down and venerate
Adam. Though God cast him out of heaven for this, some Sufis
venerated Iblis for his uncompromising refusal to bow down
before anyone save God. The Devil rarely appears in the *Nights*,
but (in an early Arab prefiguration of the story of Tartini and the
Devil's trill), in the story of 'Ibrahim of Mosul and the Devil', the
Father of Bitterness appears before Ibrahim and teaches him a new
song. Iblis also appears in 'The Tale of the Damsel Tohfat al-
Kulub'. In both stories he appears in the form of a handsome old
man. In 'The Adventures of Bulukiya', we are told that the evil
jinn are descendants of Iblis, while the good jinn are the offspring
of the six angels who did not fall.

Jinn haunted lavatories, and so it is that in 'The Tale of Nur al-

Din Ali and his Son' the *ifrit* (powerful jinn) emerges out of the tank of the lavatory to persecute the hunchback. Tohfat al-Kulub was conducted by Iblis, 'Father of the Jinn', to the land of the jinn, via a magic exit concealed in one of the lavatories of the caliph's palace. Ruins, as in 'The King's Son and the Ogress' and 'Ma'aruf the Cobbler', and cemeteries were also favoured by the jinn, particularly by the sub-category of jinn known as ghouls. A ghoul is a malevolent jinn who lives in deserted places or cemeteries. He or she is fond of human flesh (and sometimes 'ghoul' was used as a synonym for human cannibal). A ghoul could be killed with a single blow, but if the killer inadvertently hit the ghoul again, then it would come back to life. According to the nineteenth-century desert explorer Charles Doughty, ghouls lured travellers from their paths by calling to them in the voice of their mother or sister.

When it comes to the vocabulary of teratology, Arab usage was neither precise nor consistent, but in general it seems that a *marid* was a more powerful sort of jinn and that an *ifrit* was an even more powerful one yet. *Ifrits* were usually malevolent (the verbal root from which the noun is derived means to roll in the dust, i.e. to bring low). Many of the jinn encountered in the *Nights* have been imprisoned in flasks or columns of stone by Solomon, who controlled the jinn through his seal-ring and his staff and punished them for their disobedience. In 'The City of Brass', the caliph in Damascus sends out an expedition to search for such flasks. The jinn are compelled by certain objects, such as the signet ring discovered by Ma'aruf the Cobbler in an underground cave. The notion that spirits could be controlled through correct manipulation of certain magical objects probably derives from a debased form of loosely Neoplatonic ideas popular in late antiquity concerning theurgy, or the practice of magic through the control of spirits. Whereas in the medieval West it was possible for some sceptical spirits to dismiss any story concerning fairies as an old wives' tale, the medieval Muslim could not dismiss the possibility

of the existence of the jinn so easily, for they are repeatedly
attested to in the Koran — for example, in a passage about
Solomon's control of the jinn:

> And of the jinn, some worked before him
> by leave of his Lord; and such of them
> as swerved away from Our commandment,
> We would let them taste the chastisement of the Blaze.
>
> (XXXIV, 11)

Pagans in seventh-century Arabia seem to have held that the jinn
were spirits related to God. This belief was denounced in the
Koran (VI, 100):

> Yet they ascribe to God, as associates, the
> jinn, though he created them; and they impute
> to Him sons and daughters without any knowledge.

Subsequently, jinn in fiction borrowed aspects and powers both
from the demons of late antiquity and from the Indian pantheon.

Some quite specialized types of jinn and monster are noticed in
medieval Arab treatises. The *udar*, a spirit which raped men in the
desert and left them with worm-infested anuses, is a homosexual
ghoul. The *atra* is a devil which sends men to sleep during their
prayers by pissing in their ears. The *qutrub* is the Arab werewolf. In
popular belief the werewolf was a man or a woman who was
transformed into a beast by night and who fed upon corpses.
However, the great tenth-century physician al-Razi regarded
lycanthropy as mental disorder. The victims of this affliction were
melancholic, hollow-eyed, solitary folk who liked the night and
cemeteries.[41] Kabikaj was the name of the jinn in charge of
insects. Scribes sometimes wrote his name on their manuscripts to
protect them from being eaten by worms. A *nasnas* is described by
Lane as being 'half a human being; having half a head, half a
body, one arm, and one leg, with which it hops with much
agility'. In 'The Story of the Sage and the Scholar', the sage

magically applies kohl (antimony, used for eye make-up) to one of the young man's eyes and turns the young man into a *nasnas*. A *diw* was a Persian spirit of evil and darkness. A *peri*, as in the story of 'Prince Ahmad and the Fairy Peri-Banu', is a beautiful female spirit and part of Persian mythology. They are usually virtuous and therefore persecuted by the *diws*. When the *diws* and *peris* feature in the *Nights*, they are to all intents and purposes identical with the jinn.

The *rukh* in Arab folklore was a bird of vast dimensions, very similar to the equally vast and mythical Persian *simurgh*. It was capable of carrying men and even elephants in its claws. The concept probably derives from images of the Indian garuda, the half-vulture, half-man, which is shown carrying Vishnu in Indian iconography. According to a cryptic tradition in Turkish folklore, the *rukh* was a bird with a name, but no body. The *rukh* appears in 'Abd al-Rahman the Maghribi's Story of the Rukh' and again in 'The Second Voyage of Sinbad'. To some extent, stories about this bird played on the wonder of scale. Abd al-Rahman the Maghribi described the *rukh*'s egg as being a great white dome one hundred cubits long. In part, however, stories such as the one in which Sinbad is carried by the bird into the Valley of Diamonds are fantasies about the possibility of human flight; and, together with the flying carpet and the Ebony Horse, the *rukh* must be conceded a role in the imaginative prehistory of aviation. Indeed, despite the technological naïvety of the wonders of the *Nights*, some of its stories must be included in the canon of proto-science fiction.

Coleridge, reflecting on childhood origins of his own poetic imagination, observed that 'from my early reading of Faery Tales, and Genii etc. etc. – my mind had been habituated *to the Vast*'. The fairy tale shares this imagination-enlarging function with science fiction, or speculative fantasy; for fantastic voyages, distortions of time and space, alien beings, strange technologies, alternative societies, post-holocaust societies and imaginary histories, all of which are the stock-in-trade of modern science fiction, can all be found in the *Nights*. 'As one knows,' remarks the cultural essayist Gilbert Adair (perhaps a little overconfidently),

science fiction bears exactly the same relation to the future, or to any of the planet's foreseeable futures as fairy-tales do to the (crypto-medieval) past. In both genres, for instance, animals (or robots and aliens) have been invested with the at present exclusively human attributes of rational thought and speech; the control systems, laser rays, microchips and ultrasounds of science fiction – the whole dazzling cascade of what might be called (after Dufy) *la fée electronique* – constitute a vertiginous new alchemy, a Faustian near-infinite fund of knowledge and power; and one immediately recognizes in both the same narrative structures, the same Manichaean confrontations, the same elemental themes of apprenticeship, quest and redemption.[42]

Brian Stableford (in *The Encyclopedia of Science Fiction*) has put forward the claims of Mary Shelley's *Frankenstein* (1818) to be the first true work of science fiction, because it is the first to be clear on the distinction between science and magic, and the first to be cast in the form of the novel.[43] Although one must respect the purist's insistence that there could be no true genre of science fiction until Mary Shelley, Edgar Allan Poe and Jules Verne had established the ground rules of the genre, nevertheless the *Nights* and science fiction stories treat of similar themes, draw on similar techniques and share common aims. The medieval audience of wonder-tales and the modern readers of science fiction, who marvel at the scale and complexity of the universe and who speculate about how it might be otherwise, share a state of mind.

The books on *aja'ib*, or marvels, constituted a distinct genre in medieval Islamic literature.[44] The compilers of works on *aja'ib* collected tales about the marvels of Greek, Roman, Pharaonic and Sassanian antiquity. They recorded uncanny meteorological phenomena (such as downpours of blood) and the birth of monsters (such as three-headed calves). They collected details of bizarre coincidences and they described the marvels of the known universe, mingling truth and fable in their accounts of fantastic journeys. In their accounts of exotic parts of the world, Arab writers drew directly or indirectly on a pre-existing classical literature of marvels, by authors such as Lucian, Ctesias and Pseudo-Callisthenes, dealing with the wonders of India and the exploits of Alexander. (Those mendacious travellers Marco Polo and John de Mandeville also drew on this sort of material.)

The genre of the fantastic voyage goes back at least to the ancient Sumerian *Epic of Gilgamesh*. Ancient and pre-modern tales of fantastic journeys tended to be open or covert accounts of the voyage of the soul into the afterlife. In the *Nights* in 'The Adventures of Bulukiya' (which shows traces of deriving ultimately from the *Gilgamesh* epic), this aspect of the fantastic voyage is most evident.[45] Wonder is piled upon wonder. Bulukiya, in his quest for the herb of immortality, encounters speaking serpents as big as camels, captures the Queen of the Serpents, walks upon the surface of the sea, discovers the tomb of Solomon, visits strange and paradisal islands, discovers trees which bear clusters of human heads and birds on their branches as well as trees which laugh, watches mermaids sporting, enters the Garden of Eden and is expelled from it by a giant, has an audience with the King of the Jinn and is instructed by the latter as to the nature of the innumerable hells of Allah. In the least of these hells, Jahannam, there are 1,000 mountains of fire, on each mountain 70,000 cities of fire, in each city 70,000 castles of fire, in each castle 70,000 houses of fire, in each house 70,000 couches of fire and on each couch 70,000 manners of torment. This hellish image of infinity prefigures the vast imagination-stretching landscapes of galactic science fiction. Bulukiya is instructed further on the scale and structure of the cosmos when he encounters a vast angel seated on the peak of the cosmic mountain of Kaf. This angel instructs Bulukiya on the multiplicity of worlds beyond the one which Bulukiya knows (and which is encompassed within Mount Kaf). There are forty worlds, each more than forty times the size of

Bulukiya's world, lying beyond Mount Kaf, and each with its own strange inhabitants, colours and guardian angels. But the scale of these worlds is as nothing compared with the size of the angel who supports these worlds, and this angel stands on a rock which is supported by a bull which stands on a fish which swims in a mighty ocean. Bulukiya is allowed to see the fish, whose head takes three days to pass before his eyes. But the fish is small compared to the ocean, and the ocean is above an abyss of air which is above a realm of fire, and beneath all that is the cosmic serpent which can swallow up all that is above it and not notice the difference. The medieval Muslim conceived himself to be living in a universe that was vertiginous in its vastness. The grandeur of the vision of Bulukiya is the quintessence of the *aja'ib*, the astounding.

There is no space here to pursue the subject much further, but Bulukiya's cosmic journey can be compared to Islamic and gnostic speculations about alien life forms and life on other planets. For example, in the eleventh-century philosophical fantasy *Salaman wa-Absal* by Ibn Sina (better known in the West as Avicenna), Absal undertakes a journey across vast deserts and strange seas, like Bulukiya. He encounters bizarre creatures such as 'humans' who have acquired the skins of quadrupeds and on whom vegetation grows. However, Absal travels further than Bulukiya, and the reader of *Salaman wa-Absal* is introduced to the alien customs and appearances of the inhabitants of the moon and other planets. Absal even travels to the stars, to encounter the inhabitants of the zodiacal cities.[46]

While 'Sinbad' certainly draws on the (somewhat garbled) reports of real Arab seafarers in the Indian Ocean, the documentary element in the voyages of Sinbad should not be exaggerated.[47] Captain Buzurg, in his tenth-century compilation *The Book of the Wonders of India*, claimed that nine-tenths of the world's wonders were in the East. In his book Captain Buzurg did draw on real accounts by mariners and merchants of what they had seen in

India, China, Java and perhaps even Japan. However, the main impetus behind his and similar compilations was to collect instances of the *aja'ib*, so literary works were plundered to pad out these collections with tales of Amazon islands, cannibal societies, dog-headed men and human-headed trees. The further the traveller ventured from the heartlands of Islam, the stranger things became, until ultimately one came to the outermost ocean, the Green Sea. Nothing lives on or in this sea. No one has sailed in its waters. It is dark and stinking and extends for ever.

Not all science fiction takes place in space. The novels of Jules Verne and Edgar Rice Burroughs, for example, fantasized about the possibility of life under water. In this they were anticipated by the storytellers of the *Nights*. In 'Julnar the Sea-Born', King Shahriman learns from the mermaid Julnar about people who live underwater (the magic power of Solomon's seal-ring allows them to do so). Unfortunately no details are given of underwater society. However, this deficiency is remedied in 'Abdullah the Fisherman and Abdullah the Merman', where we find an alterna-tive society portrayed. It is a utopia of sorts. Utopias are rare in Islamic fiction and non-fiction. After all, it was well known that rules and norms of the ideal society had been laid down in the Koran and its details elaborated in the sayings and practice of the Prophet Muhammad, and it was commonly held that strict observ-ance of Islamic law and custom would be sufficient to bring about the ideal society. It is true that the tenth-century Arab philosopher al-Farabi, in his *Fi Mabadi ara ahl al-Madinat al-Fadila* ('On the Principles of the Views of the Inhabitants of the Good City'), set out the broad plan of an ideal society. Plato and the Koran were made to harmonize in a city-state directed by virtuous philosophers. (In Islamic thinking the ideal society is an urban one.) But the details of al-Farabi's ideal city were not fleshed out.[48]

However, the *Nights* story of 'Abdullah the Fisherman and Abdullah the Merman' does attempt to present an alternative society in some detail. At the invitation of Abdullah the Merman, Abdullah the Fisherman leaves his poor land to visit the seas of plenty. Having anointed his body with a certain miraculous fish oil, he finds that he is able to breathe underwater. Underwater society offers an inverted reflection of society on land. Everything is different; there is no buying and selling; jewels are commonplace baubles; people go about naked, clothes being unknown among them; free love is the rule; food is eaten raw; one rejoices at funerals. Or, rather, almost everything is different, for some of the merpeople are Muslims, just like Abdullah the Fisherman. However, the story is not really setting out a political programme. It offers something that is wonderful because it is strange, not something that is wonderful because it is a blueprint for the ideal of life in society. The primitive communism of submarine society is merely strange – and laughable. The same sort of point can be made about the Amazon societies which feature so frequently in the *Nights*. Stories about communities dominated by women were beguiling absurdities, but, even so, the descriptions of Amazon societies were not intended as satires on feminism. There was no feminism to satirize.

Predictions of a holocaust and speculations about what a post-holocaust society will be like have featured prominently in twentieth-century science fiction. Science fiction's imaginary societies are (usually) set in the future. In the *Nights*, however, they are located in the past, and the authors of its stories speculated about the lost technology of the ancients, vanished civilizations and the catastrophes which had overwhelmed them. The Koran abounds with examples of communities which went astray and which God destroyed, and this same theme is alluded to in the opening exordium of the *Nights* itself, in which praise is offered to God who 'destroyed the race of Thamud, Ad and Pharaoh of the vast domain'. The *Nights* offers a warning to those who will be instructed. Its audience should consider the hubris of those who sought to dwell in Iram of the Columns. King Shaddad spent 500 years building this city, but when he prepared to enter it, 'the Cry of Wrath' of the Angel of Death slew him and all his following. Or they should consider the city of Labtayt, whose king defied the ancient interdiction and opened the tower of treasures, thereby bringing about the sack of his city by the Arabs. Or the City of Brass, with its petrified inhabitants and their mummified queen (given a ghastly semblance of life by the quicksilver in her eye sockets). Or, in the cycle of 'The Porter and the Three Ladies of Baghdad', in 'The Tale of the First Lady', the city of fire-worshippers, who, all save one, failed to heed the mighty and invisible voice, did not turn to God and consequently were turned to stone. Such marvels are also warnings to those who would reflect, and a sense of wonderment is the beginning of philosophy.

9

Formal Readings

=====

For he had been as instructive as Milton's 'affable archangel'; and with something of the archangelic manner he told her how he had undertaken to show (what indeed had been attempted before, but not with that thoroughness, justice of comparison, and effectiveness of arrangement at which Mr Casaubon aimed) that all the mythical systems or erratic mythical fragments in the world were corruptions of a tradition originally revealed. Having once mastered the true position and taken a firm footing there, the vast field of mythical constructions became intelligible, nay, luminous with the reflected light of correspondences. But to gather in this harvest of truth was no light or speedy work.

George Eliot, *Middlemarch*

Enchanted castles, hands beckoning from dimly lit doors, cannibalistic ghouls, talking fish, flying horses, troglodytic bandits, one-handed dervishes . . . the reader's first impression is likely to be of the immense diversity of the stories in the *Nights* and of the free-flowing imagination, or imaginations, which shaped them. But, after a while, the reader starts to notice things – such as how many of the heroes of the *Nights* are born to elderly couples who pray for a child, how often the hero will be told, 'Whatever you do, do not open that door' (but in vain, for he will certainly open it) or how often disasters or opportunities come in threes. In time, each story comes to resemble another story, and the reader begins to recognize the patterns and permutations. Fantasy has its rules. The imaginative universe of the Arab storyteller was subject to invisible constraints.

There are peculiar problems in studying a body of fiction which is part literature and part folklore and partaking of the characteristics of both written and oral culture. We really know nothing about the authors of the tales gathered together in the *Nights*; yet many of those tales have unmistakable literary qualities, and the use of language in them precludes unthinking discussion of them as if they were all anonymous, composite, orally generated items of folk culture. Uncertainty about the status of the *Nights* and ignorance of the milieu in which it was composed have constituted a barrier to serious study of its stories both by literary critics and by folklorists. Literary verdicts used to be vague and effusive. According to the Victorian essayist Leigh Hunt: 'The *Arabian Nights* appeal to the sympathy of mankind with the supernatural world, with the unknown and the hazardous, with the possible and the remote. It fetches out the marvellous included in our common-places.'[1] Similar comments were made by other men of letters, such as William Hazlitt, Walter Bagehot and G.K. Chesterton. They tended to stress the wildness of these oriental stories, contrasting their exoticism with the drab realities of Europe in the age of the railway and the gas lamp.

Besides publishing fairy stories, the brothers Jacob and Wilhelm Grimm also pioneered the serious study of folklore in the early nineteenth century. The first folklore studies in Germany and France tended to be closely linked with philology and with theories about the Aryan sources of European languages and mythologies. Max Müller argued that mythology was 'a disease of language' and that folk-tales were the detritus of ancient myths, especially solar myths. The earliest folklorists to study the *Nights* seriously were chiefly concerned to trace the origins of its tales, and, as we have already seen, Müller's ideas strongly influenced Benfey and Cosquin in their attempts to find Indian (and therefore Aryan) sources for the *Nights*' tales. In Britain, however, the word 'folklore' developed under the overlapping shadows of antiquarianism and classical studies. (The term 'Folk Lore' was first used by W.J. Thoms, an editor of English medieval texts, in an article in

the *Athenaeum* in 1846.) Continental theories about diffusionism
and folklore as the degenerate descendant of myth were attacked
by Andrew Lang (1844–1912). A Scottish man of letters, student
of mythology and expert on the Homeric epics, Lang was able to
point to potential sources for fairy tales and other items of folklore
in the cultures of ancient Greece and Egypt. He also demolished
the solar mythology theories of Müller and his school. Lang is
chiefly known today for *The Blue Fairy Book* (1893) and its
variously coloured successors. Lang also produced an edition of
the *Nights* in 1898, based on Galland, but heavily and clumsily
expurgated for its destined juvenile audience. Lang supported
himself by his writing, and his edition of the *Nights*, like so many
others, was produced to make money. More generally, folklore
studies in the English-speaking world have until quite recent times
been carried out by literary gentlemen and Sunday historians, and
characterized by amateurism. Rituals, ballads, stories and jokes
were unsystematically collected and recorded and then unsystematically compared with one another.

It was in nineteenth-century Finland that serious work on the
classification of story-types began. Finland was the first country in
the world to have a society devoted to its national folklore.
National identity in Finland was closely identified with the national
epic, the *Kalevala* (a collection of songs about the descendants of
the legendary hero Kaleva) and more generally with Finland's
heritage of folklore. In the nineteenth century a vast mass of folk
material was collected and classified by Elias Lönnrot and others.
Taking the individual story as a unity, practitioners of what was
known as the historic-geographic method sought to register the
story's first appearance in different regions, its regional variations
and sub-types, and the basic elements which came together to
form it. Many Finnish scholars shared Lang's unhappiness with
the tendency of Benfey and others to trace every story back to
some hypothetical origin in India. However, the Finnish folklorists shared the diffusionists' preoccupation with discovering the

starting-places of stories. Antti Aarne (1867–1925) assembled a vast mass of tales, classified them in some sort of rough-and-ready order and assigned each item a number. His *Verzeichnis der Märchentypen* (1911) was a systematic catalogue of mainly Finnish items, but he included many references to parallel and earlier versions of the Finnish stories from Russia, Scandinavia, Germany and elsewhere. Subsequent revisions of the work after Aarne's death by the American folklorist Stith Thompson considerably expanded the scope of what is now known as *The Types of the Folktale*.[2] Items from all over Europe and India are included, and under some headings cross-references are occasionally made to African, North American Indian and Arab folklore, as well as reference to literary treatments of folklore themes by novelists or poets. However, though there is some overlap between Arab popular literature and the European folk-tale, Aarne's story-type classification was designed to trace relationships of borrowing and descent within European folklore. It was not designed to accommodate works of Arab literature.

A 'story-type' was defined by Stith Thompson as 'a narrative capable of maintaining an independent existence in tradition'. This is in contradistinction to a motif, which is 'any one of the parts into which an item of folklore can be analysed'. Thompson subsequently went on to extend the scope of the Finnish school's project by producing *The Motif-Index* (1932–6). This differed from the story-type index in that it was global in its coverage and also in that it regularly made reference to literary works such as Aesop's *Fables*, the *Katha Sarit Sagara* and the *Nights*. Unlike the story-type classification, the way the motif-index was compiled did not carry the built-in presupposition that any or all the items listed under a particular heading were genetically related. The motif-index just listed motifs in a sort of logical order, loosely analogous to the Dewey decimal system of library classification or to Roget's *Thesaurus*. *The Motif-Index* is an omnium gatherum in which magical and mythical people and things, marvels, riddles and taboo activities are all assigned numbers. For example, section B is devoted to animals, B 0–99 to mythical animals, B 40 to bird-beasts; B 41.2 is the number of the flying horse. Under this heading we find reference, of course, to 'The Tale of the Ebony Horse' in Burton's edition of the *Nights*, but there are also references to flying horses in Sanskrit, Indo-Chinese, German and Norse folklore.

(It would be pleasant if something like the *The Motif-Index* existed for the modern novel. Then we could look up entries like 'N.P. (novel plot) Type A 493 Middle-aged adultery, 493a adultery of successful middle-aged man in Hampstead . . . see John Braine, Margaret Drabble . . .' But, alas, this sort of formal classification is really easier to apply to folklore than to the modern novel, for the anonymous folk-tale, unlike the novels of Henry James or John Fowles, does not normally seek to surprise or disappoint expectations, but to match them. Predictability and lack of ambiguity are even more important to the folk-tale than they are to television soap operas.)

However, returning to the story-type and motif-indices as they actually exist, their relevance to the study of the *Nights* is limited. First, the *Nights* is, at best, only partly a collection of folk-tales. It is to a significant extent a deliberate literary composition, drawing on other, older literary compositions. Secondly, the *Nights* was compiled in the Semitic culture area, and, as has been noted, Aarne's and Thompson's typology of stories was not intended to be used for the study of Semitic folklore. (Hasan El-Shamy in his *Folktales of Egypt* (1980) did try to assign story-type and motif numbers to his material whenever possible, but he commented that the 'type index is, however, seriously limited with regard to the treatment of Arabic and Berber folk-tales and especially Egyptian tales'.)[3] Moreover, other, more general and theoretical objections to the Aarne–Thompson approach have been raised by students of folklore. Some have queried aspects of the classificatory layout; others have gone further and challenged its underlying assumptions. For sure, one story may be a little like another story,

but it will also be a little different. If one is going to adopt a
comparative method, then it may be more important to focus on
fundamental differences than on superficial likenesses (and,
incidentally, it is not easy to see how one's understanding of
anything is advanced by putting the eight-legged Norse flying
horse Sleipnir in the same category as the Arabian Ebony Horse).

An earlier attempt to produce a motif-index by Arthur
Christensen, a specialist in Persian legends and literature, was
judged unsatisfactory by most critics in the field; but his *Motif et
thème: Plan d'un dictionnaire des motifs des contes* (1925) served as the
model for Nikita Elisséeff's *Thèmes et motifs des Mille et une nuits:
Essai de classification* (1949), in which a fairly arbitrary selection of
themes, motifs and epic accessories from the *Nights* was listed
alphabetically in two tables. A motif was an element which
constituted a complete episode in its own right within a story,
such as a shipwreck or a fight with a jinn. A theme was the
fundamental idea expressed by a motif. An epic accessory was an
object made use of in the story, such as a flying horse or a sword.
While Elisséeff's index does little to help one understand the
Nights, it can be useful in locating stories or incidents within those
stories.

Although the works of Aarne, Thompson and Christensen went
some way towards satisfying the felt need to organize this vast
mass of material, theirs was taxonomical work, and they made
little attempt to study the deep, fiction–generating mechanisms
and genre constraints or, finally, to formulate general rules deduc-
ible from the story lore. The criticisms of the taxonomic approach
made by the Russian formalist folklore expert Vladimir Propp are
of particular interest. In *Morfologija Skazki* ('The Morphology of
the Folktale'), which was published in 1928, Propp criticized the
arbitrariness of the categories in *The Types of the Folktale*, and
criticized also the frequent confusion of story and motif found in
its listings.[4] Preconceived categories had been imposed on the
folklore materials from outside, rather than being derived from

close study of the materials themselves. Propp argued that arbitrary distinctions were often made between stories that were essentially the same, on the basis of trivial external features. He also wondered why tales about animals were treated as if they were in a separate category from ordinary tales. Should a tale about a wonderful talking animal be treated as an animal tale or a wonder-tale? Aarne's categories were perhaps useful for reference, but they were not useful to think with.

Propp himself took a very different approach to his study of Russian folk-tales. He took as the basis for his research the *Narodnya Russkye Skazki* (1855–64), a collection of over 600 Russian folk-tales made by the great ethnographer Alexander Nicolaevich Afnasyev, and within Afnasyev's collection those stories which could be classified as wonder-tales. Propp aimed to put the study of folk-tales on a scientific basis and to become the Linnaeus or the Cuvier of these narratives. He held that the quest for the 'teeth' or 'vertebrae' of stories was the necessary precondition for the development of a soundly based theory of the origins of stories. Propp believed in the primacy of myth, that is, he believed that the folk-tales he studied were the distorted and degenerate descendants of earlier pagan myths and rites. In this, Propp had been influenced by the novelist and poet Goethe's strange attempt to develop a system of botanical morphology, based on analogical reasoning. Goethe hoped to demonstrate that there was once an *Urpflanze*, a primal plant of which all later plants were degenerate descendants. It can be seen that Goethe's bizarre taxonomy gave rise to a sort of Darwinism in reverse.

Propp used as his working sample a batch of Russian folk-tales (one hundred of them) which all fell between numbers 300 and 749 in Aarne and Thompson's *Types of the Folktale* – that is, they were marvel-tales, folk-tales which involved magic or the supernatural. The delimitation is important. Propp did not set out to cover animal tales, religious tales, romantic tales, jokes and anecdotes or formulaic tales, though these too are part of folklore (and for that matter find their place in the *Nights*).

In Propp's system, heroes, villains, epic accessories, settings and themes are merely external features of the wonder-story, and study of external features is of no assistance in understanding the true nature of the wonder-story. It is of little importance whether the villain has one or three heads, whether the action of the story takes place under water or up in the air, or whether the story features a house which walks about on chicken's legs. Rather, the story's functions are what matter and they provide the story with its vertebrae. There are thirty-one possible functions in the Russian marvel-tale. There is no space here to discuss all of them or even list them, but they begin: (1) one member of the family leaves home; (2) the hero encounters a ban; (3) he breaks the ban or commits a transgression; (4) the villain makes an attempt at reconnaissance; and so on. The list of functions ends with the hero marrying and coming to the throne. Not only were there a limited number of functions, but there were a limited number of ways that one function could be linked with another. For all their superficial wildness, the plots of wonder-stories developed in an ordered progression. Functions were what carried a story on from its beginning to its end. A function's only purpose for existence was to take a story to its conclusion.

Then, instead of characters, Propp preferred to think of spheres of action. A 'sphere of action' was likely to be a person, though it could be an animal or a thing. There were seven basic spheres of action: (1) the hero, (2) the false hero, (3) the aggressor, (4) the donator, (5) the sender, (6) the auxiliary, (7) the princess. Here one may query the means by which Propp has arrived at his lucky number of seven. Why distinguish between the aggressor and the false hero? Are the donator and the sender always different? It may also be objected that Propp's method privileges plot and devalues the inventiveness of imagery and dialogue. This formalistic reductiveness has its attractions, but, if plot is as predictable as Propp makes it out to be, then what can possibly be the pleasure in listening to the story?

Be that as it may, combining spheres of action and functions, it is possible, according to Propp, to set out the development of the marvel-tale in a kind of algebraic notation. Propp believed that 'All fairy tales are uniform in their structure.' The general pattern of all Russian wonder-stories is the move from equilibrium to adventure or instability and then back again to equilibrium. Propp's views on the fairy tale seem to have been shared by the film director Pier Paolo Pasolini, who, talking about the stories in the *Nights*, remarked that each tale begins with the appearance of anomaly and ends when that anomaly and any subsequent anomalies have been removed and we return 'to the happy somnolence of everyday life'.[5] Propp's views have been influential on a number of film critics who have used Proppian ideas about functions and spheres of action to bring out the underlying meaning of the story-lines of such films as *Kiss Me Deadly* and *Sunset Boulevard*.[6] Films apart, Alan Dundes has shown how Propp's categories could be used to study children's games as well as North American Indian legends.[7] Proppian analysis also lends itself easily to analysis of certain kinds of literary fiction, even when there is nothing supernatural in them. For example, in Robert Louis Stevenson's *Treasure Island*, Jim Hawkins is the hero, Long John Silver is the aggressor, Billy Bones is the donator, Benn Gunn is a helper. When Blind Pew comes after Billy Bones's map, that is f(unction) 4 (i.e. the villain tries to obtain information); when Hawkins sets sail for Treasure Island, that is f. 11 (the hero leaves home); and so on.

Propp's typology fits some *Nights* tales quite well. In *Sept contes des Mille et une nuits* (1981), the French Arabist André Miquel has shown that 'Abu Muhammad Hight Lazy Bones' is indeed an Arab tale of wonder which conforms to the pattern detected by Propp in the Russian ones. It begins with a lack (Zubaydah's need for a jewel) and proceeds through various functions before being brought to an end when the transgression has been healed, the villain punished, and the hero has returned home with his bride.

Moving on to 'Abu'l-Husn and his Slave-Girl Tawaddud', Miquel observed that, in its very broadest outlines, this story also conformed to Propp's structure, concluding with a happy marriage as the final function, but that this way of looking at the story concealed the real weight of tale as a didactic exposé of medieval Islamic scientific knowledge. Again, the first but not the second part of 'Abdullah the Fisherman and Abdullah the Merman' obeys Propp's rules. The second part of the story is full of marvels certainly, but it entirely fails to fit a structure of lack, damage or misdeed, and ultimate reparation. In a separate study, *Un conte des Mille et une nuits: Ajib et Gharib* (1977), André Miquel analysed the plot of this lengthy wonder-story and found that it did broadly obey Proppian rules, beginning with a misdeed (Ajib ordering the murder of Gharib's future mother) and continuing through the intermediate functions to end with a restoration to the throne and a marriage (that of Gharib); then a second round of Gharib's adventures led into a second cycle of Proppian functions. However, the story was more complex than any studied by Propp, and while it seems to conform in broad outline to Propp's typology of the wonder-tale, somehow the characterization is unsatisfactory.

David Pinault, in *Story-Telling Techniques in the Arabian Nights* (1992), notes that Muhammad's tale in the 'The Mock Caliph' follows precisely 'one of the traditional patterns examined by Vladimir Propp in his *Morphology of the Folktale*: interdiction / the interdiction violated / bodily injury-mutilation / expulsion / the misfortune or lack made known'. The *Nights* story runs like this: Muhammad is made to swear not to stir from his bed by his mistress Dunya / but Muhammad, summoned by Harun al-Rashid's wife Zubaydah, leaves the house / when Dunya discoves his disobedience she has him savagely beaten / and she casts him out of her house / Muhammad tells his tale to Harun al-Rashid.[8]

However, a dot-and-pick application of Propp to the *Nights* is not really very satisfactory. Some *Nights* tales resemble Russian stories, but others do not, and Propp's restricted range of functions and spheres of action cannot accommodate them. What about heroines who take active parts, even leading parts, in the *Nights* stories in which they function, among them Miriam the Girdle Girl, Marjana and Zumurrud? Another objection which may restrict the usefulness of Propp's interpretative system is that apparently all the Russian fairy tales featured in his sample end happily. This is not the case in the *Nights*. For example, the tales of the first, second and third dervishes are surely tales of wonder and magic, but they all end unhappily. In these stories, there is no return home, no happy marriage, no restitution of a lack: quite the contrary, the bearers of these stories are celibate mendicants, all of whom have lost an eye.

Propp's categories do not work for all types of story, nor were they intended to. Propp formulated his categories for a restricted range of Russian folklore material, and critics have pointed out that even within the range of the Russian marvel-tale there are all sorts of plots which do not conform to Propp's structural rules and are difficult to register in his symbolic notation. Nevertheless, literary theorists of a formalist or structuralist persuasion were attracted by the way Propp set about his task, and some were determined to apply his insights in broader literary fields. Attempts have been made in France, particularly by structuralists like Algirdas Greimas and Claude Bremond, as well as by the Bulgarian Tzvetan Todorov, to refine or extend Propp's categories.[9] They are fascinating if rather abstruse enterprises. Occasionally they make use of the stories of the *Nights* as testing grounds for their theories.

Claude Bremond, in his *Logique du récit* (1973), attempted to simplify Propp's categories and to apply them to, among other types of narrative, the stories of the *Nights*. Bremond considered that Propp's thirty-one plot functions were excessive and he substituted pivotal functions, points where a plot could go off in a variety of directions. Bremond also replaced Propp's seven spheres of action with agents, patients, influencers, ameliorators and beneficiaries. Bremond used pivotal functions and various types of active and passive figures, as well as moderators, to draw up abstract-looking plots, all numbered like propositions in Wittgenstein's *Tractatus*. Thus II.1.3.4 is 'Satisfaction or dissatisfaction experienced by the agent who judges himself to have succeeded in his task or failed in it'. One of the examples here is a robber in Galland's version of 'Ali Baba'. This robber tried to leave a mark of identification on Ali Baba's house, but he was outwitted by Marjana and he consequently submitted to execution by one of his fellow robbers. Bremond's methodology can be used to produce incredibly complicated diagrams of the plots of stories. However, it is not clear what else one can do with it. His pivotal functions allow so much flexibility that anything becomes possible, and Propp's 'vertebrae' seem to have been dissolved into jelly.

Tzvetan Todorov took a different approach. In both the *Grammaire du Decameron* and *The Fantastic*, Todorov sought to provide a generative grammar for restricted literary genres. The *Grammaire du Decameron* (1969) sets out to investigate the constituent parts of the 'language' of Boccaccio's stories. In the 'grammar' of storytelling, a 'noun' is a person or object in the story. A 'verb' is a form of action. Todorov posited three types of 'verb': first, change (a broad category including disguise/unmasking, attack/resistance, and so on); secondly, transgression; thirdly, punishment. 'Verbs' have modes – obligatory, optative, conditional and predictive. An 'adjective' is a state, quality or condition. Todorov's construing of the grammar of the *Decameron* led him to conclude that a large number of the tales dealt with unspoken codes of values or laws which were infringed by characters in the stories, but that these characters (often adulterers) commonly went unpunished. Thus Boccaccio's stories treated of the breakdown of the medieval moral code in fourteenth-century Italy; they were the harbingers of modern capitalist individualism.

It would be surprising if Todorov's conclusions regarding the *Decameron* were not relevant to the *Nights*, for here we are comparing like with like. Both are collections of tales, both have a frame story in which stories are told under the shadow of death, and both drew on folk-tale elements, while nevertheless giving them a literary form. In neither case were many, if any, of the stories invented by those who wrote them down. Moreover, as we have already seen, the *Decameron* and the *Nights* actually have a number of stories in common. It might also be argued that fourteenth-century Cairo and Florence belonged to a common Mediterranean culture area. However, in querying Todorov's thesis, one may object that, since some of Boccaccio's tales are essentially the same as those circulating in tenth-century Baghdad or seventh-century India, must we look for a disintegration of conventional morality in those times and places too?

Although Todorov has not attempted to produce a 'grammar' of the *Nights*, it is a text on which he has had a great deal of interest to say. In an important essay, 'Les Hommes-Récits', or 'Narrative Men' (published as an appendix in the *Grammaire du Decameron*),[10] he addressed himself to the 'thinness' of a certain type of fictional character and the lack of psychological depth in such works as the *Odyssey*, the *Decameron* and the *Nights*. Todorov argues that Sinbad the Sailor's personality cannot be separated from his story. He is a story-man. In the *Nights* (described by Todorov as a 'narrative machine'), all traits of character are immediately causal. We know that Sinbad loves to travel because he does travel; we know that he travels because he loves to travel. It is as if characters in the *Nights* only know who they are by seeing what they have done. In the naïve psychology of the *Nights*, motivation is directly wedded to action. The despotic sultan kills because he is cruel; he is cruel because he kills. Since personality is defined by action, it is natural that when a new character appears within a story, he establishes himself by telling his story (hence the embedding of tales which is so characteristic of the *Nights* and other story collections). People's stories are their lives, so it is entirely appropriate that again and again in the *Nights* they save their lives by telling stories.

Todorov's book *The Fantastic: A Structural Approach to a Literary Genre* (French version 1970) was an attempt to demarcate a genre and to discover its peculiar rules. Todorov wished to define the fantastic by its deep structure, rather than by its trappings – that is, not by ghosts, creaking castles, witches, jinn, magic rings, and so on. According to Todorov, fantastic tales are set in a world in which the laws of nature appear to be being broken. However, the reader is expected to ask himself if those laws are really being broken. Ambiguity is crucial to the fantastic story, and in the truest form of the fantastic tale, as in Henry James's *The Turn of the Screw*, the ambiguity is never resolved. (Are the children really being threatened by the ghost of Quint, or is the reader the victim of the governess's unreliable narration?) If a tale's ambiguity is resolved, then how it is resolved will determine whether a particular story is to be characterized as 'uncanny' or 'marvellous'. If at the end of the story we learn that no law of nature has actually been broken (for example, the ghosts were human impostors), then the story is uncanny. If, however, the laws of nature have been broken, then the story is marvellous.[11] Most of the fantastic tales in the *Nights* resolve themselves into marvel-tales. Wicked women turn out actually to have been transformed into dogs; Abdullah the Fisherman actually travels to the kingdom under the sea; and the Ebony Horse actually flies. The ambiguities characteristic of such writers as Cazotte, Potocki and Henry James are rarely present in the *Nights*. The stock-in-trade of the *Nights* is unambiguously the marvellous – a marvellous based on hyperbole (e.g. Sinbad and the great fish), on the exotic (e.g. Sinbad and the rhinoceros) and on the instrumental (e.g. the flying carpet).

Todorov's typology of the marvellous fits some stories well enough, but it is difficult to see how it fits, say, 'The Tale of the Hunchback', 'The Sleeper and the Wakened' or 'The Mock Caliph'. At times it is hard not to feel that Todorov gets results not so much from his methodology as from close readings intelligently conducted – as in his account of 'The Second Dervish's

Tale'. In this story, which Todorov characterizes as a story about metamorphoses and magical powers, Todorov interprets the jinn who turns the man into a monkey as the personification of that man's bad luck.[12] Supernatural beings often stand in for fate or happenstance in the *Nights* stories.

Todorov's observations on the *Nights* and on other select works of European fantasy fiction are unfailingly interesting. However, only a certain kind of fantastic fiction is covered, and it is hard to see how Todorov's restrictive theory of the fantastic genre might be stretched to encompass such works as George Macdonald's *Phantastes*, Mervyn Peake's *Gormenghast* or Tolkien's *Lord of the Rings*. What is needed is a formal system that not only can account for what has been written within a particular genre, but also can indicate what the limits of the genre are and what can or cannot be written in that genre. At present, however, each attempt to give a formal or structuralist basis to the analysis of fiction seems to begin from a new starting-point.

The influence of both Propp and Todorov is evident in the Egyptian writer Ferial Ghazoul's *The Arabian Nights: A Structural Analysis* (1980). Ghazoul argues that the *Nights* stories have rules, but within those rules it is possible to construct an almost infinite variety of stories (just as English grammar has rules, but by following those rules it is possible to construct an almost infinite variety of meaningful sentences). The stories are generated by a series of binary oppositions and through *bricolage* (a term taken from another structuralist, Claude Lévi-Strauss, meaning a cunning use of those materials which come readily to hand). Thus, in the case of the *Nights*, the redactors made use of old bits and pieces of stories in order to make new ones. It is unfortunate that Ghazoul's penetrating book, which was published in Cairo, is not easy to come by in the West.

David Pinault, in *Story-Telling Techniques in the Arabian Nights* (1992), has taken quite a different approach. One of his main preoccupations has been the detection of oral characteristics in the

surviving literary versions of the *Nights*, and, like others who have
explored the frontiers between orality and literacy, he has drawn
on the work of Parry and Lord. From 1902 to 1935, Milman
Parry studied the texts of the *Iliad* and the *Odyssey*. After his
death, the work he began was completed by Albert B. Lord and
published as *The Singer of Tales* (1978). This book studied the
characteristic formulaic epithets used for the description of challenges, battles, ships, council meetings, men, and so on. Such
epithets, Parry and Lord argued, served the early Greek bards as
hand-me-down descriptions in the appropriate poetic metre. Such
formulaic adjectives and phrases, which were easy to memorize,
facilitated improvised performances by the bards. Parry and Lord
found confirmation of their Homeric thesis in twentieth-century
Yugoslavia. There they tape-recorded and analysed the performances of the illiterate Serbian *guslars*, or bards, and they also
interviewed the *guslars* themselves. In this manner they acquired
some understanding of how the bardic memory worked and how
the *guslars* could recite long epics without having recourse to a
text, by improvising (no two performances were exactly the same)
and by making use of ready-made phrases. Parry and Lord argued
that the two Homeric epics were formed by the stringing together
of shorter ballads, which were originally created by the extempore
performances of bards. Parry's and Lord's conclusions, though
widely accepted, have been challenged in some quarters. The
debate about the authorship of the Greek epics goes on, and, as a
character in Aldous Huxley's *Those Barren Leaves* facetiously
remarked: 'It's like the question of the authorship of the *Iliad* . . .
The author of that poem is either Homer or, if not Homer,
somebody else of the same name.'

Pinault argues, surely correctly, that in much the same way as
the Greek bards made use of ready-made epithets and phrases, so
those who composed the *Nights* drew on and rearranged pre-
existing material and that 'a system of formulae is also at work in
the *Arabian Nights*, though at the level of the story rather than the

epithet or phrase'. Thus plot clichés served as building blocks for the orally transmitted stories. In 'The Story of the Fisherman and the Demon', 'the redactor . . . is clearly playing with the motif of the benevolent wish-granting genie familiar to us from other tales in this genre'. However, in this particular example, the redactor reverses the convention by making the demon, or jinn, very unbenevolent indeed. Pinault goes on to examine 'The Tale of King Yunan and the Sage Duban', which is framed within 'The Story of the Fisherman and the Demon'. Evidently the two tales are thematically linked, for just as the fisherman is threatened by the demon, so the sage is threatened by the ungrateful king; but Pinault shows how the two tales are linked by the careful use of the *Leitsatz* (key sentence) 'Spare me, and God will spare you!' Even more effective is the use made of the *Leitsatz* 'It is a warning to whoso would be warned' in 'The City of Brass'. Pinault also studies the use made of the *Leitwort*, or 'leading-word', by the redactors of the *Nights*. A *Leitwort* in the *Nights* is a triliteral word root which in its various forms generates words with cognate meanings. (Most Arabic words are formed by additions to a root form consisting of three consonants.) Such linked key-words can be used repeatedly to create a stylistic effect or to emphasize a story's message. (The notion of *Leitwortstil*, which was first deployed in biblical criticism, has also been used to analyse sections of the Koran by John Wansbrough in his *The Sectarian Milieu* (1978).) Pinault shows how, in 'The Story of the Porter and the Three Ladies', 'The Tale of the First Lady' plays with the root form *s-kh-t*, with the repetitive use of *maskhut* (meaning a man turned to stone by the wrath of God or more generally metamorphosed) and *sukht* (meaning displeasure or divine wrath). In this and other studies, Pinault seeks to derive pattern from the stories, rather than impose pattern on them. The implication here is that the pattern was chosen by the storyteller rather than imposed as an unconscious constraint upon him.[13]

Although this chapter is mostly concerned with structuralist approaches to the *Nights*, this should not be taken as implying that only disciples of Propp, Todorov or Lévi-Strauss have had anything of value to say about the *Nights*. Mia Gerhardt, unlike David Pinault, is no Arabist. Nevertheless, her book *The Art of Story-Telling* (1963) is one of the best literary studies of the *Nights*, as well as being the most readable. It is possible to detect the influence on her of André Jolles's essay in structuralism, *Einfache Formen* (1969) (which offered a morphology of what Jolles held to be the universal simple forms of the legend, the saga, the myth, the riddle, the proverb, the case, the memoir, the tale and the joke). However, Gerhardt's study is not methodology-driven, nor is its approach seriously constrained by morphological considerations. Patrice Coussonet, in *Pensée mythique, idéologie et aspirations sociales dans un conte des Mille et une nuits: Le Récit d'Ali du Caire* (1989) and in a number of shorter studies, has undertaken close readings with a view to dating individual stories and thus placing them in a correct social and ideological context. Each story has to be taken on its own merits, for it may happen that an old version of an old tale may survive only in a relatively recent text (for example, in the Bulaq or Habicht recensions). Andras Hamori has produced a number of short but highly influential studies of individual stories, which serve to draw attention to aesthetic qualities (which are often neglected in the more austerely structuralist approaches to storytelling). Hamori's readings tend to discover hidden allegories in the stories. Finally, two general surveys, Suhayr al-Qalamawi's *Alf Layla wa-Layla* and Wiebke Walther's *Tausendundeine Nacht*, may also be recommended to readers of Arabic and German respectively.

Towards the end of *The Fantastic*, Todorov remarks that

psychoanalysis has replaced (and thereby made useless) the literature of the fantastic. There is no need today to resort to the devil in order to speak of an excessive sexual desire, and none to resort to vampires in order to designate the attraction exerted by corpses; psychoanalysis, and

the literature which is directly or indirectly inspired by it, deal with
these matters in undisguised forms.[14]

So far, publishers' lists hardly seem to confirm Todorov's thesis
that fantasy is obsolete, and the idea that fantastic literature has to
be useful may strike some readers as curious. Be that as it may,
psychoanalysts take the utilitarian function of fantasies for granted.
In *The Uses of Enchantment: The Meaning and Importance of Fairy
Tales* (1976), its Freudian author, Bruno Bettelheim, assumes that
children are the natural audience for fairy tales and he argues that
the function of fairy tales is to educate children for adulthood, by
dramatizing in disguised fictional forms the difficulties that they
will eventually encounter in life. Very often, the various protagonists in the stories personify different aspects of the human
personality. Fairy tales are interpreted by Bettelheim, as Freudians
interpret dreams, as having a latent as well as a manifest content.
Although most of his demonstration texts are taken from Grimm
and Perrault, tales from the *Nights* are also drawn into the argument. Thus in 'Sinbad the Seaman and Sinbad the Landsman', the
two Sinbads represent opposed parts of the human personality, for
Sinbad the Landsman embodies the ego and Sinbad the Seaman
the id, and, in a sense, Sinbad the Seaman's adventures are the
fantasies of the hard-working, landbound ego. (It could be said in
criticism here that Bettelheim gives too much prominence to
Sinbad the Landsman, for in the Arab story he features only as the
perfunctorily sketched-in audience for stories of his bolder
namesake.)

As Bettelheim reads the frame story of the *Nights*, Sheherazade
features as a medieval psychoanalyst and Shahriyar as her patient.
She tells him a great many stories to bring about his cure, because
'no single story can accomplish it, for our psychological problems
are much too complex and difficult of solution. Only a wide
variety of fairy tales could provide the impetus for such a catharsis.
It takes nearly three years of continued telling of fairy tales to free

the king of his deep depression, to achieve his cure.' Shahriyar is a disturbed id, while Sheherazade is a 'superego-dominated ego'. Thus the nightly encounter of Sheherazade and Shahriyar becomes a parable of integration.[15] Many have read the frame story in the same way as Bettelheim. However, nowhere in the medieval text is Shahriyar described as 'mad', and nowhere is it said that Sheherazade 'cured' him. If we attend to what the frame story seems to be saying, it is that Shahriyar's perception of the world in general and of women specifically is broadly speaking correct; for, if one excepts that paragon Sheherazade, it would appear that all women are indeed sexual betrayers. More generally, Bettelheim's interpretation of the stories as little dramas starring the id, ego and superego seems depressingly claustrophobic and reductive. It is hard to believe that the secrets of any medieval Arab tale can only be unlocked with the help of a twentieth-century western psychological theory.

Like the Freudians, the Jungians are eager when studying myths, legends and fairy tales, to elide the differences that separate one culture from another and one historical period from another. Thus Joseph Campbell, the Jungian mythographer, seems always to be more concerned with resemblances than differences. In his preface to a selection of stories from the *Nights* published in the United States, he remarked:

The battle scenes might comfortably appear in the *Morte d'Arthur;* the tales of enchanted castles, miraculous swords, talismanic trophies, and quest in the realms of the Jinn are reminiscent in numerous features of the favourites of Arthurian romance; the pattern of romantic love is in essence identical with that of twelfth-century Provence; the pious tales breathe the same odor of spiritual childhood and the misogynistic exempla the same monastic rancor as those of Christian Europe.

In his well-known study *The Hero with a Thousand Faces*, Campbell treated Qamar al-Zaman in 'The Tale of Kamar al-Zaman' as a hero conforming to the same essential type as Cuchulain, Moses

and Krishna. The Jungian formation apart, the influence of Propp
on Campbell is perhaps also detectable. The jinn who bring
Qamar al-Zaman and Budur together are recognizably helpers of
the Proppian sort. In Campbell's eyes, the encounter of the two
young people, engineered by the jinn, and Qamar al-Zaman's
reception of a ring from Budur signify Qamar al-Zaman's recognition of his unconscious deeps and of the equal validity of its truths
with those of ordinary waking life. 'Not everyone has a destiny:
only the hero who has plunged to touch it, and has come up again
– with a ring.'[16] (Pasolini's filmed treatment of the same story in
his *Arabian Nights* may be recommended as a counter-weight to
Campbell's unhealthily obsessive preoccupation with heroes and
heroic destiny.)[17]

Propp has remarked that the 'folktale, like any living thing, can
only generate forms that resemble itself'. Although the formalist
or structuralist approach strips a story of style, setting, characterization and imagery – of almost everything that might make it
pleasing to the reader – the dissection of the bare bones of plot
nevertheless may be useful in providing a framework for the study
of the generation and survival of stories. Moreover, Propp's regular
recourse to biological metaphors is striking. In a passage on the
survival of ideas, in *Le Hazard et la nécessité* (1970, translated 1971),
the French biologist Jacques Monod observed that ideas, like
biological organisms, 'tend to perpetuate their structures and to
multiply them; they too can fuse, recombine, segregate their
contents; in short they can evolve, and in this evolutionary selection
certainly plays an important role'.[18] It is a commonplace to speak
of the modern novel as 'evolving' from stories, such as those
found in the *Decameron* or *The Canterbury Tales*. But surely it is
time to move beyond the unconsidered use of the word 'evolving'
and time to speculate on the laws that might possibly govern the
evolution of literary forms.

Taking a lead from the geneticist Richard Dawkins, it may be
useful to think of the story as a 'selfish word-string', on the lines

of the selfish gene.[19] This word-string has no volition of its own, but it is nevertheless unconsciously engaged in a blind struggle for survival through replication. I use the word 'replicate' advisedly. Word-strings are carried from coffee-house to coffee-house, and from library to library. At present, however, many problems remain to be resolved. How does a story's 'generation' take place? And what is the unit of replication? Is it the story? Or is it the story-motif? In the latter case, would the story be merely a way for the story-motif to reproduce itself? If stories compete with one another for the attention of audiences and thus survival, what forms of adaptation will enhance a story's memorability and assist its transmission and survival? Stories must offer something to their human hosts in order to make the crucial leap from memory to memory or page to page. One way a story may commend itself to its host is if the host can make a living by telling it (and here Arab beggars' tales of legendary generosity are a particularly cogent case in point). Alternatively, a story may promote the survival of a group by promoting its cohesion and sense of common history (a saga like that of Omar bin al-Nu'uman might serve as an example). Two stories may link together in order to improve their chance of survival (as we have seen the 'weeping bitch' story-type link up with 'The Wife's Clever Response' to form 'The Tale of the Woman who Wanted to Deceive her Husband'). Similarly, by inserting themselves within a framing story, if the frame story survives, then the stories are likely to survive too. A number of quite dull and insipid tales thus survived under the umbrella of Sheherazade's narration. Stories have to adapt to the culture in which they find themselves (thus the specifically Indian features of tales taken from *Katha Sarit Sagara* – for example, Indian names and references to the Hindu pantheon – have been weeded out in the *Nights* versions). As in genetics proper, so in storytelling, error, or mutation, may occasionally enhance the viability of stories (for example, the error of transmission which caused Cinderella's fur slippers eventually to become glass ones).

The *Nights* story of 'Sinbad the Seaman and Sinbad the Lands-man' is a more complex and sophisticated tale than its (hypothetical) Pharaonic prototype, 'The Tale of the Shipwrecked Sailor'. It is plausible that blind word-strings, or stories, acquire more complex forms because these complex forms have more survival value in the complex societies of today in which old stories precariously circulate. By contrast, simpler forms, such as exempla, fables and anecdotal wisdom literature, are all but extinct in modern western society; and although the adventures of Aladdin have survived fairly well in modern popular consciousness, the story of Tawaddud with its heavy freight of Islamic lore and outdated scientific theory retains only a precarious place in the memories of a few academics. In the *Nights*, stories are the vehicle for saving lives – for example, the tales told by Sheherazade, or the tales told by the old men in order to save the life of the merchant who killed a jinn's son with a carelessly discarded date stone. In the *Nights*, knowledge of a story and the ability to tell it may assure the survival of an individual. Analogously it may be that in real life too knowledge of stories assists the survival of communities or of individuals within those communities. Monod himself believes that stories which reassure man about his destiny have a particular survival value. To engage in literary biology is, of course, only to play with a metaphor. Still, it is perhaps a fruitful metaphor.

10

Children of the Nights

From the eighteenth century onwards, translations of the *Nights* circulated so widely in Europe and America that to ask about its influence on western literature is a little like asking about the influence on western literature of that other great collection of oriental tales, the Bible. An answer to the latter question might include reference to *The Divine Comedy*, *The Private Memoirs and Confessions of a Justified Sinner*, *Middlemarch*, *Apologia pro Vita Sua*, *Anna Karenina*, *Joseph and his Brothers*, *Ben Hur* and *Boating for Beginners*, to suggest only a few obvious titles. In some cases, the Bible has been a stylistic influence. In others it has provided characters and props for a good yarn. In yet others, the authors' study of the text has set them moral and intellectual problems which they have then sought to resolve in fictional or poetic form. In countless cases, early and repeated exposure to the Bible has shaped the mentality and temperament of a writer. The Bible is so deeply embedded in western culture that there are many people today who, though they have never opened the book, still have an extensive knowledge of the Bible's teachings and stories. In the same way, people who have never sat down to read the *Nights* may know, or at least know of, the stories of Ali Baba, Aladdin and Sinbad. As Jorge Luis Borges (in characteristically paradoxical vein) observed of the *Nights*: 'It is a book so vast that it is not necessary to have read it.'[1] If one asks what was the influence of the *Nights* on western literature, then one is asking not for a single answer, but rather for a series of answers to a group of questions which relate to one another in complex ways.

Antoine Galland produced his translation of *Les Mille et une nuits* in the course of the years 1704–17. Even before his translation was completed, cheap versions and extracts from the early volumes were circulating in France and England. In France the instant success of Galland's work was marked by a rush of imitations and parodies. Thomas Simon Guellette (1683–1766) produced volumes of Tartar, Moghul and Chinese tales in mock-oriental vein. He even produced a collection of wholly bogus Peruvian tales. Popular at the time, they are rightly neglected now.[2]

Sex and satire were the staples of the pseudo-oriental story in the early eighteenth century. Anthony Hamilton (1646–1720), an Irish Cavalier and one of Charles II's courtiers, writing in French, produced such light fictions, which were highly acclaimed at the time. Hamilton's stories, which simultaneously imitate and mock his model, are characteristic examples of the impact of the *Nights* in the first few decades after their publication. Readers of the *Nights* in early-eighteenth-century France found in its pages a form of liberation, a flight from solemnity and a disregard of plausibility. *Histoire du Fleur d'Epine*, 'The Story of May-Flower', was written in parody of the *Nights* in a style which Hamilton claimed was 'more Arab than that of the Arabs'. In that work Sheherazade narrates a preposterously silly tale involving a questing sage, Pooh Pooh, as well as a musical mare, a luminous hat and a beautiful maiden who kills with a glance. Hamilton has Dunyazade criticize Sheherazade for the prolixity and confusion of her tale. (In Hamilton's case the reader may well feel that Dunyazade has right on her side.) Hamilton's *Les Quatre Facardins* was similarly silly. The four princes, who are all called Facardin (Facardin is Hamilton's rendering of the Arabic name Fakhr al-Din), attempt to give a coherent account of their magical and amorous adventures. They are not very successful, as their tales are regularly interrupted by other tales and only rarely concluded. The oriental touches in Hamilton's fabulous farrago are perfunctory, and Perrault's French fairy tales were at least as much the target of Hamilton's parody as were the stories of the *Nights*.[3]

The frivolous tone of Hamilton's stories was echoed in the pastiches of Crébillon *fils*. (His father, a weightier but dimmer figure, was also a writer.) Although he perversely worked as a government censor, Crébillon *fils* (1707–77) also specialized in the writing of erotic fictions. *Le Sopha* (1742) makes use of a frame story device and oriental settings. In the frame story, a sultan, whose grand passions are embroidery and patchwork, commands Amanzei, one of his courtiers, to entertain him with stories. The sultan works away at his patchwork and as he listens comments on Amanzei's tales. Amanzei has had a remarkable and lengthy past. He is able to recall previous lives, in particular a period when he was condemned to be incarnated as a series of sofas, until such time as he should bear the weight of two people consummating their love for the first time. Amanzei tells the sultan six stories of lovers of whose dalliances he has been an intimate witness and support. Crébillon's use of the oriental tale as a vehicle for a cynical and satirical presentation of the *amours* of contemporary libertines must have influenced Denis Diderot (1713–84). Diderot allegedly wrote *Les Bijoux indiscrets* (1748) in a fortnight for a bet, to show how easy it was to write a story in the manner of Crébillon. In Diderot's pornographic satire on the manners and pleasures of the French aristocracy, Cucufa, a genie, gives the sultan a magic ring which has the power to make his subjects' sexual organs speak and reveal what they have been up to. Hamilton, Crébillon and Diderot produced brittle fictions which made only trivial use of oriental settings, names and magical devices. The novelist's Orient was as yet only a playground and not to be taken seriously.

The deployment of oriental motifs in weightier moral tales was equally perfunctory. *Les Lettres persanes*, published by Montesquieu in 1721, is an epistolary novel in which the author uses the device of letters passing to and from two Persians travelling in Europe, Usbek and Rica, in order to expound his own views on religion, politics and law. Usbek's and Rica's accounts of the strange things they have seen in Europe alternate with letters from Persia giving an account of the increasingly tragic intrigues in Usbek's harem. Though later and dimmer readers may not always have realized this, Montesquieu was not attempting to present a serious picture of family life in Persia; the letters from the harem are really as much about France as the letters that are sent from France. However, to trap out his oriental harem, Montesquieu mainly made use of the seventeenth-century French narratives of travels in Persia by Chardin and Tavernier as sources for oriental matters. At the same time, when he presented contemporary France through the eyes of the Persians as a land of marvels and strange superstitions, Montesquieu seems to have been deliberately and playfully attempting to invest his own society with the illusory charms of one of the Arabian kingdoms, made popular by Galland's recently published translation. There is no evidence, however, that Montesquieu was an admirer of Galland's work, and the genuine oriental tales are criticized by Rica in the 137th letter for their tedium and implausibility: 'I am sure that you would not approve of an army being conjured out of the ground by a sorceress, or of another, a hundred thousand strong, being destroyed single-handed by the hero. However that is what our novels are like. The frequent repetition of these insipid adventures is boring, and the nonsensical miracles are repellent.'

Voltaire pretended to a similarly low opinion of the genuine oriental tale, though he was prepared to make use of its conventions for his own purposes. 'Enchanter of Eyes, Disturber of Hearts, Light of the Mind, I kiss not the dust from your feet, because you rarely walk, or walk only upon Iranian carpets or on roses.' This opening sentence of the dedicatory epistle to Zadig sets the light-hearted tone of his philosophic romance. Zadig ou la destinée (1748) was set in Babylon on the Euphrates in a vaguely pre-Islamic Orient. It tells of the adventures of the wise young man Zadig, of his quest for happiness and of the misfortunes he experiences through the fickleness of monarchs and of woman. Voltaire's fantasy is a satire on religious bigotry and contemporary mores, telling us much more about France in the age of the Enlightenment than it does about ancient Iraq, but it is above all a treatise in fictional form on the nature of chance and destiny. Zadig experiences the sudden reversals of fortune that are so frequently encountered by the heroes of the tales of the *Nights*. In the end, after many turns of fate and fortune and after having been instructed by an angel, Zadig concludes that, behind the appearance of chance and misfortune in the world, a divine providence does in fact rule over all things: 'there is no such thing as accident. All is either trial or punishment, reward or foresight.'⁴ However, the conclusion of *Zadig* is perhaps a little ambiguous; it was certainly provisional, and Voltaire was later ruthlessly to satirize providential explanations of evil and misfortune in his even more widely acclaimed philosophical romance, *Candide*.

Although Voltaire was steeped in the stories of the *Nights* (he claimed to have read them fourteen times) and though he lifted themes and motifs from them for use in several of his fictions, this did not prevent him from mocking the contemporary craze for them. In *Zadig* he has the Sultan Ouloug question the sultanas on their preference for such tales. '"How can you prefer stories," asked the wise Ouloug, "which have neither sense nor reason?" "But that is just why we do like them," replied the Sultanas.' Moreover, though Voltaire was perfectly familiar with Galland's tales, he was later to tell William Beckford that the chief inspiration for *Zadig* had come from the romances of Anthony Hamilton. In the hands of Hamilton, Diderot and numerous lesser figures, the mock-oriental tale had acquired a life of its own, more or less independent of its Arabian prototype.

It has been estimated that almost 700 romances in the oriental mode were published in France in the eighteenth century. Guellette, Hamilton, Crébillon and other French writers who wrote in this vein were all translated and eagerly read in eighteenth-century England, and Galland's rendering of the *Nights* was at least as

popular in England as in France.[5] An anonymous English translation of 'Aladdin' appeared, probably in 1708, and circulated as a
chap-book. More translations of selections from Galland followed
in chap-book form, and very soon English writers were engaged
in reworking, imitating and parodying the Arabian tales. It would
be a mistake, however, to regard *Les Mille et une nuits* as the only
source behind the mania for the Orient in France and England. A
taste for Galland and his imitators and parodists was only part of a
wider fashion for chinoiserie, turquerie, oriental silks and ceramics,
and architectural follies in the Egyptian or Chinese mode. The
increased consumption of opium in the eighteenth century seems
to have gone hand in hand with an interest in oriental imagery.
The translations of Sir William Jones (1746–96) from Hindu,
Persian and Arabic classics were widely read. The travel narratives
of Chardin, Tavernier, Tournefort, Sherley and Bernier were also
popular. The commercial and military ventures of Britain and
France in India stimulated an interest in Indo-Muslim culture.
Towards the very end of the century, in 1798, Bonaparte and the
French landed in Egypt, and, as Edward Said remarks, this 'inva-
sion was in many ways the very model of a truly scientific
appropriation of one culture by another'.[6]

  In general, English writers working in the oriental mode failed
to match the wit and the licentiousness of their French contemporaries.[7] Indeed, most English oriental tales tended to be leadenly
moral. Caliphs, princesses, jinn, calender dervishes and sorcerers
become fodder for what are mostly pompous and dreary sermons.
The essayist Joseph Addison (1672–1719) held the enlightened
view that every child should be encouraged to fantasize. However,
if one is to judge by his own retelling of tales from the *Nights*,
fantasy is strictly subservient to moral ends. In 'The Story of the
Graecian King and the Physician Douban', Addison strove to
civilize and Christianize his exotic materials, and as he remarked of
his version of 'Nuschar's Daydream': 'The virtue of compliance in
friendly discourse is very prettily illustrated by a little wild Arabian

tale' (only it is not so very wild in Addison's retelling). Addison's characteristic tone in his moral tales is politely sceptical, though certainly never to the point of questioning Christian truths. Indeed, his finest essay in the oriental genre, 'The Vision of Mirza', is an allegory of the Christian view of life. Though he claimed that this story, first published in the *Spectator*, was a translation from an eastern tale, the pretence was not very serious. In this grandiose allegory (which may remind some readers of the spectacular canvases of catastrophe painted by 'Mad' John Martin), Mirza looks down on the great bridge of life over which humanity must travel. Sooner or later, all who travel on the bridge lose their footing and fall, either to damnation on the rocks or to salvation in a current which carries them to the islands of the blessed. Mirza is told that he is looking on 'that Portion of Eternity which is called Time, measured out by the Sun, and reaching from the Beginning of the World to its Consummation'. Addison blends oriental fantasy with Christian preaching: '"Surely," said I, "man is but a shadow and a dream."'

Samuel Johnson's *Rasselas: Prince of Abyssinia* (1759) resembles Voltaire's *Zadig* in its use of a fabulous Orient as a field of philosophical enquiry. But its philosophical preoccupations are closer to Voltaire's other masterpiece, *Candide* (and curiously the two works were published within weeks of one another). In *Rasselas*, the eponymous Prince leaves the Happy Valley in Abyssinia, declaring that 'I shall long to see the miseries of the world, since the sight of them is necessary to happiness', and he embarks on a pilgrimage of enquiry into the meaning of life and a search for a lasting and worthwhile happiness. Johnson's melancholy temperament did not allow him to offer his readers a conclusive answer to Rasselas's enquiry. The heavy freight of moralizing and social satire in both Johnson and Voltaire is quite alien to the original Arabian tales. Johnson, like Voltaire, mocked what he perceived to be the lush ornateness of the Arabian originals. He had no real interest in Islam, the Middle East or Arab literature, but this did not stop him from pandering to the taste of the times and publishing separately sixteen oriental tales in the *Rambler* and the *Idler*, which were really sermons tricked out in oriental fancy dress.

It would seem that in the eighteenth century the English could not get enough of being preached at. Otherwise, it is hard to explain the success both of Addison's and Johnson's little tales and of Hawkesworth's rather longer *Almoran and Hamet* (1761). John Hawkesworth (1715–73), an essayist and journalist, was a friend of and collaborator with Johnson. Hawkesworth influenced Johnson, and vice versa. *Almoran and Hamet*, a Johnsonian parable about how true happiness may be found, is set in Persia.[8] Almoran is a vicious prince, and Hamet is his virtuous brother. Almoran is aided in his vile schemes by a jinn who presents him with a ring which allows him to change shape with anyone he thinks of. 'I will quench no wish that nature kindles in my bosom,' declares Almoran. The premise may be promising, but Hawkesworth throws away his opportunities. Almoran fails to deflower the blushfully virtuous Almeida, and the story turns into a dour lecture on the worthlessness of a quest for pleasure unrestrained by any considerations of morality. In the end the despotic Almoran is turned into a rock. He and the reader have learned their lessons.

Similarly boring, if improving, stuff was produced by many other hands – among them the Reverend James Ridley (*Tales of the Genii, or the Delightful Lessons of Horan, the Son of Asmar*, 1764), Hugh Kelly (*Orasmin and Elmira*, 1767) and Maria Edgeworth ('Murad the Unlucky', 1804). Though tedious, such works were popular at the time. Charles Dickens, for example, loved Ridley's stories as a child, making several allusions to them in later novels. Although Frances Sheridan's *Nourjahad* (1767) is a moral tale in the same exasperating genre, it is redeemed by the strangeness and originality of its conceit. Nourjahad is promised immortality and almost limitless riches by his guardian genius (or jinn), but at the same time he is told that these gifts carry with them a penalty.

The genius warns him that he will sometimes and without warning fall asleep for long periods of time – for several years or decades. However, Nourjahad is undeterred, and thus it is that he sleeps through the birth of his son and the death of his wife. Then again, he plans a blasphemous party in which youthful and ravishing members of his harem are to impersonate the wives of the Prophet, but, when he wakes up on what seems like the following morning, he finds that the ladies of his harem, who were to have danced before him with roses in their hair, have become stooped and withered hags. Nourjahad continues to fall asleep at inappropriate times and for inappropriate lengths of time, until Sheridan's novelette concludes with a surprise moralizing twist in the tail. *Nourjahad* offers an interesting variant of the 'years-of-experience-in-a-moment-of-time' motif; and setting the moralizing twist aside, Sheridan's story can be read as a parable on the theme of time as the destroyer of all man's hopes. As the sagacious Cozro remarks to Nourjahad: 'What have all thy misfortunes been . . . that are not common to all the race of man?'[9]

Clara Reeve took an ancient Arab legend as the basis for an oriental-cum-biblical novel, *The History of Charoba, Queen of Aegypt* (1785). This tale of a King Gebirus who invades Egypt, but who is subsequently defeated by magic and by women's wiles, was later to inspire Walter Savage Landor's epic poem *Gebir* (1798). Besides producing a novel in the oriental mode, Clara Reeve had also tried her hand at the Gothic novel, with *The Champion of Virtue: A Gothic Story* (1777). However, it was left to William Beckford to unite the two genres in a single work.

It is possible to discuss Beckford's *Vathek* as if it too was a moral tale, but, as we shall see, its conformity to the conventions of the genre was purely formal, and this novel is the first oriental tale to have any real and lasting literary worth.[10] William Beckford (1760–1844) was the son of one of England's wealthiest merchants. His father had made his fortune in Jamaican sugar and went on to become Lord Mayor of London and a leading Whig politician.

Alderman Beckford had hoped that his son would follow him into politics, but William was to achieve fame in other, less edifying areas. As a child, he had been fascinated by the *Nights* and he had begun to collect oriental paintings. His godfather, William Pitt, Lord Chatham, concerned at the boy's unhealthy interest in things oriental, wrote to his tutor instructing him to ensure that the boy have no further access to the *Nights*. Beckford's Indian paintings were burnt, but tales of oriental vice and despotism had already worked upon the boy's imagination, and Beckford's early interest in the Near East was to be reinforced later by his drawing master, the painter Alexander Cozens. Cozens (1717?–86), who claimed to be the illegitimate son of Tsar Peter the Great, had grown up in Russia, where he had met many Persians and acquired oriental interests. He was consequently nicknamed 'the Persian' by his pupil.

Beckford's parents died while he was a child. Thereafter, under the faltering guidance of tutors, he became accustomed to having his extravagant and arbitrary tastes gratified without demur. In 1781 a three-day party was held to mark his coming of age. The stage designer, painter, spy and occultist Philippe de Loutherbourg assisted in preparing the setting for one of the most magnificent masquerades to be held in eighteenth-century England. Loutherbourg's magical lighting effects transformed the family home at Fonthill in Wiltshire, and behind closed shutters and curtains Beckford's party of revellers and gilded youths wandered through an exotic dreamscape. As Beckford later put it:

The solid Egyptian Hall looked as if hewn out of a living rock – the line of apartments and apparently endless passages extending from it on either side were all vaulted – an interminable stair case, which when you looked down on it – appeared as deep as the well in the pyramid – and when you looked up was lost in vapour, led to suites of stately apartments gleaming with marble pavements – as polished as glass – and gawdy ceilings . . . Through all these suites – through all these galleries –

did we roam and wander – too often hand in hand – strains of music swelling forth at intervals.

Stagecraft helped to confer a labyrinthine *Nights* complexity upon Fonthill House:

The glowing haze investing every object, the mystic look, the vastness, the intricacy of this vaulted labyrinth occasioned so bewildering an effect that it became impossible for anyone to define – at the moment – where he stood, where he had been, or to whither he was wandering – such was the confusion – the perplexity so many illuminated storeys of infinitely varied apartments gave rise to.[11]

Beckford was later to acknowledge that it was this masquerade which inspired his novel, one of the strangest in English literature. In turn, Beckford's work on this novel, *Vathek*, inspired a further party in 1782 in which Fonthill was transformed into the Palace of Alkoremi and the Hall of Iblis. Beckford claimed that he wrote *Vathek* in three days and two nights, which may be true, but it took longer to produce a final version; and during the early 1780s, while he polished and revised the novel, he also worked with the assistance of a Turk, Zemir, on a rather loose translation into French of some stories in a manuscript of the *Nights*, which had been brought to England by Edward Wortley Montagu. (This translation, including 'The Tale of the Envier and the Envied' and 'Uns al-Wujud', was published for the first time in 1992.) There were rumours that William and his cousin Louisa Beckford had dabbled in black magic in these years. The rumours were perhaps unfounded, but in 1784 another scandal became public knowledge. It was reported in the London journals that Beckford had been discovered in bed with his young cousin, William Courtenay. Beckford was forced to travel abroad until the scandal died down, returning to England only in 1796.

Though Beckford was to publish accounts of his travels and other short pieces, from then on he concentrated on collecting books and paintings and he became an architectural patron. He had his father's mansion, Fonthill House, pulled down and used his rapidly dwindling fortune to build a palace to house his treasures. James Wyatt was commissioned to build the mock-Gothic Fonthill Abbey, described by Pevsner as 'the most prodigious romantic folly in England'. The frantic pace of building went on by day and night. As Beckford wrote to a friend: 'I listen to the reverberating voices in the stillness of the night and see immense buckets of plaster and water ascending, as if they were drawn up from the bowels of a mine, amid shouts from the depths, oaths from Hell itself, and chanting from Pandemonium or the synagogue.' Fonthill Abbey was built in the form of a cross, the arms of that cross meeting in the stucco vaulted great hall. The whole construction was overlooked by a 276-foot tower. Twelve miles of twelve-foot-high walls secluded the master of this place from the gaze of the curious, and there he ruled, like a secluded oriental despot, as 'the Caliph of Fonthill'. But debts forced him to sell the place in 1822, and the great tower, built without proper foundations, collapsed in 1825. Beckford spent the last years of his life as an increasingly eccentric and misanthropic recluse. Although he left a body of travelogues and miscellaneous writing, *Vathek* is the masterpiece for which he is remembered.

Written in French originally, in or around the year 1782 (and published in English in 1786), William Beckford's *Vathek* has become a classic of English literature. Its author announced in the preface that it was a 'story so horrid that I tremble while relating it, and have not a nerve in my frame but vibrates like an aspen'. Vathek, a young Abbasid prince, grows up bored and dissolute under the influence of his sorcerer mother, Carathis. He recognizes no good other than the achievement of his desires. 'His figure was pleasing and majestic; but when he was angry, one of his eyes became so terrible, that no person could bear to behold it; and the wretch upon whom it was fixed instantly fell backwards, and sometimes expired.' A sinister Indian *giaour* (Turkish for 'infidel') appears, acting as emissary for Eblis, the Devil. The *giaour* offers Vathek the treasures of the pre-Adamite sultans, but first Vathek must slaughter fifty innocent children. Vathek makes the atrocious sacrifice and sets out for the ruined city of Istakar where, he has been told, the treasures are to be found. On the way, Vathek rests with the Emir Fakreddin, one of his most loyal subjects. Fakreddin has a daughter, Nouronihar, who has been betrothed to her effete harem-raised cousin, Gulchenrouz:

Nouronihar loved her cousin, more than her own beautiful eyes. Both had the same tastes and amusements; the same long languishing looks; the same tresses; the same fair complexions; and, when Gulchenrouz appeared in the dress of his cousin, he seemed to be more feminine than even herself. If at any time, he left the harem, to visit Fakreddin, it was with all the bashfulness of a fawn, that consciously ventures from the lair of its dam.

Despite Fakreddin's attempts to hide Nouronihar and Gulchenrouz from Vathek, the latter abuses his hospitality by seducing the daughter and stealing away with her. Together, Vathek and Nouronihar complete the last stage of the journey: 'they advanced by moonlight till they came within view of the two towering rocks that form a kind of portal to the valley, at the extremity of which rose the vast ruins of Istakar.' Descending steps of marble and passing through ebony gates, they enter the Palace of Subterranean Fire:

The Caliph and Nouronihar beheld each other with amazement, at finding themselves in a place, which, though roofed with a vaulted ceiling, was so spacious and lofty, that, at first, they took it for an immeasurable plain. But their eyes, at length, growing familiar to the grandeur of the surrounding objects, they extended their view to those at a distance; and discovered rows of columns and arcades, which gradually diminished, till they terminated in a point as radiant as the sun, when he darts his last beams athwart the ocean.

The treasures of the pre-Adamite sultans are indeed heaped up all around, but amidst these treasures 'a vast multitude was incessantly passing, who severally kept their right hands on their hearts, without once regarding anything about them: they had all the livid paleness of death. Their eyes, deep sunk in their sockets, resembled those phosphoric meteors that glimmer by night in places of interment.' After three days of this gloomy contemplation, they are brought before Eblis: 'His person was that of a young man, whose noble and regular features seemed to have been tarnished by malignant vapours. In his large eyes appeared both pride and despair: his flowing hair retained some resemblance to that of an angel of light.' Eblis condemns Vathek and Nouronihar to wander through his halls for all eternity with their hearts in flame.

Additional episodes for *Vathek* were written but never published in Beckford's lifetime. Two and a half episodes – tales told by sufferers encountered by Vathek in the halls of Eblis – were only rediscovered in the twentieth century. These tales of the damned reveal Beckford's characteristic preoccupations. 'Histoire des deux princes amis, Alasi et Firouz' features homosexual love. 'The Story of Prince Barkariokh' includes scenes of what is effectively necrophiliac rape. 'The Story of the Princess Zulkais and Prince Kalilah' treats of incest. In this story, Zulkais joins her twin brother, who is also her lover, in hell, and she tells Vathek how

at last, I reached a chamber, square and immensely spacious, and paved with a marble that was of flesh colour, and marked as with the veins and arteries of the human body. The walls of this place of terror were hidden by huge piles of carpets of a thousand kinds and a thousand hues, and these moved slowly to and fro, as if painfully stirred by human creatures beneath their weight. All around were ranged black chests, whose steel padlocks seemed encrusted with blood.

Vathek is a weird fantasy, but since it was written by a weird man it is not difficult to see it as an autobiographical fantasy – or not wholly fantasy at all. In this *roman à clef*, Beckford's grim

Calvinist mother has been transformed into the sorceress Carathis. His father's fierce rages and intimidating gaze have been transferred to Vathek, but that caliph's quest for illicit knowledge and forbidden pleasures are based on the author's own desire to dedicate his life to unbridled pleasure and on his interest in exotic things. Nouronihar is surely based on Beckford's cousin Louisa. The effete Gulchenrouz bears more than a passing resemblance to William Courtenay. The *giaour* is perhaps, in part, a portrait of the sinister artist Alexander Cozens. The Palace of Subterranean Fires has features in common with Fonthill.

Beckford's assistant and collaborator, the Reverend Samuel Henley, took the uncorrected draft of *Vathek* to Paris, where he laboured to provide the fantasy with footnotes which had the dual purpose of establishing the fantasy's basis in genuine oriental lore and instructing the reader in the manners and customs of the Orient (in much the same way as Lane's annotations to the *Nights* were later to do). D'Herbelot's encyclopaedic *Bibliothèque orientale* was referred to frequently in the notes. It was indeed in the *Bibliothèque orientale* that Beckford had first read of the historical Abbasid Caliph Vathek (or Wathiq) and learned that 'le Khalife Vathek avoit l'oeil si terrible, qu'ayant jetté un peu avant sa mort, une oeillade de colère sur un de ses Domestiques qui avoit fait quelque manquement, cet homme en perdit contenance, & se renversa sur un autre qui étoit proche de luy'. The Koran, *The Tales of Inatuulla* (in Dow's translation) and travellers to the East such as Chardin and Thevenot are frequently cited in the notes.

The notes also suggest that Beckford was indeed indebted to the *Nights* for certain details and motifs in his novel, and the episodes certainly draw on stories from the *Nights*. 'The Story of Princess Zulkais and Prince Kalilah' borrows an episode from 'The Second Dervish's Tale', and 'The Story of Prince Barkariokh' is in part adapted from 'The Second Shaykh's Story'. But, although Beckford had some competence in Arabic and had laboured on a translation of some of the stories in the *Nights*, most of his knowledge of those stories seems to have come via Galland, and there is little or no sign of any wider influence of Arabic literature on *Vathek*. Henley's mock-learned glosses to Beckford's fantasy started a fashion for annotating oriental fictions, and *Vathek*'s example was to be followed by Southey in *Thalaba* and Moore in *Lalla Rookh*.

Vathek was the most richly realized of all oriental tales to appear in English or French up to that date and the most accurate in its details about life in the Islamic lands. Even so, it was not very accurate, and much of the erudition suggested by the footnotes was really rather bogus. The work almost certainly owes more to pseudo-oriental fictions in English and French than to Arabic sources. The Caliph Vathek in his unbridled pursuit of selfish desires and exercise of arbitrary power certainly owes something to Hawkesworth's despot, Almoran. When Almoran proclaimed, 'If I must perish, I will at least perish unsubdued. I will quench no wish that nature kindles in my bosom; nor shall my lips utter any prayer, but for new powers to feed the flame', he anticipated Vathek's carefully tended cult of the arbitrary will. Many of *Vathek*'s most striking images were borrowed from Guellette's pseudo-oriental tales. Even more pervasively, the tones of deflationary irony and mocking exaggeration which Beckford employed from time to time to punctuate a narrative of sombre terror and atrocity were surely modelled on those of his distant kinsman, the urbane and witty romancer Anthony Hamilton.

Despite the exotic detail and parade of Islamic lore, the grandiose and horrific depiction of the hellish domains of Eblis owes very little to the *Nights*, but a great deal to European literature. Vathek's temptation and his quest for the forbidden surely owes something to the Faust legend, and his interrogations of the damned must, in part, have been inspired by similar episodes in Dante's *Inferno*. Then again, Beckford's youthful but ruined Eblis recalls Milton's description of Lucifer in *Paradise Lost*:

> His form had yet not lost
> All her original brightness, nor appeared
> Less than archangel ruined and th'excess
> Of glory obscured.

Since the novel ends with Vathek and Nouronihar consigned to hellish suffering for all eternity, it might be argued that Beckford's fantasy is a moral tale in the tradition of such earlier orientalist writers as Guellette and Hawkesworth. However, such an argument can carry little conviction, for the author's intense enjoyment both of his protagonists' vices and of their punishment is not really consistent with a genuinely Christian sensibility. *Vathek*'s sombre tones, morbid themes and sinister imagery suggest affinities with such early examples of the Gothic novel as Horace Walpole's *The Castle of Otranto* (1765) and M.G. Lewis's *The Monk* (1796). Admittedly, the tone is not uniformly serious, and exaggeration and excess are at times pushed to parodic extremes. Many of Beckord's touches of Gothic horror may originally have been intended as parody; but by the time Vathek and Nouronihar reach Istakar, their creator has allowed himself to be betrayed into conviction, and private nightmares have assumed an oriental garb. Despite Beckford's multifarious borrowings from earlier tales in western and eastern languages, *Vathek* had no real precursors. However, it was to have many imitators and admirers, among them Byron, Disraeli, Poe, Melville and Lovecraft.

'Read Sinbad and you will be sick of Aeneas,' the Gothic novelist Horace Walpole had urged. Beckford's choices in reading and writing had been part of his revolt against the classics of Greek and Roman literature which 'fell flat upon his mind'. The oriental and the Gothic were closely allied in the eighteenth-century revolt against classical canons in literature. The origins of the Gothic novel in English literature should probably be sought chiefly in the growing interest in the old English ballads, in the institutions of chivalry, in the architecture of the Middle Ages and in the growing interest in antiquarianism generally. Nevertheless, Reeve and Beckford were not the only Gothic writers to have fallen under the spell of the Orient. There are traces (albeit fainter traces) of the influence of the *Nights* and other collections of genuine or pseudo-oriental tales on almost all the writers in the Gothic genre. Horace Walpole, who produced a collection of *Hieroglyphic Tales* (1785) in imitation of Anthony Hamilton, was a great enthusiast for the stories of the *Nights*, proclaiming that 'there is a wildness in them that captivates'. It is surely significant that when he produced his famous novel in the Gothic mode, *The Castle of Otranto*, he described that too as 'so wild a tale'. Familiarity with the oriental storytelling tradition had a liberating effect on writers in the late eighteenth century, freeing them from the constraints of plausibility and encouraging them to experiment with supernatural effects (as when, in *The Castle of Otranto*, Bianca rubs her ring and a giant figure appears). Matthew Gregory Lewis translated Anthony Hamilton into English and was a great admirer of *Vathek*. 'Monk' Lewis's novel *The Monk* is set in eighteenth-century Spain and is devoid of obvious oriental trappings. However, this dubiously edifying Gothic schlock-horror novel, a tale of a lascivious and murderous monk who misguidedly sells his soul to the Devil in order to escape human justice, is a romantic reworking of the story of 'Barsisa', from the old Turkish story collection *The Forty Viziers*.

The tale of the spectral bleeding nun is framed within Lewis's story of the damned monk Ambrosio, and it may be that Lewis was influenced by oriental storytelling conventions in his employment of the framing device. This same device of story-within-story was used to greater effect and more elaborately in Charles Robert Maturin's *Melmoth the Wanderer* (1820). (In this story, Melmoth, who has sold his soul to the Devil, seeks to find someone who will change places with him. Though he finds many people in horrific predicaments and learns all their stories, no one will take on his burden of damnation.) However, whatever debt the Gothic novelist may owe to the medieval Arab storyteller, the spirit of the Gothic novel, with its chain-rattling, blood-curdling horrors and its cult of the grandiose and the antique, is quite alien to the Arab sensibility. The absence of the ghost story in Arabic has already been noted, and, though there are horrors in the *Nights*, those horrors are not milked, nor did the authors of the Arabian tales interest themselves in the psychology (or psychopathology) of extreme states.

There are a number of curious resemblances between Maturin's *Melmoth the Wanderer* and Potocki's great work of fiction, *The Saragossa Manuscript*. Both open with the reading of a discovered manuscript; in each case the manuscript's contents turn out to be a series of interactive boxed stories (that is to say, of boxed stories of which developments in some stories have consequences in others); and both books feature a hero unjustly condemned by the Spanish Inquisition. It is possible that Maturin read parts at least of Potocki's remarkable masterpiece and was impressed by them. The life of the author of the *The Saragossa Manuscript* was hardly less remarkable than his fiction.[12] Jean Potocki was born in 1761, a member one of one of Poland's most distinguished families. He was educated in Switzerland and later at the Vienna Academy of Military Engineering. He proved himself to be an accomplished linguist and knew at least eight languages. (At some point in his life, he mastered Arabic.) As a young man, he travelled widely in western Europe, as well as visiting Tunisia, Constantinople, Egypt and Morocco. In 1779 he was made a Knight of Malta and he joined the Knights on a pirate hunt against Barbary corsairs. (He was later to draw on his experiences as a Knight of Malta in *The Saragossa Manuscript*.) In Constantinople in 1784, he observed the professional storytellers at work in the cafés and experimented himself in composing tales in the oriental manner. Later, in Morocco in 1791, he hunted without success for a manuscript of the *Nights*. He was told, however, that the only story collection available there went under the title of *The Three Hundred and Fifty-*

Four Nights, but there was not even any manuscript of this available for purchase. On the way back from Morocco, he passed through Spain, observing the traces of Muslim culture in Andalusia, and he crossed the desolate and bandit-ridden Sierra Morena *en route* for Madrid. Potocki was fascinated by Islamic culture. It is possible that this fascination pre-dated his visits to the Near East, for Poland in the late eighteenth century harboured substantial communities of Muslims (indeed, there are still some today), and Persian costumes and fashions were the rage among the Polish nobility.

Potocki's travels in western Europe provided as much material for his future novel as did his travels in the Islamic world. In Paris in the 1780s, he frequented the salons and met leading spokesmen of the Enlightenment. He also investigated the secret aims of the Illuminists, studied cabalism and attended spiritualist seances (this was the age of Cagliostro, Mesmer and Swedenborg). Potocki was intrigued by the occult strain in eighteenth-century rationalism. He was also, at first, sympathetic to the aims of the Enlightenment and of the reformers who were to play a leading role in the French Revolution. In 1788 he returned to Poland, filled with ideas about progress and reform. In the same year, he became the first Pole to go up in a balloon, ascending over Warsaw with M. Blanchard. They were accompanied by Osman, a Turkish valet Potocki had brought back with him from Istanbul, and by his dog Lulu. Though Potocki was later to become disillusioned with the bloody progress of the Revolution in France, as late as 1791 he still had friendly contacts with the Jacobin Club in Paris.

In 1798 Potocki travelled through the Caucasus. He was a pioneer in the study of the ancient cultures and languages of that region. In particular, he learned the secret language reserved for the use of the Circassian nobility. Potocki wrote volumes on the ethnography and archaeology of the Slavic and Caucasian peoples. Among his non-fiction were such imposing works of scholarship as the *Essai sur l'histoire universelle et recherches sur la Sarmatie* and the *Principles of Chronology for the Ages Anterior to the Olympiads.* In 1805 he was sent by Tsar Alexander on an embassy to Peking. Though the mission was turned back by the Chinese in Mongolia, he made many valuable observations on the manners and customs of the Siberian and Mongol peoples. In his last years he retired to his estate in Podolia and succumbed to acute boredom and melancholia. It seems that one of his fantasies was that he had become a werewolf, and it is said that when he finally decided to commit suicide he melted down a samovar to obtain silver for the fatal bullet. He shot himself on 20 November 1815.

During the 1780s and 1790s, Potocki had written some short fictions in the oriental mode. (Like Gérard de Nerval later, he embedded them in his travel narratives.) He began work on his masterpiece *Le Manuscrit trouvé à Saragosse* (*The Saragossa Manuscript*) in 1797. Although the work was, in a superficial sense, completed by the time of his death in 1815, the ending is somewhat rushed and perfunctory; and it is possible that, if its author had been able to persuade himself to live a little longer, then *The Saragossa Manuscript* might have had quite a different ending.

Potocki's narrative is divided into days, perhaps on the model of the *Nights*. The story begins in 1739, when a young Walloon officer, Alphonse Van Werden, is travelling across the Sierra Morena, hoping to reach Madrid. However, he is foolish enough to spend the night in a haunted inn, and thereafter he plunges into a series of mysterious and nightmarish adventures. In the course of the first night he becomes entangled with the sweetly seductive Moorish sisters Emina and Zubeida, who claim to be his cousins, but who may be emissaries of the Devil at work to persuade Alphonse to renounce his chance of Christian salvation. Whoever they may be, Alphonse drifts off to sleep in their bed, dreaming of the charms of the seraglio, but when he awakes he finds that he is not in bed in the inn with the bewitching sisters, but is instead lying under a gibbet, which has been used to hang two bandits. Moreover: 'The bodies of Zoto's brothers were not strung up, they were lying by my side. I had apparently spent the night with them. I was lying on pieces of rope, bits of wheels, the remains of human carcasses and on the dreadful shreds of flesh that had fallen away through decay.' As strange encounter follows strange encounter and mystery is piled on mystery, Alphonse wonders if he may not be the victim of dreams, impostures or, perhaps, hallucinations brought on by drugs. He is never sure what to believe, and neither is the reader.

The perplexing adventures of Alphonse serve as a frame for other tales told by people he encounters, including a demoniac, a cabalist, a gypsy chief, a mathematician, a bandit and the Wandering Jew. Their tales in turn serve as frames for yet other stories – of love, honour, revenge, adultery and magic, featuring soldiers, lovers, Inquisitors and supernatural apparitions. The labyrinthine complexity of Potocki's story collection outdoes even such set pieces in the *Nights* as the boxed tales of the Hunchback cycle, for Potocki's tales interlock and overlap, the plot of one story determining the outcome in another. Somewhere, buried in all these stories, is the promise of secret knowledge. Alphonse Van Werden's interlocutors introduce him to a world of mysteries, initiatic secrets and buried treasure. Emina and Zubeida are subterranean creatures, first encountered in a cellar. Their father, the Sheikh of the Gomelez, masterminds a vast plot, which mirrors and parodies the alleged and real conspiracies of the Illuminists and other politico-occult groups of the late eighteenth century.

Some of the mysteries confronted by Alphonse are sexual ones. In particular, the dangerous delights of troilism are dangled before Alphonse and his companions, first in one form and then in another, in a long series of eerie doublings. Both Emina and Zubeida declare their wish to marry Alphonse (but perhaps their charms are deceitful and their bodies the reanimated corpses of the Zoto brothers). Alphonse is tempted and he will later find his temptation echoed when he hears the story of Pacheco the demoniac about his ill-fated love for the sisters Camille and

Inesille; and Pacheco's story is in turn echoed on a higher plane by Rebecca's tale of the cabalistic raising of two mystical entities known as the Celestial Twins. And so on. Thus doubles are redoubled in a series of uncanny distorting mirrors. What is going on? Just as in Cazotte's *Le Diable amoureux* (to be discussed shortly), the horror lies in the ambiguity. Potocki's treatment of this ingredient of the fantastic is masterly, and for most of the narrative Alphonse, like Abu al-Hasan in 'The Sleeper and the Wakened', is never sure whether he is awake or dreaming.

Oriental themes, Gothic horrors and occult doctrines and practices fascinated Potocki, but they also repelled him. His mysterious horrors are not entirely serious, and at times mystification gives way to pure comedy, as in the tale of the man in Madrid who wished to contribute to literature but, lacking the talent to write himself, dedicated his life to making ink to serve the literati. Potocki the *philosophe* kept an ironic distance from his materials and used the props of Romanticism (gypsies, succubi, cabalists and bandits) in the service of Enlightenment values. *The Saragossa Manuscript* is to some extent a tract on the virtues of tolerance and a satire on outmoded feudal codes of honour. Potocki wished to instruct as well as to entertain, and there is space in over 800 pages for an encyclopaedic collection of discourses on strange customs, ethical systems and contemporary philosophy.

The story of the writing and publication of Potocki's tales is, if anything, more confusing than the tales themselves. According to a contemporary source, the origins of the work lay in Potocki's reading of the *Nights* and his wish to entertain his sick wife by telling stories in the same vein. He started to put the stories on to paper in 1797. In 1804–5 he had the first part of the work (the first thirteen days) printed on his own printing press for distribution among friends. The second section of the work was subsequently commercially published in Paris as *Avadoro, histoire espagnole* in 1813. Then the two printed versions were joined together in a three-volume edition produced in St Petersburg in 1814. (Pushkin toyed with the idea of a verse translation into Russian.) The last part of the work seems to have been written before his abortive journey to China. The collection of stories had not been fully revised by the time of his death. *The Saragossa Manuscript* was written in French. In 1847 a complete version was discovered by Edmund Chojecki and translated by him into Polish. Subsequently the original French manuscript was lost, and the integral French edition published in Paris only in 1989 is, for the most part, a retranslation from the Polish into French. Printed versions of Potocki's tales were only fragmentarily available in western Europe in the nineteenth century. They were nevertheless ruthlessly plagiarized by Maurice Cousin in his *Memoirs of Cagliostro*, by Washington Irving in *Wolfert's Roost and Other Stories*, by Jean Nodier in *Ines de las Sierras* and by Gérard de Nerval in *Les Infernales*.

Beckford and Potocki are two of the founding fathers of modern fantasy literature. It is time now to consider a third key figure, Jacques Cazotte (1719–92).[13] Cazotte has already been mentioned in an earlier chapter as the collaborator with the Syrian priest Dom Chavis on an early translation of the *Nights* into French. Cazotte was educated by Jesuits and subsequently employed by the French Ministry of the Marine. In Martinique he landed himself in all sorts of trouble and ended up in prison, broken in health and financially ruined. He returned to France in 1759 and began a new career as a writer. Perrault, D'Aulnoy and Galland had popularized the fairy tale in France, and Cazotte followed the trend. In his *La Patte du chat* (1741), Armadil, a courtier, is banished by the queen for stepping on the paw of her cat. He subsequently encounters a siren, is lured by her into a lake and travels in strange regions, before he returns to court and, forgiven by the queen, marries the princess. A year later, Cazotte produced a parody of the *Nights*, *Les Mille et une fadaises*, in which an abbot is required to cure a society lady's insomnia by telling her stories. He is very successful in this, as the stories he tells are so dull that they invariably send his audience to sleep. The tales which Cazotte has the abbot tell are light-hearted and gallantly sentimental in the manner of Guellette and Hamilton. Indeed, pseudo-oriental fabulists are one of the targets of Cazotte's parody. *Les Mille et une fadaises* and the later and rather similar work *Le Lord impromptu* (1767) were immensely popular at the time, but are of only historic interest now.

The same cannot be said of Cazotte's masterpiece, *Le Diable amoureux* ('The Devil in Love') (1772). Some critics have argued that this book is the first fantasy novel to have been written in France. The young hero, Alvaro, after practising cabalistic rituals to raise the Devil in a graveyard, is confronted by an apparition of a camel which cries out in a terrrible voice, 'Che vuoi?' ('What do you want?) A little later Alvaro becomes acquainted with a young woman, Biondetta, whose sole apparent desire is to serve him. Entering Avadoro's service, she clings devotedly to him. She is never anything but slavishly devoted and sweetly loving, but Alvaro is tormented by doubts. Is she what she seems or is she the Devil in human form? After two months with her, Alvaro is still not sure. In an echo of 'The Sleeper and the Waker' theme in the *Nights*, he muses: 'But what could I make of my entire adventure? It all seems a dream, I kept telling myself; but what else is human life? I am dreaming more extravagantly than other men, that is all.' Everything is cast in doubt, everything ambiguous almost to the very end of the novel. Even if Alvaro, and we, could be certain that Biondetta was the Devil, it would be the Devil in a new and unusual light: 'I am a woman by choice, Alvaro, but still I am a woman, and subject to all the weaknesses of one.' It may be that *Le Diable amoureux* was intended as a strange parable on the vulnerability of evil.

Cazotte's text warned of the dangers of dabbling in the occult. After the book's publication, he was contacted by Martinists and Illuminists who thought that they could detect elements of genuine occult lore in the fantasy. Martinists followed the teachings of the obscure eighteenth-century visionary Martinez de Pasqually (1727–74). Organized in secret lodges on masonic lines throughout France, they believed in a world of unseen spirits and in the possibility of making these spirits visible and having contact with them. They held that all men were spirits once, but that since the Fall their souls have been trapped in the world of matter. In performing magical rituals, Martinist initiates sought to raise man's status by contact with the spirit world and to secure the help of good spirits in combating evil ones. They strove to redeem the fallen state of man since his expulsion from Eden and through psychic reintegration to return to man's original godlike status. In the late eighteenth century, the success of cults such as Martinism and Swedenborgianism, as well as the careers of figures like Casanova and Cagliostro, can, to some extent, be seen as evidence of a revolt against the values of the Enlightenment. But the more one investigates the links between Enlightenment thinking and occult philosophy, the less appropriate does any crudely drawn contrast between reason and superstition seem. (European Free-masons, for example, combated the superstitions of the Catholic Church, while inventing new myths and rituals of their own.) In the latter part of his life Cazotte acquired a reputation as a visionary, and stories circulated about his prophetic powers. His friend La Harpe relates that at a dinner in 1788 Cazotte predicted the execution of Louis XVI and Marie Antoinette, as well as the fates of those who sat around the table, including also the execution of the Marquis de Condorcet and himself. In 1792 Cazotte, who had become a mystical monarchist, was arrested and guillotined as a counter-revolutionary.

Presumably it was Cazotte's taste for the supernatural and the erotic which drew him to the *Nights*. As has been noted, Chavis and Cazotte's *Suite des mille et une nuits* (which was published as volumes 38 to 41 of the fairy tale anthology *Cabinet des fées*, 1788–90) is, in part, a genuine translation of Arab tales (being based on the Paris Bibliothèque nationale MS arabe 1723). Chavis provided a crude word-for-word translation which Cazotte then turned into elegant French, modelled on the style of Galland. However, Cazotte also reworked the authentic tales to turn them into mystical Martinist allegories. Moreover, it seems that four of the stories in the Chavis and Cazotte collection were composed by Cazotte himself: 'The Story of Xailoun the Idiot', 'The History of Alibengiad, Sultan of Herak, and of the False Birds of Paradise', 'The History of the Family Schebanad of Surat' and 'The History of Maugraby, or the Magician'. The last of these stories is the most impressive and the most mystical. In it, Habed-il-Kalib, King of Tadmur, engages in spiritual combat with Maugraby, an agent of Satan. Maugraby specializes in kidnapping children, whom he takes to the caverns of Domdaniel under the roots of the sea where they may be brainwashed and trained in the evil arts of sorcery. Habed receives guidance in dreams, studies magic and undergoes ordeals of initiation, in preparation for his battle with the shape-shifting Maugraby. This weird and grim tale was unmistakably intended by Cazotte to serve as a parable about the Martinist programme for spiritual reintegration and salvation.

Chavis and Cazotte's work was translated into English by Robert Heron as *The Arabian Tales, or a Continuation of the Arabian Nights* in 1792, and it was from the translated text of 'Maugraby the Magician' that the poet Robert Southey took the story-line for his epic poem *Thalaba the Destroyer* (1800).[14] Southey, having read Galland (or perhaps indeed Cazotte), had declared: 'The Arabian tales certainly abound with genius, they have lost their metaphorical rubbish in passing through the filter of a French translation.' The poet, who thought that Arab literature, and for that matter the art and the religion of the Arabs, was worthless, turned the fantastic story into an allegory of Christian duty and endeavour. Cazotte's Habed-il-Kalib is christened Thalaba by Southey, and Thalaba sets out to battle with the sorcerers who dwell in the submarine domain of Domdaniel, 'under the Roots of ocean', encountering all sorts of *Nights* marvels, before his final triumph and apotheosis. Despite the strong story-line and the vivid imagery, the poetry is not actually very good. Imitating Beckford's procedure with *Vathek*, Southey equipped his romance with a massive quantity of orientalist footnotes – they take up more space than the poem. Despite his hostility to Islam and his contempt for Arab literature, Southey remained fascinated by oriental themes and in *The Curse of Kehama* (1810) replanted the Wandering Jew theme in a Hindu setting.

Southey's poetic renderings of oriental stories were much criticized when they were published and did not sell well. By contrast, Thomas Moore's *Lalla Rookh* (1817) was immensely popular and went through repeated reprintings in the decades after its first appearance.[15] In Moore's book, the eponymous princess is being escorted by a certain Feramorz on her way to an undesired marriage with the King of Bukharia. In order to while away the journey, Feramorz tells the princess stories. This prose story frames four tales told by Feramorz in verse. (Moore took as his model here Inayat Allah's *Bahari Danish*, or 'Garden of Knowledge', an Indo-Persian story collection, which was also cited in the footnotes of Beckford's *Vathek* and Southey's *Thalaba*.) The tales are 'The Veiled Prophet of Khorassan' (which furnished the main source for Borges's 'The Masked Dyer, Hakim of Merv'), 'Paradise and the Peri', 'The Fire Worshippers' and 'The Light of the Haram'. Lalla Rookh, in the course of listening to these tales, which are saturated with lush oriental imagery, has fallen in love with Feramorz, and fortunately when they arrive in Bukharia she discovers that he is none other than the King of Bukharia, so they are happily wed.

Certainly, Moore was to some extent inspired by the wildness and the imagery of the *Nights*. However, *Lalla Rookh* owes a heavier debt to translations of such medieval Persian poets as Sadi and Hafiz of Shiraz. By the early nineteenth century, an increasing amount of Persian and Arabic literature was being made available in English, French and German translations, and writers were no longer so dependent on the *Nights* as their source of oriental inspiration. As can be seen by the foregoing discussion, besides authentic works of Middle Eastern literature, novelists and poets were also finding inspiration in the burgeoning body of pseudo-oriental literature, by Anthony Hamilton, Frances Sheridan, Jacques Cazotte, William Beckford and others. Moreover, the Middle East was now more open to western travellers than ever before. Although the poet Lord Byron deployed imagery from the *Nights* in a number of his poems, most notably in *Don Juan, Vathek*, which he reverenced, was probably a greater influence on him: 'For correctness of costume, beauty of description, and power of imagination, it far surpasses all European imitations' (and Byron also imitated the *Vathek*ian footnote).[16]

However, Byron's own travels in the eastern Mediterranean lands were yet more important still in shaping such poems as *The Giaour* (1813) and *The Corsair* (1814). In the nineteenth century, English works of 'orientalist' literature, such as Thomas Hope's *Anastasius* (1819), James Morier's *Hajji Baba of Isfahan* (1824), Alexander Kinglake's *Eothen* (1844), William Makepeace Thackeray's *Notes of a Journey from Cornhill to Grand Cairo* (1845) and Benjamin Disraeli's *Tancred* (1847), drew on their authors' travels in the Ottoman lands. Contemporary realities there often disappointed those whose image of the Levant had been formed by Galland's courtly version of the *Nights*. (Kinglake, who travelled through Syria and Egypt, decided that the *Nights* 'cannot have owed their conception to a mere oriental, who, for creative purposes, is a thing dead and dry – a mental mummy that may have been a live king just after the Flood, but has since lain balmed in spice'. Kinglake decided that the *Nights* must have been written by Greeks instead.) Some writers now thought of the *Nights* as something that should be put away with other childish things when they attained maturity.

Children take unpredictable things away from what they have read, and not all of them found unalloyed delight in the *Nights*.

Coleridge and De Quincey found sinister things there. According to Samuel Taylor Coleridge (1772–1834):

One tale . . . (the tale of a man who was compelled to seek for a pure virgin) made so deep an impression on me (I had read it in the evening while my mother was mending stockings) that I was haunted by spectres, whenever I was in the dark – and I distinctly remember the anxious and fearful eagerness, with which I used to watch the window, in which the books lay – & whenever the sun lay upon them, I would seize it, carry it by the wall & bask & read –. My Father found out the effect, which these books had produced – and burnt them.[17]

Coleridge claimed to have read the *Nights* at the age of six. Coleridge was not always the most reliable witness about his own life, but, at whatever age he read the stories, it is hard to know what it was that so terrified him in the story of 'Zayn al-Asnam' (one of Galland's 'orphan stories'), in which the Lord of the Jinn, who has taken the form of a beautiful young man, orders Zayn al-Asnam to find a beautiful girl, who has never lusted after a man, and bring her to him.[18]

More generally, Coleridge saw dark things in the oriental tales. In 1800 he had an opium-laced dream of 'a Woman whose features were blended with darkness catching hold of my right eye & attempting to pull it out – I caught hold of her arm fast – a horrid feel . . . the Woman's name Ebon Ebon Thalud – When I awoke, my right eye swelled.' This nightmare vampire seems to derive partly from Ebn Thaher, a drug dealer in one *Nights* story, and partly from a female ghoul in another.[19] The *Nights* was associated in Coleridge's mind with acts of justice so cruel and arbitrary that they can hardly be seen as acts of justice at all. Challenged about the frightfulness of the ordeal of the Ancient Mariner and his companions which began with the killing of the albatross, he compared their fate to that of the merchant who tosses away a date stone and then finds himself condemned to death by a jinn.

Though steeped in the *Nights*, Coleridge also found inspiration in pseudo-oriental literature. 'The Adventures of Abduah the Merchant', in James Ridley's *Tales of the Genii*, presented 'Kubla Khan' with the key image of a houri separated from her lover by a dismal chasm from the bottom of which rose 'Wild notes of strange uncouth warlike music'. The Orient was for Coleridge a repository of weird and nightmarish images and, beyond imagery, the source of something grander and more impalpable. From reading the *Nights*, his mind had 'been habituated to the Vast — and I never regarded *my senses* in any way as the criteria of my belief'. But the influence of the *Nights* went even wider yet. In John Livingston Lowes's fine study of the sources of Coleridge's imagination, *The Road to Xanadu* (1927), Lowes wrote that 'to attempt to trace the prints of the *Arabian Nights* . . . in "The Rime of the Ancient Mariner," and "Christabel," and "Kubla Khan," were like seeking the sun and the rain of vanished yesterdays in the limbs and foliage of the oak. But the rain and sun are there.'[20]

Like Coleridge, Thomas De Quincey (1785–1859) had been terrorized as a child by the *Nights*. De Quincey was not an admirer of the *Nights* in general, considering the stories to be lacking in psychological depth and artistic unity, and he remarked of Sinbad, for example, that 'it is not a story at all, but a mere series of adventures, having no unity of interest whatsoever'. However, in his *Autobiography*, he made an exception for 'Aladdin' and for one particular incident in that story which had terrified him when young and was to exercise a complex and rather sinister influence over the patterns of his adult thinking. The magician in the depths of Africa seeks the child Aladdin, the one fated child who can lead him to the treasure:

Where shall such a child be found? Where shall he be sought? The magician knows: he applies his ear to the earth; he listens to the innumerable sounds of footsteps that at the moment of his experiment are tormenting the surface of the globe; and amongst them all, at a distance of six thousand miles, playing in the streets of Baghdad, he distinguishes the peculiar steps of the child Aladdin.

For the magician 'has the power, still more unsearchable, of reading in that hasty moment an alphabet of new and infinite symbols . . . The pulses of the heart, the motions of the will, the phantoms of the brain, must repeat themselves in secret hiero-glyphics uttered by the flying footsteps.'[21]

De Quincey found in this passage an allusion to the notion (common to Arab diviners and physiognomists) that everything has grammar and meaning and that 'the least things in the universe must be secret mirrors to the greatest'. It is a remarkable passage in De Quincey's memoirs – not least because a description of the sorcerer, such as he recalls, listening to the myriad footsteps of the world is not to be found in any surviving edition of the *Nights*. It is perhaps a false memory, deriving from one of the writer's opium reveries (which were always rich in sinister oriental imagery), and so this reminiscence of De Quincey's may be reckoned to be his own contribution to the corpus of the *Nights* and part of its disconcertingly large pseudepigrapha. De Quincey consistently associated the *Nights* with images of horror and despair-ing inevitability. In *Suspiria de Profundis*, he reveals how (slightly distorted) memories of 'The Second Dervish's Tale' – in which the young man who has slept with the jinn's woman is tracked down by the jinn – were for ever associated in his own mind with the guilty sensation of being found out: 'It appeared, then, that I had been reading a legend concerning myself in the *Arabian Nights*. I had been contemplated in types a thousand years before on the banks of the Tigris. It was horror and grief that prompted that thought.'

In a brief discussion of the impact of the *Nights* on English literature, Edward Said observed (somewhat sourly) that 'the *Arabian Nights*, for example, are regularly associated with child-hood, beneficent fantasies, it is true, but ones occurring in a sense so that they may be left behind'.[22] Said was surely thinking of such passages as that which occurs in the fifth book of Wordsworth's *The Prelude*:

> I had a precious treasure at that time,
> A little, yellow canvas-cover'd book,
> A slender abstract of Arabian Tales;
> And when I learn'd, as now I first did learn,
> From my Companions in this new abode,
> That this dear prize of mine was but a block
> Hewn from a mighty quarry; in a word,
> That there were four large Volumes, laden all
> With kindred matter, 'twas, in truth, to me
> A promise scarcely earthly.

Tennyson evoked similar childhood delights in his 'Recollections of the *Arabian Nights*':

> When the breeze of a joyful dawn blew free
> In the silken sail of infancy,
> The tide of time flow'd back with me,
> The forward-flowing tide of time;
> And many a sheeny summer-morn,
> Adown the Tigris I was borne,
> By Bagdat's shrines of fretted gold,
> High-walled gardens green and old;
> True Mussulman was I and sworn,
> For it was in the golden prime
> Of good Haroun Alraschid.

In Dickens, too, the linkage between the stories of the *Nights* and the lost delights of innocent childhood is strong indeed. In *A Christmas Carol*, the Ghost of Christmas Past introduces Scrooge to the forgotten delights of infancy:

'Why it's Ali Baba!' Scrooge exclaimed in ecstasy. 'It's dear old honest

Ali Baba ... And what's his name who was put down in his drawers, asleep, at the Gate of Damascus; don't you see him! And the Sultan's Groom turned upside-down by the Genii; there he is upon his head! Serve him right. I'm glad of it. What business had *he* to be married to the Princess!'

In *Hard Times*, the soulless and materialistic Gradgrind confronts Sissy Jupe and asks her what she has been reading to her father: '"About the fairies, sir, and the Dwarf, and the Hunchback, and the Genies," she sobbed out . . . "Hush!" said Mr Gradgrind, "that is enough. Never breathe a word of such destructive nonsense any more."'

But though it is not difficult to find *pièces justificatives* for Said's observation, it is still a selective reading. Even in Dickens, imagery from the *Nights* is not always used to summon up the innocent and the childlike. The first paragraph of the first chapter of *The Mystery of Edwin Drood* presents an opiate vision of the city of Cloisterham, in which the spire of Cloisterham's cathedral loses its Englishness and becomes old Baghdad:

What IS the spike that intervenes, and who has set it up? Maybe, it is set up by the Sultan's orders for the impaling of a horde of Turkish robbers, one by one. It is so, for cymbals clash, and the Sultan goes by to his palace in long procession. Ten thousand scimitars flash in the sunlight, and thrice ten-thousand dancing girls strew flowers.

The orientalizing transfiguration of an English provincial town prefigures the part played by crime and opium in this mystery novel.[23]

Not all those who read the *Nights* as children were inspired to become novelists or poets. Some became bank clerks or grocers; and, if they found inspiration or consolation in the stories, it was a private matter and is now forgotten. For many readers the *Nights* offered the first introduction to ancient and alien cultures. Edward Gibbon (1737–94) was introduced to the *Nights* at an early age. He found it to be a book 'which will always please by the moving picture of human manners and specious miracles'. In the words of his biographer G.M. Young: 'his imagination moved most freely in the East, and the work of his manhood is shot with a child's vision of grave and bearded Sultans who only smiled on the day of battle, the sword of Alp Arslan, the mace of Mahmoud, Imaus and Caf, and Altai, and the Golden Mountains, and the Girdle of the Earth'. It is probably due to Gibbon's childhood reading of the *Nights* that his account of the medieval Near East, and especially of the court of the Abbasids, in the later volumes of *The Decline and Fall of the Roman Empire*, glows with an imaginative sympathy, something which is often lacking in his portrayal of feudal Europe.[24] In much the same way as a reading of Homer's *Iliad* inspired Schliemann to look for the historical ruins of Troy, so Sir Henry Layard's childhood reading of tales about the Ebony Horse and the City of Brass led him as an adult in the 1840s to uncover the ruins of ancient Nineveh. (Those same fantastic dead Arabian cities are, of course, the ghostly precursors of such morbidly poetic Victorian necropolises as Christina Rossetti's 'The Dead City' (1847) and James Thomson's 'The City of Dreadful Night' (1874).)

No two people ever read the same book, and the stories which led Layard to archaeology hinted to Newman of divine mysteries. Cardinal Newman, looking back on his childhood in *Apologia pro Vita Sua* (1864), remembered that he 'used to wish the Arabian Tales were true: my imagination ran on unknown influences, magic powers and talismans'. It seems that the numinous and the miraculous qualities of the Arabian fairy tales left an imprint on the youthful mind of John Henry Newman that was to lead him as an adult to accept the Catholic faith, a faith in which the numinous and the miraculous are indeed true for its believers. (In a similar manner, in the next century, C.S. Lewis's childhood enthusiasm for Norse myths and legends was to lead him as an adult to accept the Incarnation of Christ as God as a myth, but a myth which had the advantage of being true.) Mock-oriental literature also had a part in setting Newman on the spiritual path that he was to follow. Southey's epic poem on the theme of spiritual testing, *Thalaba*, impressed Newman greatly and influenced his spiritual mission: '*Thalaba* has ever been to my feelings the most sublime of English poems – I mean *morally* sublime.'

While the *Nights* continued to exercise a sway over the imaginations of poets, novelists and others in the Victorian period, the writing of oriental tales, in the manner of Hamilton or Beckford, had quite gone out of fashion in Britain. The only full-length mock-oriental novel of note to be published in this period was the eccentric and now little-read *Shaving of Shagpat: An Arabian Entertainment* (1855).[25] George Meredith (1828–1909) read the *Nights* as a child. It was his favourite book, and *The Shaving of Shagpat*, his first novel, was modelled on it. In the preface, he told his readers that his book was an attempt to reproduce 'the style and manner of Oriental Story-tellers'. (As far as style is concerned, it was of course more closely modelled on Lane's translation of the *Nights*, which had been published in 1838–41.) Meredith used to make up Arabian tales to tell to his young stepdaughter, and it may be that elements in *The Shaving of Shagpat* derive from these nightly inventions. However, the novel was really written for adults:

Now, the story of Shibli Bagarag, and of the ball he followed, and of the subterranean kingdom he came to, and of the enchanted palace he entered, and of the sleeping king he shaved, and of the two princesses he released, and of the Afrite held in subjection by the arts of one and bottled by her, is it not known as 'twere written on the finger-nails of men and traced in their corner-robes . . .?

Bagarag, the humble barber, finds himself engaged in a heroic series of quests and ordeals in his struggle to shave an enchanted hair from the head of Shagpat the clothier and so free the city, also called Shagpat, from subjection to the man.

The telling of the story is parodically prolix and extended by the insertion of framed stories and inserted fragments of verse. Though Shibli Bagarag is a humble barber, his speech is grandiose indeed. Faintly ludicrous mock-oriental similes abound, and high sentence is played off against low comedy. Humble Bagarag is both assisted and hindered in his ordeals by high-born women. Meredith's Asian queens are *femmes fatales*. In the framed 'Story of Bhanavar the Beautiful', Bhanavar possesses a jewel which gives her power over the serpents and, alone in her chamber,

she arose, and her arms and neck and lips were glazed with the slime of the serpents, and she flung off her robes to the close-fitting silken inner vest looped across her bosom with pearls, and whirled in a mazy dance-measure among them, and sang melancholy melodies, making them delirious, fascinating them; and they followed her round and round, in twines and twists and curves, with arched heads and stiffened tails; and the chamber swam like an undulating sea of shifting sapphire lit by the moon of midnight.

Rabesqurat is Mistress of Illusions, 'surrounded by slaves with scimitars, a fair Queen, with black eyes, kindlers of storms, torches in the tempest, and with floating tresses, crowned with a circlet of green-spiked precious stones and masses of crimson weed with flaps of pearl'. Similarly, the Princess Goorelka is a poisoner and sorceress who keeps men in enchanted captivity as birds and torments them when they displease her. Noorna bin Noorka, on the other hand, is the barber's guiding good spirit and the woman he will eventually marry.

Today *The Shaving of Shagpat* is a forgotten novel by an unfashionable novelist. In some respects, the novel deserves its neglect. If it is taken as a pastiche or parody of the *Nights*, it is not a very good one. As an adventure story, it is confused and rambling. Many current sword-and-sorcery romances have a better grip on narrative. If one reads *The Shaving of Shagpat* as an allegory, as many critics have done, then the allegory is obscure.

In general terms, it is plain that Shagpat, with his magical hair, stands for oppression based on the power of illusion, but whether the oppression is social and class-based or whether it rests on some form of intellectual deceit, or clinging to outmoded ideas, is unclear, and further details of the allegory are impenetrable. However, some of the imaginative imagery in the book, such as Rabesqurat's mirror made from human eyes, or the bridge of eggs, is brilliant.

Meredith's novel of Arabian sword and sorcery was inspired by Lane's translation. Curiously, though, the appearance first of Lane's and then of Burton's translations coincided with a decline in the grip of the *Nights* on the English literary imagination. It may be that those translations, stylistically unattractive and bottom-heavy with annotation, were actually responsible for that decline. Paradoxically, a fuller and more accurate knowledge of the *Nights* led to a closing of the gates of imagination. From the late nineteenth century onwards, the *Nights* ceased to be part of the common literary culture of adults. As for children, they now read selected and heavily expurgated versions of the stories. 'Sinbad', 'Ali Baba', 'Aladdin', 'The Ebony Horse' and a handful of other stories continued to be read, but it was a much reduced corpus, and the *Nights* had increasingly to compete for attention with books written specifically for children by Dean Farrar, George MacDonald, Frederick Marryat, E. Nesbit and many others. (Of course, the *Nights* was often a major influence on this new breed of writer; for example, Nesbit's Psammead stories obviously owe a great deal to the Arab tales.)

Robert Louis Stevenson wrote both for children and for adults, and it is often difficult to determine whom his stories were intended for. Meredith's books were a strong influence on him, and like *The Shaving of Shagpat*, Stevenson's *New Arabian Nights* (1882) pastiched the style of the *Arabian Nights Entertainments* — that is, the style of the commonly available English translation of Galland. Stevenson's book also has a frame story of sorts, in which

Prince Florizel and Colonel Geraldine wander the streets of nineteenth-century London in disguise, as Harun al-Rashid and Jafar had done in old Baghdad. Their wanderings frame six rather good stories of adventure, murder and suicide. In the *New Arabian Nights* and in its sequel *More New Arabian Nights: The Dynamiter*, the stress is on plot and on colourful settings, rather than psychological or social verisimilitude (and this was indeed what late-nineteenth-century readers found in the medieval *Nights*). A later story by Stevenson, 'The Bottle Imp', in *Island Nights Entertainments* (1893), reverses the quest formula, in that the wonder-working bottle is something which must be got rid of, a curse which must be lifted, rather than sought. This inversion of the quest formula echoes the frame story of the Hunchback cycle in the *Nights* (and it also has affinities with the frame of Maturin's *Melmoth the Wanderer*).[26]

In the nineteenth century, merchants in the United States carried on a surprisingly extensive commerce with Muslim Zanzibar. Later, American shipping in the Mediterranean was to suffer from the depredations of the Barbary corsairs, prompting the United States government to action. However, unlike Britain, the United States did not rule over an empire of Muslims. It is not surprising, then, that the influence of the *Nights* on nineteenth-century American literature was relatively slight. Though the influence was slight, however, it was there.[27]

Washington Irving (1783–1859) has already been mentioned as one of the plagiarists who made use of Potocki. *The Conquest of Granada* (1829) and *Legends of the Alhambra* (1832, revised and expanded 1857) are based on his three-month sojourn in Spain in 1829. *Legends of the Alhambra* is a scrapbook compilation of travel reminiscences, inconsequential encounters and framed stories. Irving was enchanted by the Old World and the vestiges of vanished civilizations. In particular, the Moors of Spain, mysterious and forgotten as the inhabitants of the City of Brass, haunted his imagination. The moonlit ruins of the Moorish palace of the

Alhambra served as the setting for moralistic and melancholy reflections that are rich in atmosphere and cliché. The framed tales are of ghosts, hidden treasures, sorcerers, bandits and gypsies. In Irving (as with Cazotte, Potocki, Maturin and Richard Burton) a cult of the Orient went hand in hand with a fascination with gypsies.

'The Legend of the Moorish Astrologer' is perhaps the best thing in the book. This is a retelling of a story found in al-Maqqari's *Nafh al-Tib* (a romantic history of the lost Muslim realm of Andalusia written in Damascus in the early seventeenth century). An earlier version of al-Maqqari's story is found in the *Nights*. A Muslim Spanish ruler employs an astrologer to use his magic powers to defend the kingdom. The astrologer uses his occult lore to construct a bronze talismanic statue of an armoured horseman as well as armies of miniature figurines. The astrologer's operation of these miniature figures in the tower secures victories for the king's armies in the field. When the astrologer seeks his reward, the king is unresponsive, but the astrologer has his revenge, and the kingdom is ruined. 'The Legend of Prince Ahmed el Kamel or the Pilgrim of Love' borrows motifs from the *Nights*, including such stock features as the young prince who is secluded to protect him from a prophesied evil fate, learning the language of birds, falling in love with birds, a magic carpet and a flying horse.[28]

Although Edgar Allan Poe published a collection entitled *Tales of the Grotesque and Arabesque* in 1840, the influence of the *Nights* on his writing appears decidedly superficial. In characterizing some of his tales as 'Arabesque', Poe intended no specific reference to the Arab manner of telling stories. He only used the term to refer to intricately patterned tales (intricate as the design of an oriental carpet) in which the centre of interest lay in the cunningly crafted plot, rather than in the exploration of the characters in the tales. (More generally, words like 'arabesque', 'carbuncle', and 'talisman' and phrases like 'Barmecide feast' and 'Aladdin's cave' were part of the age's common stock of literary bric-à-brac from a cultural attic.)

Poe's short story 'The Thousand-and-Second Tale of Scheherezade' is a lightweight, though heavily laboured, sketch in which Sheherazade starts to tell Shahriyar a story, one of the hitherto untold adventures of Sinbad, featuring an ironclad steamship, an automaton chessplayer, Babbage's Calculating Machine, the telegraph, the daguerreotype, and so forth. Shahriyar finds her account of the technological wonders of nineteenth-century civilization so preposterous that he loses patience and gives orders for her to be strangled. 'She derived, however, great consolation (during the tightening of the bowstring) from the reflection that much of the history remained still untold, and that the petulance of her brute of a husband had reaped for him a most righteous reward, in depriving him of many inconceivable adventures.' It is possible that Poe, as an early writer of science fiction, found similar difficulties in interesting his audience in stories about future marvels of science.

On the face of it, it is improbable that Arabian or pseudo-Arabian themes should play much part in a novel about a whaling ship out of Nantucket. However, it is fairly clear that Herman Melville's *Moby Dick* (1851) does draw heavily on such material. Like every other educated westerner in the nineteenth century, Melville read the *Nights* as a child. He also travelled in the East and read widely both in other accounts of oriental travel and in such novels as *Vathek* and *Anastasius*. In particular, the two despots, Captain Ahab and the Caliph Vathek, share the terrible and intimidating eye, and Ahab's damned hunt for the thing which should not be sought has a certain affinity with Beckford's caliph's quest for forbidden treasure. The seas across which Ahab roams teem with marvels, spirits and omens. Ahab's favoured harpoonist and familiar, the turbaned Fedallah, is 'such a creature as civilized, domestic people in the temperate zone only see in their dreams, and that but dimly; but the like of whom now and then glide among the unchanging Asiatic communities, especially the Oriental isles to the east of the continent'. It is hinted that Fedallah may be a descendant of the jinn. The text of *Moby Dick* is enriched by covert embedded references to the *Nights* and other sources of nineteenth-century culture. In an earlier novel, *Mardi and a Voyage Thither* (1849), the influence of the *Nights* is more obvious and more superficial. The book draws heavily on story-motifs that Melville had encountered in his reading of Lane's translation of the stories. *Mardi* tells of a quest for an abducted princess in a fantastic archipelago in the South Seas and of the strange societies that are found on those islands. It is a modern version of the voyages of Sinbad, but in Melville political, social and religious allegory takes precedence over wonder.[29]

In the nineteenth century English and French writers plundered the *Nights* for oriental props and knick-knacks. The engagement of twentieth-century writers has been more cerebral, and the *Nights*, containing as it does early and exotic examples of framing, self-reference, embedded references, hidden patterns, recursion and intertextuality, has become a source book for modernist fiction in its playful mode. It has also served as an advertisement for grand pretensions on the part of modern writers.

James Joyce (1882–1941), horribly well read, owned a copy of the translation of the *Nights* by Burton (or 'Old Bruton' as he is called in *Finnegans Wake*). His masterpiece, *Ulysses* (1922) gives an account of a single day (Bloomsday, 16 June 1904) in the lives of Stephen Dedalus and Leopold and Molly Bloom. Although Joyce's narrative is set in Dublin, it is obvious that both the novel's structure and many of its more detailed allusions derive from Homer's *Odyssey*. But behind the wanderings of Odysseus, there is a second range of reference to another tempest-driven, roving seafarer – Sinbad. (It may be recalled that already at the beginning of the eighteenth century Galland had speculated that the Sinbad cycle of stories might have taken some of its details from the Homeric epic.) In Joyce's novel, mirages of old Baghdad and

Basra are discernible in twentieth-century Dublin. In the 'Proteus' chapter, a chapter of transformations and disguises, Stephen awakes groggy from sleep and dreaming. One thought he manages to catch at: 'Remember. Haroun al Raschid.' It is a prefiguration of Stephen's encounter with Bloom, who like Haroun al-Rashid wanders round the streets of his city incognito. Will Stephen Dedalus, like Sinbad, return safely to port? Eventually, yes. Towards the end of the book, in the 'Ithaca' chapter, Leopold Bloom, who has offered Stephen safe haven, reflects on Stephen's current sleeping state:

He rests. He has travelled.

  With?

  Sinbad the Sailor and Tinbad the Tailor and Jinbad the Jailor and Whinbad the Whaler and . . . [and so on].

Finnegans Wake (1939), a linguistically rich and notoriously taxing phantasmagoria, treats, among other things, of the cyclical nature of history and myth. The dreams of Humphrey Chimpden Earwicker frame stories, in the same way as does one of the novel's models and sources, 'the 'unthowsent and wonst nice' or, as it is also known, the 'arubyat knychts, with their tales within wheels and stucks between spokes' or, again, 'this scherzarade of one's thousand and one nightinesses'. In alluding to the omnium-gatherum richness of the *Nights*, Joyce was laying claim to the same quality for his *Finnegans Wake* and he was setting himself up in competition with the medieval Arab storytellers: 'Not the king of this age could richlier eyefeast in oriental longuardness with alternate nightjoys of a thousand kinds but one kind. A shahryar cobbler on me when I am lying!' By the time Joyce wrote *Finnegans Wake*, he had become familiar with the translation of Mardrus, who appears as 'the Murdrus dueluct', and Joyce tells us elsewhere that 'the author was in fact mardred'. And so the teasing references continue, 'until there came the marrer of mirth'.[30]

  'Prost bitte!' *Finnegans Wake* also contains many allusions to

Proust, and Proust's masterpiece, *A la recherche du temps perdu* (translated in English as *Remembrance of Things Past*) is also studded with references to the *Nights*. Early in the first chapter of its first volume, *Swann's Way*, the narrator speculates that if his great-aunt had learned of the secret amatory life of the outwardly eminently respectable Charles Swann, whom she used to entertain to dinner, then she might have found it as extraordinary 'as the thought of having had to dinner Ali Baba, who as soon as he finds himself alone and unobserved, will make his way into the cave, resplendent with its unsuspected treasures', a scene she was familiar with, 'for she had seen it painted on the plates we used for biscuits at Combray'. Towards the very end of the last chapter of the last volume, *Time Regained*, the narrator broods on his approaching death and the possible termination of his storytelling task:

If I worked, it would be only at night. But I should need many nights, a hundred perhaps, or even a thousand. And I should live in the anxiety of not knowing whether the master of my destiny might not prove less indulgent than the Sultan Shahriyar, whether in the morning, when I broke off my story, he would consent to a further reprieve and permit me to resume my narrative the following evening.

Like the *Nights*, Proust's novel is a story told against death.

In between Proust's commencement and his conclusion runs a skein of allusions and comparisons which conduct the narrator's memory inevitably back to childhood. Comparisons with characters and incidents in the *Nights* are also used to make the otherwise familiar bizarre and exotic. Thus, to those who do not know her, the Princesse de Guermantes seems as fantastic as the Princess Badroul Boudour. The narrator, wandering at a loss by night in the strange city of Venice, compares himself to a character in the *Nights*. Paris defamiliarized by wartime and the presence of Senegalese troops and Levantine taxi-drivers similarly appears like old Baghdad. Contrariwise, Bassorah of the *Nights* has become the Basra from which British troops in Mesopotamia are conducting their campaign against the Ottoman Turks. Then again, the narrator compares his glimpse of Baron de Charlus being flogged in a homosexual brothel to a tale in the *Nights*, 'the one in which a woman who has been turned into a dog willingly submits to being beaten in order to recover her former shape' (that is, 'The Porter and the Three Ladies of Baghdad').

As noted above, the *Nights* first appears in Proust's novel in a non-literary form, as images on the cake plates in his childhood home in Combray. The plates feature scenes from 'Ali Baba', 'Aladdin', 'Sinbad' and 'The Sleeper and the Waker'. Subsequently the much loved plates are irretrievably lost. Although the oriental images displayed on the cake plates are less famous than the madeleine dipped in tea, they too play a recurring role in conducting the narrator back to his lost past. Later, in mid-life, his mother talks to him of his childhood in Combray and of his childhood reading there, and the narrator expresses the wish to reread the *Nights*. His mother sends him copies of the translations by Galland and by Mardrus, though she is hesitant about including the Mardrus version; for not only do the older generation disapprove of the licentiousness of Mardrus, but also Mardrus's new-fangled manner of transliteration (one can hardly call it a system of transliteration) has a defamiliarizing effect. Even the title is different – not *The Thousand and One Nights*, as in Galland, but *The Thousand Nights and One Night*.

Proust loved the *Nights*, but he was emphatic that *Remembrance of Things Past* was not intended as a pastiche or some other form of reworking of the *Nights* in modern dress. In the final sequence of meditations on his end and the end of the book, he argues that 'you can make a new version of what you love only by renouncing it. So my book, though it might be as long as the *Thousand and One Nights*, would be entirely different.' And yet it may be that, in renouncing the beloved fictions of childhood in favour of the truth, the narrator has indeed (and paradoxically) written a *Thousand and One Nights* for his own times.

If the length of Proust's novel challenges comparison with the story collection of the *Nights*, the brevity of Borges's fictions matches that of most of the stories in that collection. The views of the Argentinian short-story writer and poet Jorge Luis Borges (1899–1986) on the merits of the various translations of the *Nights* have already been discussed. Apart from his essay on its translators, he also wrote an essay on the stories themselves. '*The Thousand and One Nights*' (published in *Siete noches*, or 'Seven Nights', in 1980). The *Nights* is a key text, perhaps the key text, in Borges's life and work. At an early age Borges discovered the Burton translation in his father's library and devoured it, together with the works of Thomas De Quincey, Robert Louis Stevenson, G.K. Chesterton and others. (The key authors and texts which influenced this famous modernist writer are, for the most part, curiously old-fashioned ones.) Later on, in Spain in 1919, Borges met and was befriended by Rafael Cansinos-Assens, the polyglot poet and translator of the *Nights* into Spanish. Borges's stories, like most of the stories in the *Nights*, are extremely short; and like the *Nights* stories they are strong in plot and aim to provoke a sense of wonder in the reader, but they usually have little psychological depth. To borrow Edgar Allan Poe's terminology, Borges wrote 'Arabesques'.

Borges's version of the *Nights* is an anglophile and anglophone one. Not only did he approach the *Nights* through Burton's translation, but his responses to the stories were almost certainly conditioned by the responses of his beloved Stevenson and Chesterton. (G.K. Chesterton, who wrote a critical study of Stevenson, was, like Stevenson, a master of short and highly coloured fictions.) Of course, the *Nights* furnished Borges with a treasure-house of oriental props on which he drew for stories like 'The Search of Averroes', 'The Ascent of al-Mutasim' and 'The Masked Dyer of Merv'. Occasionally, Borges restricted himself to the retelling of stories from the *Nights* – for example, the stories in *A Universal History of Infamy* of 'The Chamber of Statues' and

'The Tale of the Two Dreamers'. However, stories that have one meaning in the context of an anonymous medieval Arab story collection acquire another meaning when related by a twentieth-century modernist and Argentinian fabulist. (In the same way, *Don Quixote* when narrated by Borges's invention, the twentieth-century littérateur Pierre Menard, is not at all the same book as the one written by Cervantes, even though the two versions are word for word identical.) The *Nights* tale of 'The City of Labtayt' is a tale of *aja'ib*, of the wonders of pre-Islamic Spain; Borges's version of it is essentially a story about the recursive nature of destiny. It is possible to discover one's fate, but one would not have encountered that fate if one had not enquired about it in the first place. The paradox is there in the Arab version, but Borges's version, because it is by Borges, makes the paradox the central feature of the story. Again, 'The Ruined Man who Became Rich Again through a Dream' is an Arab story about prophecy fulfilled; but when essentially the same story appears in Borges's *A Universal History of Infamy*, it becomes a parable about recursion. Thus the cultural attic of the *Nights* furnished Borges with metaphysical themes, and Borges found in the *Nights* precisely what he was hoping to find – *doppelgängers*, self-reflexiveness, labyrinthine structures and para-doxes, and especially paradoxes of circularity and infinity.

The night on which Sheherazade started to tell Shahriyar the story of herself and her storytelling particularly fascinated Borges. He has Albert refer to this passage in 'The Garden of the Forking Paths'. Albert, meditating on the ways in which books could be infinite, 'remembered that night which is at the middle of the Thousand and One Nights when Scheherezade (through a magical oversight of the copyist) begins to relate word for word the story of the Thousand and One Nights, establishing the risk of coming once again to the night when she must repeat it, and thus on to infinity'. The same horrifying problem is discussed in 'Partial Magic in *Quixote*'. Italo Calvino, failing to find the episode in the *Nights*, later accused Borges of making it up – a plausible charge,

given Borges's penchant for playful literary forgery. In fact,
Sheherazade does tell 'The Tale of the Two Kings and the Wazir's
Daughters' in the Breslau version of the *Nights* (and it is translated
by Burton in the second of his supplementary volumes), but
Borges's reading of what is going on was a misreading and
perhaps a wilful misreading, though a fruitful one. Although 'The
Tale of the Two Kings and the Wazir's Daughters' is followed by
more stories in the Burton translation, in the original Breslau text
Sheherazade's telling of her own story is her last story and it
brings the story cycle to an end; it was not intended to plunge its
audience into a new and potentially infinite sequence of stories
within stories. But Borges may have the last word on the subject
of misreadings: 'I think that the reader should enrich what he is
reading. He should misunderstand the text; he should change it
into something else.'

The function of the 'frame' in literature fascinated Borges. It is
not merely that one tale may frame another tale, which in turn
may frame another, suggesting the possibility of an infinitely
prolonged descent through tales within tales. Borges also argued
that the fascination of framing stems from the possibility that the
reader, as he reads a story framed within another story, may
become himself uneasily aware that he too may be framed, that is,
part of a story that someone else is telling. The reader as he reads
may suspect that he is as much a fiction as the characters in the
Nights who tell stories but are themselves inventions of
Sheherazade.

'The South' is one of several of Borges's stories in which the
Nights plays a overt role, albeit an enigmatic one. It begins with
the protagonist, Dahlmann, buying an imperfect copy of Weil's
translation of the *Nights*. His purchase of this volume sets in train a
mysterious series of events, beginning with an assault on a staircase
during which Dahlmann is injured by some unknown thing.
Apparently recovered, Dahlmann sets out by train, heading south.
He carries with him the first volume of *The Thousand and One*

Nights, 'which was so much a part of the history of his ill-fortune, was a kind of affirmation that his ill-fortune had been annulled; it was a joyous and secret defiance of the frustrated forces of evil'. Dahlmann seems to die in a knife duel on the Argentinian pampas, but the early appearance of the fantastic Arabian text is perhaps a warning that all of Dahlmann's experiences on the pampas may be a fantasy.

Again, in 'Doctor Brodie's Report' the fact that that report is discovered in the pages of one of the volumes of Lane's translation of the *Nights* – a translation which was lavishly furnished by Lane with annotations on Muslim manners and customs – warns the reader that the Borges story which follows is an ethnographic fantasy. Similarly, it is not by chance that in 'Tlon Uqbar, Orbis Tertius', among the volumes of the encyclopaedia devoted to the strange alternative world of Tlon Uqbar, the eleventh volume has 1,001 pages. For Borges, as for the medieval Arabs, 1,001 is the number of infinity. Thus the non-existent encyclopaedia opens the way into infinite alternative possibilities. (But though the *Nights* may be considered to be a literary labyrinth, its anonymous authors did not share Borges's preoccupation with mazes, and there is no word in medieval Arabic for a maze.)

Besides drawing on the *Nights* itself, Borges also reworked western stories which derived from the *Nights* or pastiched it in the pseudo-oriental manner. Borges's 'The Sorcerer Postponed' in *A Universal History of Infamy* is a treatment of the years-of-experience-in-a-moment motif. Although the same motif is found in the *Nights* 'Tale of the Warlock and the Young Cook of Baghdad', Borges did not take his inspiration from there but from 'The Tale of Don Illan' in the medieval story collection *Conde Lucanor* by Don Juan Manuel. (Don Juan Manuel reworked his originally Arab material to tell a moral tale, warning against the sin of ingratitude, but the same tale told by Borges becomes a paradoxical parable about the nature of storytelling; for however long it takes a man to live his life, that life may be recounted as a story in ten minutes or so.) Similarly, in the same collection, 'The Masked Dyer of Merv' takes its story from the first framed tale in Moore's poem *Lalla Rookh*.

Borges read the *Nights* as a child and many times subsequently as an adult. He quotes the *Nights*, he rewrites tales from the *Nights* and he often strives for the same imaginative effects as the medieval authors of the *Nights* achieved. Clearly, in several senses (all of them naïve) Borges has been influenced by the *Nights*, but what does this mean? Influence does not just pass down from ancient writers to more modern writers, like a stream running downhill. Writers are not passive receptacles. Being influenced is an active process, and writers actually hunt for the books they wish to be influenced by, making choices among the thousands of books that they might be influenced by. Sometimes they are seeking the retrospective authorization of past precedent for something they were going to write anyway – or, if not that, then an ancient set of references to provide a familiar form for something new. Writers choose those whom they will be influenced by and they also choose how they will be influenced.

Not only do writers find their influences; in doing so, they modify our vision of the works they have been influenced by. When Borges read the *Nights*, he did not read what a medieval Egyptian had read; instead he read the stories that Stevenson and Chesterton read. As Borges himself remarks in 'Kafka and his Precursors' (in *Other Inquisitions*): 'The word "precursor" is indispensable in the vocabulary of criticism, but one should try to purify it from every connotation of polemic or rivalry. The fact is that each writer *creates* his precursors. His work modifies our conception of the past, as it will modify the future.'[31] In his novel *Small World* (1984), David Lodge has some gentle but serious fun with this notion. Persse, Lodge's questing knight in academia, announces that he has been doing a thesis on Shakespeare and T.S. Eliot:

'It's about the influence of T.S. Eliot on Shakespeare.'

'That sounds rather Irish, if I may so,' said Dempsey, with a loud guffaw. His little eyes looked anxiously around for support.

'Well, what I try to show,' said Persse, 'is that we can't avoid reading Shakespeare through the lens of T.S. Eliot's poetry. I mean, who can read *Hamlet* today without thinking of "Prufrock"? Who can hear the speeches of Ferdinand in *The Tempest* without being reminded of "The Fire Sermon" section of *The Waste Land*?'[32]

So it is that those of us who have read Borges find ourselves reading quite a different *Nights* from the text that admirers of *Vathek* or of *The Shaving of Shagpat* used to read. John Barth (b. 1930) is the American author of long, ambitious and somewhat chaotic novels, such as *The Sot-Weed Factor* and *Giles Goat-Boy*. Barth's intertextual games-playing with the *Nights* would certainly have baffled Addison or Hawkesworth. (Even Borges might have found him a bit difficult.) In 1974 Barth's novel *Chimera* appeared. In part a reworking of the Greek legends about Pegasus and Bellerophon, it is also a meditation on the nature of storytelling, a meditation in which the author inserts himself in his narrative and, masquerading as a time-travelling genie, communes with Sheherazade ('Sherry') and her sister Dunyazade ('Doony'). Barth shares Borges's preoccupation with problems of literary self-reference. According to Barth, the *Nights* is a book which begins by quoting itself: 'There is a book which is called *The Thousand and One Nights*.' In Barth's book, the Genie's message to Sheherazade is that 'the key to the treasure is the treasure'. It is not entirely clear what the Genie, or Barth, intends by this cryptic formulation, but perhaps the sense is that the story of the telling of the story is itself the story – or that the solution to writer's block is to write fiction about fiction. The former formulation is somewhat reminiscent of Tzvetan Todorov's observation that, in the thirteenth-century work *The Quest of the Holy Grail*, the quest for the Grail is in the deepest sense the quest for the story of that quest.[33] Barth pursues his own quest for the narrative of narrative in a series of dizzying spirals.

In the first part of *Chimera*, the 'Dunyazadiad', Barth is much preoccupied with the ways in which framed stories can operate on the stories which frame them. Sheherazade and the Genie speculate on whether one might go beyond the normal conventions of framed stories to create something more dynamic 'and conceive a series of, say, *seven* concentric stories-within-stories, so arranged that the climax of the innermost would precipitate that of the next tale out, and that of the next, et cetera, like a string of firecrackers or the chains of orgasms that Shahriyar could sometimes set my sister catenating'. In fact, the Genie has already suggested a limited precedent for all this in the *Nights* tale of 'The Ensorcelled Prince', which is framed within 'The Fisherman and the Jinni', but whose outcome determines the outcome of the story which frames it. In the latter parts of the book, the 'Perseid' and the 'Bellerophoniad', Barth goes on to execute this programme suggested by the Genie. The results are spectacularly bewildering.

The pervasive imagery of the spiral signifies the self-reflexive nature of the book. However, Barth's sense of the erotic nature of fiction prevents the 'Perseid' and the 'Bellerophoniad' from becoming excessively cerebral. Barth works through climaxes and orgasms to adumbrate feminist themes (in what is perhaps a conscious echo of Lally-Hollebecque's vision of the *Nights* as feminist document). In these later sections of the book, where Perseus and Bellerophon are centre stage, there is also some playful exploration of the folklore classification systems of Vladimir Propp and Stith Thompson. The tone of *Chimera* is throughout slangy and breezy.

The breeziness continues in Barth's volume of essays, *The Friday Book, or Book-Titles Should Be Straightforward and Subtitles Avoided* (1984). In this volume, Barth offers snippets of autobiography, such as the fact that he discovered the *Nights* and *The Ocean of Story* while a student doing library work at Johns Hopkins University. He also comments on both the *Nights* and *Chimera* and devotes a separate essay to *The Ocean of Story*. As far the *Nights* are concerned, he was particularly exercised by two problems: why does Sheherazade's storytelling take precisely 1,001 nights, and what is the significance of her three pregnancies? The fruits of his meditations on the sexual nature of Sheherazade's storytelling emerged in yet another fictional cat's cradle, *Tidewater Tales* (1987). In this complex farrago of tales within tales, Sheherazade belatedly returns the Genie's call, turns up to join a boating and storytelling party on Chesapeake Bay and then finds herself trapped in the twentieth century. 'Good readers read the lines and better readers read the spaces.' Prior to her time-travelling appearance, Barth, picking up on the question he had asked in *The Friday Book*, rather implausibly deduces from hints and silences in the *Nights* that the limit of 1,001 nights is tightly and directly linked to the sequence of Sheherazade's pregnancies and to her menstrual cycle. *Tidewater Tales* as a whole is playful and clever, but by comparison with *Chimera* really rather shallow. Barth's parasitic procedures may have sucked his literary host-body dry.

Salman Rushdie, asked on the BBC radio programme *Desert Island Discs* what book (apart from the Bible and Shakespeare) he would have with him on his island, chose the *Nights*, but Rushdie has discovered in this, his favourite book, something different again from what Borges and Barth found. Rushdie's *Nights* represents an alternative tradition in Islamic literature, something to set against the dour decrees of the mullahs of the Middle East and the dictators of the Indian subcontinent. References to the *Nights* abound in all of Rushdie's books. In *Midnight's Children* (1981), Saleem Sinai, one of 1,001 children born on the night of India's independence, at an early age immerses himself in the stories of Sinbad, Aladdin and the Genie of the Lamp, before embarking on his own magical adventures. In *The Satanic Verses* (1988) the stories of his protagonists, Gibreel Farishta and Saladin Chamcha, frame yet other stories of wonder and magic, and images from the *Nights* are given a surrealistic reworking – as for example the glass genie who is his own bottle. Finally, Rushdie's intertextual children's book, *Haroun and the Sea of Stories* (1990), sports with both the *Nights* and *The Ocean of Story*. But ultimately the question he asks, though sarcastically phrased, is a serious one and it is addressed to adult holders of power: 'What's the use of stories which aren't even true?'

Barth and Rushdie are unusual now in their knowledge of and involvement with the text of the *Nights*. Most people in the West today encounter a few bowdlerized versions of stories from the *Nights* as children. Later, as adults, they are likely to forget even those few stories. Borges observed: 'All great literature becomes children's literature.' This observation has some truth, and doubtless Borges was thinking of such classics as *Gulliver's Travels* and *Robinson Crusoe*: equally certainly, he had conveniently forgotten such works as *The Brothers Karamazov* and *Remembrance of Things Past*, which show no signs of becoming popular with children. In order for the *Nights* to regain some of the status it once held in European intellectual life, it will probably be necessary to commission a new translation of all or most of the stories in the fullest recension (so that Burton's version can at last be relegated to the repository shelves). Obviously, further studies of both the content and the influence of the *Nights* would also be helpful. In this chapter, a highly selective and idiosyncratic look has been taken at selected instances of various types of influence exerted by the *Nights* on a heterogeneous body of writers. In place of the writers discussed above, one might have substituted Goethe, Walter Scott, Thackeray, Wilkie Collins, Elizabeth Gaskell, Nodier, Flaubert, Stendhal, Dumas, Gérard de Nerval, Gobineau, Pushkin, Tolstoy, Hofmannsthal, Conan Doyle, W.B. Yeats, H.G. Wells, Cavafy, Calvino, Georges Perec, H.P. Lovecraft, A.S. Byatt and Angela Carter, for all these writers too have been influenced in one way or another by the *Nights*. Indeed, it might have been an easier, shorter chapter if I had discussed those writers who were not influenced by the *Nights*. A discussion of the lack of influence of the *Nights* on, say, William Blake, Evelyn Waugh and Vladimir Nabokov might have been just as rewarding. But enough . . .

Although better and fuller translations of the *Nights* may well be produced in the next hundred years, it still seems unlikely that the *Nights* will regain all of the status and the popularity it enjoyed in Britain and Europe in the eighteenth and nineteenth centuries. In part, this is because, as has been indicated above, the *Nights* has had an important role in engendering its own competition. In England, for example, translations of the *Nights* started to circulate at the beginning of the eighteenth century. The first novels only started to appear somewhat later – Defoe's *Robinson Crusoe* in 1719, Richardson's *Pamela* in 1741 and Fielding's *Joseph Andrews* in 1742. From the late eighteenth century onwards, as we have seen, the *Nights* influenced the development of the novel in many important ways. Any edition of the *Nights* published today faces competition from science fiction, sword-and-sorcery fantasy, horror, romance, crime and thrillers. These are mass-market genres which had not been thought of when the first English versions of the *Nights* began to circulate, but in their origins all these types of the literature of entertainment surely owe something to the ancient oriental story collection. To quote John Livingston Lowes (on Coleridge) again and to give his words a more general application: 'to attempt to trace the prints of the *Nights* . . . were like seeking the sun and rain of vanished yesterdays in the limbs and foliage of the oak. But the rain and sun are there.'

Today, of course, any edition of the *Nights* also has to compete with film and television for the public's attention. However, the 'selfish word-strings' which comprise the stories of the *Nights*, in continuing to mutate, have made the successful transition on to film. As early as 1905 the pioneer film-maker Georges Méliès drew on the pantomime tradition to present in *Le Palais des Mille et une nuits* an opulent, if now quaintly dated, vision of the gorgeous East. Other films have followed, with such titles as *A*

Tale of the Harem, *The Cobbler and the Caliph*, *Kismet* and *The Seventh Voyage of Sinbad*. Most filmed adaptations of stories from the *Nights* are frankly trashy, but a few, including the two versions of *The Thief of Baghdad* (1924 and 1940) and Pasolini's *Il fiore delle Mille e una notte* (1974), rank high among the masterpieces of world cinema. Thus the *Nights* continues to adapt, increasing in bulk and replicating its stories in new and strange forms. As much a cultural amphibian in the modern West as it was in the medieval Near East, the inspiration of the *Nights* flourishes not only in novels by intellectuals but also in films aiming at mass entertainment. Pier Paolo Pasolini's epigraph for his wonderful film will serve for this book as well:

La verità non sta in un solo sogno, ma in molti sogni.

(One does not find truth in a single dream, but rather in many dreams.)

Chronology

===

c. 18th–16th centuries BC	Westcar Papyrus.
5th century BC	Oldest surviving version of the *Jataka*.
AD *c.* 250	Seng-Houei's *Kieou Tsa P'iyu King*.
630	The Prophet Muhammad conquers Mecca.
632	Death of Muhammad.
630s and 640s	Defeat of Byzantine and Sassanian Persian armies and occupation of their lands by the Arabs.
661	Beginning of Umayyad dynasty.
710	Muslim invasion of Spain.
711	Muslim occupation of Transoxania and northern India.
750	Beginning of Abbasid dynasty of caliphs.
c. 750	*Kalila wa-Dimna* translated from Persian into Arabic.
762–6	Baghdad is founded and becomes Abbasid capital.
c. 800	*Sindibad* cycle put together.
c. 800–900	*Kitab Hadith Alf Layla* put together.
831	The poet al-Asma'i dies.
836	Samarra is founded and becomes Abbasid capital for a while.
c. 850?	Earliest surviving fragment of the *Nights* written.

869	The essayist al-Jahiz dies.
910	Fatimid caliphate founded in North Africa.
942	Al-Jahshiyari, compiler of a no-longer-extant rival story collection, dies.
956	The cosmographer and historian al-Mas'udi dies.
969	Fatimid occupation of Egypt and foundation of Cairo. *Rasa'il Ikhwan al-Safa* ('Letters of the Brethren of Purity') written.
987	Ibn al-Nadim's *Fihrist*, a catalogue of books, completed.
994	Al-Tanukhi, compiler of the story collection *Faraj ba'd al-Shidda*, dies.
1085	Somadeva's *Katha Sarit Sagara*.
early 12th century	Heroic epic *Sirat Antar* put together.
1110	Petrus Alfonsi, compiler of the *Disciplina clericalis*, dies.
1122	Al-Hariri dies.
1143	Koran translated into Latin.
1171	Saladin brings to an end Fatimid caliphate in Egypt and founds Ayyubid dynasty.
1200	Ibn al-Jawzi dies.
early 13th century	Al-Jawbari's exposé of rogues' tricks, the *Kashf al-Asrar*, written.
1250–60	Collapse of Ayyubid principalities in Egypt and Syria and their replacement by Mamluke sultanate.

1252–84	Alfonso the Wise reigns in Castile.
1253	The pornographer al-Tayfashi dies. *Sindibad* translated into Spanish.
1258	Mongols sack Baghdad. Execution of last Abbasid caliph of Baghdad.
1260–77	Mamluke Sultan al-Zahir Baybar reigns over Egypt and Syria.
1311	Shadow-play author Ibn Daniyal dies.
1330	Nakhshabi's *Tutinameh*.
1353	Boccaccio's *Decameron* written.
1367	Al-Yafi'i, collector of Sufi tales, dies.
1384	Don Juan Manuel dies.
1387	Chaucer begins *Canterbury Tales*.
c. 1410	The pornographer al-Nafzawi *floruit*.
1412	Al-Ghuzuli, compiler of the *belles-lettres* collection *Matali al-Budur*, dies.
1424	Sercambi dies.
1486	Ahmad al-Danaf, notorious Egyptian criminal, executed.
1516	Ottoman Turkish occupation of Mamluke Syria. Ariosto's *Orlando Furioso* published.
1517	Ottoman Turkish occupation of Mamluke Egypt. Execution of Tumanbay, last of Mamluke sultans.
1549–59	*Heptameron* compiled by Margaret of Navarre.
1634–6	Basile's *Pentamerone*.
1646	Birth of Antoine Galland.
1697	D'Herbelot's *Bibliothèque orientale* posthumously published under Galland's supervision. Perrault's *Contes de la mère l'Oye* published.

1704	Galland begins publishing his translation, *Les Mille et une nuits*. (The last volume appears in 1717.)
1708	Probable date of first chap-book edition of Galland in English translation.
1715	Death of Galland.
1721	Montesquieu's *Lettres persanes*.
1742	*Le Sopha* by Crébillon *fils*. *Les Mille et une fadaises*.
1748	Diderot's *Les Bijoux indiscrets*. Voltaire's *Zadig*.
1759	Johnson's *Rasselas*.
1761	Hawkesworth's *Almoran and Hamet*.
1764	Ridley's *Tales of the Genii*.
1764	Walpole's *Castle of Otranto*.
1767	Sheridan's *Nourjahad*.
1772	Cazotte's *Le Diable amoureux*.
1776	Richardson's *Grammar of the Arabick Language*.
1786	English edition of Beckford's *Vathek*.
1792	Cazotte guillotined.
1794	Alexander Russell's *Natural History of Aleppo*.
1795	Foundation of the Ecole des langues orientales vivantes, Paris.
1796	Death of the orientalist Sir William Jones. M.G. Lewis's *The Monk*.
1798–1801	French occupation of Egypt.
1799	Von Hammer-Purgstall in Istanbul.
1801	Southey's *Thalaba*.
1804	Maria Edgeworth's 'Murad the Unlucky'.

1804–5	First part of Potocki's *Saragossa Manuscript*.
1810	Silvestre de Sacy's *Grammaire arabe*. Southey's *The Curse of Kehama*.
1811	Jonathan Scott's translation of the *Nights*.
1812–22	Grimms' *Kinder und Hausmärchen*.
1812–32	Byron's *Giaour*.
1813	Brothers Grimm publish their *Märchen*.
1814–18	Calcutta I edition of the *Nights*.
1815	Suicide of Potocki.
1817	Moore's *Lalla Rookh*.
1820	Maturin's *Melmoth the Wanderer*.
1824–43	Breslau edition of the *Nights*.
1825	Al-Jabarti dies. Habicht begins to publish his version of the *Nights*. German version of von Hammer-Purgstall's translation of the *Nights* published.
1832	Washington Irving's *Legends of the Alhambra*.
1835	Bulaq edition of the *Nights*.
1836	Lane's *Manners and Customs of the Modern Egyptians*.
1837	Weil begins his translation of the *Nights*.
1838	Torrens's translation of the *Nights*.
1838–41	Lane's translation of the *Nights*.
1839–42	Calcutta II edition of the *Nights*.
1840	Poe's *Tales of the Grotesque and Arabesque*.
1844	Kinglake's *Eothen*.

1851	Nerval's *Voyage en Orient*. Melville's *Moby Dick*.
1855	Meredith's *The Shaving of Shagpat*.
1863–93	Lane's *Arabic–English Lexicon*.
1882	Stevenson's *New Arabian Nights*.
1882–4	Payne's translation of the *Nights*.
1885–8	Burton's translation of the *Nights*.
1899–1904	Mardrus's translation of the *Nights*.
1911	Aarne's *Verzeichnis der Märchentypen*.
1921–8	Littmann's German translation of the *Nights*.
1928	Vladimir Propp's *Morfologija Skazki*.
1943	Death of D.B. Macdonald.
1974	John Barth's *Chimera*.
1978	Albert B. Lord's *The Singer of Tales*.
1984	Mahdi's edition of *Alf Layla wa-Layla*.

Notes

Introduction

1 Jorge Luis Borges, 'The Garden of the Forking Paths', in *idem*, *Labyrinths* (London, 1970), p. 48; *idem*, '*The Thousand and One Nights*', in *idem*, *Seven Nights* (London, 1980), p. 50.

2 R.A. Nicholson, *A Literary History of the Arabs* (London, 1907), pp. 456–9; H.A.R. Gibb, *Arabic Literature: An Introduction* (2nd revised edn, Oxford, 1963), pp. 148–9.

3 Mia I. Gerhardt, *The Art of Story-Telling: A Literary Study of the Thousand and One Nights* (Leiden, 1963).

4 Muhsin Mahdi, *Alf Layla wa-Layla* (Leiden, 1984), 2 vols.

5 Husain Haddawy, *The Arabian Nights* (London and New York, 1990). For famous tales (such as 'Sinbad', 'Aladdin' and 'Ma'aruf the Cobbler') which are not found in the oldest manuscript and therefore do not feature in Haddawy's translation, the reader may wish to consult the modern translation, in Penguin Books, by N.J. Dawood, *Tales from the Thousand and One Nights* (London, 1973).

6 Richard Burton, *A Plain and Literal Translation of the Arabian Nights Entertainments, Now Entitled the Book of the Thousand Nights and a Night* (Benares = Stoke Newington, London, 1885), 10 vols; and *Supplemental Nights to the Book of the Thousand Nights and a Night* (Benares = Stoke Newington, London, 1886–8), 6 vols. (In later reprints of the *Supplemental Nights* it is common to find that the third volume has been split into two. However, the pagination in supplemental volumes 3 and 4 is continuous.)

1 Beautiful Infidels

1 On the Arabic language in general, see A.F.L. Beeston, *The Arabic Language Today* (London, 1970); and *Encyclopedia of Islam* (2nd edn), s.v. 'Arabiyya'.

2 On the life and work of Galland, see Mohamed Abdel-Halim, *Antoine*

Galland, sa vie et son ouevre (Paris, 1964); Georges May, *Les Mille et une nuits d'Antoine Galland* (Paris, 1986); Claude Hagège, 'Traitement du sens et fidelité dans l'adaptation classique: Sur le texte arabe des *Mille et une nuits* et la traduction du Galland', *Arabica*, 27 (1980), pp. 114–39.

3 On the life and work of d'Herbelot, see Henry Laurens, *Aux sources de l'orientalisme: La Bibliothèque orientale de Barthélemi d'Herbelot* (Paris, 1978).

4 On Beckford and Southey, see Chapter 10.

5 On translations of the *Nights* in general, see D.B. Macdonald, 'On Translating the *Nights*', *The Nation* (1900), pt 1, pp. 167–8, and pt 2, pp. 185–6; *idem*, 'A Bibliographical and Literary Study of the First Appearance of the *Arabian Nights* in Europe', *Library Quarterly*, 2 (1932), pp. 387–420; Nikita Elisseef, *Thèmes et motifs des Mille et une nuits* (Beirut, 1949), pp. 69–84; Hagège, 'Traitement du sens et fidelité'; Jorge Luis Borges, 'The Translators of *The 1001 Nights*', in *Borges: A Reader*, ed. E.R. Monegal and A. Reid (New York, 1981), pp. 73–86; Wiebke Walther, *Tausendundeine Nacht* (Munich, 1987), pp. 36–53.

6 On English translations of Galland, see especially C. Knipp, 'The *Arabian Nights* in England', *Journal of Arabic Literature*, 5 (1975), pp. 44–54.

7 On the life and works of von Hammer-Purgstall, see Baher Mohammed Elgohary, *Joseph Freiherr von Hammer-Purgstall, 1774–1856: Ein Dichter und Vermittler orientalischer Literatur* (Stuttgart, 1979); Bernard Lewis, *The Assassins* (London, 1967), pp. 12–13; Peter Partner, *The Murdered Magicians: The Templars and their Myth* (Oxford, 1982), pp. 138–45.

8 On Habicht's translation, see D.B. Macdonald, 'Maximilian Habicht and his Recension of *The Thousand and One Nights*', *Journal of the Royal Asiatic Society* (1909), pp. 685–704.

9 On the life and works of Lane, see Leila Ahmed, *Edward W. Lane: A Study of his Life and Works and of British Ideas of the Middle East* (London, 1978); A.J. Arberry, *Oriental Essays* (London, 1960), pp. 87–121; R. Irwin, 'The Garden of Forking Paths', *Times Literary Supplement* (26 April, 1985), p. 474.

10 On the life and work of John Payne, see Thomas Wright, *The Life of John Payne* (London, 1919).

11 On nineteenth-century British pornographers, see Steven Marcus, *The Other Victorians* (London, 1966), esp. ch. 2.

12 Wright, *Life of John Payne*, p. 269.

13 There are four modern biographies of Burton in English worthy of consideration (each has its own slant and its particular problems): Byron Farewell, *Burton* (London, 1963); Fawn M. Brodie, *The Devil Drives* (New York, 1967); Edward Rice, *Captain Sir Richard Francis Burton* (New York, 1990); Frank McLynn, *Burton: Snow upon the Desert* (London, 1990). For reviews of the latter two books, see R. Irwin, 'The Many Lives of Ruffian Dick',

Washington Post Book World (20 May, 1990), pp. 3, 6; and *idem*, 'A Passion for the Unknowable', *Times Literary Supplement* (12 October, 1990), pp. 1089–90. Richard Francois Gournay's *L'Appel du Proche-Orient: Richard Francis Burton et son temps* is a more penetrating study than any of the English biographies. James A. Casada's *Sir Richard F. Burton: A Bibliographical Study* (London, 1990) is excellent.

14 On Urquhart, see Sir Thomas Urquhart, *The Jewel*, ed. R.D.S. Jack and R.J. Lyall (Edinburgh, 1983); Richard Boston (ed.), *The Admirable Urquhart: Selected Writings* (London, 1975).

15 Borges, 'The Translators of *The 1001 Nights*', pp. 73–86.

16 Husain Haddawy, *The Arabian Nights* (London and New York, 1990), p. xxv.

17 Rana Kabbani, *Europe's Myths of Orient* (London, 1986), pp. 45–66; cf. Edward W. Said, *Orientalism* (London, 1978), pp. 194–7.

18 Henry Reeve, '*The Arabian Nights*', *Edinburgh Review*, 164 (1886), p. 184.

19 On the life and works of Mardrus, see Emile-François Julia's (to all intents and purposes unreadable) *Les Mille et une nuits et l'enchanteur Mardrus* (Paris, 1935); and cf. Rana Kabbani, 'Turkish Delight', *Observer* (13 July 1986), p. 53. For less rhapsodic views of Mardrus and his translation, see Macdonald, 'On Translating the *Nights*', pt 2, pp. 185–6; V. Chauvin, '*Les Mille et une nuits* de M. Mardrus', *Revue des bibliothèques et archives de Belgique*, 3 (1905), pp. 290–95; I. Cattan, 'Une traduction dite "littérale": *Le Livre des mille et une nuits* par le docteur J.-C. Mardrus', *Revue tunisienne*, 13 (1906), pp. 16–23; Abdel-Halim, *Antoine Galland*, pp. 208–13; Suhayr al-Qalamawi, *Alf Layla wa-Layla* (Cairo, 1976, in Arabic), p. 23; Hagège, 'Traitement du sens et fidelité', pp. 129–32.

20 Jeremy Wilson, *Lawrence of Arabia* (London, 1989), p. 719.

21 Borges, 'Translators', p. 86.

22 Francesco Gabrieli, 'Le *Mille e una notte* nella cultura europeana', in *idem*, *Storia e civiltà Musulmana* (Naples, 1947), pp. 99–107.

23 N.J. Dawood (trans.), *Tales from the Thousand and One Nights* (London, 1973). Michael Beard, in a review of Haddawy's translation in the *Journal of the American Oriental Society*, 112 (1992), pp. 144–5, while praising Haddawy's work, contrasted it with the Dawood translation in the following terms: 'in general, Dawood is nimbler, choosing to frame clusters of action between strong pauses which allow the reader to stand back from the action. Haddawy's tendency is to accumulate actions in small unsorted units, sometimes confusingly'. Of course, it must be borne in mind that the two translators are working from different texts; and, in the end, it all depends what you are looking for in a translation.

2 The Book without Authors

1 On the rise of orientalism, see Raymond Schwab, *La Renaissance orientale* (Paris, 1950) (though Schwab concentrates mainly on India). Also: Maxime Rodinson, *Europe and the Mystique of Islam* (Seattle and London, 1987); Albert Hourani, *Islam in European Thought* (Cambridge, 1991). Edward W. Said's *Orientalism* (London, 1978) is a stimulating book. For some of the criticism it has stimulated, see B. Lewis, 'The Question of Orientalism', *New York Review of Books* (24 January 1982), pp. 49–56; R. Irwin, 'Writing about Islam and the Arabs: A Review of E.W. Said, *Orientalism*', *I & C* (formerly *Ideology and Consciousness*), 9 (Winter 1981–2), pp. 103–12; E. Sivan, 'Edward Said and his Arab Reviewers', in *idem, Interpretations of Islam, Past and Present* (Princeton, 1985), pp. 133–54.

2 *The Arabian Nights Entertainments in the Original Arabic: Published under the Patronage of the College of Fort William by Sheykh Uhmud bin Moohummud Sheerwanee ool Yumunee* (Calcutta, 1814, 1818), 2 vols. On the early printed editions in general, see Nikita Elisseef, *Thèmes et motifs des Mille et une nuits* (Beirut, 1949), pp. 65–8; Muhsin Mahdi, *Alf Layla wa-Layla* (Leiden, 1984), vol. 1, pp. 14–22.

3 *Tausend und Eine Nacht Arabish: Nach einer Handschrift aus Tunis Herausgegeben von Dr Maximilian Habicht* (Breslau, 1825–38), 8 vols. Four further volumes were published by R. Fleischer in 1842–3.

4 Silvestre de Sacy, 'Compte-rendu du tome 1er de la première edition de Calcutta', *Journal des savants* (November 1817), pp. 667–86; *idem*, 'Mémoire sur l'origine du recueil de contes intitulés les *Mille et une nuits*', *Mémoires de l'Académie des inscriptions et belles-lettres*, 10 (1829), pp. 30–64.

5 *Alf Layla wa-Layla* (Bulaq, Cairo, 1835), 2 vols.

6 *Book of the Thousand and One Nights Commonly Known as the 'Arabian Nights Entertainments' Now for the First Time Published Complete in the Original Arabic*, ed. W.H. Macnaghten (Calcutta, 1839–42).

7 Richard Burton, *A Plain and Literal Translation of the Arabian Nights Entertainments, Now Entitled the Book of the Thousand Nights and a Night* (Benares = Stoke Newington, London, 1885), vol. 10, pp. 66–94 (pt 1 of the 'Terminal Essay').

8 On the manuscripts of the *Nights*, see H. Zotenberg, 'Notice sur quelques manuscrits des *Mille et une nuits* et la traduction de Galland', *Notices et extraits des manuscrits de la Bibliothèque nationale de Paris*, 28 (1888), pp. 167–320; D.B. Macdonald, 'Lost Manuscripts of the *Arabian Nights* and a Projected Edition of Galland', *Journal of the Royal Asiatic Society* (1911), pp. 219–26; *idem*, 'A Preliminary Classification of Some Mss of the *Arabian Nights*', in *Volume of Oriental Studies Presented to E.G. Browne* (Cambridge,

1922), pp. 304–21; *idem*, 'The Earlier History of the *Arabian Nights*', *Journal of the Royal Asiatic Society* (1924), pp. 355–97; Elisseef, *Thèmes et motifs*, pp. 55–64; Mahdi, *Alf Layla wa-Layla*, vol. 1, pp. 25–36 (in Arabic).

9 Al-Mas'udi, *Les Prairies d'or*, ed. and trans. C. Barbier de Meynard (Paris, 1861–77), vol. 4, pp. 89–90.

10 Ibn al-Nadim, *The Fihrist of al-Nadim*, trans. Bayard Dodge (New York, 1970), vol. 2, pp. 713–14.

11 Ibid., p. 718; cf. R. Irwin, 'The Image of the Byzantine and the Frank in Arab Popular Literature of the Late Middle Ages', in Benjamin Arbel, Bernard Hamilton and David Jacoby (eds), *Latins and Greeks in the Eastern Mediterranean after 1204* (London, 1989), p. 230.

12 S.D. Goitein, 'The Oldest Documentary Evidence for the Title *Alf Laila wa-Laila*', *Journal of the American Oriental Society*, 78 (1959), pp. 301–2.

13 Al-Maqrizi, *Kitab al-Khitat* (Cairo, 1854), vol. 1, p. 485.

14 Richard Burton, *Supplemental Nights to the Book of the Thousand Nights and a Night* (Benares = Stoke Newington, London, 1886–8), vol. 3, pp. 41–2; Nabia Abbott, 'A Ninth-Century Fragment of the *Thousand Nights*', *Journal of Near Eastern Studies*, 8 (1949), p. 157n.

15 Abbott, 'A Ninth-Century Fragment', pp. 129–64.

16 On the career of Macdonald, see William Douglas Mackenzie, 'Duncan Black Macdonald: Scholar, Teacher and Author', in *The Macdonald Presentation Volume* (Princeton, London and Oxford, 1933), pp. 3–10; Jean-Jacques Waardenburg, *L'Islam dans le miroir de l'Occident* (The Hague, 1962), pp. 132–5. For some of his writings on the *Nights*, see note 8 above.

17 On textual criticism and the editing of manuscripts, see Paul Maas, *Textual Criticism* (Oxford, 1958); M.L. West, *Textual Criticism and Editorial Technique* (Stuttgart, 1973); E.J. Kenny, *The Classical Text: Aspects of Editing in the Age of the Printed Book* (Berkeley and Los Angeles, 1974); Sebastiano Timpanaro, *The Freudian Slip* (London, 1976). On the editing of Arabic manuscripts (including the *Nights*), see Jan Just Witkam, 'Establishing the Stemma: Fact or Fiction?', *Manuscripts of the Middle East*, 3 (1988), pp. 88–101.

18 Mahdi, *Alf Layla wa-Layla*. Although the text, introduction and critical apparatus are all in Arabic, Mahdi has provided a very brief statement in English of his aims and conclusions at the end of the first volume.

19 *Idem*, 'Exemplary Tales in the *1001 Nights*', in *The 1001 Nights: Critical Essays and Annotated Bibliography/Mundus Arabicus*, 3 (1983), pp. 1–24.

20 Ibid., p. 23.

21 For the unedifying life of this adventurer, see Jonathan Curling, *Edward Wortley Montagu, 1713–1776* (London, 1954). On the manuscript, see Fatma Moussa-Mahmoud, 'A Manuscript Translation of the *Arabian Nights* in the Beckford Papers', *Journal of Arabic Literature*, 7 (1976), pp. 7–23.

22 On dating the *Nights*, see Macdonald, 'The Earlier History of the *Arabian Nights*', pp. 353–97; W. Popper, 'Data for Dating a Tale in the *Nights*', *Journal of the Royal Asiatic Society* (1926), pp. 1–14; Wiebke Walther, *Tausendundeine Nacht* (Munich, 1987), pp. 16–18.

23 Mahdi, *Alf Layla wa-Layla*, vol. 1, p. 235; Husain Haddawy, *The Arabian Nights* (London and New York, 1990), p. 255.

24 Mahdi, *Alf Layla wa-Layla*, vol. 1, p. 290; Haddawy, *The Arabian Nights*, p. 215.

25 Mahdi, *Alf Layla wa-Layla*, vol. 1, p. 319; Haddawy, *The Arabian Nights*, p. 241. On the career of Sudun, see Gaston Wiet, *Les Biographies du Manhal safi* (Cairo, 1932), p. 162 (no. 1133).

26 Mahdi, *Alf Layla wa-Layla*, vol. 1, p. 319. Haddawy in his translation of *The Arabian Nights* renders the key phrase (on p. 241) as 'two dinars', rather than as 'two Ashrafi dinars'. It is one of the rare trivial blemishes in a fine translation.

27 H.T. Norris, review of Haddawy's *Arabian Nights, Bulletin of the School of Oriental African Studies*, 55 (1992), pp. 330–31.

3 Oceans of Stories

1 Richard Burton, *A Plain and Literal Translation of the Arabian Nights Entertainments, Now Entitled the Book of the Thousand Nights and a Night* (Benares = Stoke Newington, London, 1885), vol. 3, p. 158; E.L. Ranelagh, *The Past We Share: The Near Eastern Ancestry of Western Folk Literature* (London, 1979), pp. 205–7.

2 Burton, *Nights*, vol. 6, pp. 152–5; Eberhard Hermes (trans. and ed.), *The Disciplina Clericalis of Petrus Alfonsi* (London, 1977), pp. 124–5; Dorothee Metlitzki, *The Matter of Araby in Medieval England* (New Haven and London, 1977), pp. 97–103; Ranelagh, *The Past We Share*, pp. 182–8.

3 Burton, *Nights*, vol. 5, pp. 1–32; M. Gaudefroy-Demombynes, *Les Cent et une nuits* (Paris, 1982), pp. 182–98, 299–302; Metzliki, *The Matter of Araby*, pp. 140–41.

4 On the Sanskrit story collections, see A.B. Keith, *History of Sanskrit Literature* (Oxford, 1928).

5 On the *Panchatantra* and *Kalila wa-Dimna*, see T. Benfey, *Pantschatantra* (Leipzig, 1859), 2 vols; Ion G.N. Falconer, *Kalilah and Dimnah, or the Fables of Bidpai* (Cambridge, 1885); *Encyclopedia of Islam* (2nd edn), s.v. 'Kalilah wa-Dimnah'.

6 Somadeva, *The Ocean of Story*, trans. C.H. Tawney, ed. N. Penzer (London, 1924–8), 10 vols.

7 Louis Renou (trans.), *Contes du vampire* (Paris, 1963), is a complete translation with notes.

8 Emmanuel Cosquin, *Etudes folkloriques: Recherches sur les migrations des contes populaires et leur point du départ* (Paris, 1920).

9 B.E. Perry, 'The Origin of the Book of Sindbad', *Fabula*, 3 (1960), pp. 26–7n.

10 On Homer and the *Nights*, see Armand Abel, *Les Enseignements des Mille et une nuits* (Brussels, 1939), p. 113; Mohamed Abdel-Halim, *Antoine Galland, sa vie et son ouevre* (Paris, 1964), p. 296; Gustave E. von Grunebaum, 'Greece in the *Arabian Nights*', in *idem, Medieval Islam: A Study in Cultural Orientation* (Chicago, 1953), pp. 303–4.

11 On the possible legacy of classical literature generally (and of Plautus specifically) on the *Nights*, see Edward Rehatsek, 'A Few Analogies in the *Thousand and One Nights* and in Latin Authors', *Journal of the Bombay Branch of the Royal Asiatic Society*, 14 (1880), pp. 74–85; Abel, *Les Enseignements*, pp. 111–3; von Grunebaum, 'Greece in the *Arabian Nights*', pp. 294–319; *idem*, 'Greek Form Elements in the *Arabian Nights*', *Journal of the American Oriental Society*, 62 (1942), pp. 277–92; Perry, 'The Origin of the Book of Sindbad'; *idem*, 'Two Fables Recovered', *Byzantinische Zeitschrift*, 54 (1961), pp. 4–14; *idem*, 'Some Traces of Lost Medieval Story Books', in *Humaniora: Essays in Literature, Folklore, Bibliography, Honouring Archer Taylor* (Locust Valley, NY, 1960), pp. 150–60.

12 Ibn al-Nadim, *The Fihrist of al-Nadim*. trans. Bayard Dodge (New York, 1970), vol. 2, p. 718.

13 See Chapter 2, note 27.

14 On the survival of Pharaonic stories, see Hasan El-Shamy, *Folktales of Egypt* (Chicago, 1980), pp. 248, 259, 275, 281; *Encyclopedia of Islam* (2nd edn), s.v. 'Alf Layla wa-Layla'. On ancient Egyptian literature in general, see Gaston Maspero, *Popular Stories of Ancient Egypt* (London and New York, 1915); Ernest A.W. Budge, *Egyptian Tales and Romances: Pagan, Christian, and Muslim* (London, 1931); W.K. Simpson (ed.), *The Literature of Ancient Egypt* (New Haven, 1972); Stith Thompson, *The Folktale* (Berkeley and Los Angeles, 1977), pp. 273–6.

15 Stephanie Dalley, 'Gilgamesh in the *Arabian Nights*', *Journal of the Royal Asiatic Society* (1991), pp. 1–17.

16 O.R. Gurney, 'The Tale of the Poor Man of Nippur and its Folktale Parallels', *Anatolian Studies*, 22 (1972), pp. 149–58.

17 Nikita Elisseef, *Thèmes et motifs des Mille et une nuits* (Beirut, 1949), p. 48.

18 On the *Sindibadnama*, see Perry, 'The Origin of the Book of Sindbad'; S. Belcher, 'The Diffusion of the Book of Sindbad', *Fabula*, 28 (1987), pp. 34–58.

19 H. Zotenberg, 'Histoire de Gal'ad et Chimas, roman arabe', *Journal asiatique*, 6 (1885), p. 551, and 7 (1886), pp. 97–123; Perry, 'The Origin of the Book of Sindbad', pp. 1–94, *passim*.

20 J.R. Walsh, 'The Historiography of Ottoman–Safavid Relations in the Sixteenth and Seventeenth Centuries', in Bernard Lewis and P.M. Holt (eds), *Historians of the Middle East* (London, 1962), p. 197.

21 On the translation movement, see L.E. Goodman, 'The Translation of Greek Materials into Arabic', in M.L.J. Young, J.D. Latham and R.B. Serjeant (eds), *Religion, Learning and Science in the Abbasid Period* (Cambridge, 1990), pp. 477–97.

22 Perry, 'Some Traces', pp. 156–7.

23 On Ibn al-Muqaffa and *Kalila wa-Dimna*, see Esin Atil, *Kalila wa Dimna: Fables from a Fourteenth-Century Arabic Manuscript* (Washington, 1981); J.D. Latham, 'Ibn al-Muqaffa and Early Abbasid Prose', in Julia Ashtiany, T.M. Johnstone, J.D. Latham, R.B. Serjeant and G. Rex Smith (eds), *Abbasid Belles-Lettres* (Cambridge, 1990), pp. 48–77; *Encyclopedia of Islam* (2nd edn), s.v. 'Ibn al-Muqaffa' and 'Kalilah wa-Dimnah'; R. Irwin, 'The Arabic Beast Fable', *Journal of the Warburg and Courtauld Institutes*, 55 (1992), pp. 36–50.

24 On the *Maqamat* of al-Hamadhani and al-Hariri, see R.A. Nicholson, *A Literary History of the Arabs* (Cambridge, 1930), pp. 328–36; Abdelfattah Kilito, *Les Séances* (Paris, 1983); A.F.L. Beeston, 'Al-Hamadhani, al-Hariri and the *Maqamat* Genre', in Ashtiany *et al.* (eds), *Abbasid Belles-Lettres*, pp. 125–35; Shmuel Moreh, *Live Theatre and Dramatic Literature in the Medieval Arab World* (Edinburgh, 1992), pp. 104–22.

25 R.A. Nicholson, *A Literary History of the Arabs* (London, 1907), p. 332.

26 On the origins and development of *adab*, see Barbara Daly Metcalf (ed.), *Moral Conduct and Authority: The Place of Adab in South Asian Islam* (Berkeley and Los Angeles, 1984) (esp. chapters by Peter Brown, Ira M. Lapidus and Gerhard Bowering); S.A. Bonebakker, '*Adab* and the Concept of *Belles-Lettres*', in Ashtiany *et al.* (eds), *Abbasid Belles-Lettres*, pp. 16–30.

27 Al-Nadim, *The Fihrist of al-Nadim*, vol. 2, pp. 712–24, 734–5.

28 Ibid., p. 714; cf. *Encyclopedia of Islam* (2nd edn), s.v. 'Djashiyari'.

29 Hans Wehr (ed.), *Al-Hikayat al-Ajibah wa'l-Akhbar al-Gharibah* (Wiesbaden, 1956).

30 F.C. Seybold (ed.), *Geschichte von Sul und Schumul. Unbekannte Erzahlungen aus Tausend und Einer Nacht* (Leipzig, 1920).

31 On al-Tanukhi, see D.S. Margoliouth, *Table Talk of a Mesopotamian Judge* (London, 1922); *Encyclopedia of Islam* (1st edn), s.v. 'Tanukhi'; Wiebke Walther, *Tausendundeine Nacht* (Munich, 1987), pp. 19, 24.

32 On al-Ghuzuli, see C. Torrey, 'The Story of el-Abbas and his Fortunate Verses', *Journal of the American Oriental Society*, 16 (1896), pp. 43–70; *idem,*

'A Story of a Friend in Need: The Arabic Text Edited from the Vienna Manuscript of al-Ghuzuli and Translated for the First Time', *Journal of the American Oriental Society*, 26 (1905), pp. 296–305; *Encyclopedia of Islam* (2nd edn), s.v. 'Ghuzuli'.

33 On al-Ayni, see *Encyclopedia of Islam* (2nd edn), s.v. 'Ayni'.

34 On Ibn Arabshah, see Freytag (ed.), *Fakihat al-Khulafa wa Mafakihat al-Zurafa* (Bonn, 1832), 2 vols, reviewed by Sylvestre de Sacy in *Journal des savants* (1835), pp. 602–12, 652–67; Clement Huart, *A History of Arabic Literature* (London, 1903), pp. 363–4; El-Shamy, *Folktales of Egypt*, pp. 263, 275–6; *Encyclopedia of Islam* (2nd edn), s.v. 'Ibn Arabshah'.

35 On al-Ibshihi, see *Encyclopedia of Islam* (2nd edn), s.v. 'Ibshihi'.

36 On al-Yafi'i, see Mia I. Gerhardt, *The Art of Story-Telling: A Literary Study of the Thousand and One Nights* (Leiden, 1963), pp. 369, 372n., 374, 465; *Encyclopedia of Islam* (1st edn), s.v. 'Yafi'i'.

37 D. Ayalon, 'The Historian al-Jabarti and his Background', *Bulletin of the School of Oriental and African Studies*, 23 (1960), p. 246.

38 Huart, *A History*, pp. 425–6; Ayalon, 'The Historian al-Jabarti'.

39 Franz Rosenthal, *A History of Muslim Historiography* (Leiden, 1962), pp. 42–3.

40 On the medieval Arab folk-epics, see R. Paret, *Die Geschichte des Islams im Spiegel der Arabischen Volksliteratur* (Tübingen, 1927); *idem, Der Ritter-Roman von Umar an-Numan und seine Stellung zur Sammlung von 1001 Nacht* (Tübingen, 1927); R. Goossens, 'Autour du *Digenis Akritas*: La "Geste d'Omar" dans les *Mille et une nuits*', *Byzantion*, 7 (1932), pp. 303–16; M. Canard, 'Delhemma: Epopée arabe des guerres arabo-byzantines', *Byzantion*, 10 (1935), pp. 283–300; N. Christides, 'An Arabo-Byzantine Novel: *Umar B. al-Nu'man* compared with *Digenis Akritas*', *Byzantion*, 22 (1962), pp. 549–604; U. Steinbach, *Dhat al-Himma. Kulturgeschichteliche Untersuchungen zu einem arabischen Volksroman* (Wiesbaden, 1972); G. Canova, 'Gli studi sull'epica popolare araba', *Oriente moderno*, 57 (1977), pp. 211–26; P. Heath, 'A Critical Review of Modern Scholarship on *Sirat Antar* ibn Shaddad and the Popular Sira', *Journal of Arabic Literature*, 15 (1984), pp. 19–44; B. Connelly, *The Arab Folk Epic and Identity* (Berkeley, Los Angeles and London, 1986).

41 Edward William Lane, *An Account of the Manners and Customs of the Modern Egyptians. Written in Egypt during the Years 1833–1835* (London, 1836), chs 21–3. (See also Chapter 4 for more detail on Lane's observations.)

42 M. Gaudefroy-Demombynes, *Les Cent et une nuits* (Paris, 1982).

43 On medieval European translations from Arabic generally, see R.W. Southern, *Western Views of Islam in the Middle Ages* (Cambridge, Mass., 1962); James Kritzek, *Peter the Venerable and Islam* (Princeton, 1964); Norman

Daniel, *The Arabs and Mediaeval Europe* (London, 1975); Juan Vernet, *Ce que la culture doit aux Arabes d'Espagne* (Paris, 1978); Maxime Rodinson, *Europe and the Mystique of Islam* (Seattle, 1987), pp. 3–37.

44 Hermes, *The Disciplina Clericalis of Petrus Alfonsi*, p. 104.

45 On the influence of the *Disciplina*, see Metlitzki, *The Matter of Araby*, pp. 95–106.

46 On translation from Arabic in Spain, see Angel Gonzalez Palencia, *Historia de la literatura arabigo-española* (Barcelona, 1928); Vernet, *Ce que la culture doit aux Arabes d'Espagne*.

47 On Don Juan Manuel, see Palencia, *Historia*, pp. 313–4; Vernet, *Ce que la culture doit aux Arabes d'Espagne*, pp. 320–1; T. Montgomery, 'Don Juan Manuel's Tale of Don Illan and its Revision by Jorge Luis Borges', *Hispania*, 47 (1964), pp. 464–6.

48 Nai-tung Ting, 'Years of Experience in a Moment: A Study of a Tale Type in Asian and European Literature', *Fabula*, 22 (1981), pp. 210–11 (and cf. pp. 190–19 on Don Juan Manuel).

49 On Lull, see E. Allison Peers, *Ramón Lull: A Biography* (London, 1929).

50 Ferial J. Ghazoul, '*The Arabian Nights* in Shakespearean Comedy: "The Sleeper Awakened" and *The Taming of the Shrew*', in *The 1001 Nights: Critical Essays and Annotated Bibliography/Mundus Arabicus*, 3 (1983), pp. 58–70.

51 On the diffusion of Arab tales and motifs in Europe, see Metlitzki, *The Matter of Araby*; Ranelagh, *The Past We Share*.

52 On some Arab sources for *The Canterbury Tales*, see Chaucer Society, *Originals and Analogues of Chaucer's Canterbury Tales* (London, 1872–88); W.F. Bryan and Germaine Dempster, *Sources and Analogues of Chaucer's Canterbury Tales* (Chicago, 1941); Metlitzki, *The Matter of Araby*.

53 On the *Decameron*, see A.C. Lee, *The Decameron: Its Sources and Analogues* (London, 1909).

54 On Sercambi, see Cosquin, *Etudes folkloriques*, pp. 286–8; Bryan and Dempster, *Sources*, pp. 21–2; *Encyclopedia Iranica*, s.v. 'Alf Layla wa-Layla'. Quite a few of Sercambi's stories seem to derive from oriental sources, including the *Nights*.

55 Ariosto, *Orlando Furioso*, trans. Guido Waldman (Oxford, 1974), pp. 339–51.

56 Italo Calvino, *Italian Folktales* (London, 1980), p. xv.

57 On the Brothers Grimm and their sources, see Otto Spies, *Orientalische Stoffe in den Kinder – und Hausmärchen der Bruder Grimm* (Waldorf-Hessen, 1952); J.M. Ellis, *One Fairy Story Too Many* (Chicago, 1983).

58 Ernest Gellner, in *Times Literary Supplement* (22 August 1986), p. 903.

59 El-Shamy, *Folktales of Egypt*, p. xlii.

4 The Storyteller's Craft

1 Elias Canetti, *The Voices of Marrakesh* (London, 1978), p. 77.

2 On *khurafa*, see E.W. Lane, *Arabic–English Lexicon* (Cambridge, 1984, reprinted from edn of 1863), vol. 1, p. 726; D.B. Macdonald, 'The Earlier History of the *Arabian Nights*', *Journal of the Royal Asiatic Society* (1924), pp. 362–76; Nabia Abbott, 'A Ninth-Century Fragment of the "Thousand Nights": New Light on the Early History of the *Arabian Nights*', *Journal of Near Eastern Studies*, 8 (1949), pp. 155–8.

3 On preaching, see *Encyclopedia of Islam* (2nd edn), s.v. 'khatib' and 'khutba'. On popular preachers, see Ibn al-Jawzi, *Kitab al-Qussas wa'l-Mudhakkirun*, ed. and trans. M.L. Swartz (Beirut, 1986); Adam Mez, *The Renaissance of Islam* (London, 1937), pp. 326–7, 351; Ignaz Goldziher, 'The Hadith as a Means of Edification and Entertainment', in *idem, Muslim Studies* (London, 1971), vol. 2, pp. 145–63; Johannes Pedersen, 'The Criticism of the Islamic Preacher', *Die Welt des Islams*, n.s. 2 (1953), pp. 215–31; Khalib Athamina, 'Al-Qasas: Its Emergence, Religious Origin and Socio-Political Impact on Early Muslim Society', *Studia Islamica*, 76 (1992), pp. 53–74; *Encyclopedia of Islam* (2nd ed), s.v. 'kass'.

4 B.E. Perry, 'The Origin of the Book of Sindbad', *Fabula* 3 (1960), p. 11.

5 On live theatre in the pre-modern Arab world, see Shmuel Moreh, *Live Theatre and Dramatic Literature in the Medieval Arab World* (Edinburgh, 1992); cf. Peter J. Chelkowski (ed.), *Taziyeh: Ritual and Drama in Iran* (New York, 1979).

6 Charles Pellat (ed. and trans.), *The Life and Works of Jahiz* (Berkeley and Los Angeles, 1969), p. 101; cf. Moreh, *Live Theatre*, pp. 87–9; cf. *Encyclopedia of Islam* (2nd edn), s.v. 'hikaya'.

7 Al-Mas'udi, *The Meadows of Gold: The Abbasids*, trans. and ed. Paul Lunde and Caroline Stone (London, 1989), pp. 352–4.

8 Barhebraeus, *The Laughable Stories: The Syriac Text*, ed. and trans. E.A.W. Budge (London, 1897).

9 Al-Maqrizi, *Kitab al-Khitat* (Cairo, 1854), vol. 1, p. 485.

10 Roger Le Tourneau, *Fez in the Age of the Marinides* (Norman, Okla, 1961), p. 71.

11 Ibn Taghribirdi, *Al-Nujum al-Zahira* (Cairo, n.d.), vol. 7, pp. 813–14.

12 Richard Burton, *A Plain and Literal Translation of the Arabian Nights Entertainments, Now Entitled the Book of the Thousand Nights and a Night* (Benares = Stoke Newington, London, 1885), vol. 7, pp. 308–14.

13 E. Lévi-Provençal (ed. and trans.), *Seville Musulmane au début du XIIe siècle: Le Traité d'Ibn Abdun sur la vie urbaine et les corps des métiers* (Paris, 1947), pp. 60–61 and cf. p. 147n.

14 On this theme of *ibra*, or warning, in the *Nights*, see Abdelfattah Kilito, *L'Oeil et l'aiguille*, (Paris, 1992); David Pinault, *Story-Telling Techniques in the Arabian Nights* (Leiden, 1992), pp. 148–239.

15 On the guild of storytellers, see André Raymond, 'Une liste des corporations au Caire en 1801', *Arabica*, 4 (1957), p. 158; Gabriel Baer, *Egyptian Guilds in Modern Times* (Jerusalem, 1964), p. 116.

16 Katib Chelebi, *The Balance of the Truth* (London, 1957), p. 61. On the Middle Eastern coffee-house generally, see Antoine Galland, *De l'origine et du progrès du café: Sur un manuscrit arabe de la Bibliothèque du Roy* (Paris, 1699); Ralph S. Hattox, *Coffee and Coffee Houses: The Origins of Social Beverage in the Medieval Near East* (Seattle and London, 1985).

17 Alexander Russell, *The Natural History of Aleppo* (London, 1794), pp. 148–9.

18 Burton, *Nights*, vol. 10, pp. 164–6.

19 Edward William Lane, *An Account of the Manners and Customs of the Modern Egyptians: Written in Egypt during the Years 1833–1835* (London, 1836), chs 21–3.

20 Macdonald, 'The Earlier History of the *Arabian Nights*', p. 370.

21 On storytelling in Turkey, see Wolfram Eberhard, *Minstrel Tales from South Eastern Turkey* (Berkeley and Los Angeles, 1955); Ahmet O. Evin, *Origins and Development of the Turkish Novel* (Minneapolis, 1983), pp. 26, 30–39; Metin And, *Culture, Performance and Communication in Turkey* (Tokyo, 1987), pp. 74–5, 110–14; *Encyclopedia of Islam* (2nd edn), s.v. 'maddah'.

22 On storytelling in Persia, see Jiri Cepek, 'Iranian Folk-Literature', in Jan Rypka (ed.), *History of Iranian Literature* (Dordrecht, 1968), pp. 608–61; Elwell Sutton, 'Collecting Folklore in Iran', *Folklore*, 93 (1982), pp. 98–104; Peter Chelkowski, 'Popular Entertainment, Media and Social Change in Twentieth-Century Iran', in Peter Avery and Gavin Hambly (eds), *The Cambridge History of Iran* (Cambridge, 1991), vol. 7, pp. 766, 782–3.

23 John Malcolm, *Sketches of Persia* (London, 1845), p. 175.

24 Annemarie Schimmel, *The Triumphal Sun: A Study of the Works of Jalaloddin Rumi* (London and The Hague, 1978), esp. pp. 40–41; cf. Marshall S.G. Hodgson, *The Venture of Islam* (Chicago, 1974), vol. 2, pp. 244–9.

25 C.J. Wills, *In the Land of the Lion and the Sun, or Modern Persia: Being Experiences of Life in Persia from 1866 to 1881* (London, 1891), pp. 44–5.

26 Mary Ellen Page, 'Professional Storytelling in Iran: Transmission and Practice', *Iranian Studies*, 12 (1979), pp. 195–215.

27 M. Akar, 'The Arab Story-Teller: Nacer Khemir and the Revival of a Tradition', in *The Arab Cultural Scene* (*Literary Review*, special supplement, London, 1982), pp. 105–9.

28 Hasan El-Shamy, *Folktales of Egypt* (Chicago, 1980), p. xlviii.

29 Richard Hughes, *In the Lap of Atlas* (London, 1979), p. 41.
30 Iain Finlayson, *Tangier: City of the Dream* (London, 1992), p. 167.

5 Street Entertainments

1 For general histories of Islamic societies in pre-modern times, see M.G.S. Hodgson, *The Venture of Islam* (Chicago, 1974), 3 vols; Ulrich Haarmann, *Geschichte der arabischen Welt* (Munich, 1987); I.M. Lapidus, *A History of Muslim Societies* (Cambridge, 1988); Albert Hourani, *A History of the Arab Peoples* (London, 1991).

2 On Abbasid history, see Hugh Kennedy, *The Prophet and the Age of the Caliphates: The Islamic East to the Eleventh Century* (London, 1986). On Baghdad and social life in the eighth, ninth and tenth centuries, see Adam Mez, *The Renaissance of Islam* (London, 1937), an exceptionally lively book, full of recondite snippets and anecdotes; Gaston Wiet, *Baghdad: Metropolis of the Abbasid Caliphate* (Norman, Okla, 1974); M.M. Ahsan, *Social Life under the Abbasids* (London, 1979); Jacob Lassner, *The Topography of Baghdad in the Early Middle Ages* (Detroit, 1970); Louis Massignon, *The Passion of al-Hallaj, Mystic and Martyr of Islam* (Princeton, 1982), vol. 1, esp. pp. 224–94.

3 Oleg Grabar, *The Formation of Islamic Art* (New Haven and London, 1973), p. 173.

4 Richard Burton, *A Plain and Literal Translation of the Arabian Nights Entertainments, Now Entitled the Book of the Thousand Nights and a Night* (Benares = Stoke Newington, London, 1885), vol. 9, pp. 193–4.

5 Husain Haddawy, *The Arabian Nights* (London and New York, 1990), p. 66.

6 Ibn Jubayr, *The Travels of Ibn Jubayr*, trans. R.J.C. Broadhurst (London, 1952), p. 226.

7 On the history of the Mamlukes of Egypt and Syria, see Robert Irwin, *The Middle East in the Middle Ages: The Early Mamluk Sultanate 1250–1382* (Beckenham, Kent, 1986); P.M. Holt, *The Age of the Crusades: The Near East from the Eleventh Century to 1517* (London, 1986); U. Haarmann, 'Der arabische Osten im späten Mittelalter 1250–1517', in *idem* (ed.), *Geschichte der arabischen Welt* (Munich, 1987), pp. 217–63. On medieval Cairo, see Gaston Wiet, *Cairo: City of Art and Commerce* (Norman, Okla, 1964); S.D. Goitein, 'Cairo: An Islamic City in the Light of the Geniza Documents', in I.M. Lapidus (ed.), *Middle Eastern Cities* (Berkeley and Los Angeles, 1969), pp. 80–96; I.M. Lapidus, *Muslim Cities in the Later Middle Ages* (Cambridge, Mass., 1967).

8 Haddawy, *The Arabian Nights*, pp. 215–18, 221–2.

9 Ibid., pp. 239–41.

10 Edward William Lane (trans.), *The Thousand and One Nights, Commonly Called, in England, the Arabian Nights Entertainments* (London, 1877), vol. 1, p. 67; cf. *idem, An Account of the Manners and Customs of the Modern Egyptians: Written in Egypt during the Years 1833–1835* (London, 1836), pp. 291–2.

11 Richard Burton, *Supplemental Nights to the Book of the Thousand Nights and a Night* (Benares = Stoke Newington, London, 1886–8), vol. 2, p. 72.

12 Haddawy, *The Arabian Nights*, p. 69.

13 Ibn Khaldun, *The Muqaddimah: An Introduction to History*, trans. Franz Rosenthal (London, 1958), vol. 2, p. 348.

14 On the strangely neglected topic of the professional farter in the Middle Ages, see now Shmuel Moreh, *Live Theatre and Dramatic Literature in the Medieval Arab World* (Edinburgh, 1992), pp. 65–6. It is odd that Burton, for all his immense interest in the subject in general, restricts himself in his annotations to commenting on amateurs.

15 On the Banu Sasan, see Clifford Edmund Bosworth's marvellous book, *The Mediaeval Islamic Underworld* (Leiden, 1976), 2 vols.

16 There is as yet neither a decent edition of al-Jawbari's bizarre masterpiece, nor a scholarly translation. However, in the meantime, al-Jawbari, *Kashf al-Asrar* (Cairo, 1918?), and Abd al-Rahmane al-Djawbari, *Le Voile arraché: L'Autre Visage de l'Islam*, trans. René R. Khawam (Paris, 1979), 2 vols, may be used with caution. On al-Jawbari, see S. Wild, 'Jugglers and Fraudulent Sufis', in *Proceedings of the VIth Congress of Arabic and Islamic Studies* (Stockholm, 1975), pp. 58–63; Bosworth, *Mediaeval Islamic Underworld*, vol. 1, pp. 106–18; *Encyclopedia of Islam* (supplementary fascicule), s.v. 'Djawbari'.

17 On medieval Arab conjuring, see Wild, 'Jugglers and Fraudulent Sufis'; *idem*, 'A Juggler's Programme in Medieval Islam', in *La Signification du bas moyen age dans l'histoire et la culture du monde musulman: Actes du 8ième congrés de l'union européenne des arabisants et islamisants* (Aix-en-Provence, 1976), pp. 161–72.

18 Muhammad ibn Abu Bakr al-Zakhruri, 'Zahr al-Basatin fi Ilm al-Mashatin', British Library, Supp. MS 1210, f. 42a–b.

19 Ibid., ff. 92b–93b.

20 Massignon, *Passion of al-Hallaj*, vol. 1, pp. 155–61.

21 Du Camp is cited in Francis Steegmuller (trans. and ed.), *Flaubert in Egypt* (London, 1972), pp. 87–9.

22 On al-Muzaffar Hajji, see Irwin, *Middle East*, pp. 133–4.

23 On live theatre, see Moreh, *Live Theatre, passim*.

24 Burton, *Nights*, vol. 4, p. 193.

25 On shadow plays, see P. Kahle, 'The Arabic Shadow Play in Medieval

Egypt (Old Texts and Old Figures)', *Journal of the Pakistan Historical Society*
(1954), pp. 85–115; *idem*, 'The Arabic Shadow Play in Egypt', *Journal of the
Royal Asiatic Society* (1940), pp. 21–34; M.M. Badawi, 'Medieval Arabic
Drama: Ibn Daniyal', *Journal of Arabic Literature*, 13 (1982), pp. 83–107;
Shmuel Moreh, 'The Shadow Play (*Khayal al-Zill*) in the Light of Arabic
Literature', *Journal of Arabic Literature*, 18 (1987), pp. 46–61; *Three Shadow
Plays by Ibn Daniyal*, ed. Paul Kahle, Derek Hopwood and Mustafa Badawi
(Cambridge, 1992); Moreh, *Live Theatre, passim*.

6 Low Life

1 There is very little secondary literature on crime in the medieval Near East.
  However, see Clifford Edmund Bosworth, *The Mediaeval Islamic Underworld*
  (Leiden, 1976), 2 vols; Muhammad Rajab al-Najjar, *Hikayat al-Shuttar wa'l-
  Ayyarin fi'l-Turath al-Arabi* (Kuwait, 1981); *Encyclopedia of Islam* (2nd edn),
  s.v. 'liss'. On crime fiction, see Fadwa Malti-Douglas, 'Classical Crime
  Narratives: Thieves and Thievery in *Adab* Literature', *Journal of Arabic
  Literature*, 19 (1988), pp. 108–27; and cf. *idem*, 'The Classical Arabic Detec-
  tive', *Arabica*, 35 (1988), pp. 59–81. There are also some extremely interesting
  remarks about the medieval Arab origins of certain detection techniques in
  Carlo Ginzburg's 'Clues: Roots of an Evidential Paradigm', in his *Myths,
  Emblems, Clues* (London, 1986), pp. 96–125.
2 Al-Mas'udi, *The Meadows of Gold: The Abbasids*, trans. and ed. Paul Lunde
  and Caroline Stone (London, 1989), pp. 356–7.
3 Charles Pellat (ed. and trans.), *The Life and Works of Jahiz* (Berkeley and Los
  Angeles, 1969), p. 145.
4 Al-Mas'udi, *Meadows*, pp. 348; cf. pp. 350, 356.
5 Ibid., pp. 150, 154–5, 156–7, 160–61. On urban militias and related groups,
  see Claude Cahen, 'Mouvements populaires et autonomisme urbain dans
  l'Asie musulmane du moyen âge', *Arabica*, 5 (1958), pp. 225–50, and 6
  (1959), pp. 25–56, 223–65.
6 For this and other criminal scandals, see Ulrich Haarmann, *Quellenstudien
  zür fruhen Mamlukenzeit* (Freiburg im Breisgau, 1970), pp. 172–3.
7 Abd al–Latif al-Baghdadi, *The Eastern Key: Kitab al-Ifadah wa'l-Itibar*, trans.
  Kamal Hafuth Zand and John A. and Ivy E. Videan (London, 1965),
  pp. 223–79. One learns from the introduction to this edition (Arabic and
  English on facing pages) that, centuries after his death, Abd al-Latif, desperate
  to get his book into circulation again, contacted the Videans at a London
  seance presided over by a Mrs Ray Welch.

8 Al-Maqrizi, *Le Traité des famines de Magrizi*, trans. Gaston Wiet (Leiden, 1962), p. 37.

9 See Chapter 5.

10 On the *Sira* or 'Romance' of al-Zahir Baybars, see E.W. Lane, *An Account of the Manners and Customs of the Modern Egyptians: Written in Egypt during the Years 1833–1835* (London, 1836), pp. 367–80; H. Wangelin, *Das arabische Volksbuch vom Konig Azzahir Baibars* (Stuttgart, 1936); M.C. Lyons, 'The Sirat Baybars', in *Orientalia hispanica*, 1 (Leiden, 1974), pp. 490–503. The *Sira* was printed in forty-eight parts in Cairo, 1908–9. *Les Enfances de Baibars*, trans. Georges Boulas and Jean-Patrick Guillaume (Paris, 1985), is the first volume of an ongoing translation of a modern Syrian manuscript.

11 *The Subtle Ruse: The Book of Arabic Wisdom and Guile* (London and The Hague, 1980).

12 On *tufaylis* and the science of gate-crashing, see Ahmad ibn Ali al-Khatib al-Baghdadi, *Al-Tatfil wa Hikayat al-Tufaylyyin* (Damascus, 1927); al-Mas'udi, *Meadows*, pp. 303–5; *idem, Les Prairies d'or*, ed. and trans. C. Barbier de Meynard (Paris, 1874), vol. 8, pp. 13–19; *Encyclopedia of Islam* (1st edn), s.v. 'tufaili'. Abu Zayd, the picaresque protagonist of al-Hariri's *Maqamat*, was of course a *tufayli par excellence*.

13 On the cycle of crime stories incorporated into the *Nights*, see Nikita Elisseef, *Thèmes et motifs des Mille et une nuits* (Beirut, 1949), p. 51; Mia I. Gerhardt, *The Art of Story-Telling* (Leiden, 1963), pp. 167–90; André Miquel, *Sept contes des Mille et une nuits, ou Il n'y a pas de contes innocents* (Paris, 1981), pp. 51–78.

14 On thieves' guilds in medieval and in Ottoman times, see Lane, *Modern Egyptians*, p. 113; Bernard Lewis, 'The Islamic Guilds', *Economic History Review*, 8 (1937–8), p. 35; Gabriel Baer, *Egyptian Guilds in Modern Times* (Jerusalem, 1964), pp. 9, 13, 35, 81; *idem, Fellah and Townsman in the Middle East* (London, 1982), p. 151.

15 On *futuwwa*, see Cahen, 'Mouvements populaires'; *Encyclopedia of Islam* (2nd edn), s.v. 'futuwwa'. However, academic interest so far has concentrated almost exclusively on the respectable side of *futuwwa*.

16 For hostile accounts of *futuwwa*, see e.g. I. Goldziher, 'Eine Fetwa gegen die Futuwwa', *Zeitschrift der Deutschen morgenlandischen Gesellschaft*, 73 (1919), pp. 127–8; Joseph Schacht, 'Zwei neue Quellen zur Kenntnis Futuwa', in *Festschrift Georg Jacob* (Leipzig, 1932), pp. 276–87; al-Turkomani, *Kitab al-Luma*, ed. S.Y. Labib (Stuttgart, 1986), pp. 54–62, 113–19.

17 On *shuttar*, see Louis Massignon, *The Passion of al-Hallaj, Mystic and Martyr of Islam* (Princeton, 1982), vol. 1, pp. 270–71; I.M. Lapidus, *Muslim Cities in the Later Middle Ages* (Cambridge, Mass., 1967), p. 272; al-Turkomani, *Kitab al-Luma*, pp. 63–8, 125–33; al-Najjar, *Hikayat al-Shuttar wa'l-Ayarrun*.

18 On the sect, see Bernard Lewis, *The Assassins* (London, 1967).

19 On the *zu'ar*, see Lapidus, *Muslim Cities*, pp. 153–64, 173–7.

20 On the *harafish*, see ibid., pp. 177–83.

21 On the etiquette of mendicancy, see M.L.J. Young, J.D. Latham and R.B. Serjeant (eds), *Religion, Learning and Science in the Abbasid Period* (Cambridge, 1990), p. 506.

22 Pellat, *Life and Works of Jahiz*, p. 255.

23 Lane, *Manners*, p. 299.

24 On drug-taking, see Franz Rosenthal, *The Herb: Hashish versus Medieval Muslim Society* (Leiden, 1971); Sami-Ali, *Le Haschisch en Egypte: Essai d'anthropologie psychoanalytique* (Paris, 1988); Michael Dols, *Majnun: The Madman in Medieval Islamic Society* (Oxford, 1982), pp. 101, 105–8.

25 On the Sufi use of drugs, see J. Spencer Trimmingham, *The Sufi Orders in Islam* (Oxford, 1971), p. 199n.; Annemarie Schimmel, *Mystical Dimensions of Islam* (Chapel Hill, NC, 1975), pp. 335–6; Peter Lamborn Wilson, *Scandal: Essays in Islamic Heresy* (New York, 1988), pp. 195–213.

26 On wine and its celebration in the Middle East, see Wilson, *Scandal*, pp. 123–151; F. Harb, 'Wine Poetry (*Khamriyyat*)', in Julia Ashtiany, T.M. Johnstone, J.D. Latham, R.B. Serjeant and G. Rex Smith (eds), *Abbasid Belles-Lettres* (Cambridge, 1990), pp. 219–34; Dols, *Majnun*, pp. 104–5; *Encyclopedia of Islam*, (2nd edn), s.v. 'khamr'.

27 *The Assemblies of al-Hariri Retold by Amina Shah* (London, 1980), p. 51.

28 On gambling, see Franz Rosenthal, *Gambling in Islam* (Leiden, 1975); *Encyclopedia of Islam* (2nd edn), s.v. 'kimar'.

29 On the police and law enforcement, see Reuben Levy, *The Social Structure of Islam* (Cambridge, 1969), pp. 331–8; Lapidus, *Muslim Cities*, p. 270.

30 On executions, see Adam Mez, *The Renaissance of Islam* (London, 1937), pp. 367–74; Max Meyerhof and Joseph Schacht, *The Theologus Autodidactus of Ibn al-Nafis* (Oxford, 1968), pp. 81–2; Boaz Shoshan, *Popular Culture in Medieval Cairo* (Cambridge, forthcoming).

7 Sexual Fictions

1 On the alleged madness of Shahriyar, and on Sheherazade as a medieval psychoanalyst, see Chapter 9. Although, in *Majnun: The Madman in Medieval Islamic Society* (Oxford, 1992), p. 172, Michael Dols has adduced one eighteenth-century French source which suggests that inmates of Cairo's lunatic asylum were told stories, evidence for the therapeutic use of storytelling in the medieval Near East is extremely slight.

2 Rana Kabbani, *Europe's Myths of Orient: Devise and Rule* (London, 1986), p. 48.

3 The secondary literature on sex in Islamic societies is quite extensive. See, in particular, Afaf Lutfi al-Sayyid-Marsot (ed.), *Society and the Sexes in Medieval Islam* (Malibu, 1979); B.F. Musallam, *Sex and Society in Islam: Birth Control before the Nineteenth Century* (Cambridge, 1983); Abdelwahab Bouhdiba, *Sexuality in Islam* (London, 1985); Fedwa Malti-Douglas, *Woman's Body, Woman's Word: Gender and Discourse in Arabo-Islamic Writing* (Princeton, 1991); Nikkie R. Keddie and Beth Baron (eds), *Women in Middle Eastern History: Shifting Boundaries in Sex and Gender* (New Haven and London, 1991). Salah al-Din Munajjid's *Al-Hayat al-jinsiyya ind al-Arab* [Sexual Life among the Arabs] (Beirut, 1958) deserves to be translated into English.

4 S.D. Goitein, *A Mediterranean Society* (Berkeley and Los Angeles, 1988), p. 308.

5 On this issue, see Musallam, *Sex and Society*.

6 On the *Hikayat al-Ajiba*, see Chapter 3.

7 On erotica, see Manfred Ullman, *Die Medizin im Islam* (Leiden, 1970), pp. 193–8; Munajjid, *Al-Hayat*, esp. pp. 149–72; Bouhdiba, *Sexuality*, pp. 140–58. Luce López-Baralt, *Un Kama Sutra español* (Madrid, 1992), offers both the text of an erotic treatise written by a seventeenth-century Spanish Muslim exile in Tunisia, and what is now the most important survey of Arabic erotic literature, as well as of knowledge of that literature in the medieval West.

8 On al-Tayfashi, see Ahamad al-Tayfashi, *Surur al-Nafs*, ed. Ihsan Abbas (Beirut, 1980); Ahmad al-Tifachi, *Les Délices des coeurs*, trans. René R. Khawam (Paris, 1981); Musallam, *Sex and Society*, pp. 91–3; Munajjid, *Al-Hayat*, p. 161.

9 Ali al-Baghdadi, *Les Fleurs éclatantes dans les baisers et l'accolement*, trans. René R. Khawam (Paris, 1973). Although Khawam does not say so, he appears to be translating the Paris Bibliothèque nationale MS arabe 3671 of *Kitab al-Zahr al-Aniq*.

10 For al-Nafzawi, see *The Perfumed Garden of the Shaykh Nefzawi*, trans. Sir Richard Burton, ed. Alan Hull Walton (London, 1963); al-Nafzawi, *The Glory of the Perfumed Garden: The Missing Flowers* (London, 1975). Burton's translation of al-Nafzawi was a really a plagiaristic rendering of an earlier French translation. The older literature misdates al-Nafzawi. For the correct century, see Robert Brunschvig, *La Berberie orientale sous les Hafsides* (Paris, 1947), pp. 372–3.

11 Richard Ettinghausen, *Arab Painting* (New York, 1977), p. 32.

12 Bouhdiba, *Sexuality*, pp. 75, 171, 202–3. Bottoms also feature prominently in the Nobel Prize-winning novelist Naguib Mahfouz's *Cairo Trilogy*.

13 On *tasmina*, see Bouhdiba, *Sexuality*, p. 202; Huda Lutfi, 'Manners and Customs of Fourteenth-Century Cairene Women: Female Anarchy versus Male Shar'i Order in Muslim Prescriptive Treatises', in Keddie and Baron, *Women*, p. 110.

14 On *ghulumiyyat*, see Ahmad Abd ar-Raziq, *La Femme au temps des Mamlouks en Egypte* (Cairo, 1973), p. 183; Bouhdiba, *Sexuality*, p. 201.

15 Ibn Khaldun, *The Muqaddimah: An Introduction to History*, trans. Franz Rosenthal (London, 1958), vol. 2, pp. 295–6.

16 On homosexuality in the medieval Near East, see *Encyclopedia of Islam* (2nd edn), s.v. 'liwat'. Burton's theories about the 'sotadic zone' (found in the *Nights*, 'Terminal Essay', vol. 10) tell one a lot about Burton's phobias and nothing about anything else.

17 On the distinction between active and passive homosexuality, and on the latter considered as an illness in the Middle Ages, see Franz Rosenthal, 'Ar-Razi on the Hidden Illness', *Bulletin of the History of Medicine*, 52 (1978), pp. 45–60; Dols, *Majnun*, pp. 95–9, 106. For a similar distinction in a pre-Islamic culture, see K.J. Dover, *Greek Homosexuality* (London, 1979).

18 A translation exists by René R. Khawam; see note 8 above. However, as Khawam refrains from revealing what manuscript he is translating, it is impossible to assess the translation's accuracy; cf. Munajjid, *Al-Hayat*, p. 161.

19 Leo Africanus, *The History and Description of Africa of Leo Africanus* (London, 1896), vol. 2 (Hakluyt Society, vol. 93), p. 458. On lesbianism more generally, see Bouhdiba, *Sexuality*, pp. 44–5.

20 Al-Jahiz, *The Epistle on Singing Girls* (Oxford, 1980), p. 32.

21 Al-Mas'udi, *The Meadows of Gold*, trans. Paul Lunde and Caroline Stone (London, 1989), p. 264.

22 Robert Irwin, *The Middle East in the Middle Ages: The Early Mamluk Sultanate 1250–1382* (Beckenham, Kent, 1986), pp. 130, 133.

23 On prostitution, see Abd ar-Raziq, *La Femme*, pp. 45–8; Bouhdiba, *Sexuality*, pp. 189–95; *Encyclopedia of Islam* (2nd edn), s.v. 'bigha'.

24 Richard Burton, *A Plain and Literal Translation of the Arabian Nights Entertainments, Now Entitled the Book of the Thousand Nights and a Night* (Benares = Stoke Newington, London, 1885), vol. 9, p. 194.

25 On the *udar*, see *Encyclopedia of Islam* (2nd edn), s.v. 'liwat'.

26 Bernard Lewis, *Race and Slavery in the Middle East* (Oxford, 1990), p. 20.

27 On the *adab* of love, see Lois Anita Giffen, *Theory of Profane Love among the Arabs* (London and New York, 1972).

28 On the Banu Udhra, see Burton, *Nights*, vol. 2, p. 304n.; Giffen, *Theory*, pp. 29, 33, 75; J.C. Burgel, 'Love, Lust and Longing: Eroticism in Early Islam as Reflected in Literary Sources', in Marsot, *Society and the Sexes*, pp. 91–6; A. Hamori, 'Love Poetry (*Ghazal*)', in Julia Ashtiany, T.M.

Johnstone, J.D. Latham, R.B. Serjeant and G. Rex Smith (eds), *Abbasid Belles-Lettres* (Cambridge, 1990), pp. 205–6. See also Burton, *Nights*, vol. 7, pp. 117–24, for the story of 'The Lovers of Banu Uzrah'.

8 The Universe of Marvels

1 *Encyclopedia of Islam* (2nd edn), s.v. 'Balinus'.

2 Jorge Luis Borges, 'Narrative Art and Magic', in *Borges: A Reader*, ed. E.R. Monegal and A. Reid (New York, 1981), pp. 34–8.

3 Useful literature on Islamic occultism is not easy to come by. Even readers of Arabic are not well served. However, see Edmond Doutté, *Magie et religion dans l'Afrique du nord* (Algiers, 1908); Paul Kraus, *Jabir Ibn Hayyan: Contribution à l'histoire des idées scientifiques dans l'Islam* (Cairo, 1942–3), 2 vols; Toufic Fahd, *La Divination arabe* (Strasburg, 1966); Manfred Ullman, *Die Natur-und Geheimwissenschaften im Islam* (London, 1972); Sylvie Matton (ed.), *La Magie arabe traditionelle* (Paris, 1977); *Encyclopedia of Islam* (1st edn), s.v. 'sihr'. Armand Abel's 'La Place des sciences occultes dans la décadence', in R. Brunschvig and G.E. von Grunebaum (eds), *Classicisme et déclin culturel dans l'histoire de l'Islam* (Paris, 1957), pp. 291–311, is an exceptionally stimulating *tour d'horizon*.

4 Tanya Luhrmann, *Persuasions of the Witch's Craft* (Oxford, 1989), p. 87.

5 [Pseudo-] al-Majriti, *Ghayat al-Hakim*, ed. H. Ritter (Leipzig and Berlin, 1933), pp. 139–40; David Pingree (ed.), *Picatrix: The Latin Version of the Ghayat al-Hakim* (London, 1986). The medieval Latin translation omits this anecdote, contenting itself with remarking: 'eorum tanta fuere mirabilia que si narrare vellemus essent auditoribus et narrantibus difficilia'. See also Ibn Khaldun, *The Muqaddimah: An Introduction to History*, trans. Franz Rosenthal (London, 1958), vol. 1, p. 221; Ibn al-Nadim, *The Fihrist of al-Nadim*, ed. Bayard Dodge (New York, 1970), vol. 2, p. 753. For some interesting ideas on the background to parts of pseudo-al-Majriti's strange and extremely sinister text, see J. Hjarpe, *Analyse critique des traditions arabes sur les Sabeens harraniens* (Uppsala, 1972).

6 On al-Mamun and the pyramids, see Richard Burton, *A Plain and Literal Translation of the Arabian Nights Entertainments, Now Entitled the Book of the Thousand Nights and a Night* (Benares = Stoke Newington, London, 1885), vol. 5, pp. 105–7; Ulrich Haarmann (ed.), *Das Pyramidenbuch des Abu Ga'far al-Idrisi* (Beirut, 1991) (Arabic text), pp. 128–9.

7 Richard Burton, *Supplemental Nights to the Book of the Thousand Nights and a Night* (Benares = Stoke Newington, London, 1886–8), vol. 6, pp. 135–42;

A. Schimmel, 'Some Glimpses of the Religious Life in Egypt during the Later Mamluk Period', *Islamic Studies* (Rawlapindi), 7 (1965), pp. 373–4; cf. Nai-tung Ting, 'Years of Experience in a Moment: A Study of a Tale Type in Asian and European Literature', *Fabula*, 22 (1981), pp. 183–211.

8 A book on *aja'ib* by Roy Mottahedeh is forthcoming. It should be good. In the meantime, see Mohammed Arkoun, Jacques Le Goff, Tawfiq Fahd and Maxime Rodinson (eds), *L'Etrange et le merveilleux dans l'Islam médiéval* (Paris, 1978).

9 On the Sinbad the Sailor cycle and related Islamic nautical yarns, see Francesco Gabrieli, 'I viaggi di Sinbad', in *idem, Storia e civiltà Musulmana* (Naples, 1947), pp. 83–9; Jean Sauvaget (ed. and trans.), *Akhbar as-Sin wa l-Hind: Relation de la Chine et de l'Inde* (Paris, 1948); Mia I. Gerhardt, *The Art of Story-Telling: A Literary Study of the Thousand and One Nights* (Leiden, 1963), pp. 236–63; Michel Gall, *Le Secret des Mille et une nuits* (Paris, 1972), pp. 17–72; Captain Buzurg ibn Shahriyar of Ramhormuz, *The Book of the Wonders of India* (London and The Hague, 1981); André Miquel, *Sept contes des Mille et une nuits, ou Il n'y a pas de contes innocents* (Paris, 1981), pp. 79–109.

10 On medieval European ghosts, see M.R. James, 'Twelve Medieval Ghost-Stories', *English Historical Review*, 37 (1922), pp. 413–22; Keith Thomas, *Religion and the Decline of Magic* (London, 1971), pp. 701–2; R.C. Finucane, *Appearances of the Dead: A Cultural History of Ghosts* (London, 1982), pp. 29–89.

11 Fabri, *Le Voyage en Egypte de Felix Fabri, 1483*, trans. J. Masson (Paris, 1975), vol. 2, pp. 445–6.

12 Burton, *Nights*, vol. 3, p. 252n.

13 Ibid., vol. 5, pp. 166–86.

14 On the *mihna*, see *Encyclopedia of Islam* (2nd edn), s.v. 'mihna'.

15 On Aladdin considered as a tomb robber, see C.R. Long, 'Aladdin and the Wonderful Lamp', *Archaeology*, 9 (1956), pp. 210–14. On Islamic treasure-hunting, see G. Maspero, 'L'Abrégé des merveilles', *Journal des savants* (1899), pp. 69–81, 155–72; Doutté, *Magie*, pp. 265–70; Haarmann, *Pyramidenbuch, passim*.

16 Burton, *Nights*, vol. 6, pp. 213–56; cf. Gerhardt, *Art of Story-Telling*, pp. 328–33.

17 Abd al-Rahmane al-Djawbari, *Le Voile arraché: L'Autre Visage de l'Islam*, trans. R. Khawam (Paris, 1979), pp. 243–54.

18 On Arab automata, see Banu-Musa, *The Book of Ingenious Devices*, trans. Donald R. Hill (Dordrecht, 1979); al-Jazari, *The Book of Knowledge of Ingenious Mechanical Devices*, trans. Donald R. Hill (Dordrecht, 1974). However, the Banu Musa and al-Jazari provided specifications for machines

which could actually have worked. There is, as far as I know, no literature on their fictional counterparts.

19 Burton, *Nights*, vol. 9, p. 324.

20 Husain Haddawy, *The Arabian Nights* (New York and London, 1990), p. 119.

21 Burton, *Nights*, vol. 3, pp. 269–70.

22 On Islamic geomancy, see Stephen Skinner, *Terrestrial Astrology: Divination by Geomancy* (London, 1980), pp. 30–52; E. Savage-Smith and Marion B. Smith, *Islamic Geomancy and a Thirteenth-Century Divinatory Device* (Malibu, 1980); *Encyclopedia of Islam* (2nd edn), s.v. 'khatt'.

23 On *firasa*, see Yasin Mourad, *La Physiognomie arabe* (Paris, 1939); Fahd, *Divination*, pp. 369–429; *Encyclopedia of Islam* (2nd edn), s.v. 'firasa'.

24 Carlo Ginzburg, *Myths, Emblems, Clues* (London, 1990), p. 125.

25 On dreams and dream interpretation in the Middle East, see N. Bland, 'On the Muhammedan Science of Tabir or Interpretation of Dreams', *Journal of the Royal Asiatic Society* (1856), pp. 118–71; G.E. von Grunebaum and R. Caillois (eds), *The Dream and Human Societies* (Berkeley, 1966); K. Brackertz (trans.), *Das Traumbuch des Achmet ben Sirin* (Munich, 1986); Fadwa Malti Douglas, 'Dreams, the Blind and the Semiotics of the Biographical Notice', *Studia Islamica*, 51 (1980), pp. 137–62; cf. Peter Burke. 'L'Histoire sociale des rêves', *Annales: Economies, sociétés, civilizations*, 28 (1973), pp. 329–42.

26 Burton, *Nights*, vol. 4, p. 289. Essentially the same story features as non-fiction in a fourteenth-century chronicle by Ibn al-Dawadari; see Ulrich Haarmann, 'Der Schatz im Haupte des Gotzen', in U. Haarmann and P. Bachmann (eds), *Die Islamische Welt zwischen Mittelalter und Neuzeit* (Beirut, 1979), pp. 198–229, esp. pp. 208–9n.

27 Thomas Mann, *Joseph and his Brothers*, trans. H.T. Lowe-Porter (London, 1959), pp. 892–3. More generally, Mann's great fictional tetralogy is an excellent guide to many aspects of old Semitic culture.

28 On al-Tanukhi, see Chapter 3.

29 Burton, *Supplemental Nights*, vol. 4, pp. 341–66. Maria Edgeworth's schoolmistressy *Murad the Unlucky* (1804) reads as if it was written specifically in opposition to this *Nights* tale.

30 On Todorov, see Chapter 9.

31 C.S. Lewis, 'On Stories', in *idem, Of This and Other Worlds* (London, 1982), p. 39.

32 Julian Barnes, *Flaubert's Parrot* (London, 1984), pp. 66–7.

33 Paul Willemen (ed.), *Pier Paolo Pasolini* (London, 1977), p. 74.

34 Walter Benjamin, 'Fate and Character', in *idem, One Way Street* (London, 1979), p. 126.

35 Jacques Monod, *Chance and Necessity* (London, 1972), pp. 154–5.

36 Burton, *Nights*, vol. 8, p. 9.

37 Most of the works of Abu'l-Qasim remain in mauscript only. However, on him, see P. Casanova, 'Alphabets magiques arabes', *Journal asiatique*, ser. 11, 18 (1921), p. 38; E.J. Holmyard, 'Abu'l-Qasim al-Iraqi', *Isis*, 8 (1926), pp. 403–26; Stefan Wild, 'A Juggler's Programme in Mediaeval Islam', in *La Signification du bas moyen âge dans l'histoire et la culture du monde musulman: Actes du 8me congrès de l'union européenne des arabisants et islamisants* (Aix-en-Provence, 1976), pp. 353–60; Ullman, *Die Natur- und Geheimwissenschaften*, pp. 125, 237, 412.

38 On the jinn, see Toufy Fahd, 'Anges, démons et djinns en Islam', in D. Bernot *et al.* (eds), *Génies, anges et démons* (Paris, 1971), pp. 153–214; *Encyclopedia of Islam* (2nd edn), s.v. 'djinn'.

39 Abdelwahab Bouhdiba, *Sexuality in Islam* (London, 1985), p. 50.

40 *Encyclopedia of Islam* (2nd edn), s.v. 'Iblis'.

41 On lycanthropy as mental illness, see Michael W. Dols, *Majnun: The Madman in Medieval Islamic Society* (Oxford, 1992), pp. 61, 64–6, 84, 87, 89.

42 Gilbert Adair, *Myths and Memories* (London, 1986), p. 75.

43 Brian Stableford, 'Proto Science Fiction', in Peter Nicholls and John Clute (eds), *The Encyclopedia of Science Fiction* (London, 1979), pp. 476–8. However, Pierre Versins took the view that science fiction is not a genre to be narrowly defined and dated, but is rather 'a state of mind'. See his magnificent *Encyclopédie de l'utopie, des voyages extraordinaires et de la science fiction* (Paris, 1972), esp. s.v. 'Arabe (culture)'.

44 See note 8 above.

45 Stephanie Dalley, '*Gilgamesh* in the *Arabian Nights*', *Journal of the Royal Asiatic Society* (1991), pp. 1–17.

46 Ibn Sina's visionary tale survives only fragmentarily in a thirteenth-century commentary on it by the Persian philosopher Nasir al-Din al-Tusi, *Hall Mushkilat al-Isharat* (Tehran, 1926). On *Salaman wa-Absal*, see Henry Corbin, *Avicenna and the Visionary Recital*, trans. W.R. Trask (Princeton, 1960), pp. 223–41; Hossein Nasr, *An Introduction to Islamic Cosmological Doctrines: Conceptions of Nature and Methods Used for its Study by the Ikhwan al-Safa, al-Biruni and Ibn Sina* (Cambridge, Mass., 1964), pp. 181, 263n., 265–6, 274; I. Strousma, 'Avicenna's Philosophical Stories: Aristotle's *Poetics* Reinterpreted', *Arabica*, 39 (1992), pp. 183–206.

47 See note 9 above.

48 On al-Farabi, see E.I.J. Rosenthal, *Political Thought in Medieval Islam* (Cambridge, 1962), pp. 122–42.

9 Formal Readings

1 *Leigh Hunt's Literary Criticism*, p. 246, cited in Muhsin Jassim Ali, *Scherezade in England: A Study of Nineteenth-Century English Criticism of the Arabian Nights* (Washington, 1981), p. 83.

2 Stith Thompson, *The Types of the Folktale: Antti Aarne's Verzeichnis der Marchentypen Translated and Enlarged* (Helsinki, 1932–6).

3 Hasan M. El-Shamy, *Folktales of Egypt* (Chicago, 1980), p. 237.

4 Vladimir Propp, *The Morphology of the Folktale* (Austin and London, 1968). See also *idem, Theory and History of Folklore* (Manchester, 1984).

5 Paul Willemen (ed.), *Pier Paolo Pasolini* (London, 1977), p. 74.

6 On Proppian approaches to film, see Pam Cook (ed.), *The Cinema Book* (London, 1985), pp. 234–8.

7 Alan Dundes, *The Morphology of North American Indian Tales* (Helsinki, 1964); *idem*, 'On Game Morphology', *New York Folklore Quarterly*, 20 (1964).

8 David Pinault, *Story-Telling Techniques in the Arabian Nights* (Leiden, 1992), p. 131.

9 On the response of literary theorists to Propp, see Robert Scholes, *Structuralism in Literature*, (New Haven and London, 1974), pp. 59–69, 91–117; Jonathan Culler, *Structuralist Poetics: Structuralism, Linguistics and the Study of Literature* (London, 1975), pp. 207–9, 212–13, 232–4.

10 An English translation of 'Les Hommes-Récits' appears in Tzvetan Todorov, *The Poetics of Prose* (Ithaca, 1977), pp. 66–79.

11 Tzvetan Todorov, *The Fantastic: A Structural Approach to a Literary Genre* (Ithaca, 1975), pp. 107–10.

12 Ibid., pp. 160–61.

13 Pinault, *Story-Telling Techniques, passim*.

14 Todorov, *The Fantastic*, pp. 160–61.

15 Bruno Bettelheim, *The Uses of Enchantment: The Meaning and Importance of Fairy Tales* (New York, 1976), pp. 86–90.

16 Joseph Campbell, *The Hero with a Thousand Faces* (London, 1975), p. 197.

17 Pasolini's film *Il fiore delle Mille e una notte / The Arabian Nights* was released in 1974. Despite the merits of various other film adaptations of the *Nights*, notably that of Powell and Pressburger, Pasolini's is the only version made for adults.

18 Jacques Monod, *Chance and Necessity* (London, 1971), p. 154.

19 Dawkins's ideas about selfish genes are found in *The Selfish Gene* (Oxford, 1976).

10 Children of the Nights

1 Jorge Luis Borges, 'The Thousand and One Nights', in idem, Seven Nights (London, 1984), p. 57.

2 On Thomas Guellette and his rivals and imitators, see M.-L. Dufrenoy, L'Orient romanesque en France 1704–1789 (Montreal and Amsterdam, 1946–7, 1975), 3 vols; Martha Pike Conant, The Oriental Tale in England in the Eighteenth Century (New York, 1908).

3 See note 2 above.

4 See W.H. Trapnell, 'Destiny in Voltaire's Zadig and the Arabian Nights', International Journal of Islamic and Arabic Studies, 4 (1987), pp. 1–15.

5 On the early appearance of Galland in English versions, see Sheila Shaw, 'Early English Editions of the Arabian Nights: Their Value to Eighteenth-Century Literary Scholarship', Muslim World, 49 (1959), pp. 232–8; C. Knipp, 'The Arabian Nights in England: Galland's Translation and its Successors', Journal of Arabic Literature, 5 (1974), pp. 44–54.

6 Edward W. Said, Orientalism (London, 1978), p. 42.

7 On Addison and other 'orientalist' writers in England in this period (Samuel Johnson, John Hawkesworth, Joseph Crabtree, etc.), see Conant, The Oriental Tale.

8 Hawkesworth's Almoran and Hamet has recently been reprinted, together with Frances Sheridan's The History of Nourjahad, Clara Reeve's The History of Charoba, Queen of Egypt and Maria Edgeworth's Murad the Unlucky, in Robert L. Mack (ed.), Oriental Tales (Oxford, 1972).

9 See note 8 above.

10 The literature on Beckford is vast, but André Parreaux, William Beckford, Auteur de Vathek [1760–1844]: Etude de la création littéraire (Paris, 1960), is fundamental. See also Fatma Moussa-Mahmoud (ed.), William Beckford of Fonthill 1760–1844: Bicentenary Essays (New York, 1960); Boyd Alexander, England's Wealthiest Son: A Study of William Beckford (London, 1962); Fatma Moussa-Mahmoud, 'A Manuscript Translation of the Arabian Nights in the Beckford Papers', Journal of Arabic Literature, 7 (1976), pp. 7–23. Vathek has appeared in innumerable editions. Beckford's Suite de contes arabes, ed. Didier Girard, was published for the first time in Paris in 1992.

11 J.W. Oliver, The Life of William Beckford (London, 1932), pp. 89–90, 91.

12 Very little has been written about Potocki (except perhaps in Polish). However, see Edouard Krakowski, Le Comte Jean Potocki: Un témoin de l'Europe des Lumières (Paris, 1963); Czeslaw Milosz, The History of Polish Literature (London, 1969), pp. 192–4; 'Jean Potocki et le Manuscrit trouvé à

Saragosse', in *Actes du colloque organisé par le Centre de civilisation française de l'Université de Varsovie, Avril, 1972* (Warsaw, 1974); Franz Rottensteiner, *The Fantasy Book* (London, 1978), pp. 21–2; Tzvetan Todorov, *The Fantastic: A Structural Approach to a Literary Genre* (Ithaca, 1975), *passim*; Marcel Schneider *Histoire de la littérature fantastique en France* (Paris, 1985), pp. 114–19. A complete version of the novel has only recently been published: *Manuscrit trouvé à Saragosse*, ed. René Radrizzani (Paris, 1989). An English translation of this edition is forthcoming. In the meantime, see *Tales from the Saragossa Manuscript* (*Ten Days in the Life of Alphonse Van Worden*), trans. Christine Donougher, ed. Brian Stableford (Sawtry, Cambs., 1991). Some of his travel writings have been published as Jean Potocki, *Voyages* (Paris, 1980), 2 vols. Dominic Triaire, *Potocki* (Arles, 1991), came to hand too late for me to use it here.

13 Jacques Cazotte, *The Devil in Love*, trans. Judith Landry, ed. Brian Stableford (Sawtry, Cambs., 1991). On Cazotte, see Richard Burton, *Supplemental Nights to the Book of the Thousand Nights and a Night* (Benares = Stoke Newington, London, 1868–88), vol. 6, pp. i–xii; Edward Pease Shaw, *Jacques Cazotte (1719–1792)* (Cambridge, Mass., 1942); Schneider, *Histoire*, pp. 99–107;

14 On Southey, see Byron Porter Smith, *Islam in English Literature* (2nd edn, New York, 1975), pp. 179–87; Peter L. Caracciolo, 'Introduction', in *idem* (ed.), *The Arabian Nights in English Literature: Studies in the Reception of the Thousand and One Nights into British Culture* (London, 1988), p. 9. Caracciolo's book, and particularly its introduction, is fundamental to the study of the influence of the *Nights* on British literature.

15 On Moore, see Smith, *Islam*, pp. 195–201; M. Asfour, 'Thomas Moore and the Pitfalls of Orientalism', *International Journal of Arabic and Islamic Studies*, 4 (1987), pp. 75–92.

16 On Byron, see Smith, *Islam*, pp. 127–8, 189–95; Wallace Cable Brown, 'Byron and English Interest in the Near East', *Studies in Philology*, 34 (1937), pp. 55–64; Harold S.L. Wiener, 'Byron and the East: Literary Sources of the *Turkish Tales*', *Nineteenth-Century Studies* (1940), pp. 89–129; Caracciolo, 'Introduction', p. 20.

17 Samuel Taylor Coleridge, *Collected Letters*, vol. 1, p. 347, cited in John Beer, *Coleridge's Poetic Intelligence* (London, 1977).

18 Burton, *Supplemental Nights*, vol. 3, pp. 3–38. On Coleridge and the *Nights*, see Allan Grant, 'The Genie and the Albatross: Coleridge and the *Arabian Nights*', in Caracciolo (ed.), *The Arabian Nights*, pp. 111–29.

19 Aletha Hayter, *Opium and the Romantic Imagination* (London, 1968), p. 207.

20 John Livingston Lowes, *The Road to Xanadu* (Boston, 1927), p. 416.

21 Thomas De Quincey, *Autobiography* (Edinburgh, 1889), pp. 128–9; cf. Hayter, *Opium*, p. 128. On De Quincey and the Orient, see John Barrell, *The Infection of Thomas De Quincey: A Psychopathology of Imperialism* (New Haven and London, 1991).

22 Edward W. Said, 'Islam, Philology and French Culture', in *idem*, *The World, the Text and the Critic* (London, 1984), p. 271.

23 On Arabian themes in Dickens, see Harry Stone, *Dickens and the Invisible World: Fairy Tales, Fantasy and Novel-Making* (London, 1979), pp. 21–5; Michael Slater, 'Dickens in Wonderland', in Caracciolo (ed.), *The Arabian Nights*, pp. 130–42.

24 G.M. Young, *Gibbon* (London, 1932), pp. 13–14.

25 On *Shagpat*, see Cornelia Cook, 'The Victorian Scheherazade: Elizabeth Gaskell and George Meredith', in Caracciolo (ed.), *The Arabian Nights*, pp. 201–17.

26 On Stevenson, see Leonee Ormond, 'Cayenne and Cream Tarts: W.M. Thackeray and R.L. Stevenson', in Caracciolo (ed.), *The Arabian Nights*, pp. 178–96.

27 On 'orientalist' literature in the United States, see Luther S. Luedtke, *Nathaniel Hawthorne and the Romance of the Orient* (Bloomington and Indianapolis, 1989).

28 On Washington Irving, see E.L. Ranelagh, *The Past We Share* (London, 1979), pp. 247–58; M.M. Obeidat, 'Washington Irving and Muslim Spain', *International Journal of Islamic and Arabic Studies*, 4 (1987), pp. 27–44.

29 On oriental themes in *Moby Dick*, see Dorothee Finkelstein, *Melville's Orienda* (New Haven, 1961).

30 On oriental themes in Joyce, see Robert G. Hampson, 'The Genie out of the Bottle: Conrad, Wells and Joyce', in Caracciolo (ed.), *The Arabian Nights*, pp. 229–43.

31 Jorge Luis Borges, *Other Inquisitions, 1937–1952* (New York, 1966), p. 113.

32 David Lodge, *Small World* (London, 1984), pp. 51–2.

33 Tzvetan Todorov, 'The Quest of Narrative', in *idem*, *The Poetics of Prose* (Ithaca, 1977), pp. 120–42.

Index